To Miranda

You saw what this could be

before I ever picked up the pen.

First Edition
ISBN: 978-0-9916352-7-6
Library of Congress Control Number: 2025938029

Published by
Scribble & Sons Publishing
Windsor, Colorado
www.ScribbleAndSons.com

Design, Illustration & Text by Mark Ludy
Cover art features Mel & Moose (@mr.moosehakes)

For more on this book and upcoming volumes, visit
www.MarkLudy.com

Printed in Canada
10 9 8 7 6 5 4 3 2 1

SCRIBBLE
& SONS PUBLISHING

PETS

and Their People

Volume One

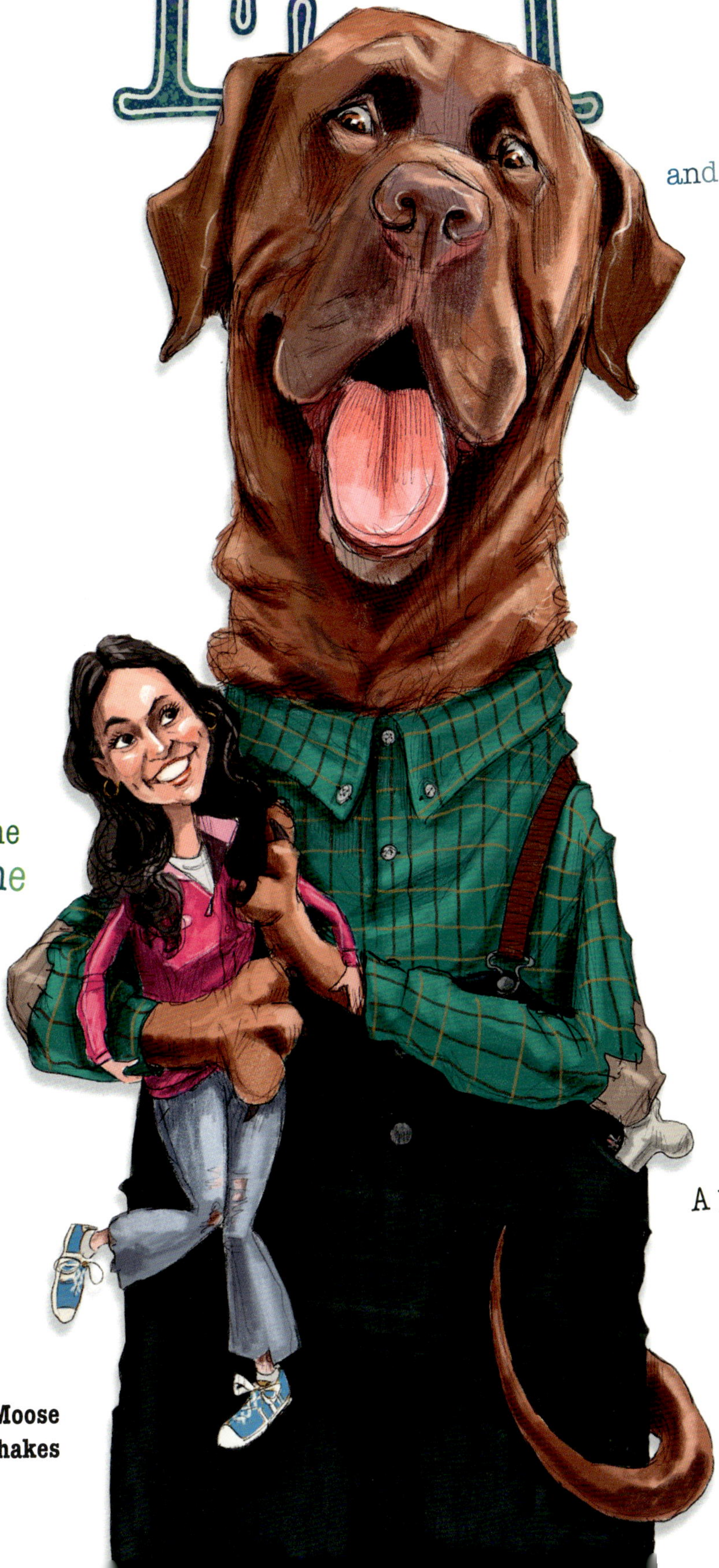

Mel & Moose
@mr.moosehakes

A Portrait Collection of Curious Companions

by

Mark Lüdy

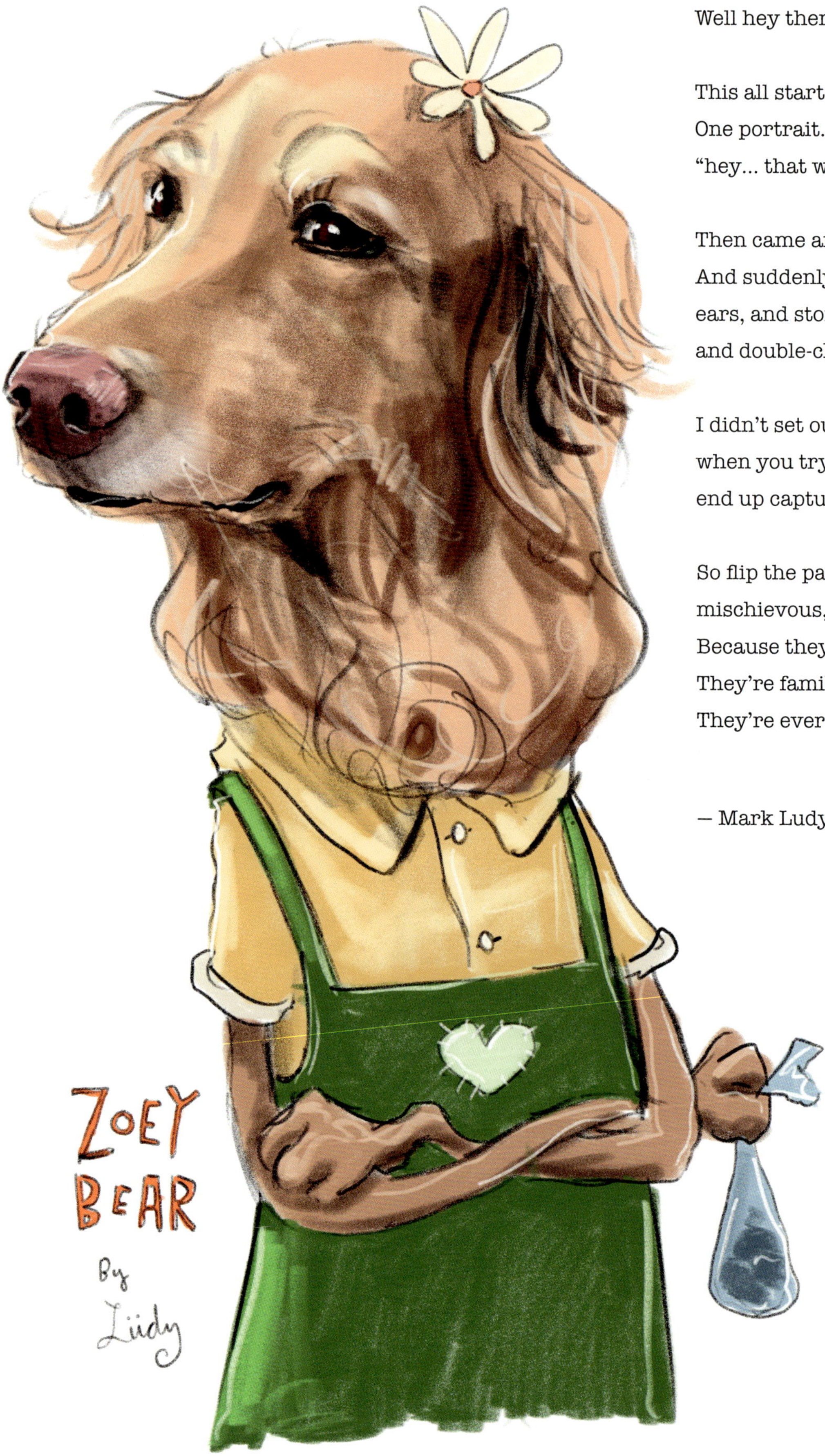

Well hey there—

This all started with a doodle. One pet. One portrait. One moment of "hey... that was fun."

Then came another. And another. And suddenly, I was knee-deep in fur, floppy ears, and stories that made me laugh, cry, and double-check my spelling of "Shih Tzu."

I didn't set out to make a book. But turns out, when you try to capture the heart of a pet— you end up capturing the hearts of their people too.

So flip the page. Meet these marvelous, mischievous, one-of-a-kind companions. Because they're not just pets. They're family. They're art. They're everthing.

— Mark Ludy

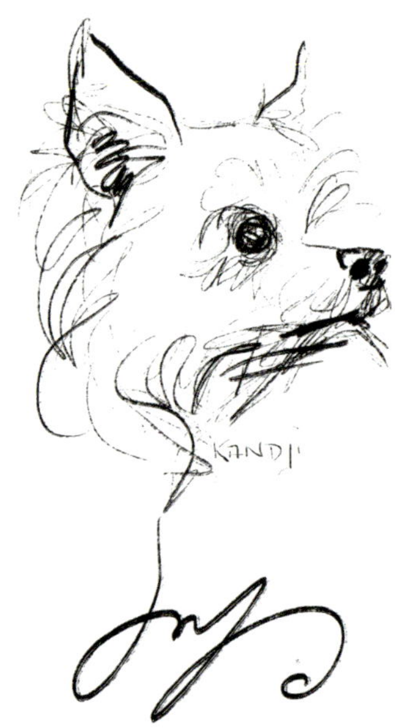

*Kandji was the first pet drawn

They say they're just pets...

But we know better.

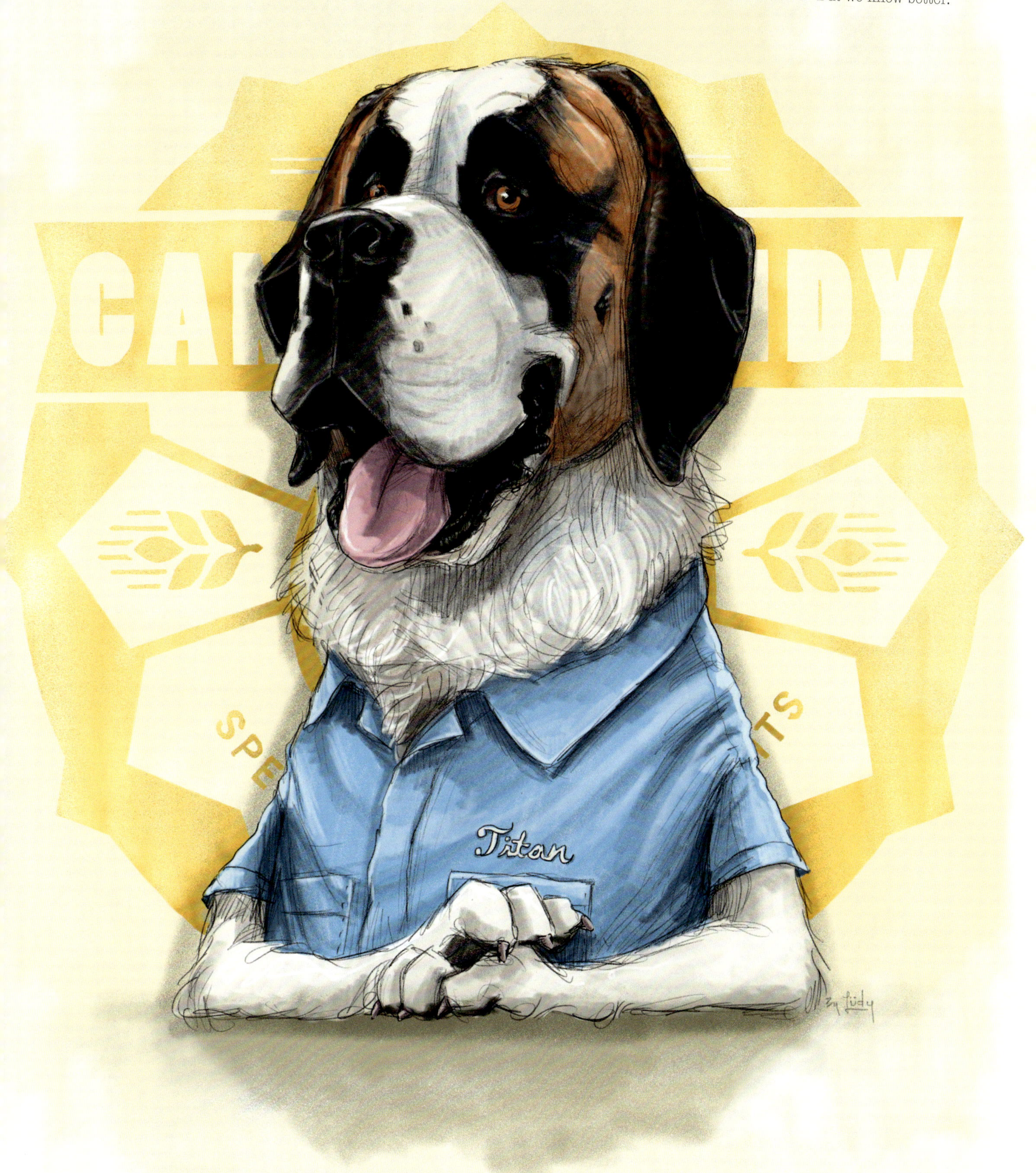

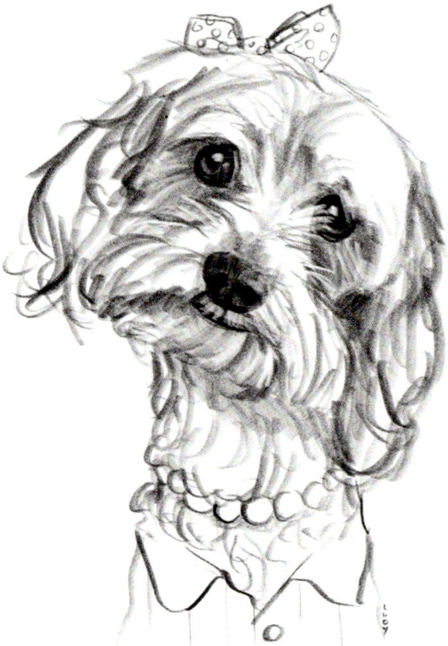

PHOEBE

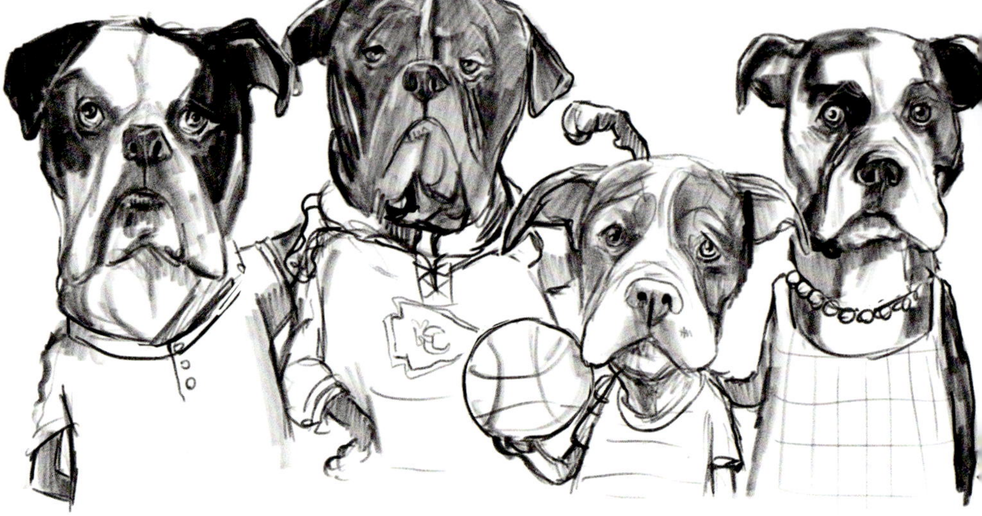

MOE LOU OPAL NORA

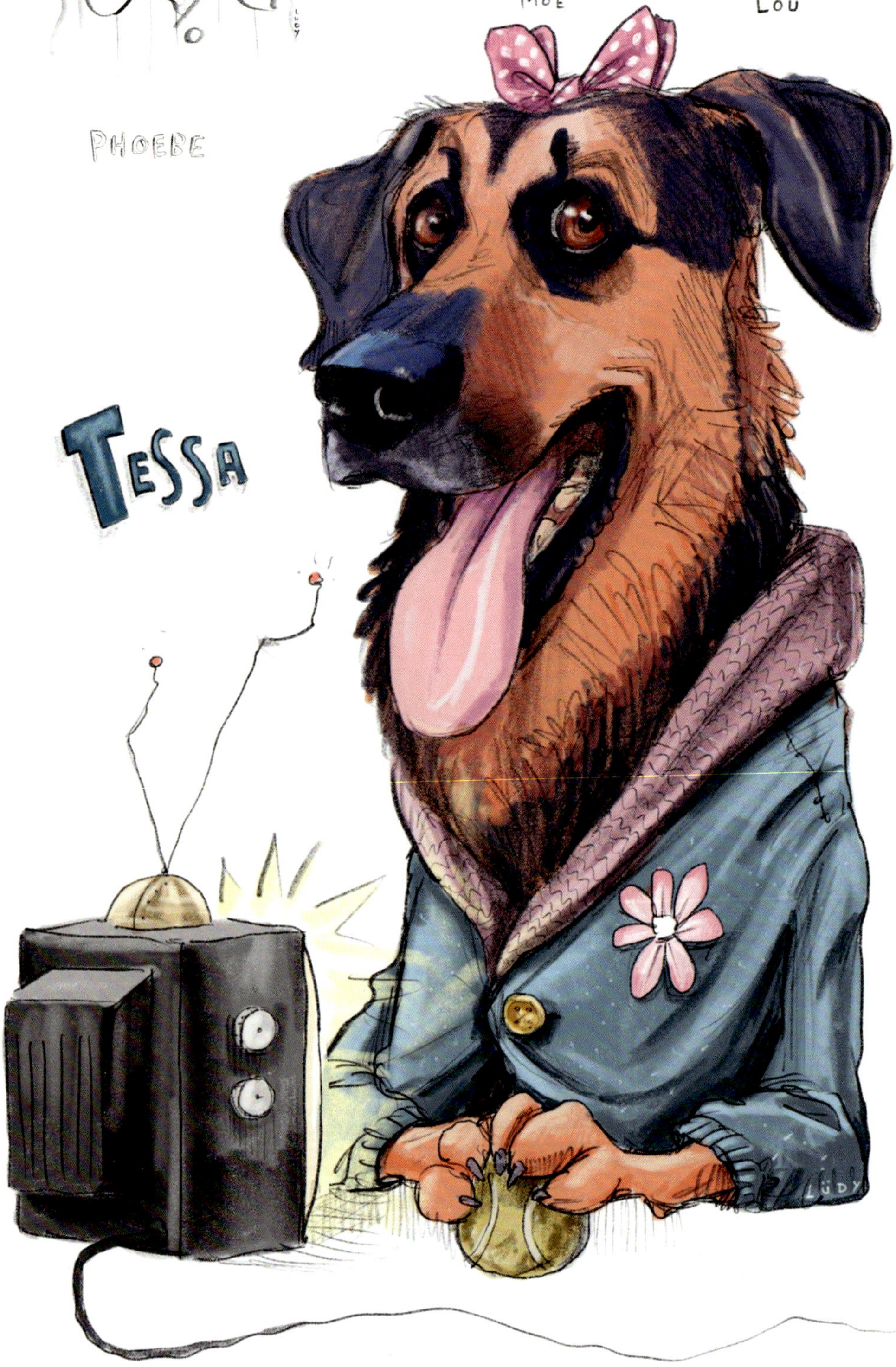

TESSA

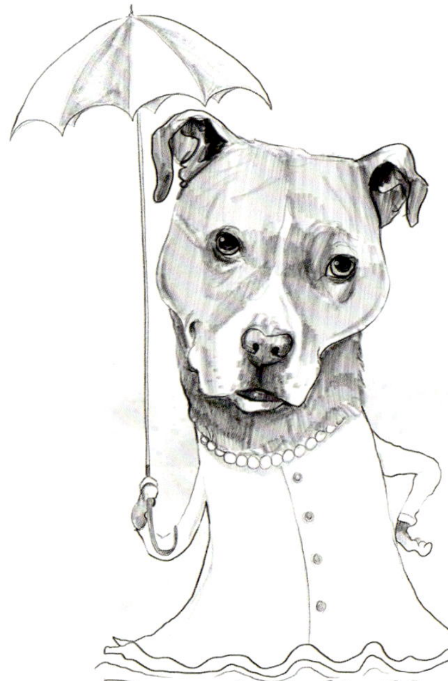

PRINCESS IZABELLA

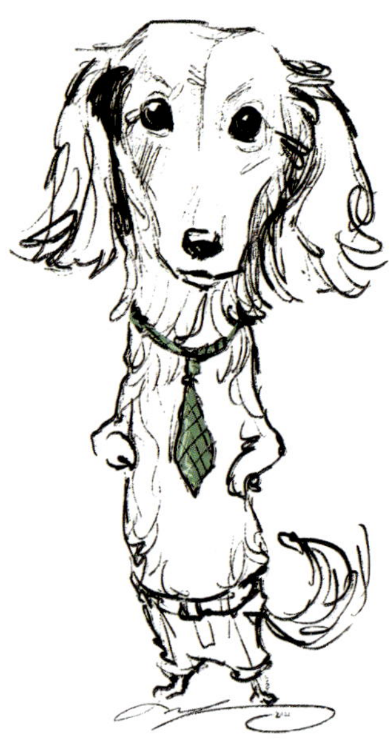

Every crew has a ringleader, a wild card, and the one who (mostly) holds it together.

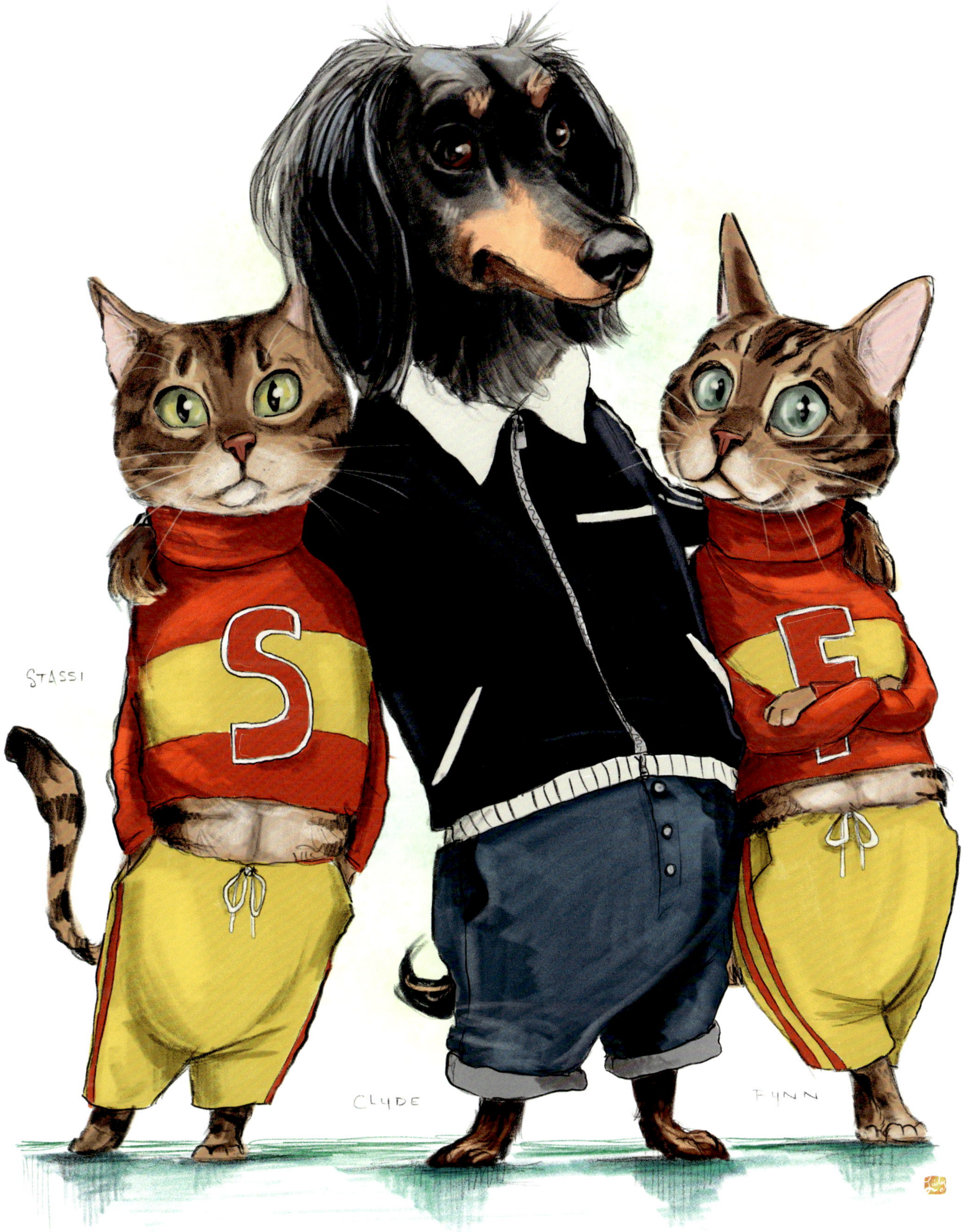

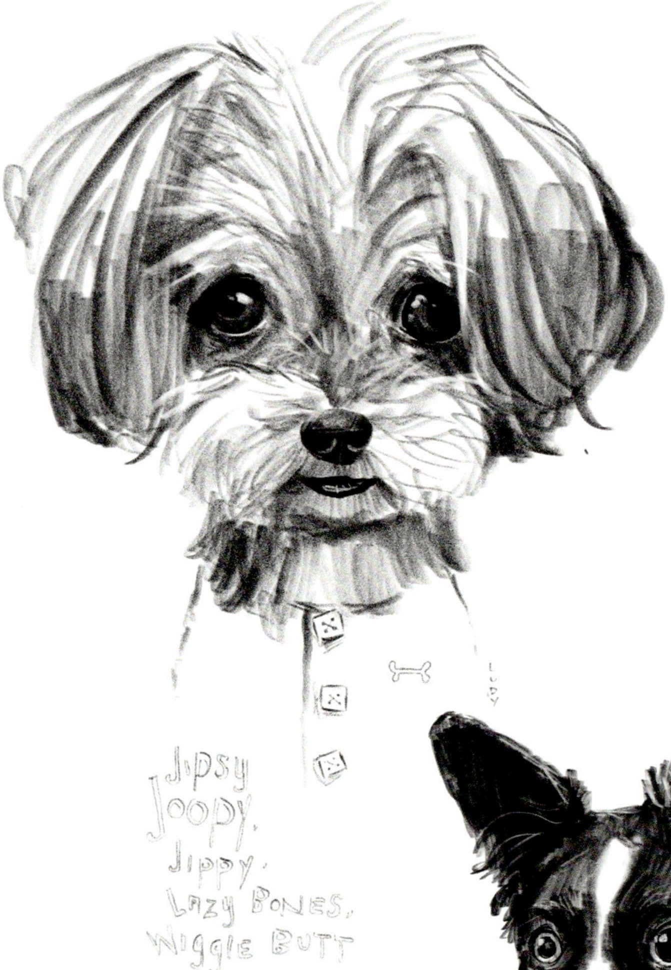
Jipsy
Joopy,
Jippy,
Lazy Bones,
Wiggle Butt

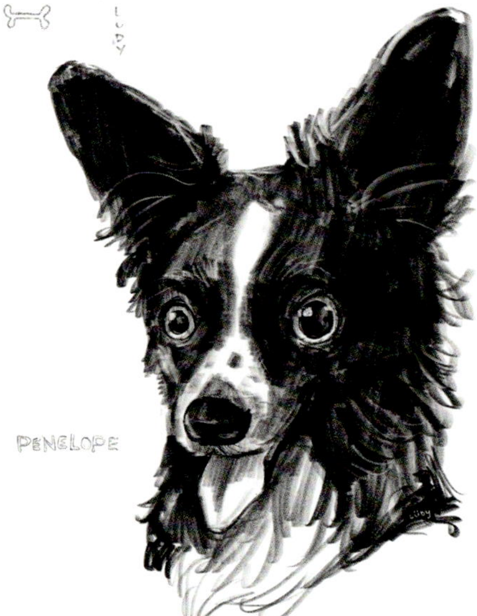
PENELOPE

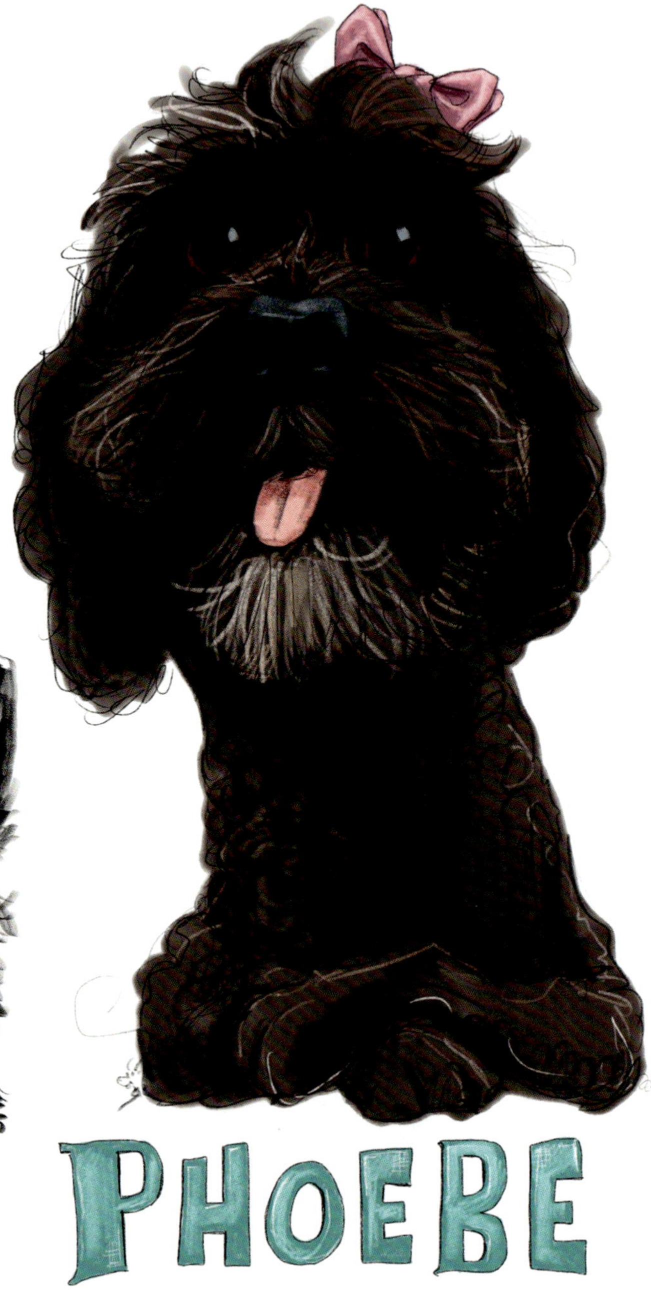
PHOEBE

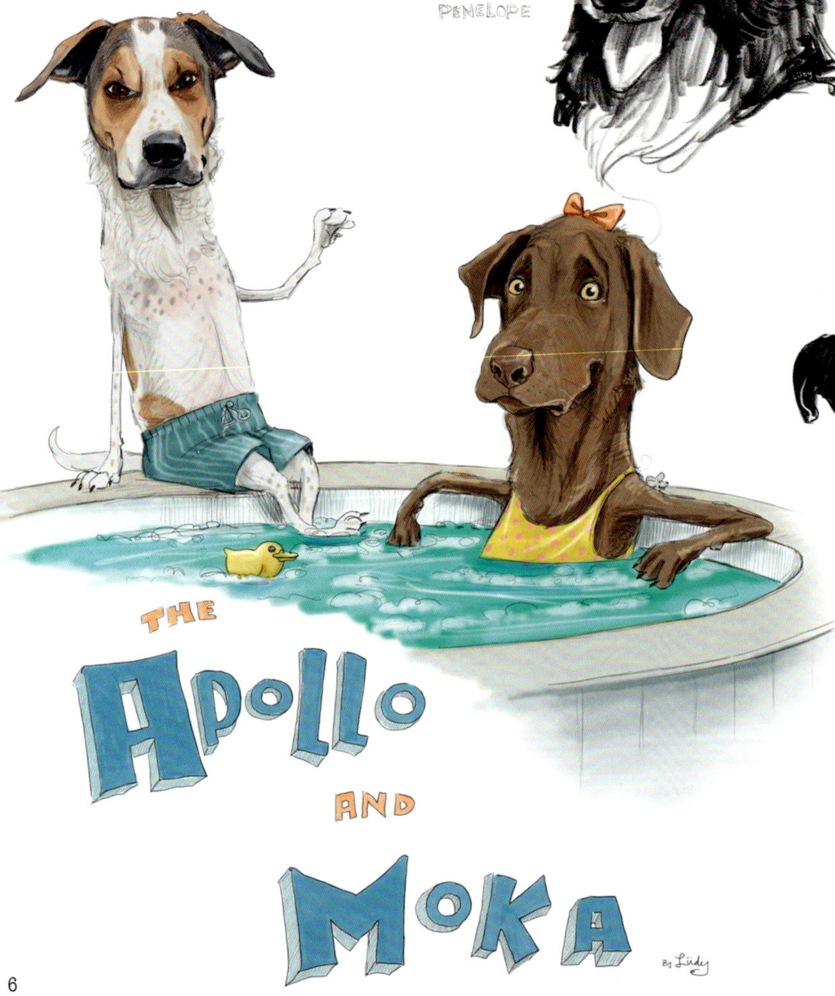
THE
Apollo
AND
Moka
By Lidy

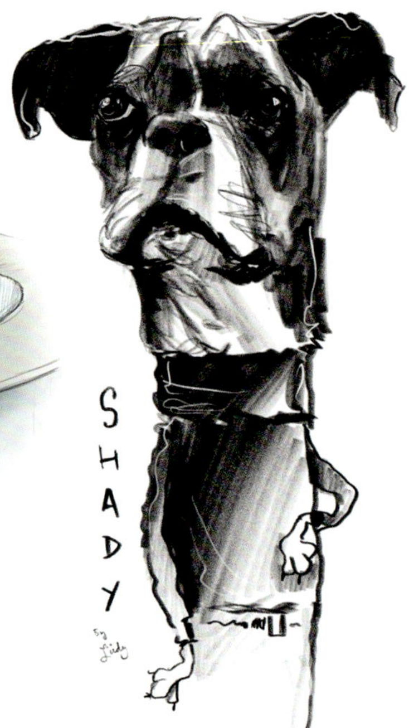
SHADY

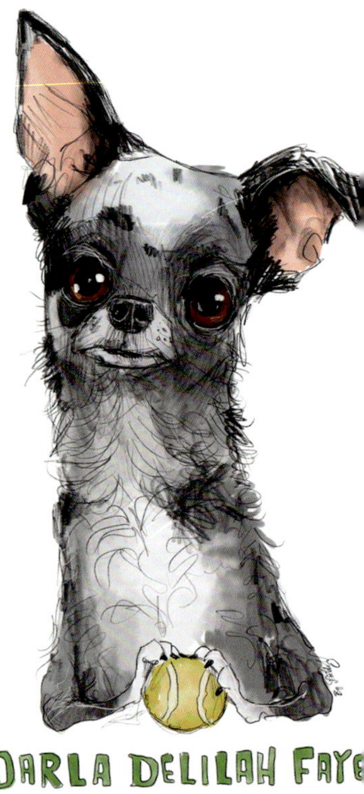
DARLA DELILAH FAYE

"The greatness of a nation can be judged by the way its animals are treated."

– Mahatma Gandhi

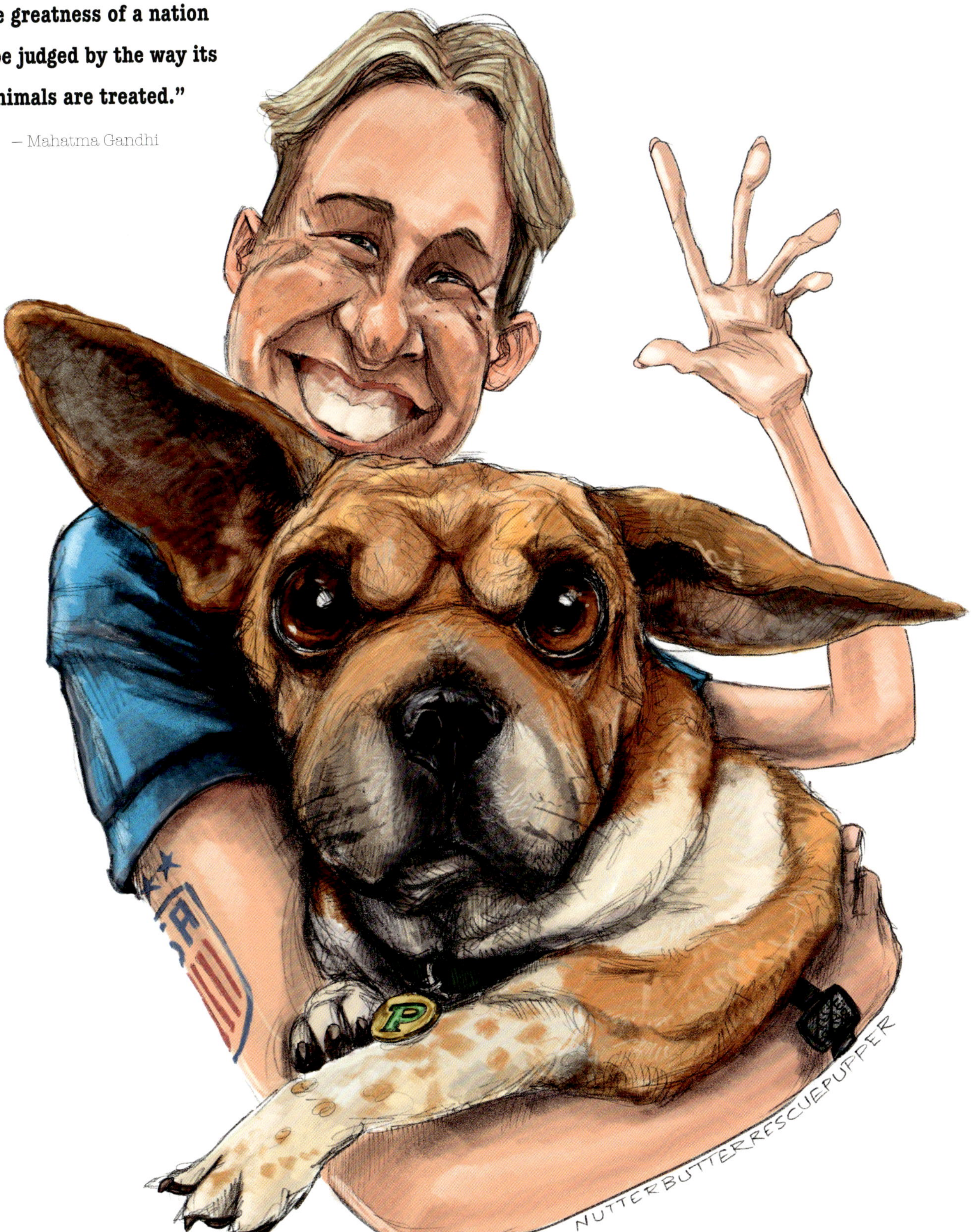

PEANUT

AND HIS KRISTEN

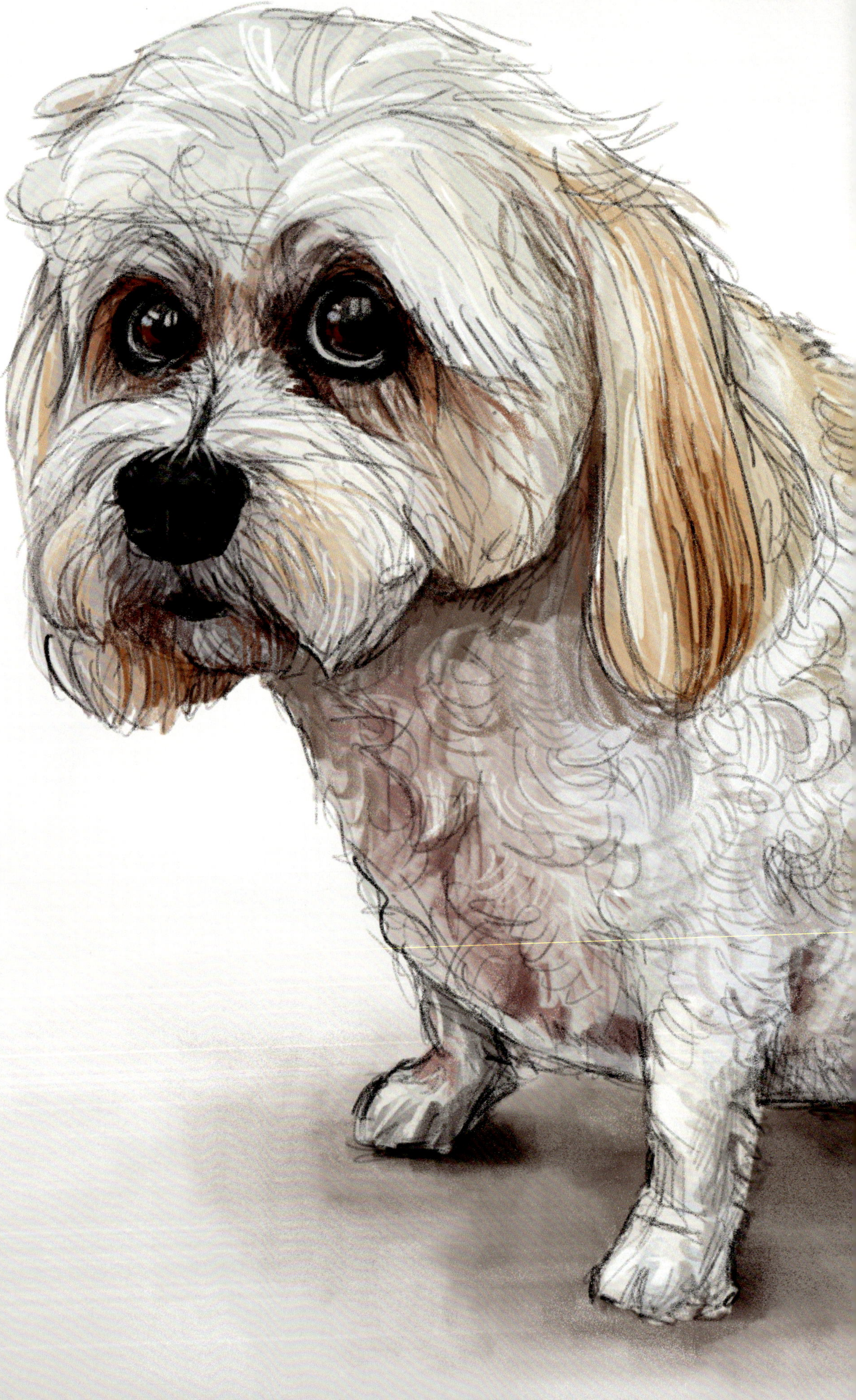

You don't have to be loud

to be unforgettable.

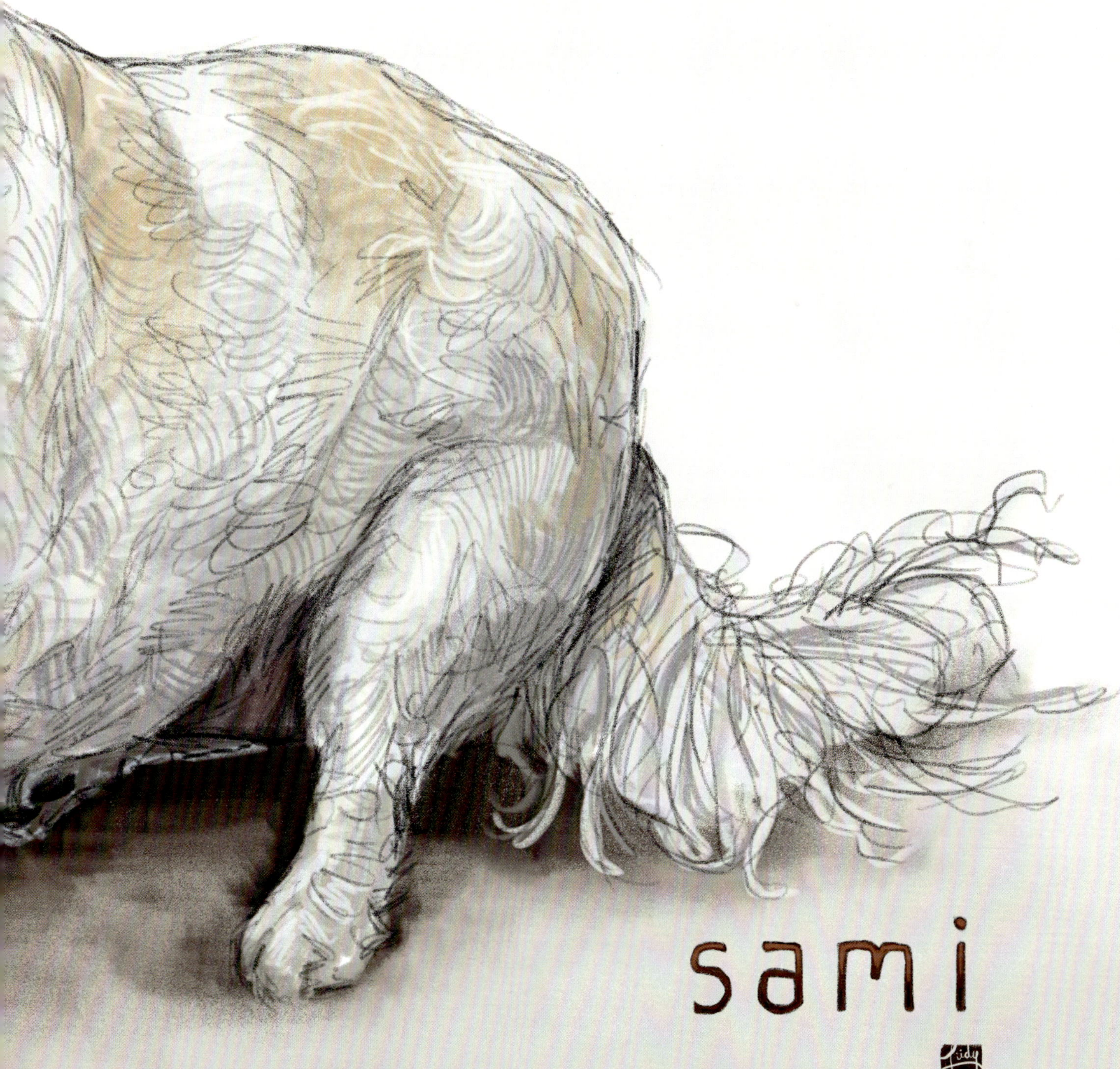

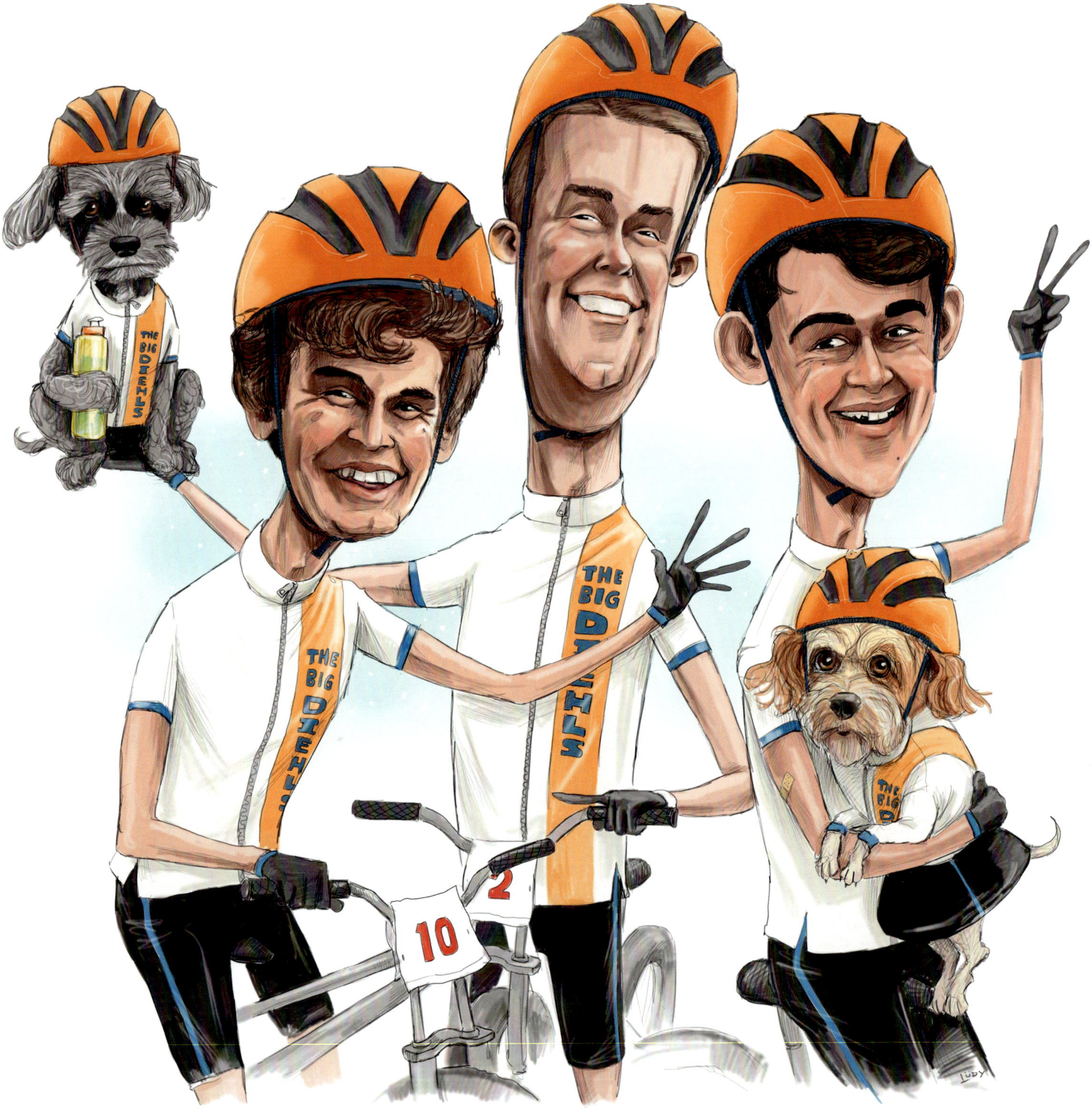
THE BIG DIEHLS
THE BIG DIEHLS
THE BIG DIEHLS
10
2
LÜDY

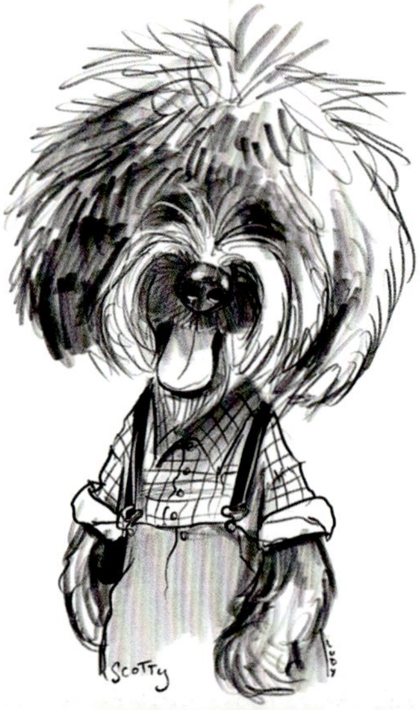
SCOTTY

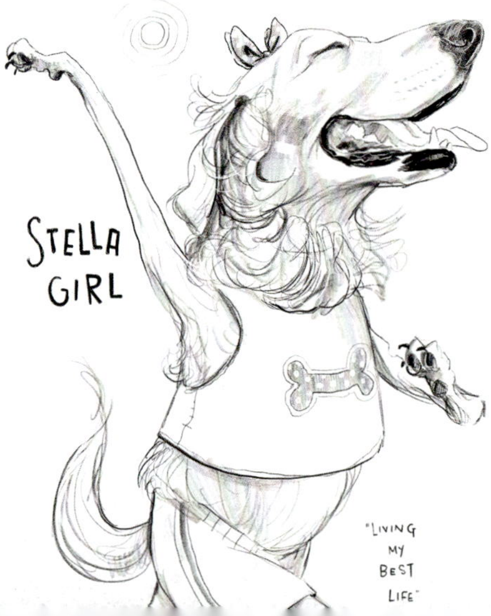
STELLA GIRL
"LIVING MY BEST LIFE"

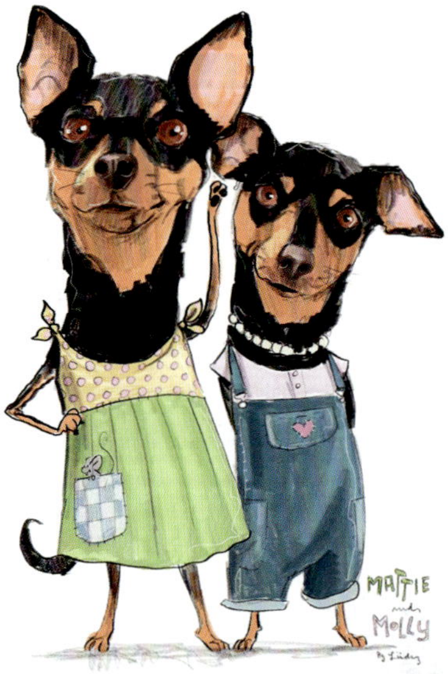
MATTIE
Molly

SHERIFF AND ZUMA

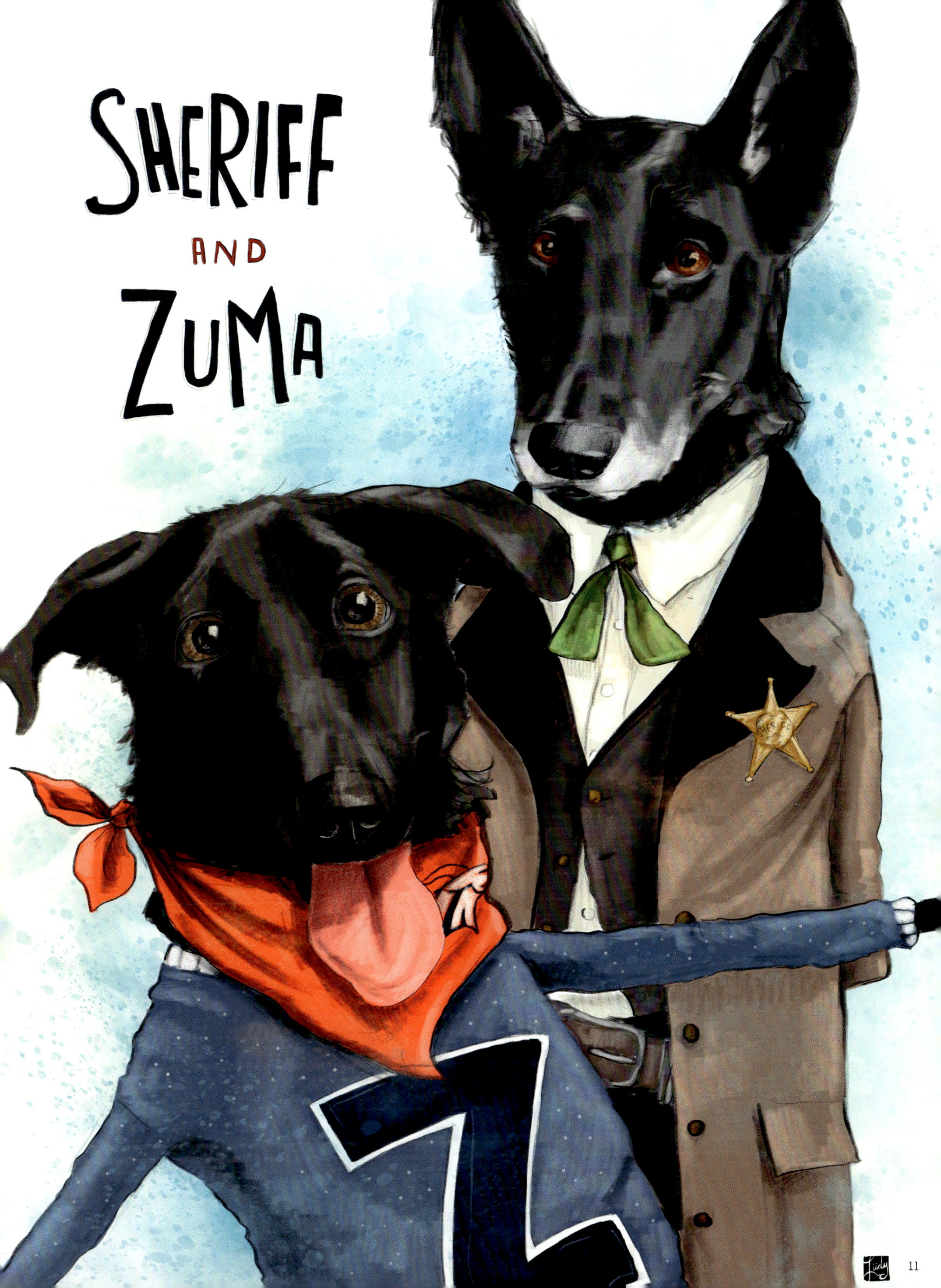

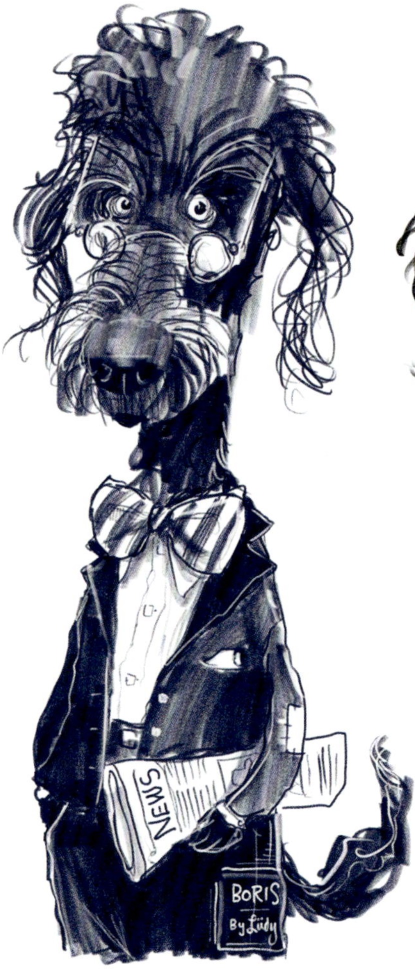
NEWS
BORIS
By Lüdy

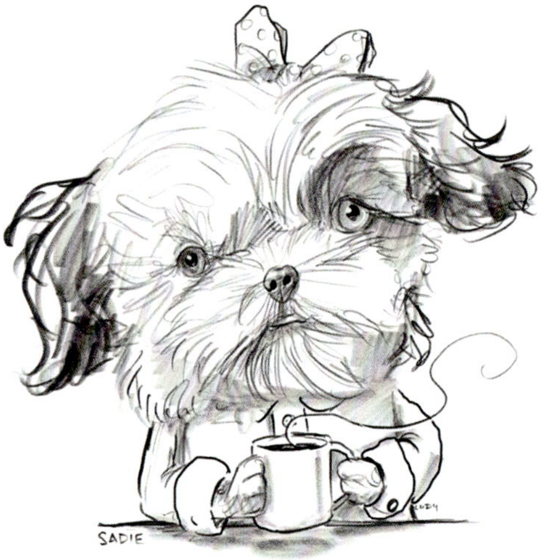
SADIE

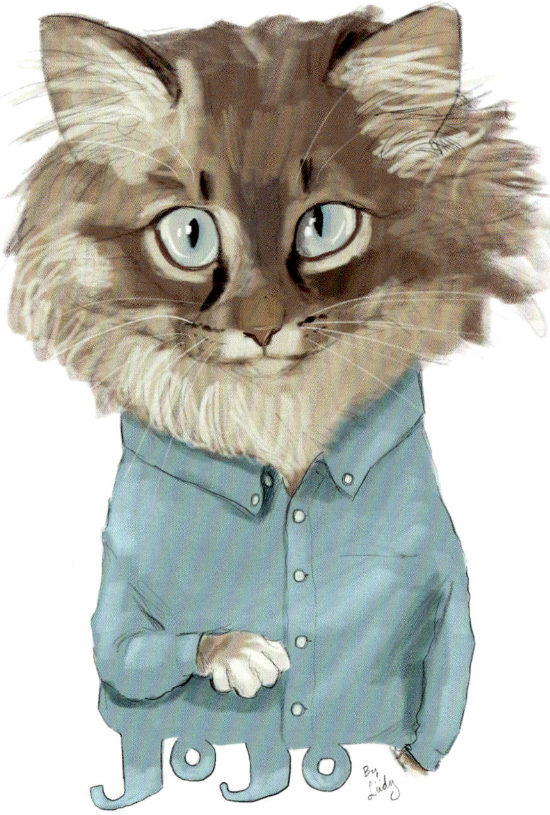
JOJO
By Lüdy

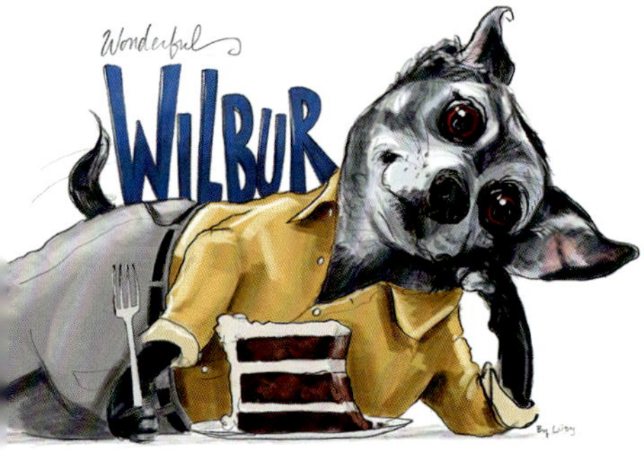
Wonderful
WILBUR

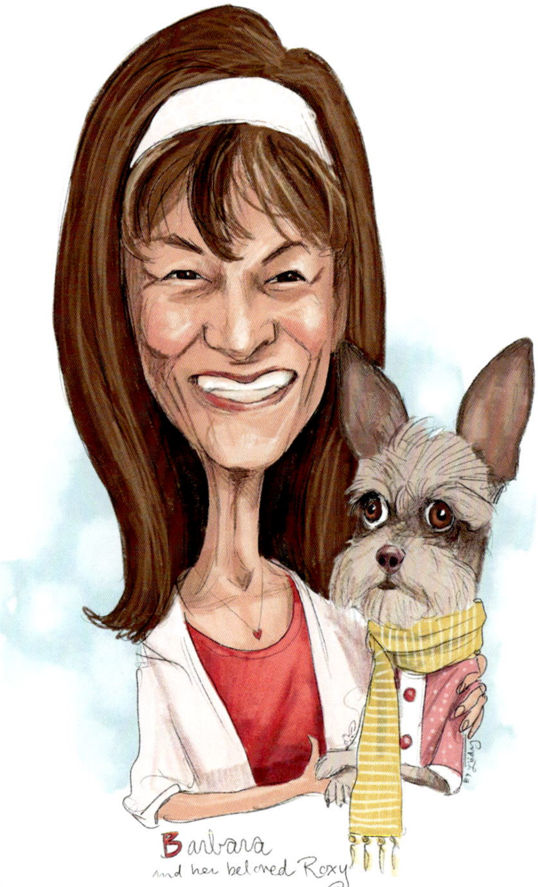
Barbara
and her beloved Roxy

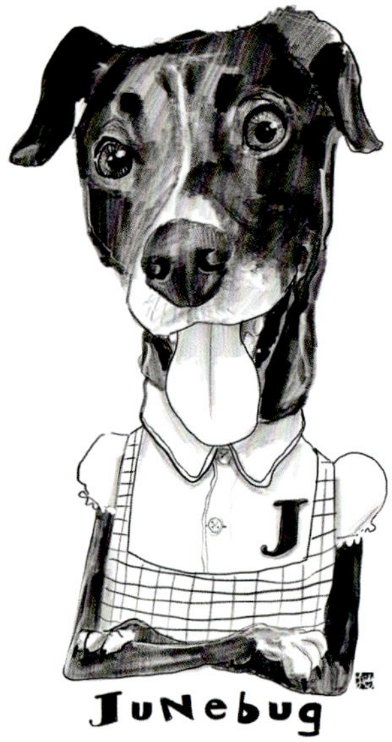
J
JuNebug

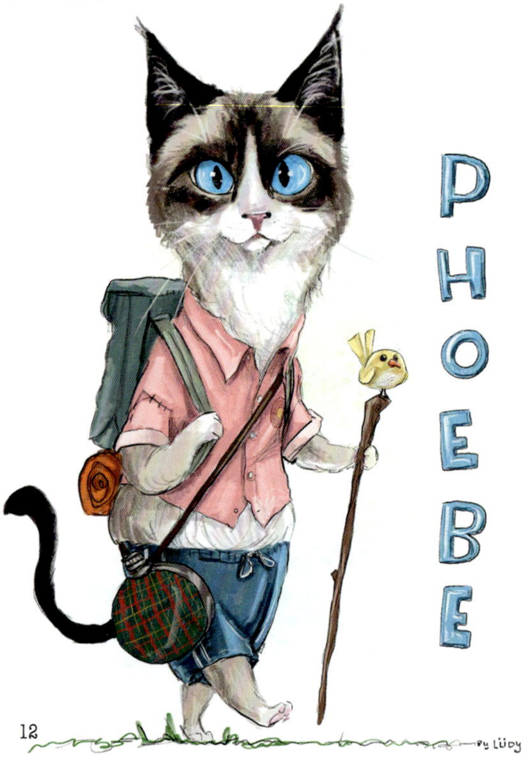
PHOEBE
By Lüdy

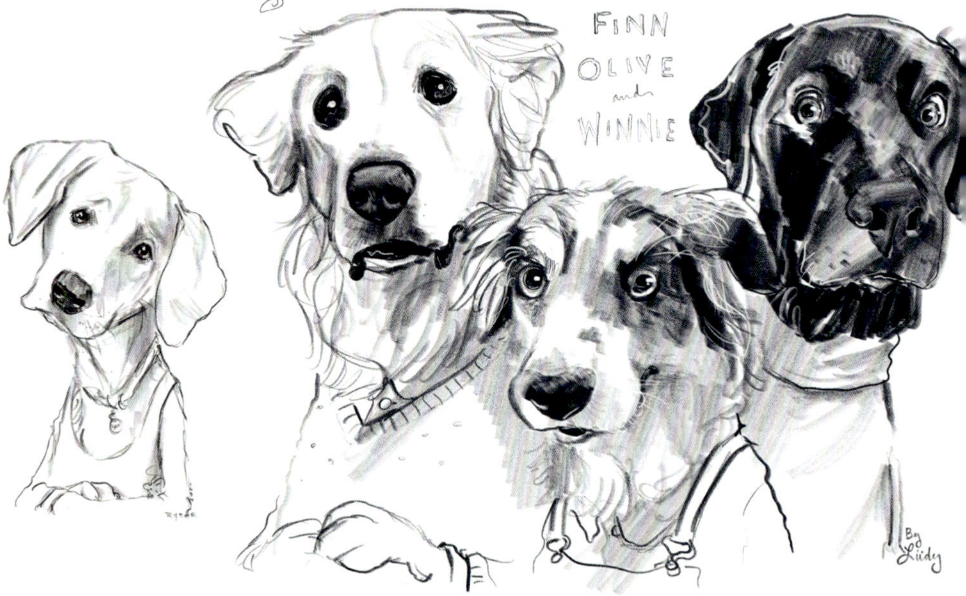
FINN
OLIVE
and
WINNIE
By Lüdy

"In ancient times cats were worshipped as gods;

they have not forgotten this."

— Terry Pratchett

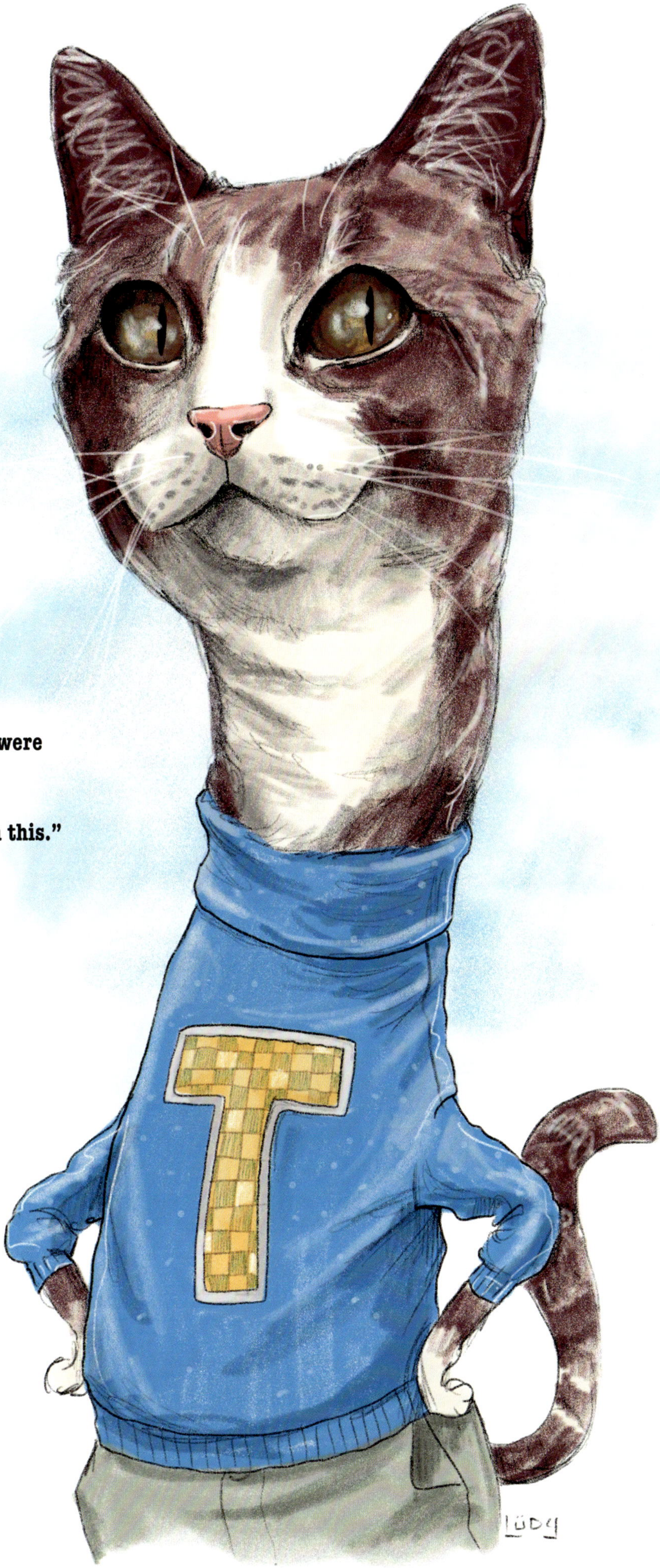

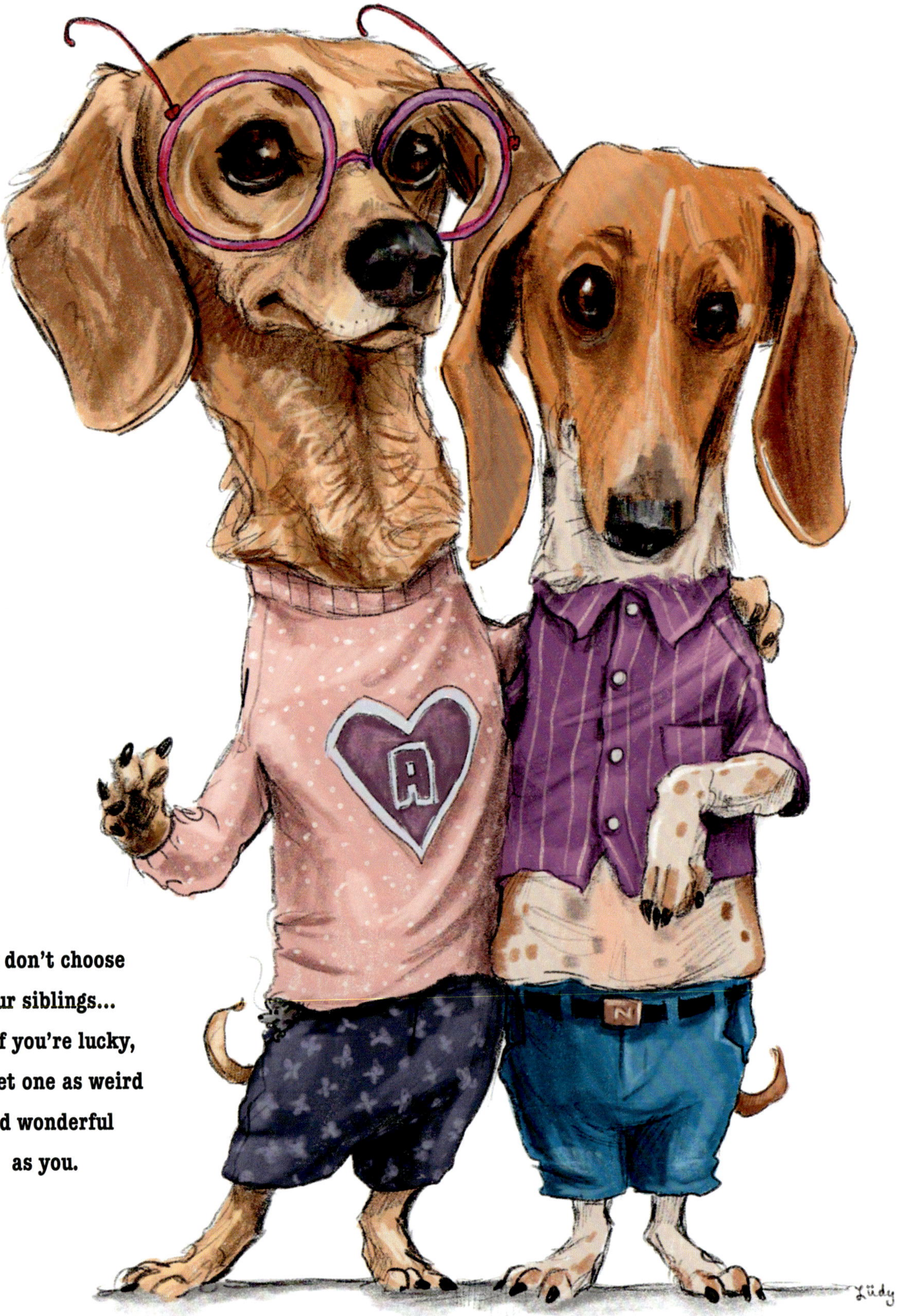

You don't choose
your siblings...
but if you're lucky,
you get one as weird
and wonderful
as you.

Anna and Nico

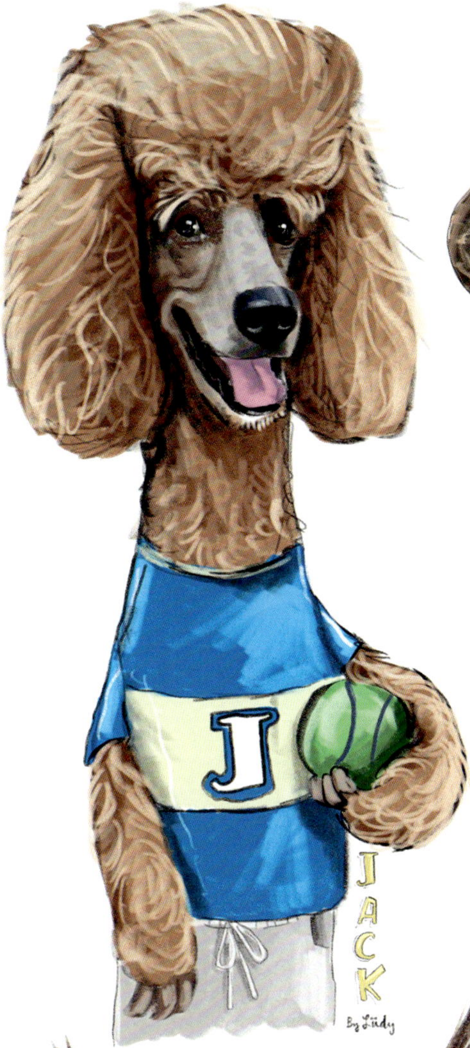
J
JACK
By Lüdy

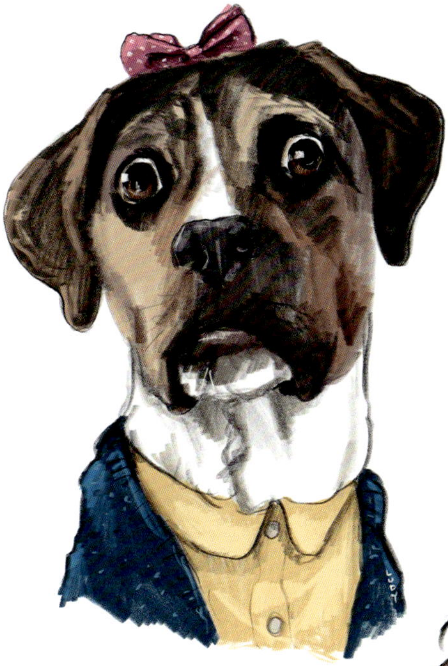

PENNY LANE

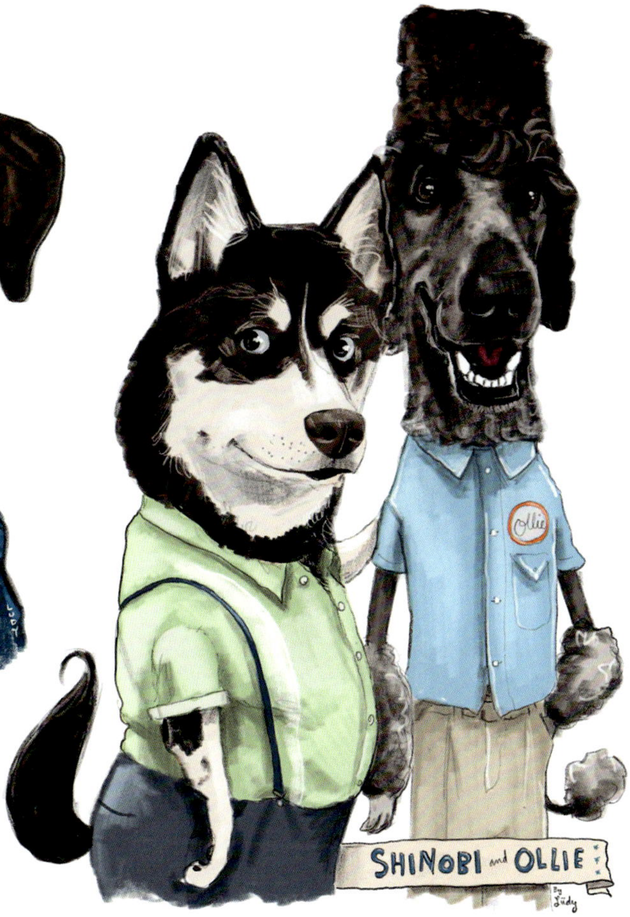
SHINOBI and OLLIE
By Lüdy

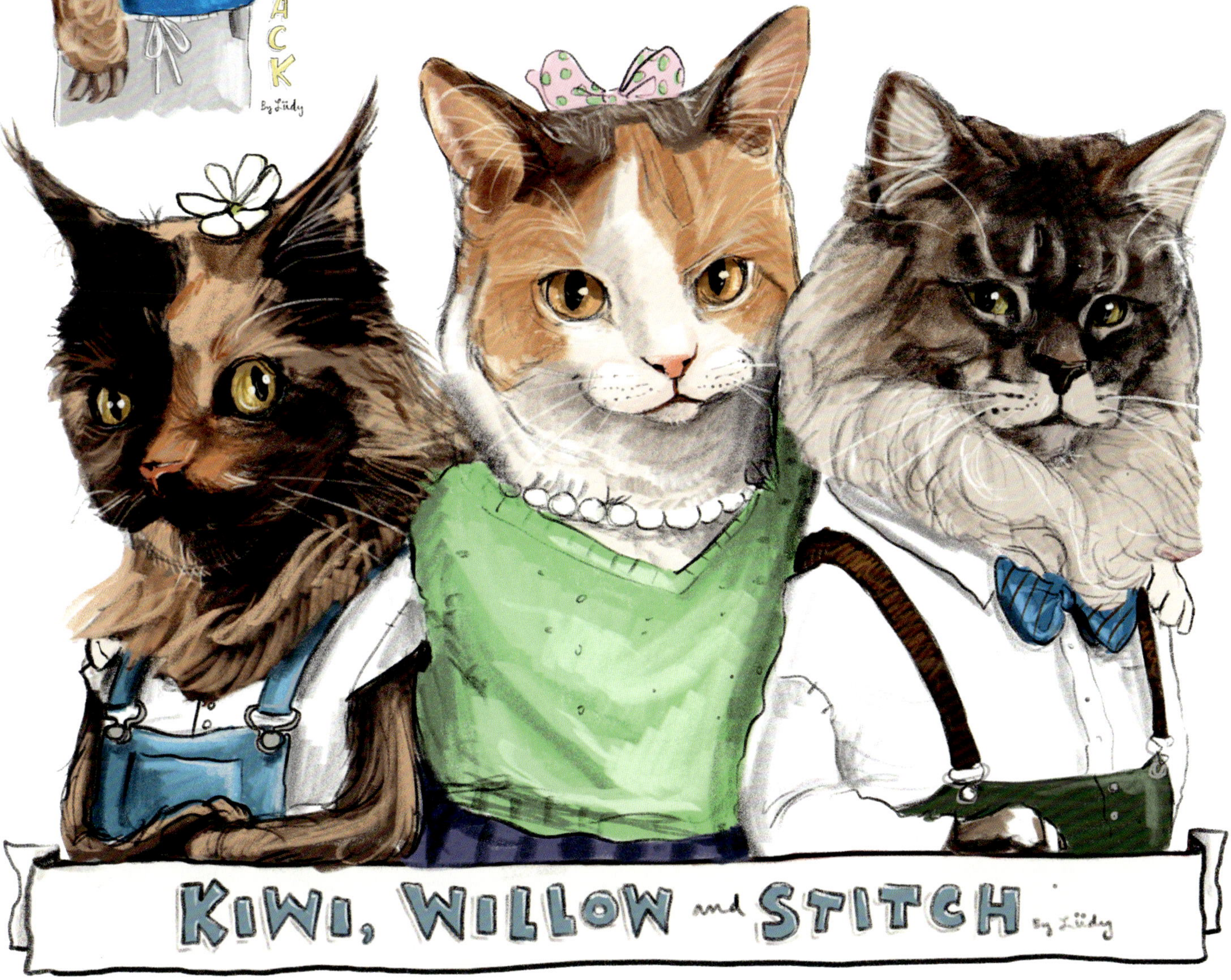
KIWI, WILLOW and STITCH
By Lüdy

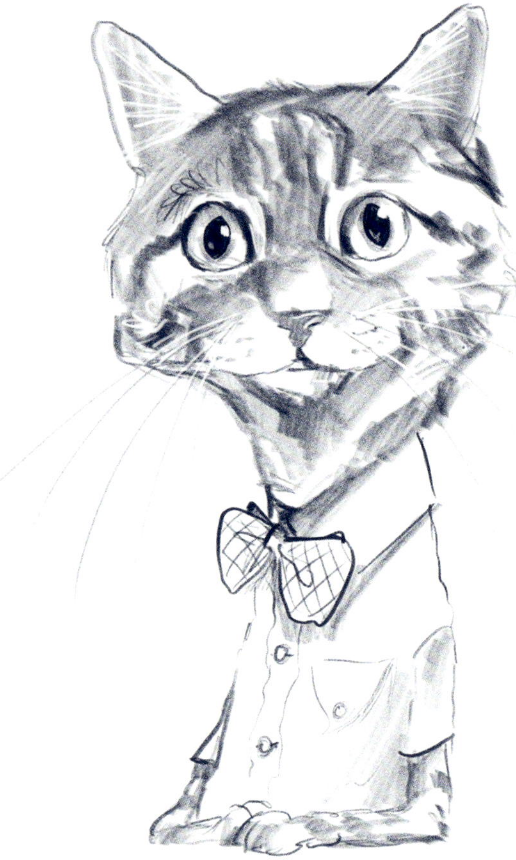

DIESEL

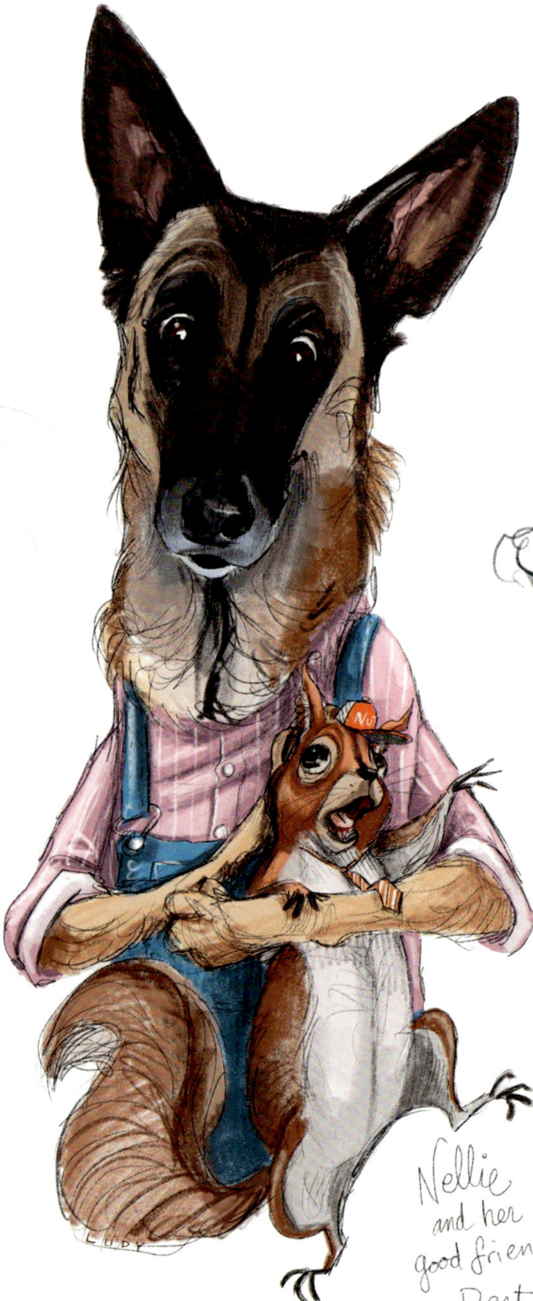

Nellie and her good friend Bert.

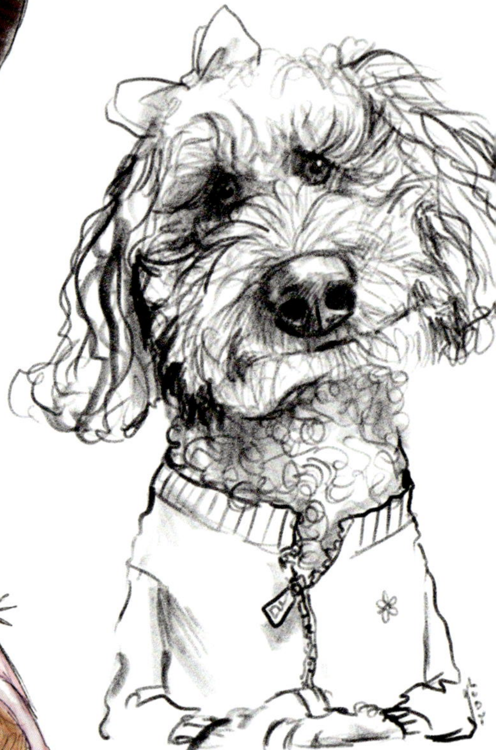

Clementine.

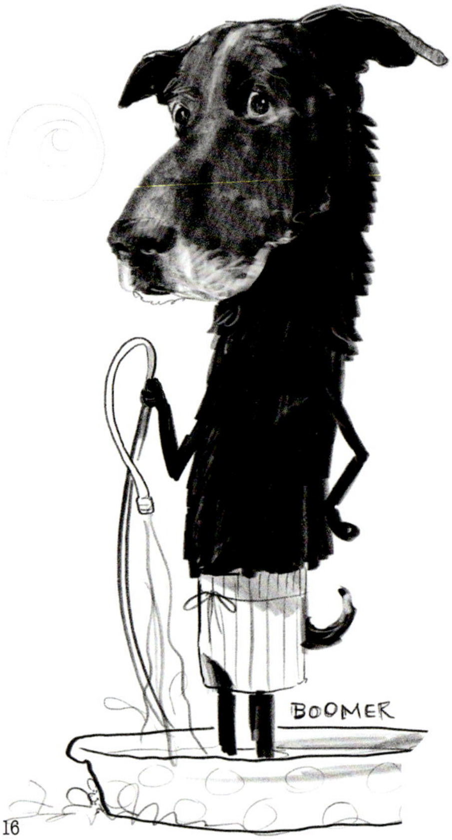

BOOMER

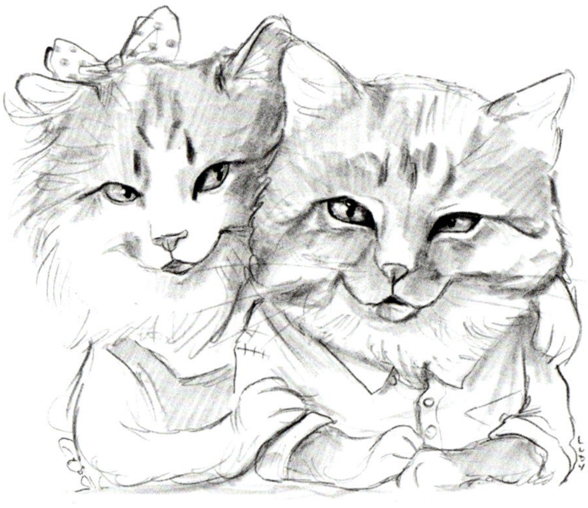

Maggie and Andrew

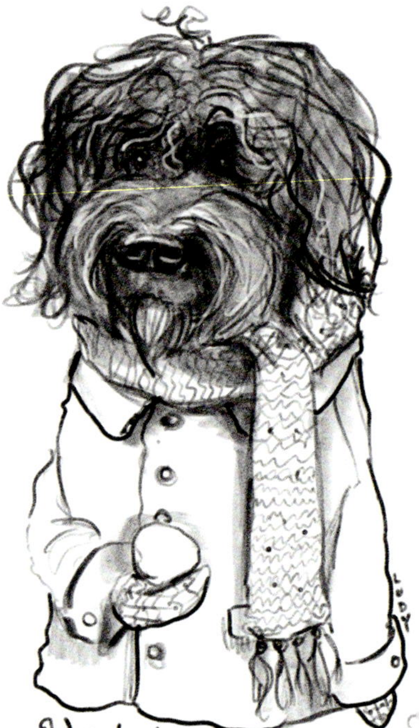

Wonderful PHELPS

Not all heroes
wear capes.
Some wear
bandanas
and
answer to
'Steve.'

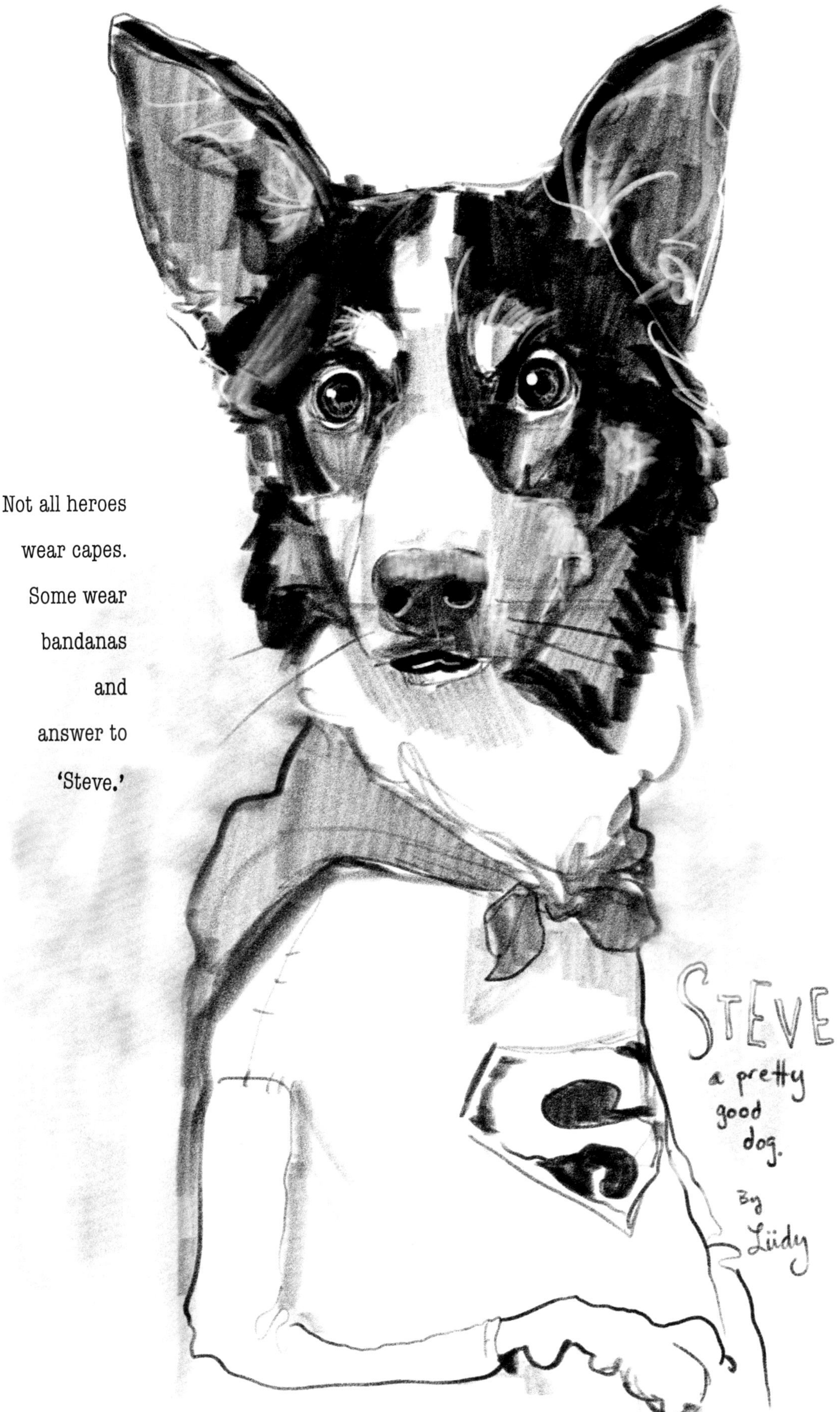

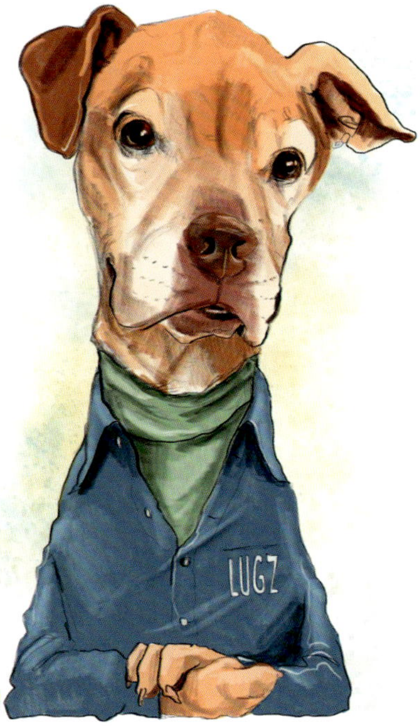
LUGZ

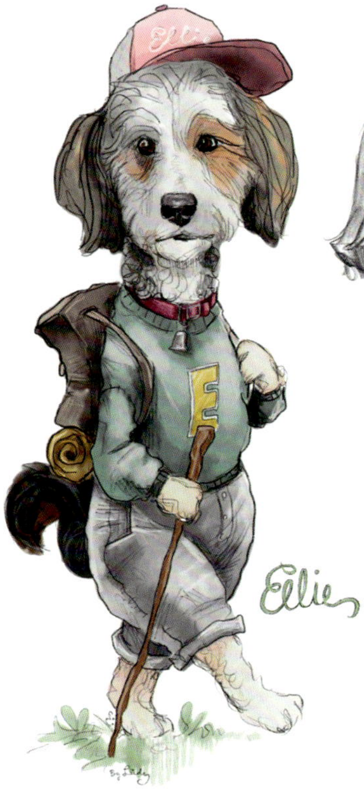
Ellie

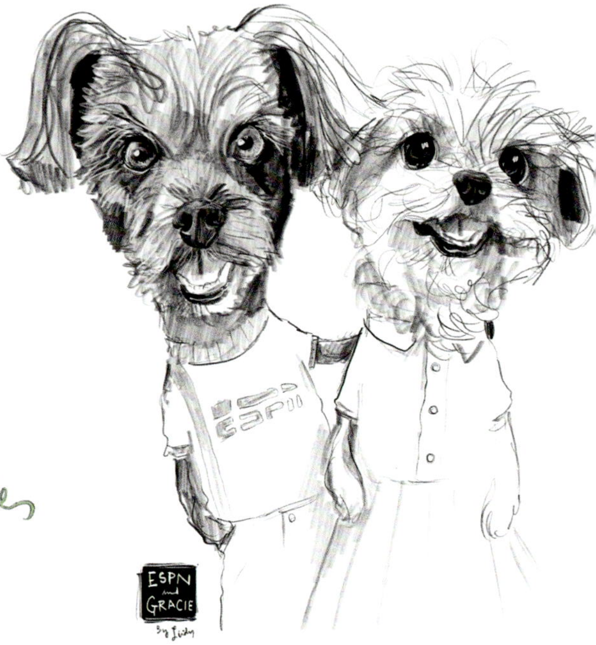
ESPN
and
GRACIE

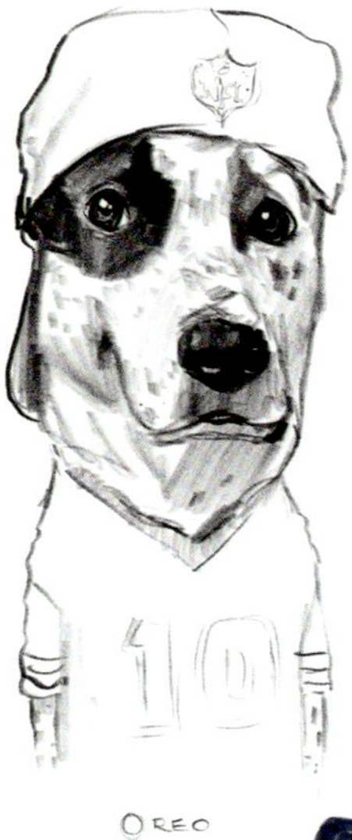
OREO

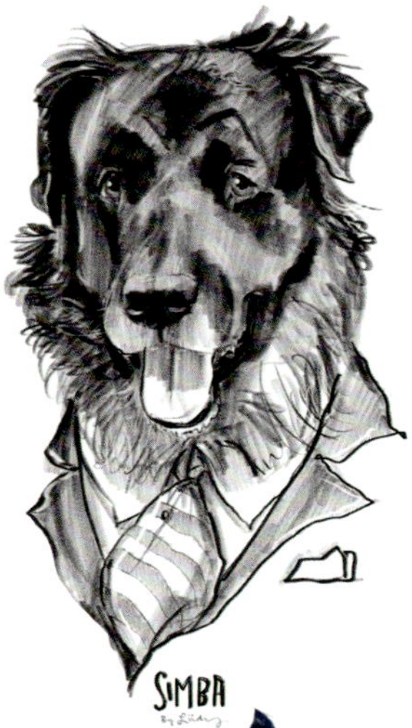
SIMBA

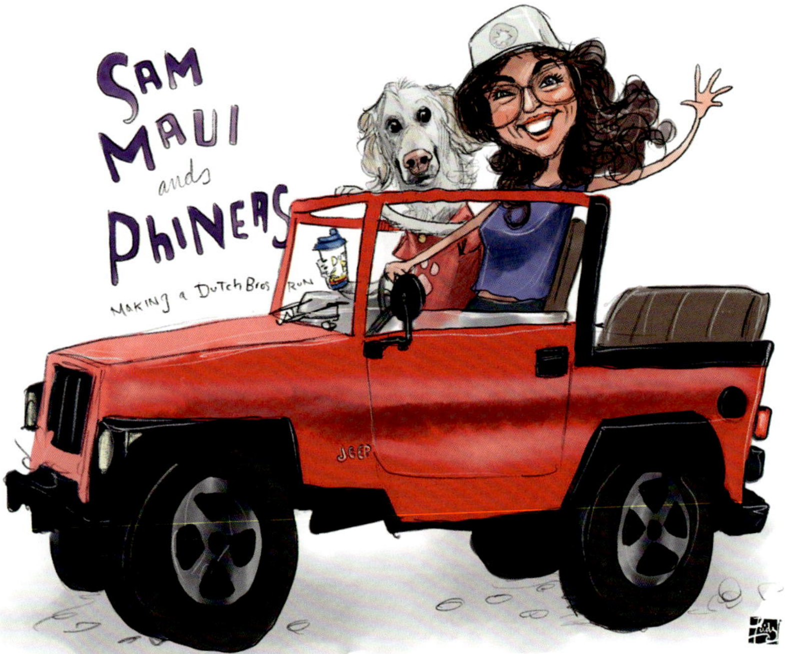
SAM
MAUI
and
PHINEAS
MAKING a Dutch Bros RUN
JEEP

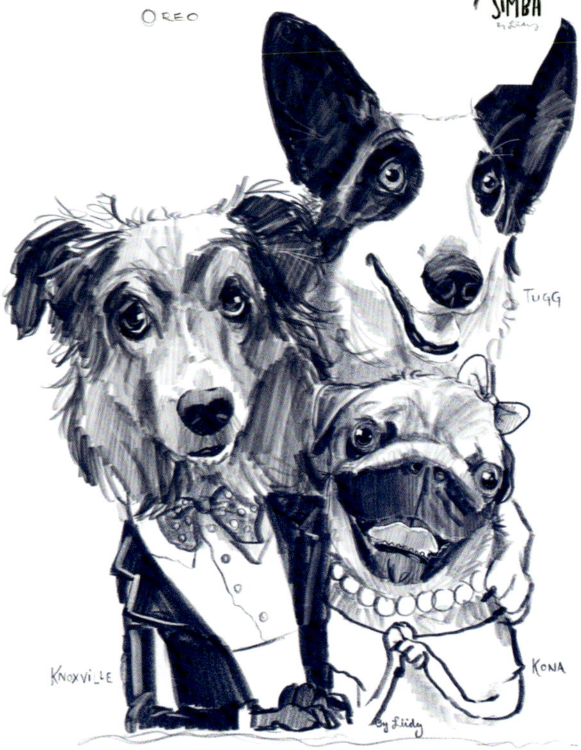
TUGG
KNOXVILLE
KONA

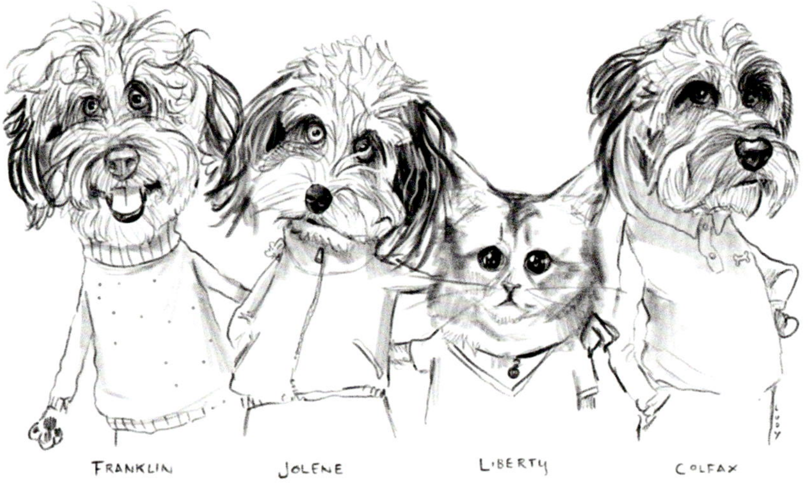
FRANKLIN
JOLENE
LIBERTY
COLFAX

"Animals are such agreeable friends— they ask no questions; they pass no criticisms."

— George Eliot

Dego

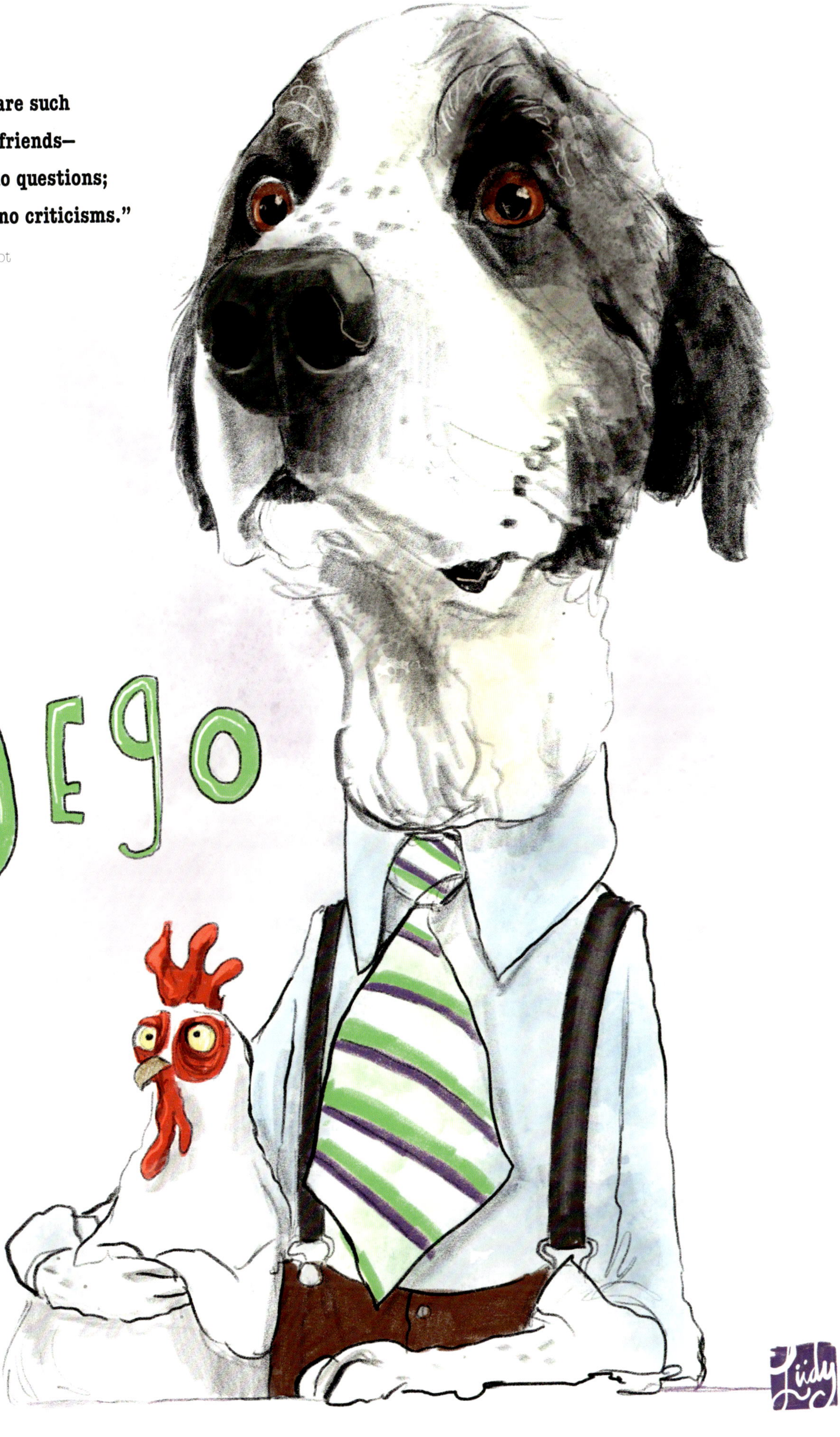

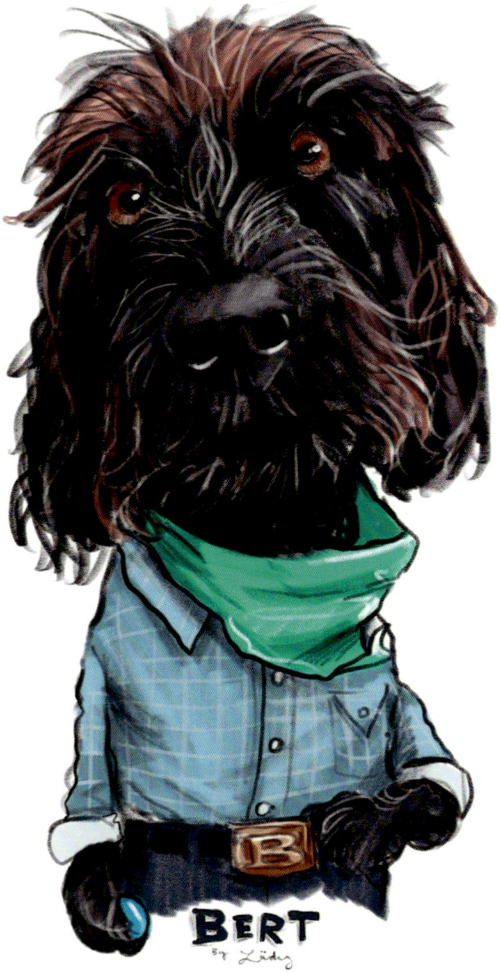
BERT
By Lüdy

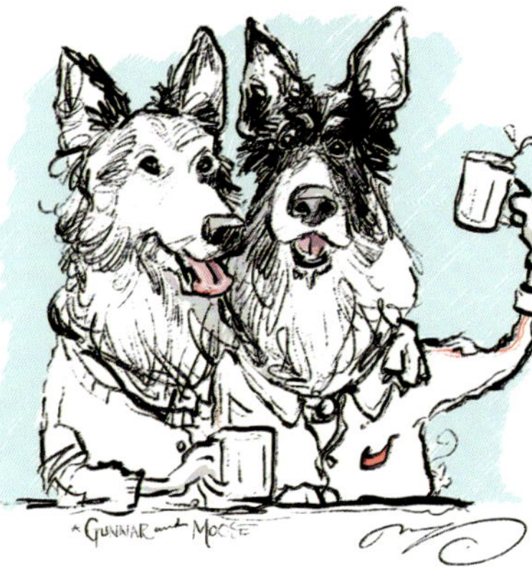
Gunnar and Moose

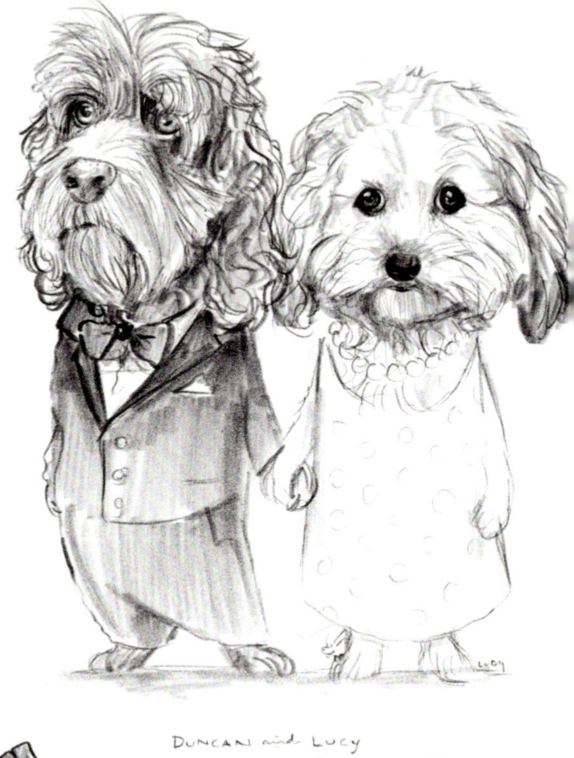
DUNCAN and LUCY

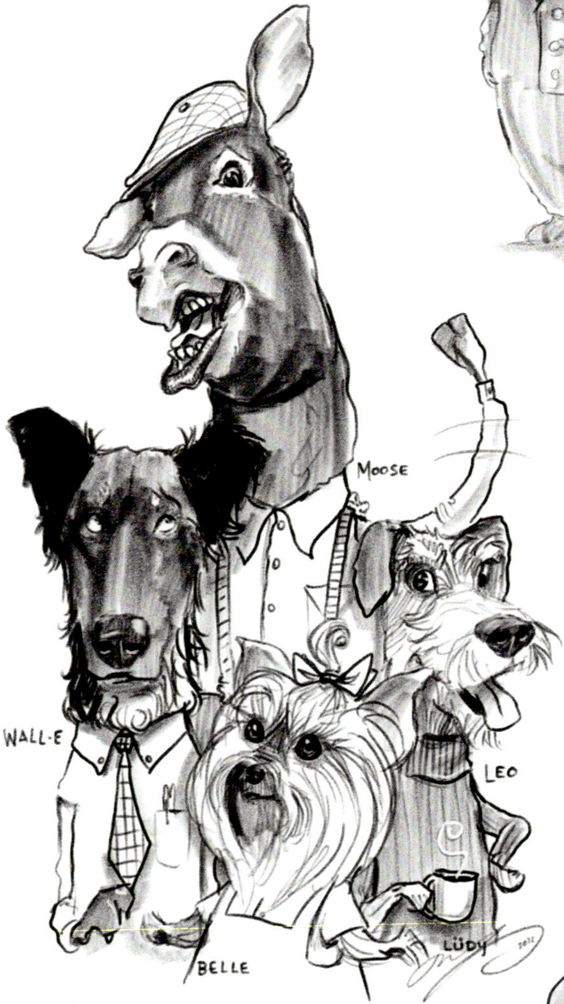
MOOSE
WALL-E
LEO
BELLE
LÜDY 2012

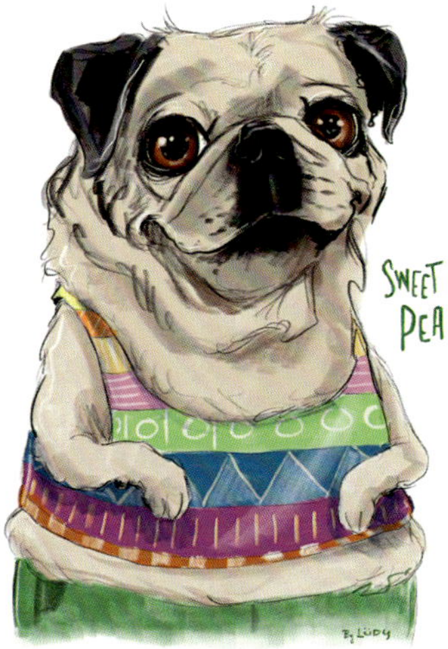
SWEET PEA
By Lüdy

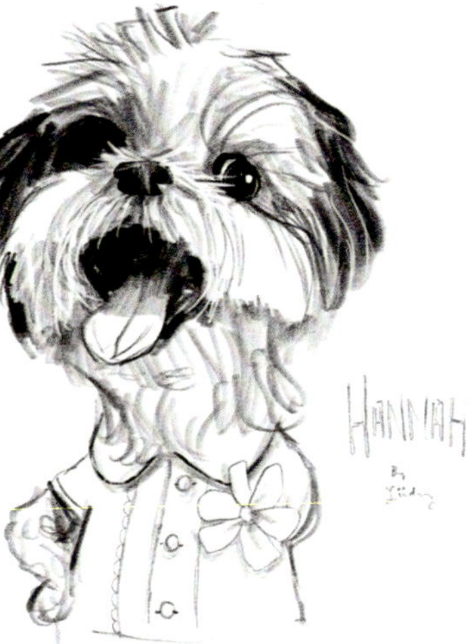
Hannah
By Lüdy

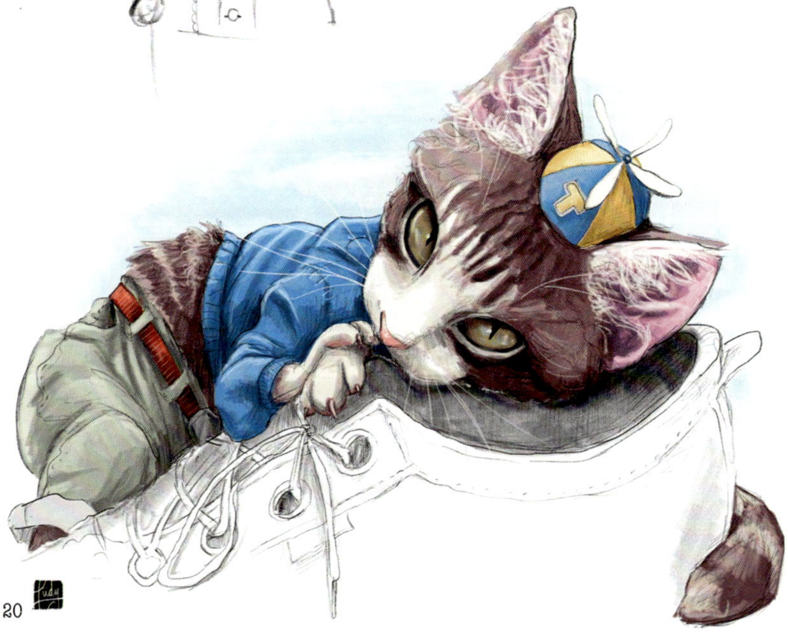

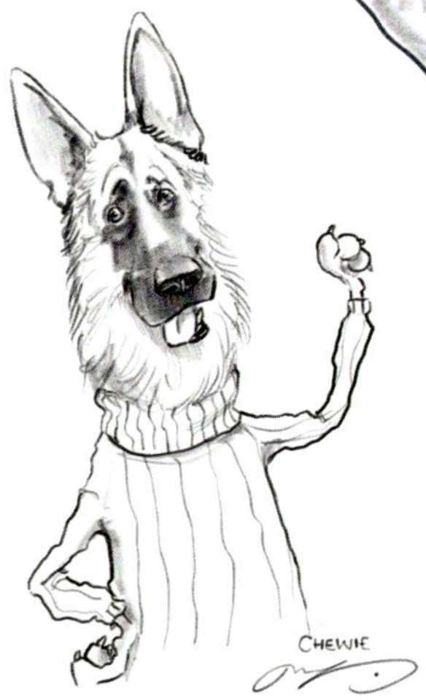
CHEWIE

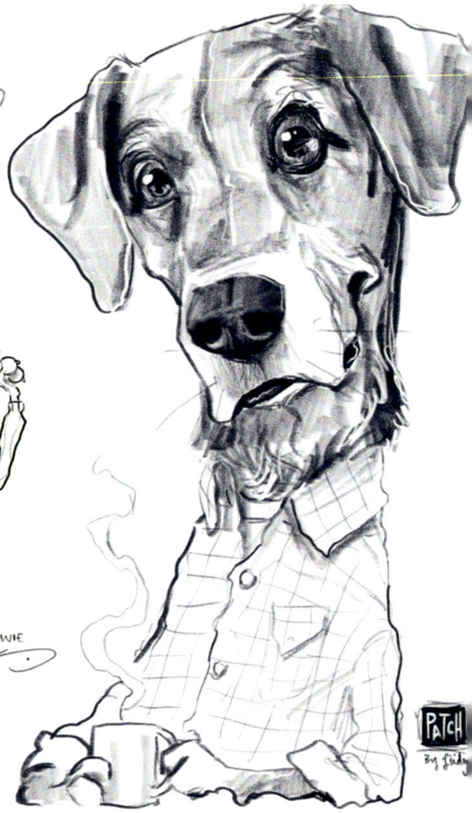
PATCH
By Lüdy

"A friend is someone who knows all about you and still loves you."

—Elbert Hubbard

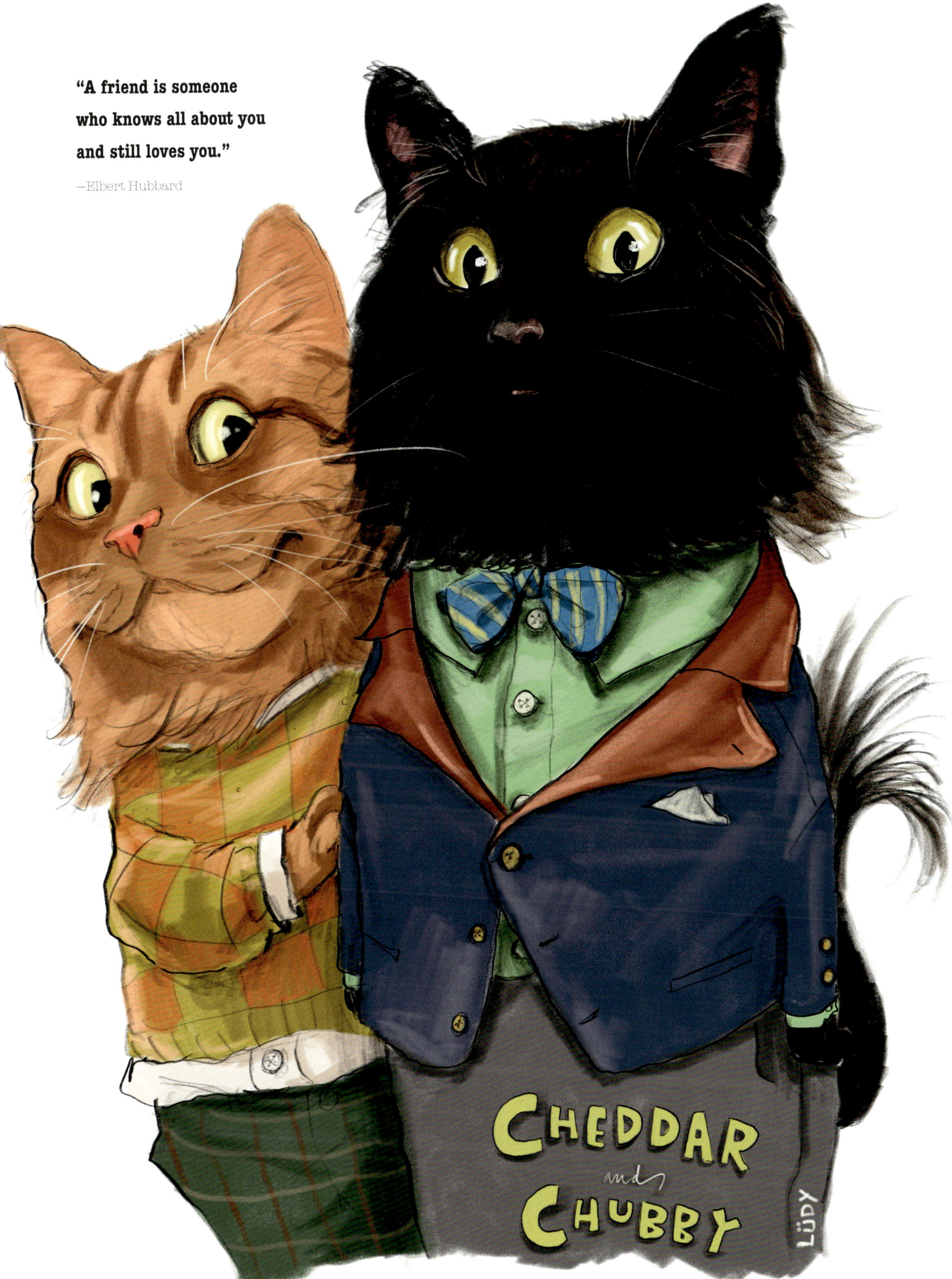

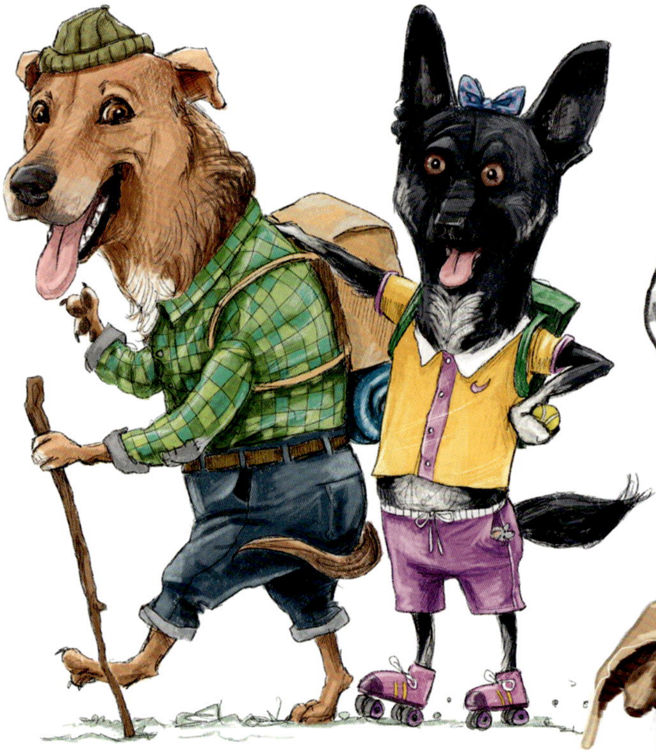

LINK and SHEIK

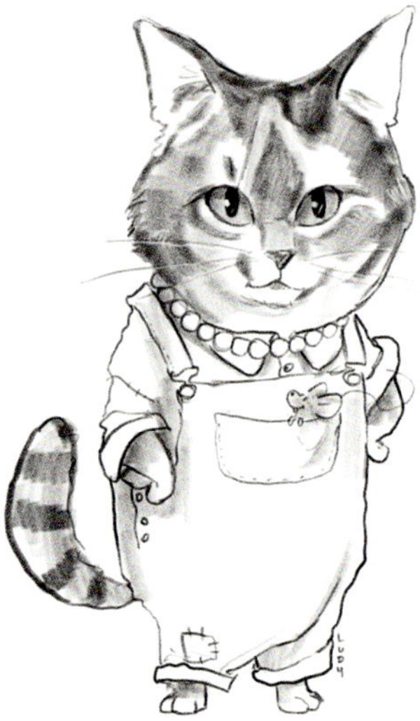

Musette

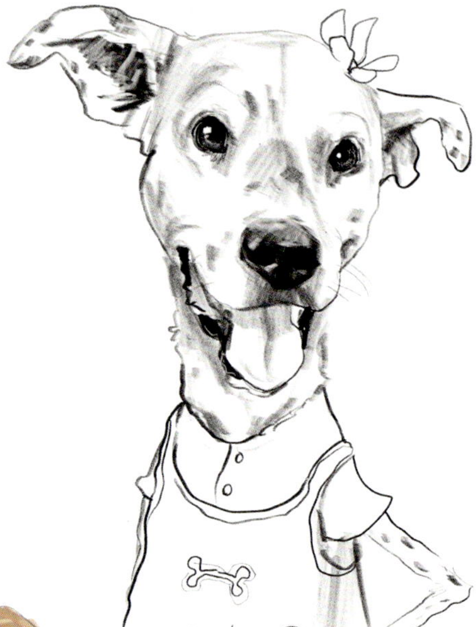

Sweet DOTTIE

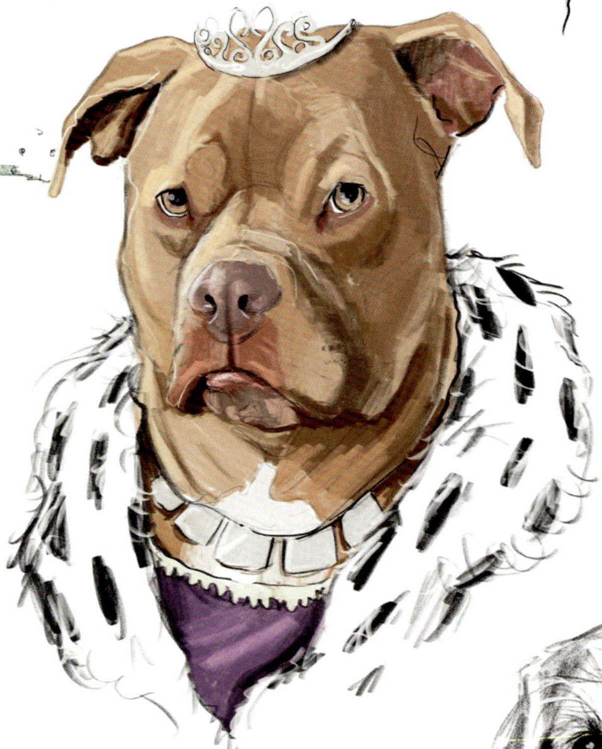

AMEENA Reine

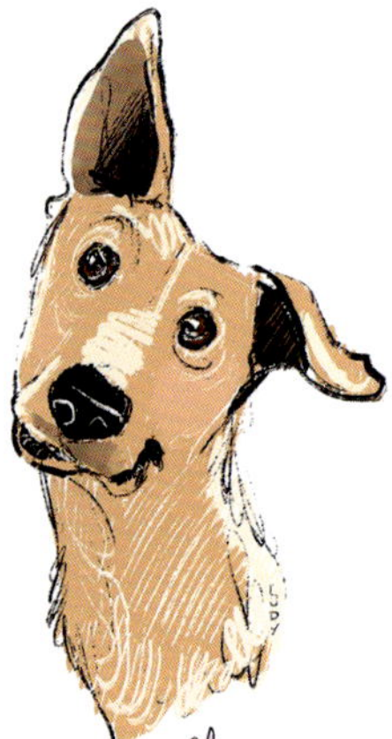

Molly

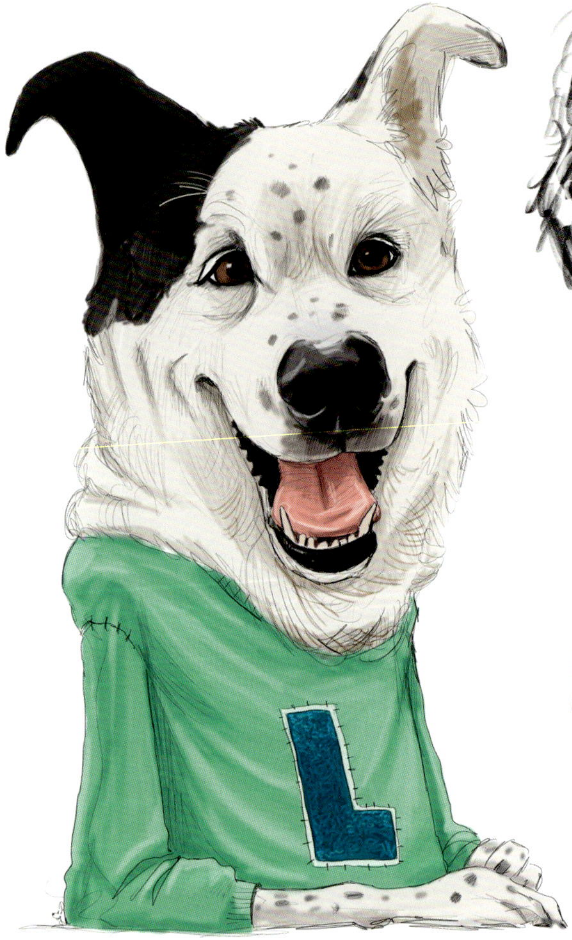

Wonderful LUCY

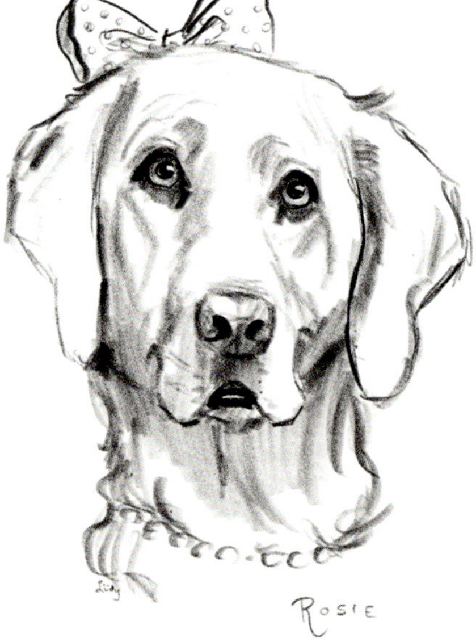

ROSIE

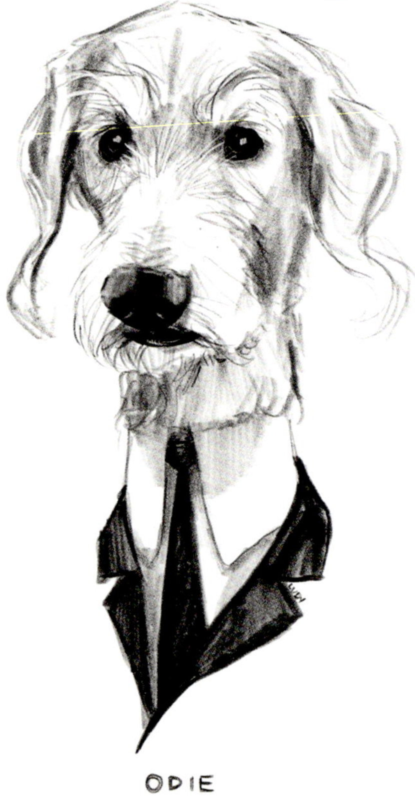

ODIE

"Pugs are living proof that God has a sense of humor."

— Margot Kaufman

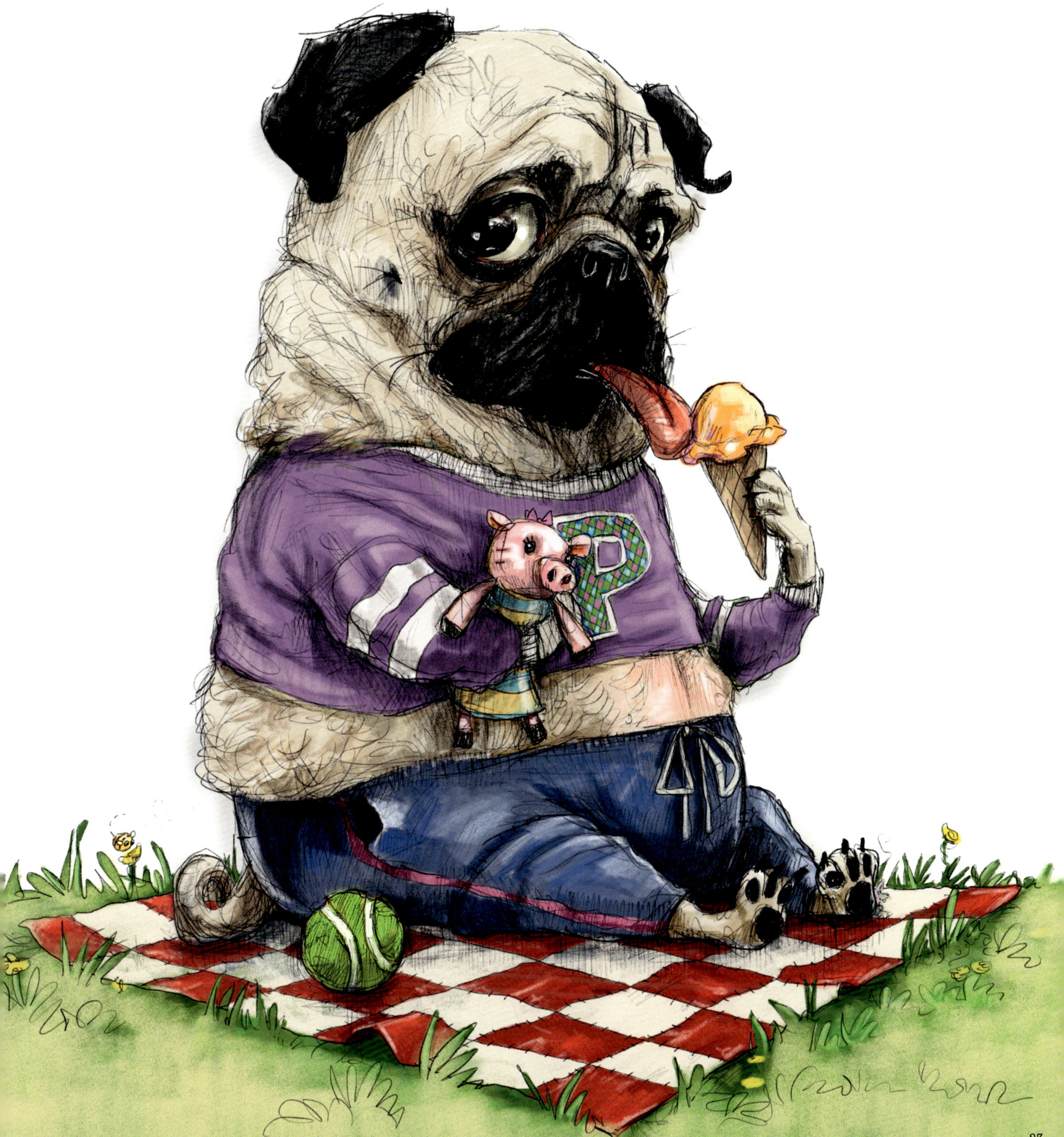

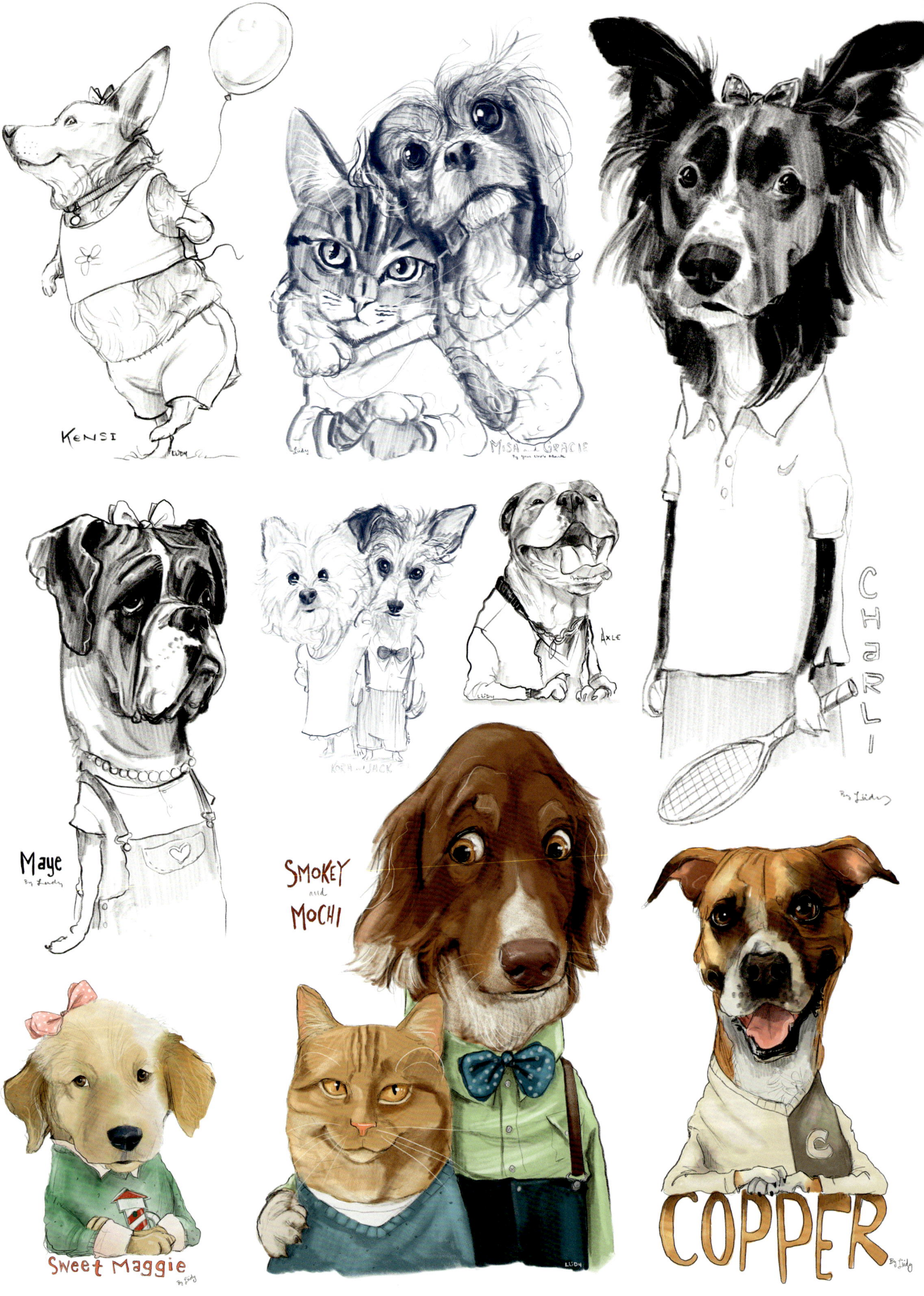
KENSI
CHARLI
Maye
AXLE
SMOKEY
and
MOCHI
Sweet Maggie
COPPER

When pets and their people come together, even ordinary days start to feel like adventures.

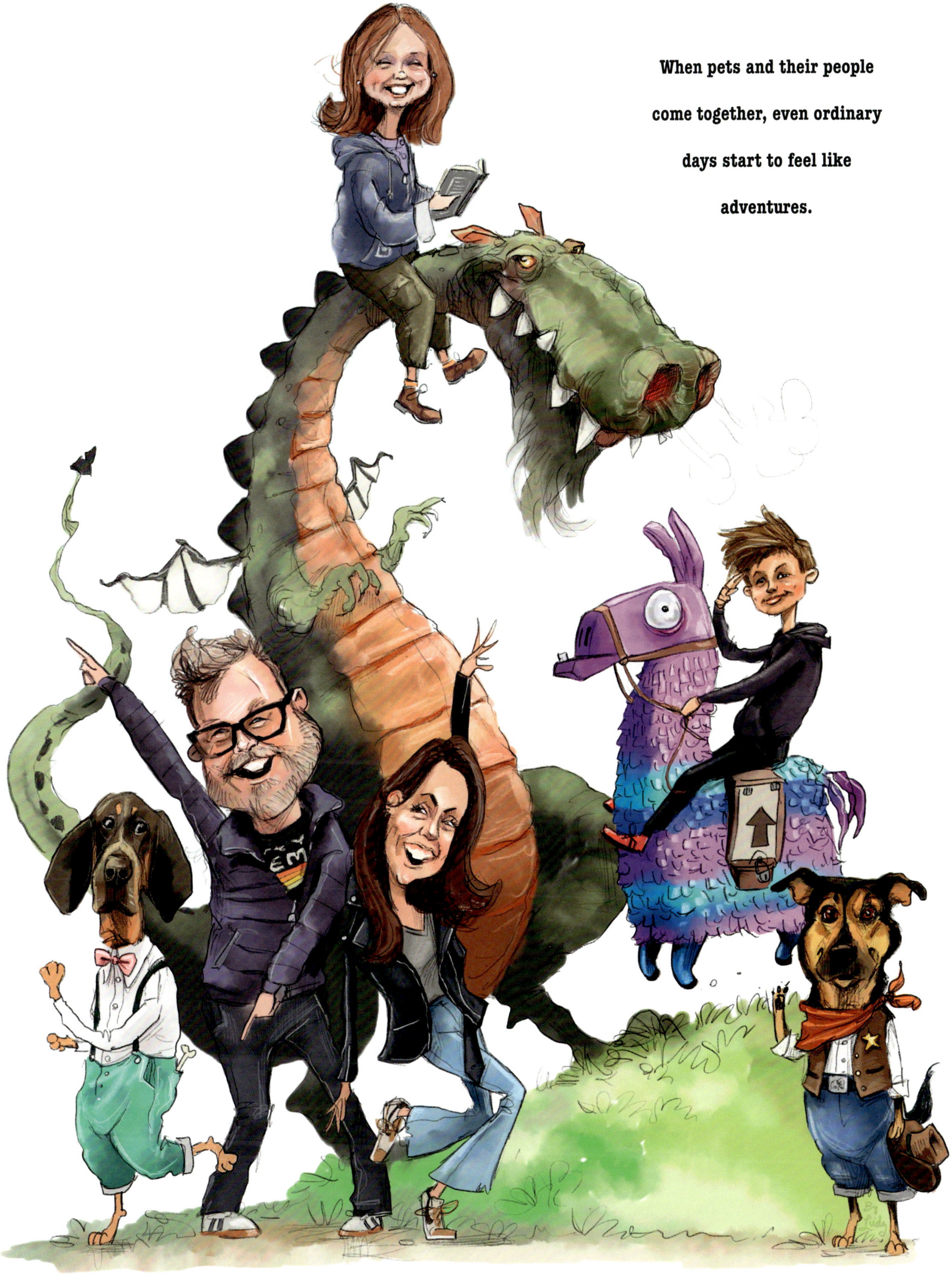

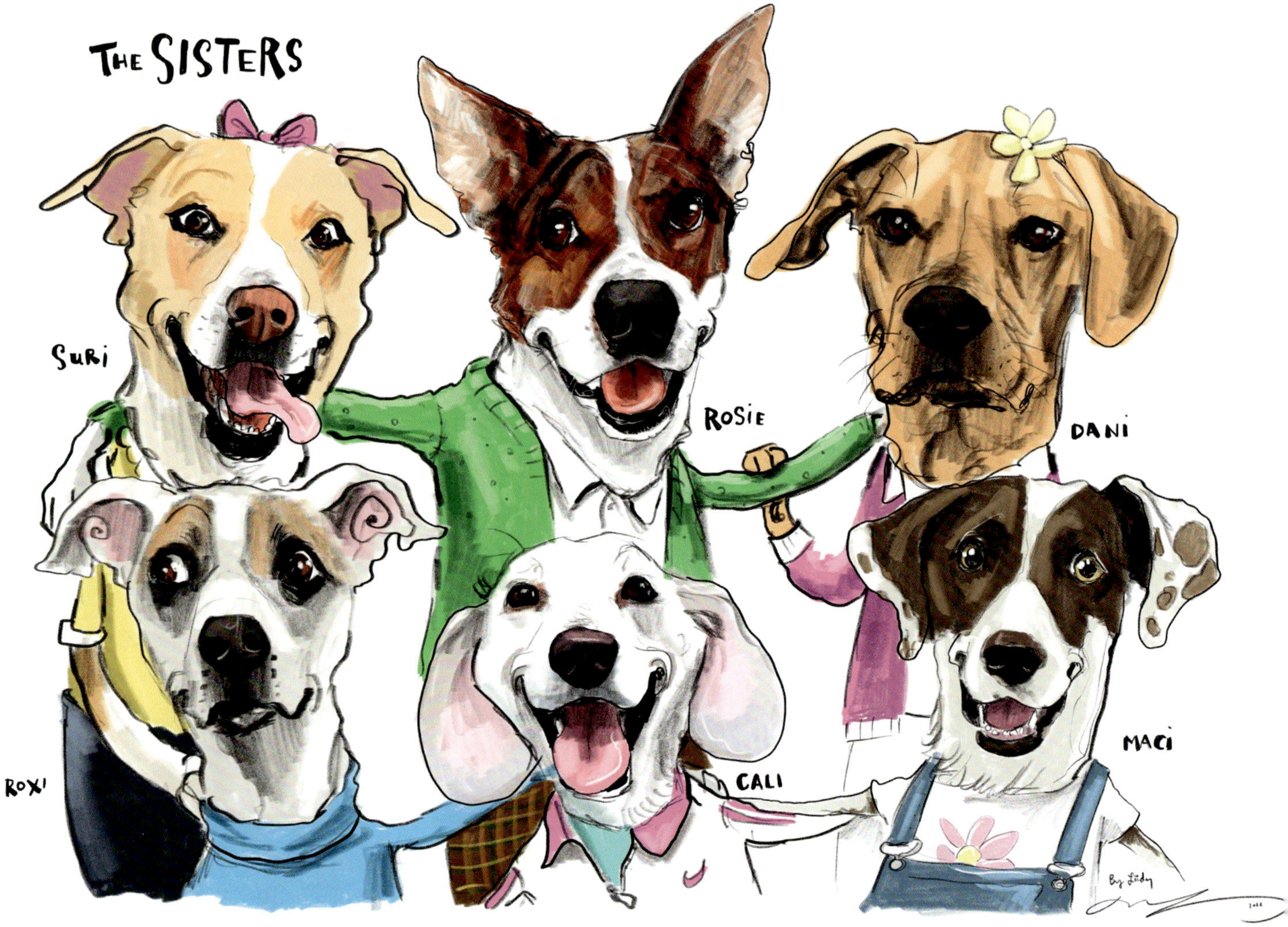
THE SISTERS
SURI
ROSIE
DANI
ROXI
CALI
MACI
By Jüdy

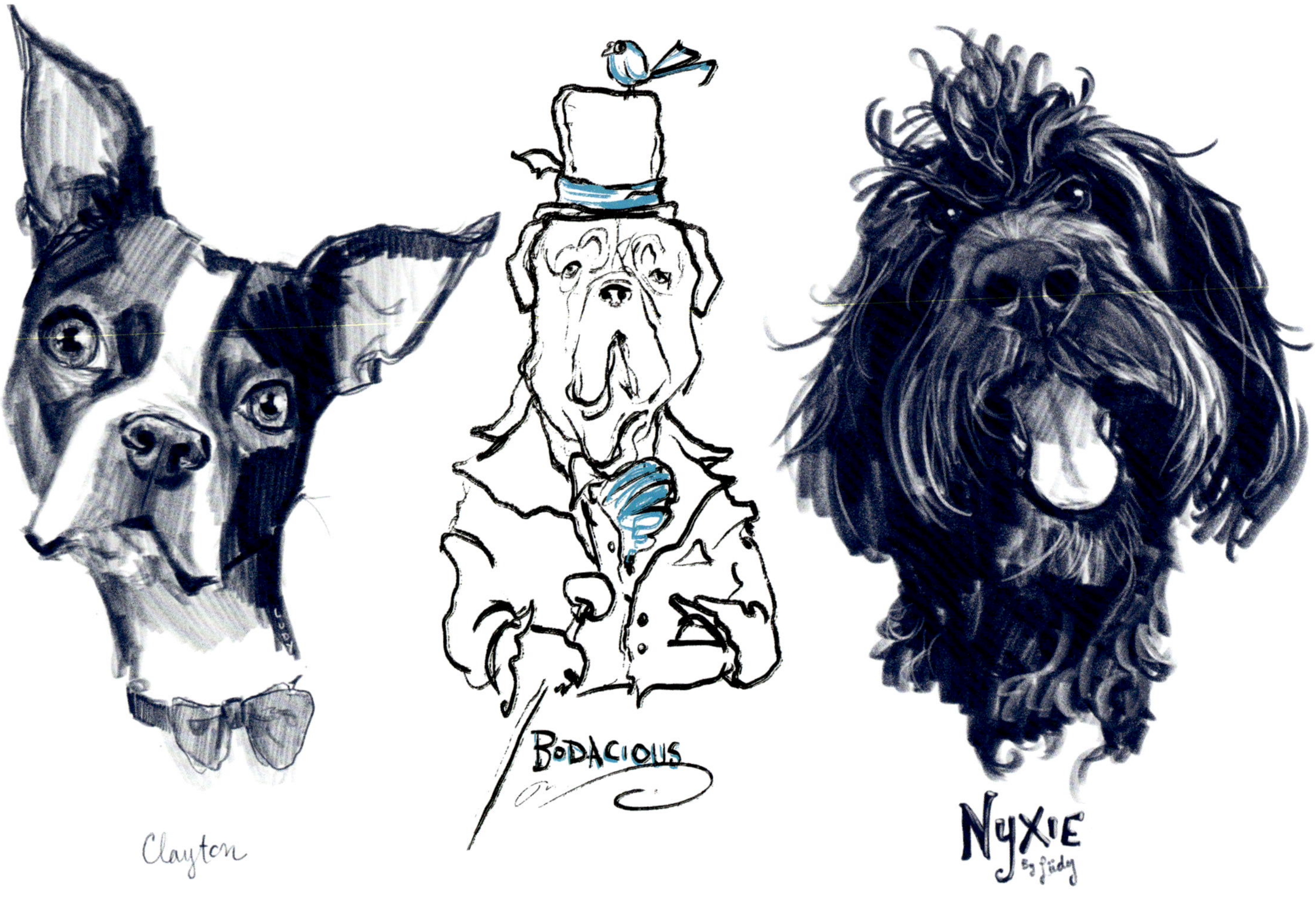
Clayton
BODACIOUS
NYXIE
By Jüdy

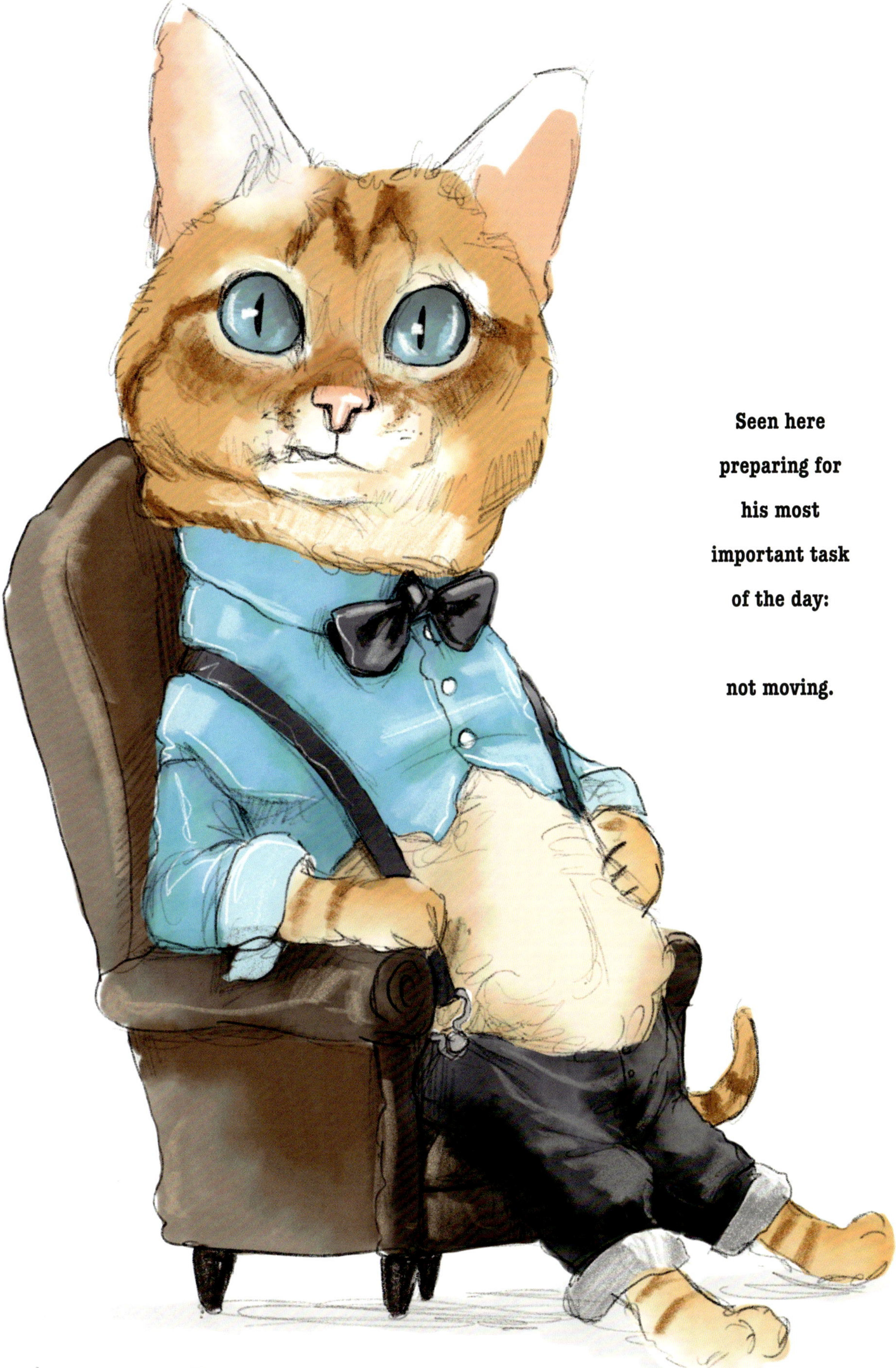

Seen here
preparing for
his most
important task
of the day:

not moving.

George

by Lüdy

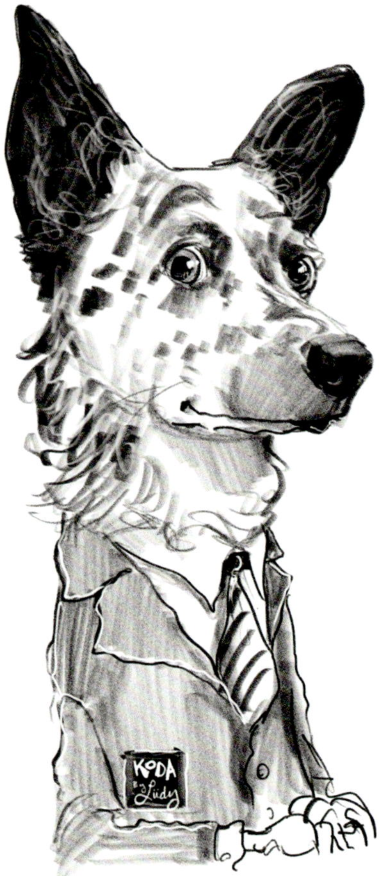

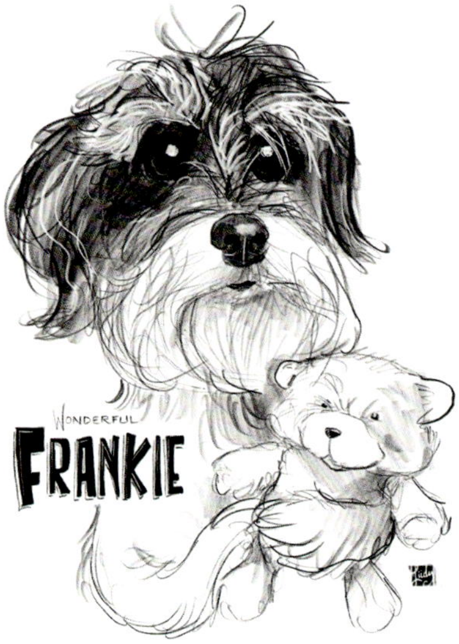

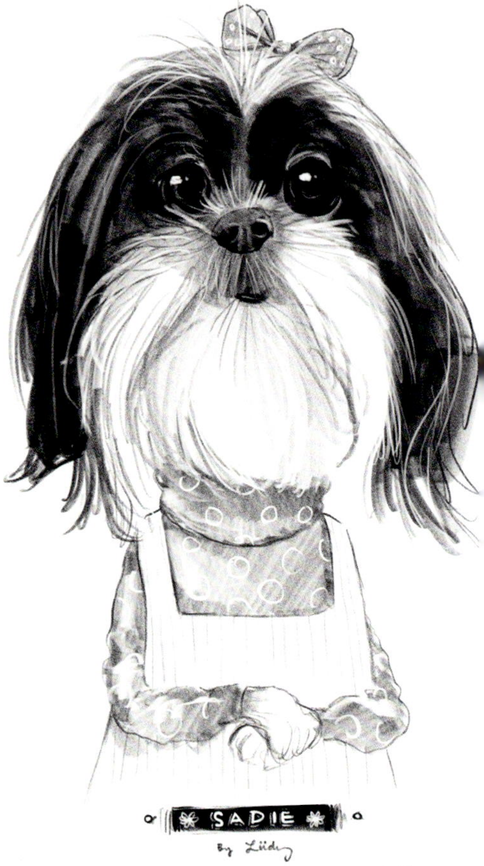

They don't ask for much.
A walk. A window. A crumb.
A corner of the couch.
And yet—somehow—
they give us everything.
They give us mornings
with meaning.
Evenings with laughter.
They remind us to chase joy.
To nap boldly.
To show up with our whole tail.

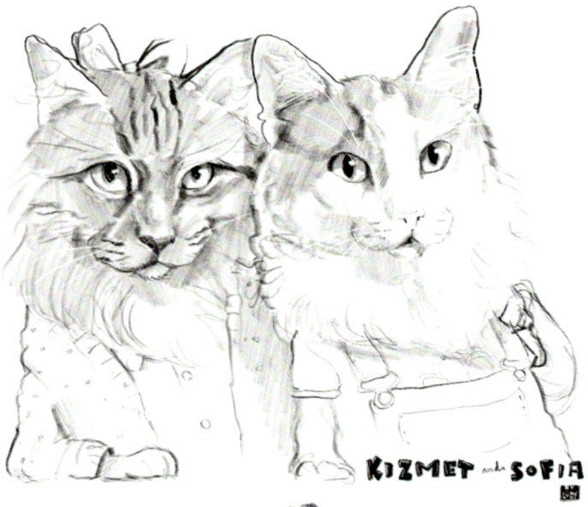

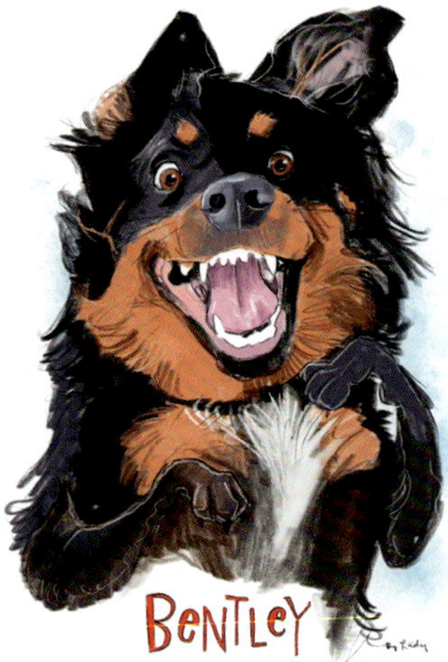

They love us through the mess,
the noise,
and that one time
we ran out of treats.
They are the heartbeat beside us—
Furry, finned, feathered,
or otherwise—
And life is simply better
with them in it.

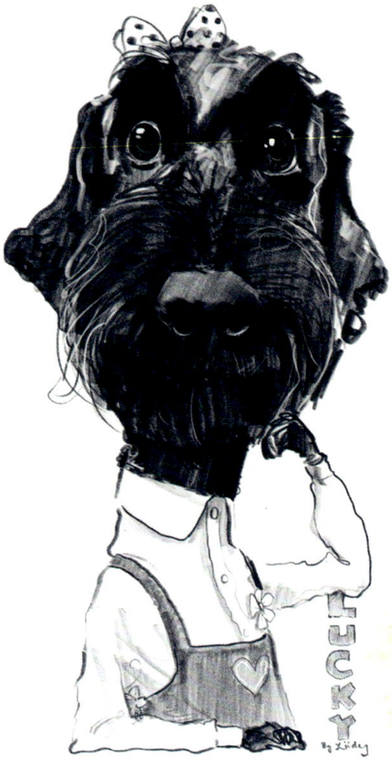

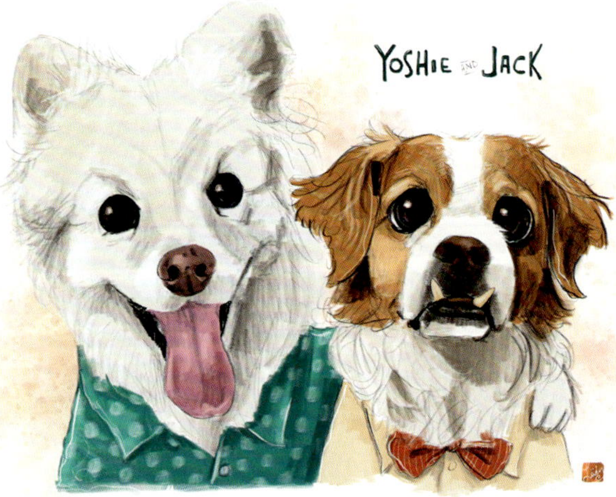

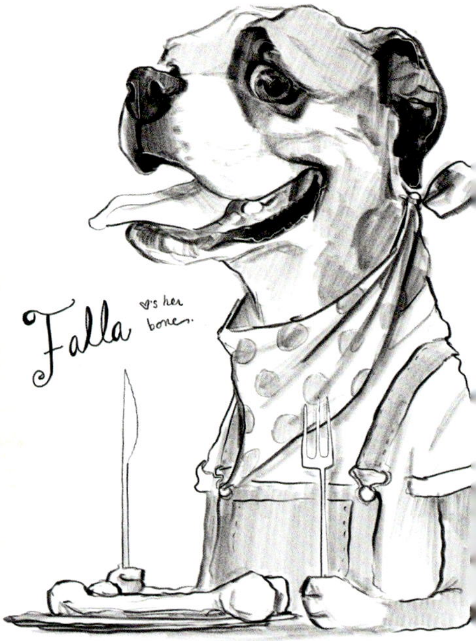

BABALU and FRANKIE

By Lindy

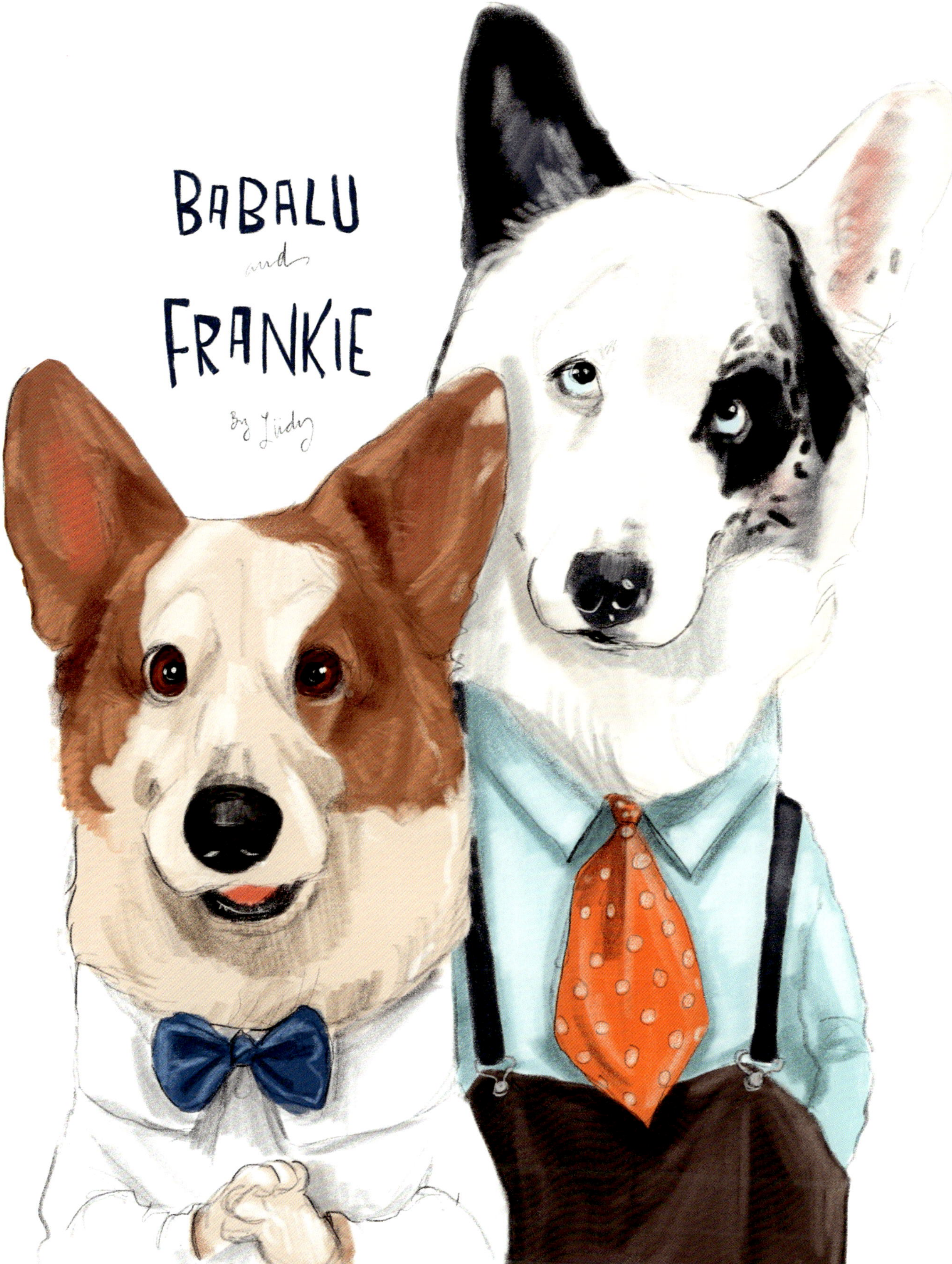

Met on a Monday. Sniffed on a Tuesday. Inseparable ever since.

Dora, Howard and Norman

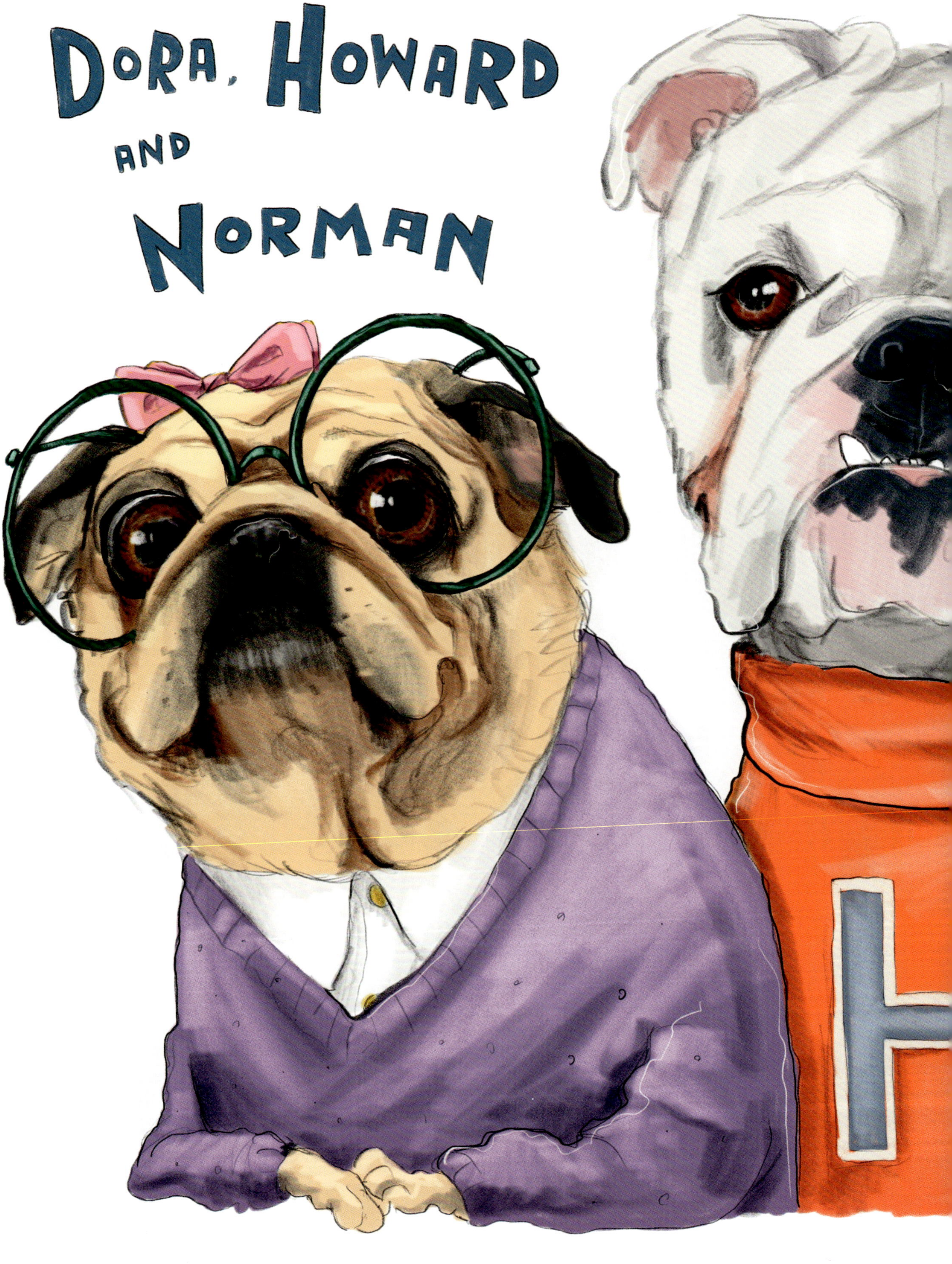

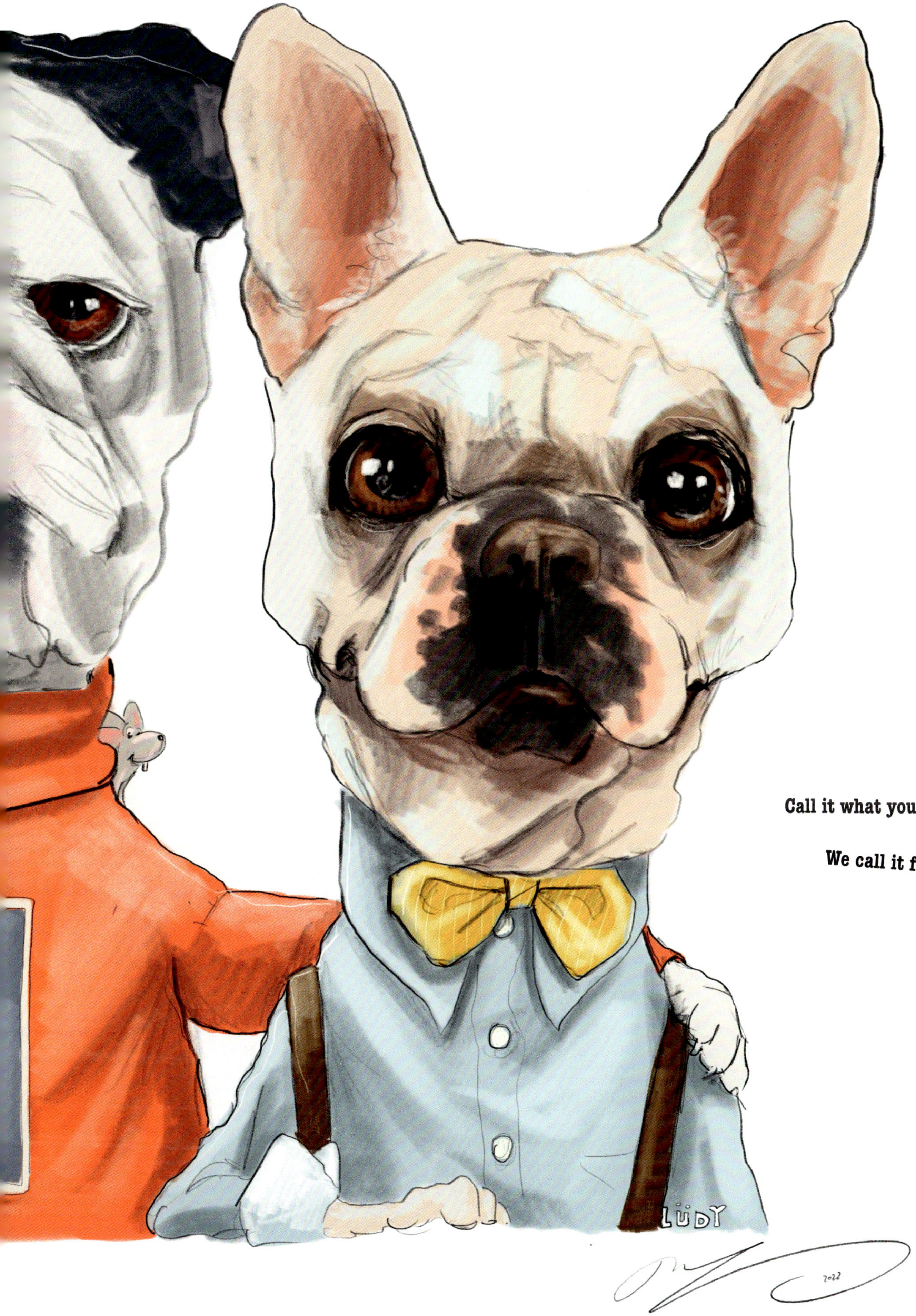

Call it what you want.

We call it family.

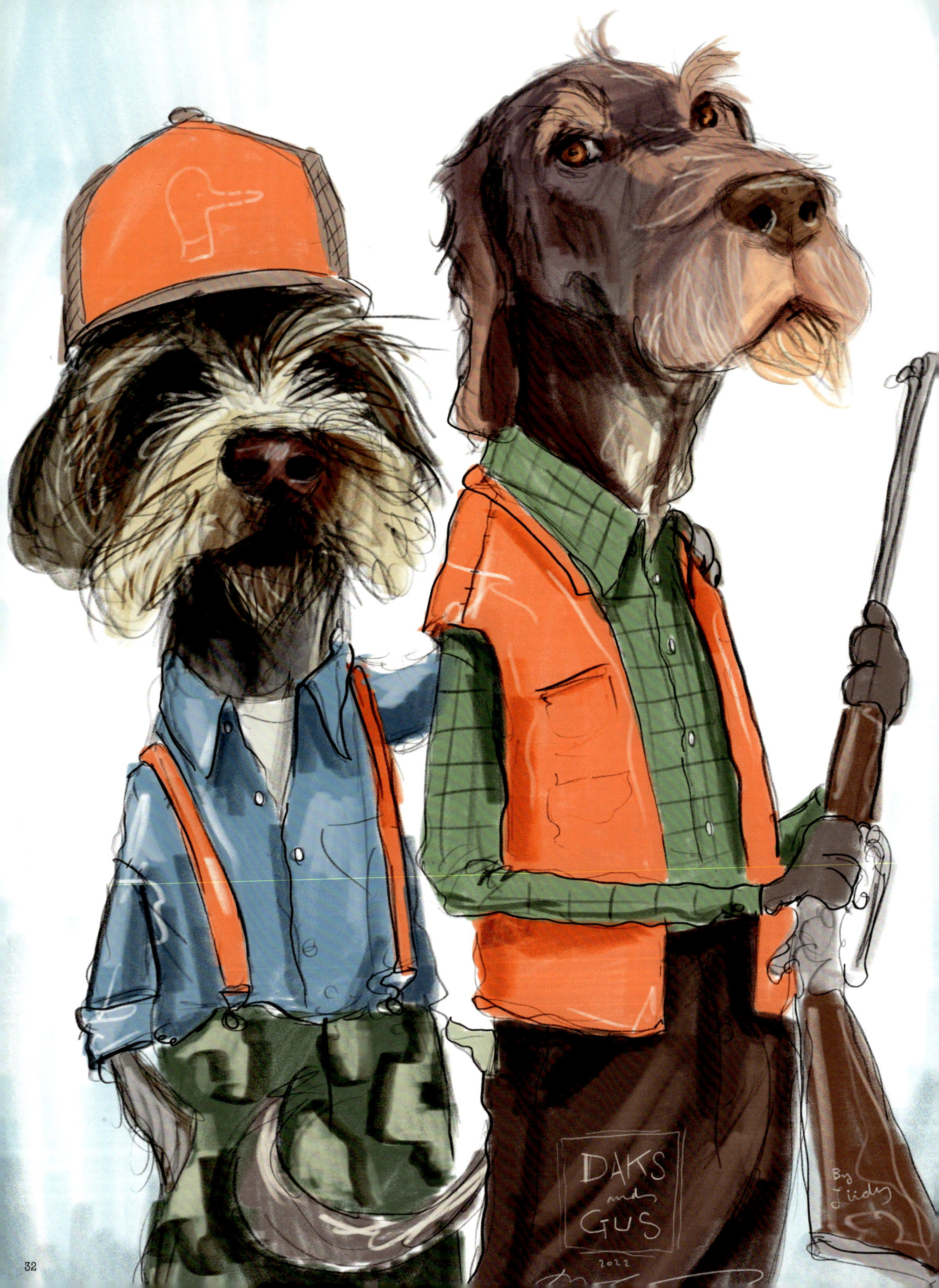
DAKS and GUS
2022
By Liidy

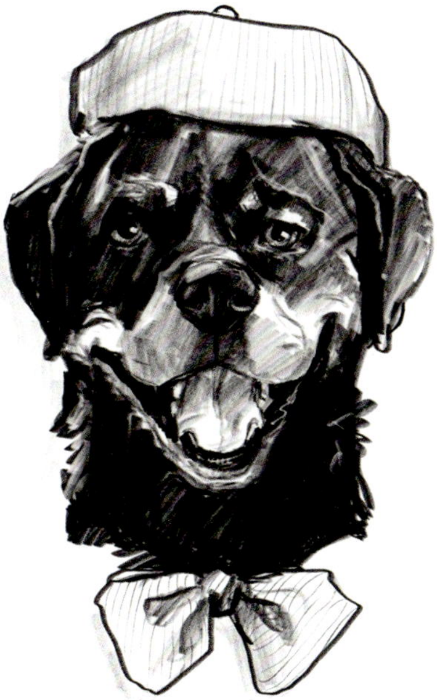

GUINNESS

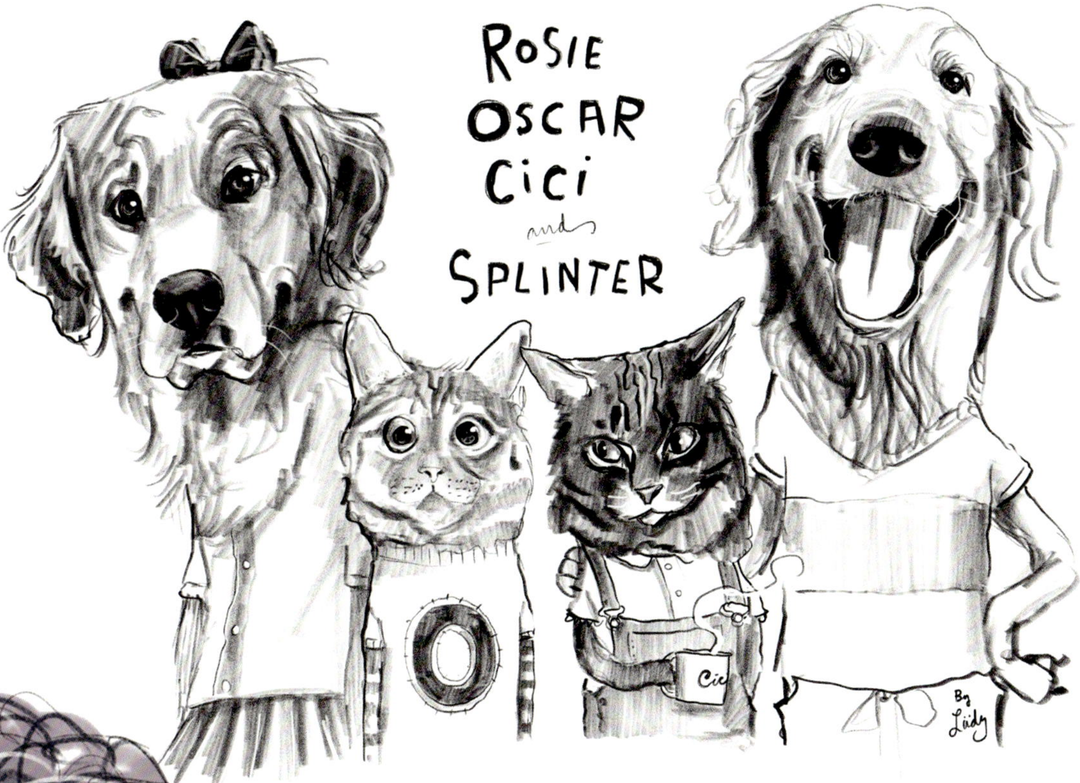
ROSIE
OSCAR
CICI
and
SPLINTER
Cici
By Lüdy

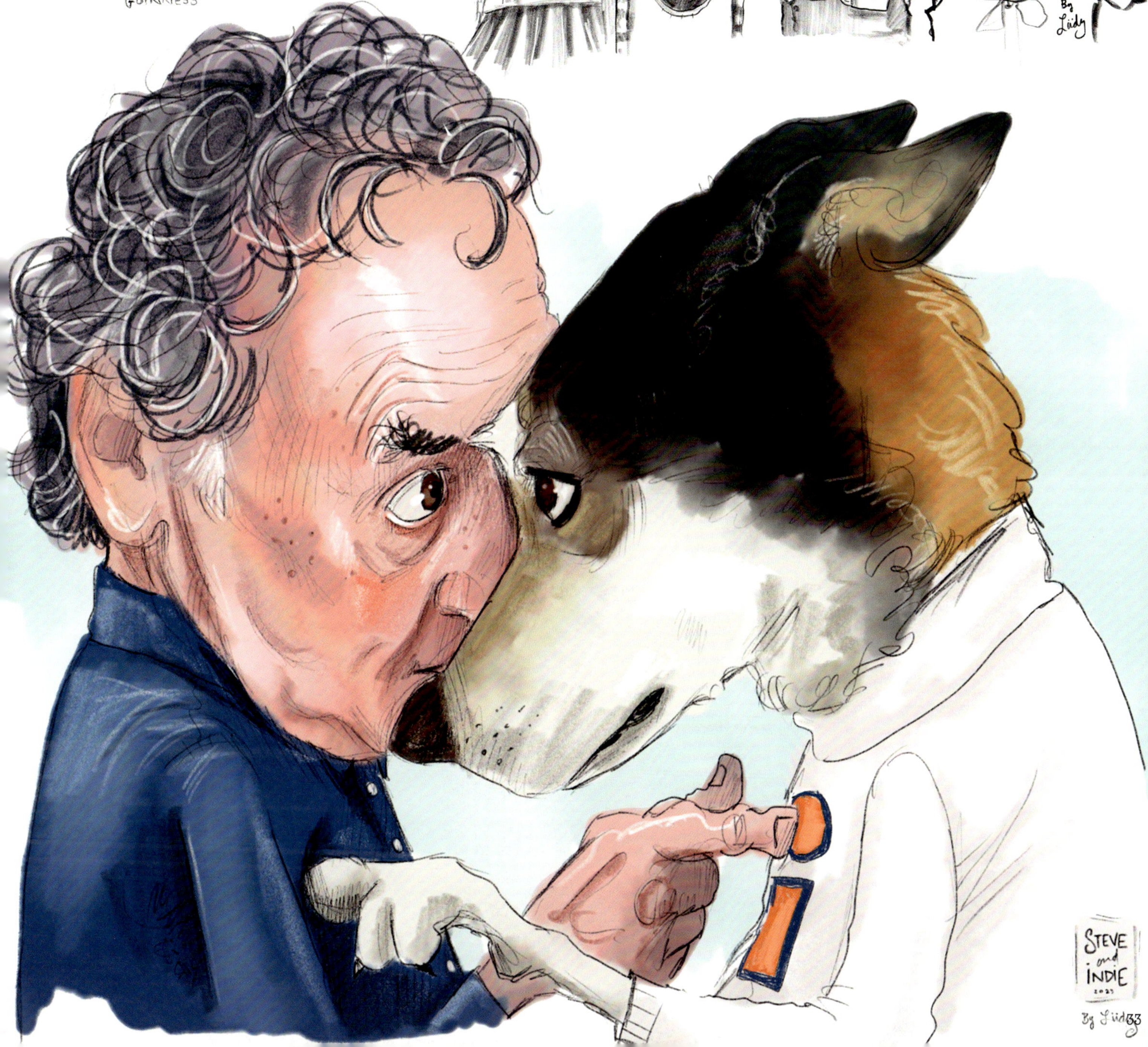
STEVE and INDIE 2023
By Lüdy83

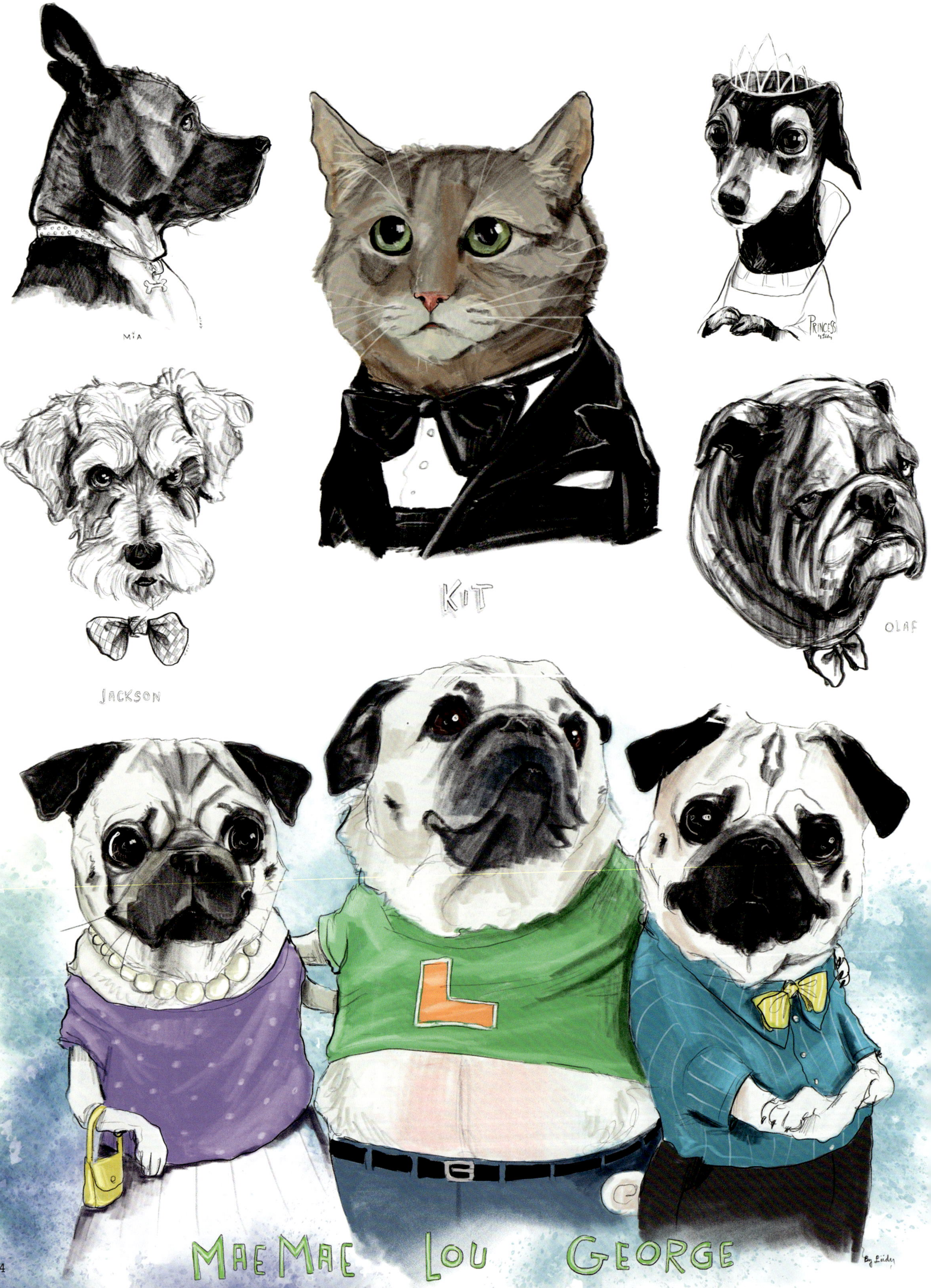
MIA
KIT
PRINCESS
JACKSON
OLAF
MAEMAE
LOU
GEORGE

Some friendships
are written in stories.
Theirs is scribbled
in sidewalk chalk,
tugged through park grass,
and whispered
in quiet snuggles
when no one
else is watching.

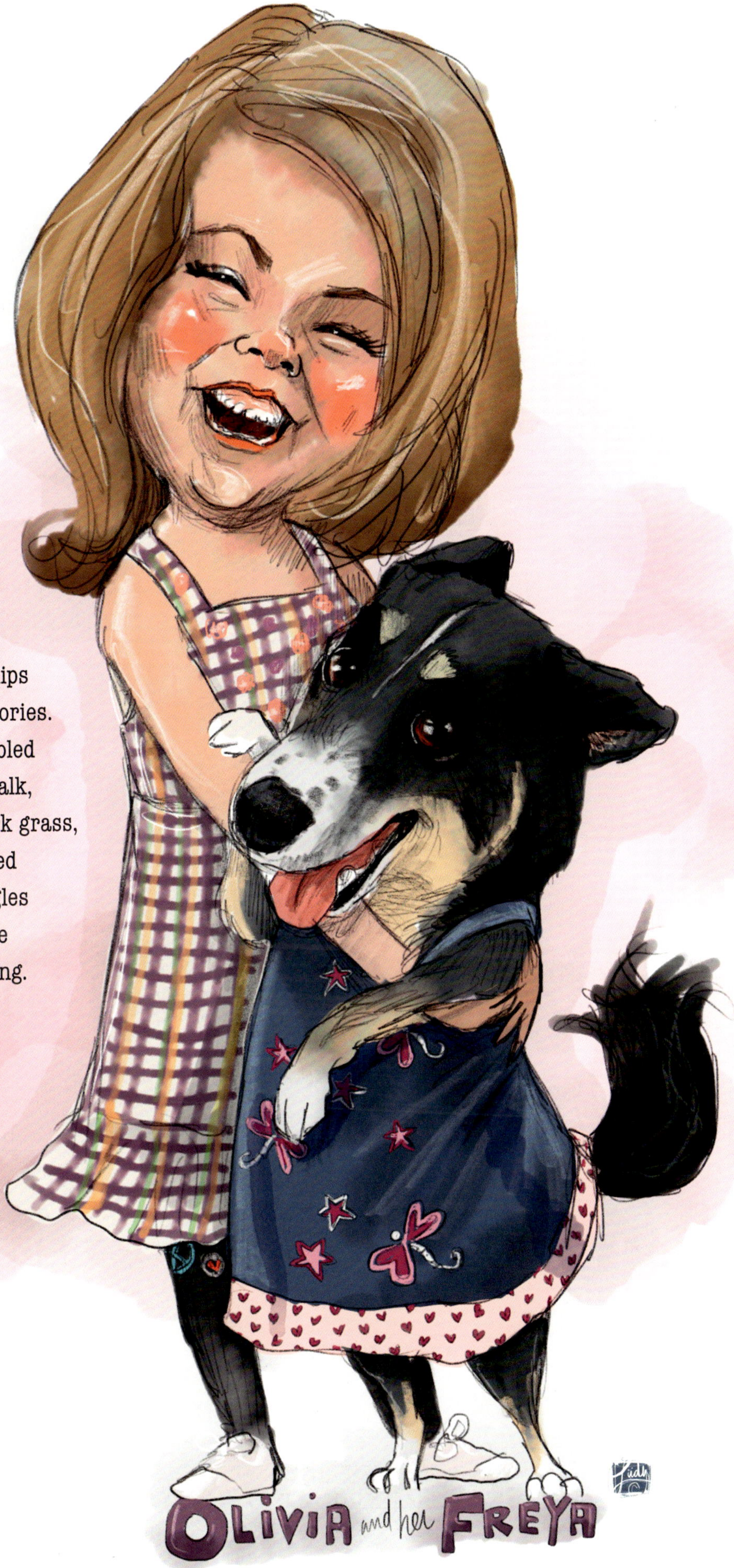

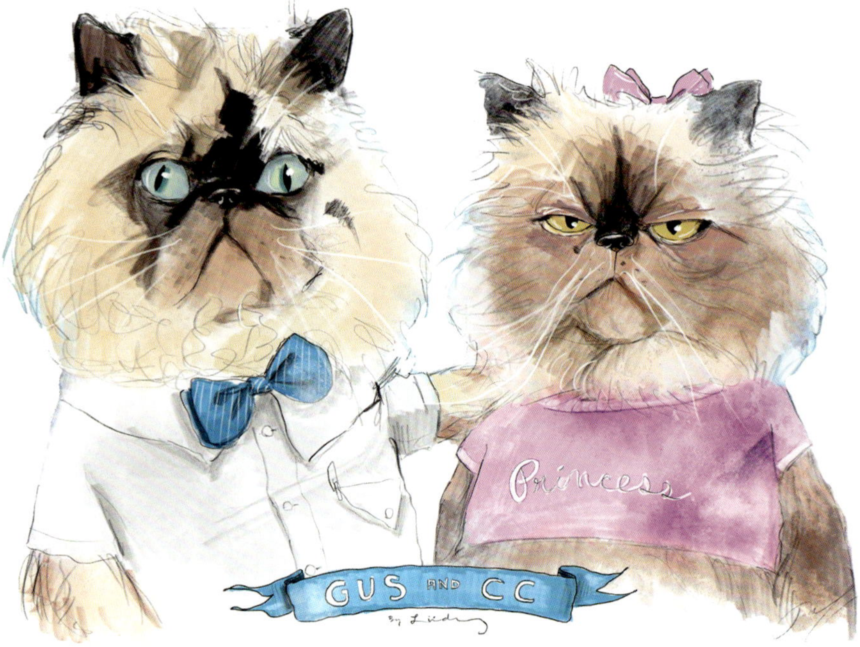
Princess
GUS AND CC

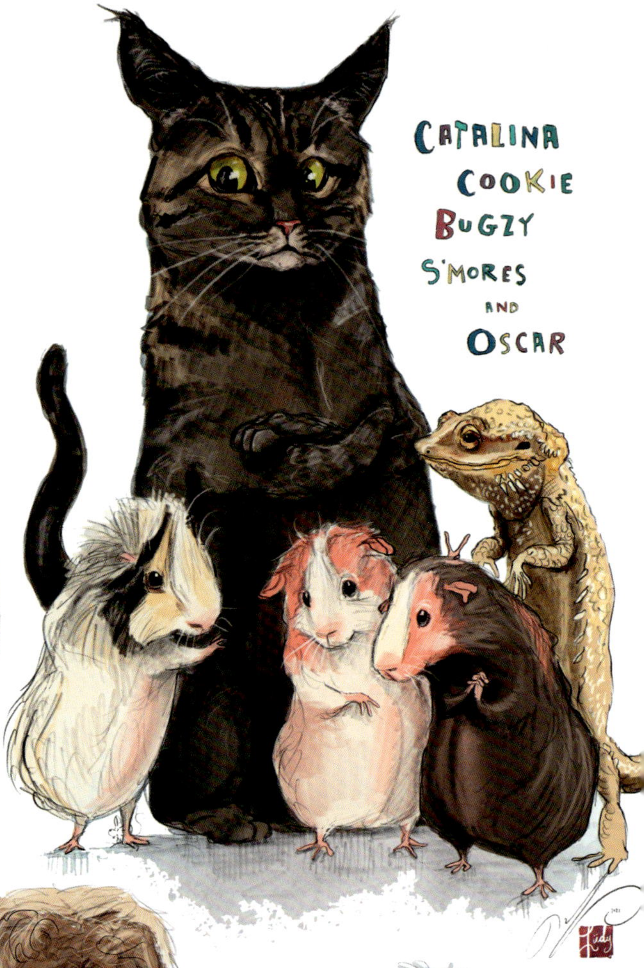
CATALINA
COOKIE
BUGZY
S'MORES
AND
OSCAR

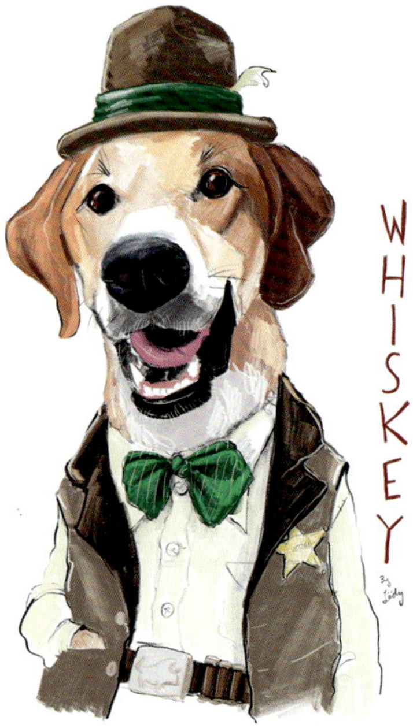
WHISKEY

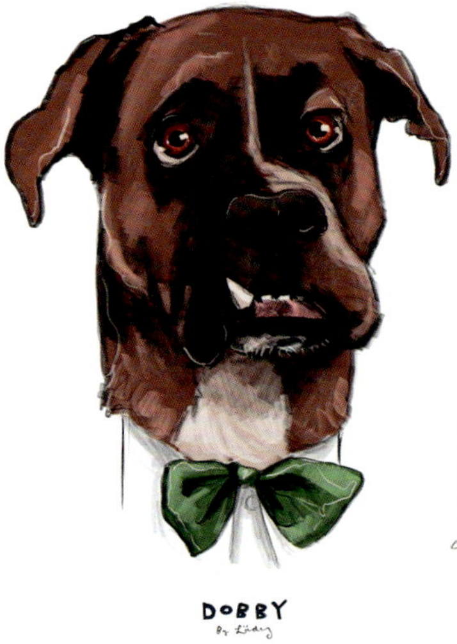
DOBBY

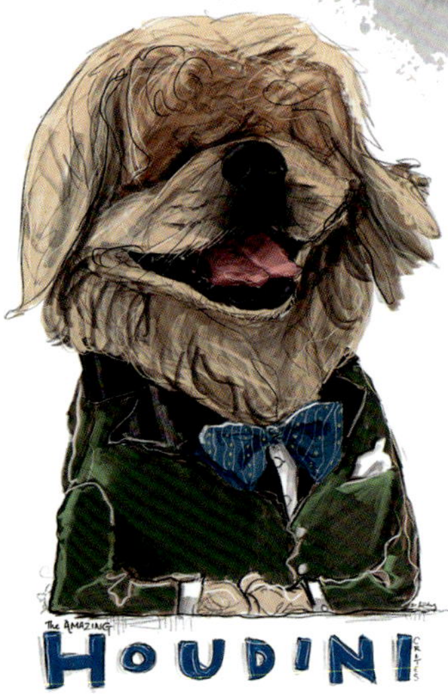
The Amazing
HOUDINI

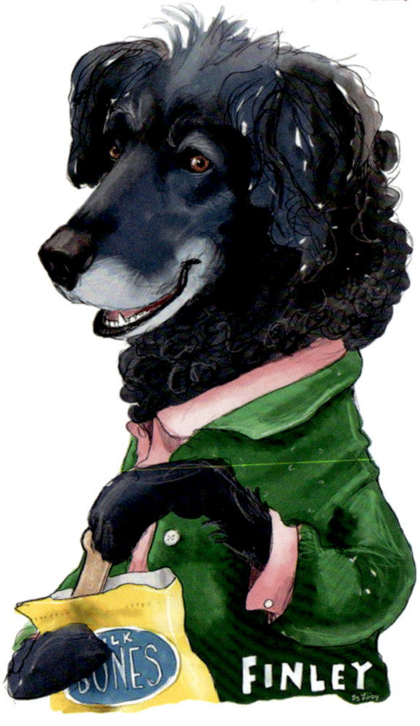
BONES
FINLEY

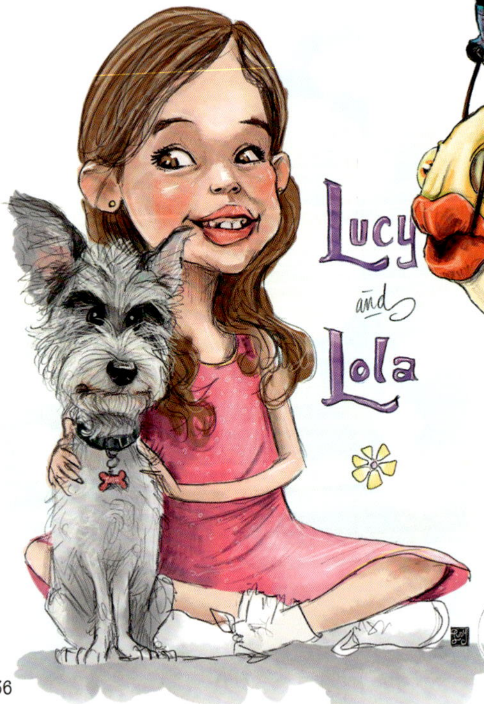
Lucy
and
Lola

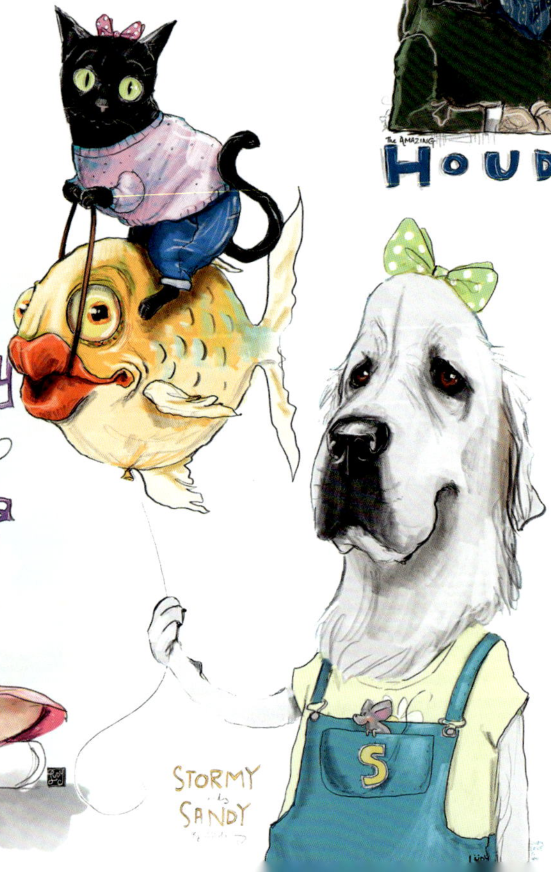
STORMY
SANDY

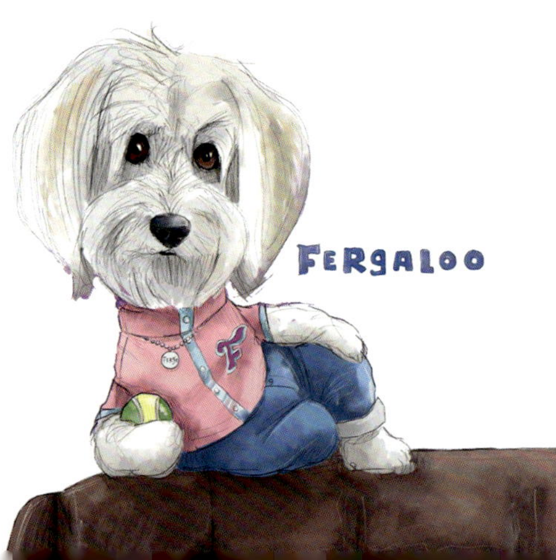
FERGALOO

Love hard.

Nap often.

Protect

the chicken.

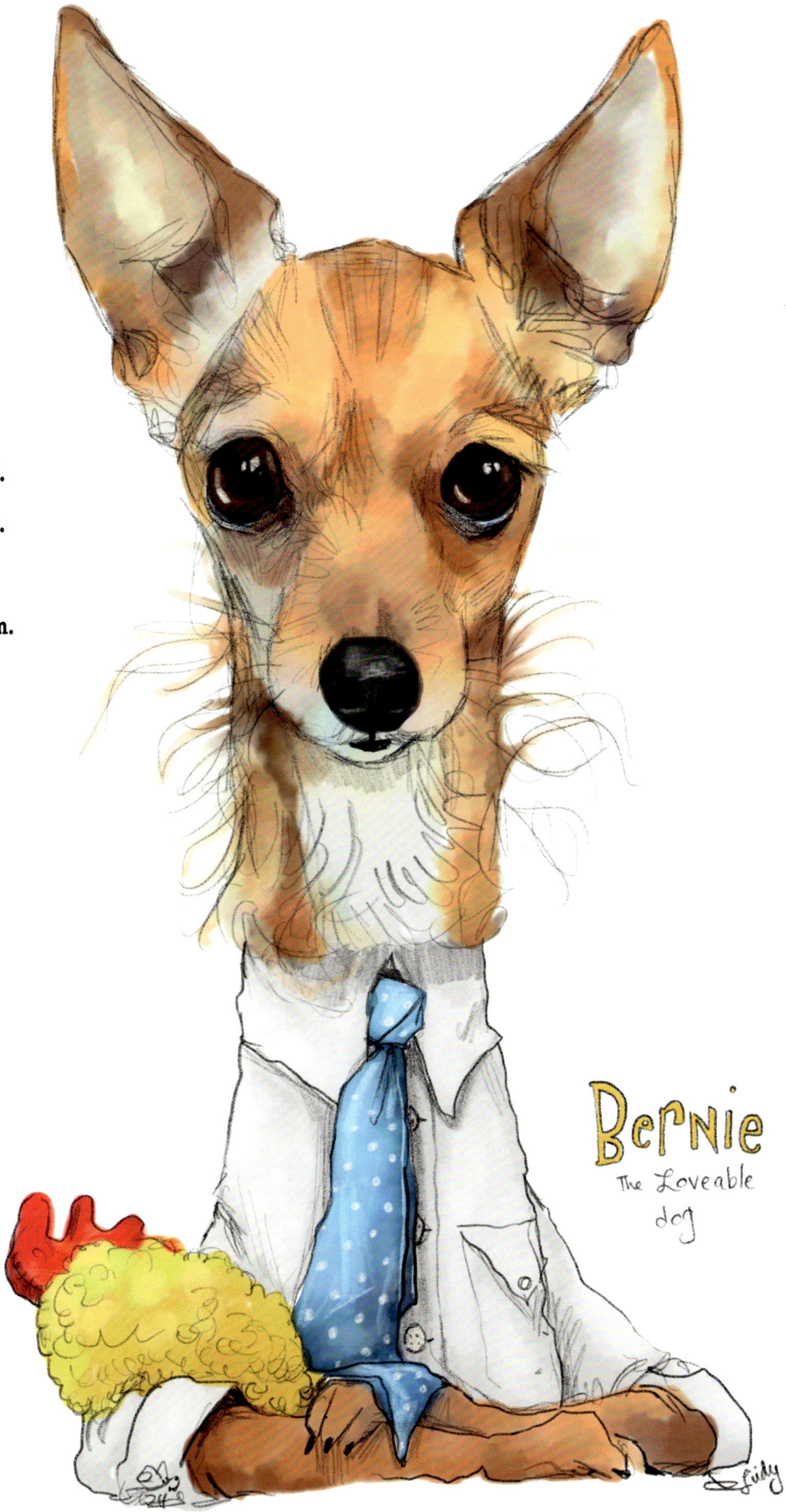

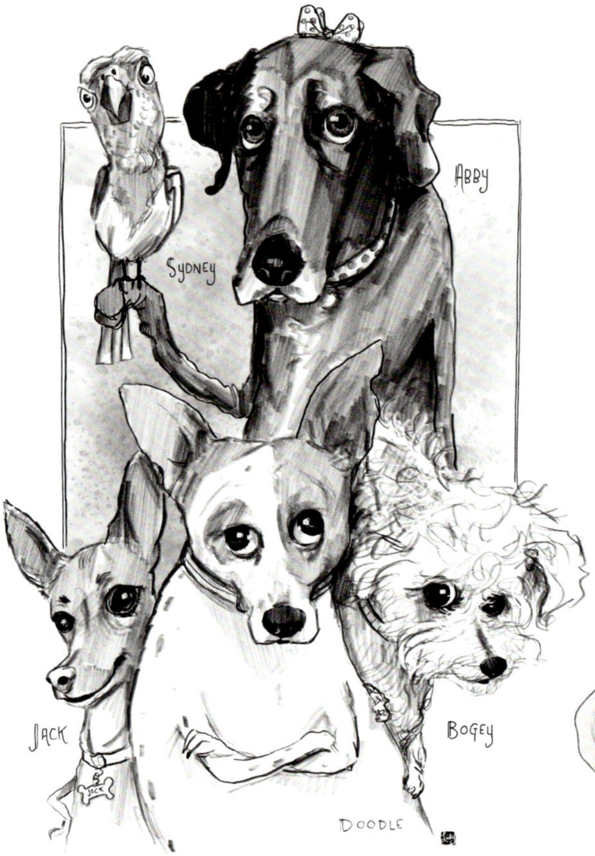
Sydney
Abby
Jack
Bogey
Doodle

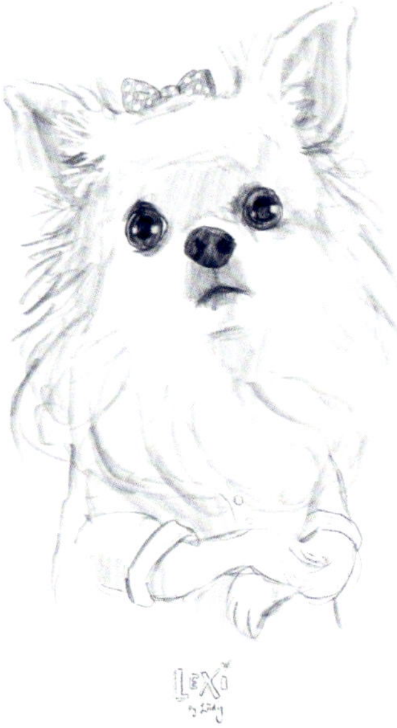
Lexi

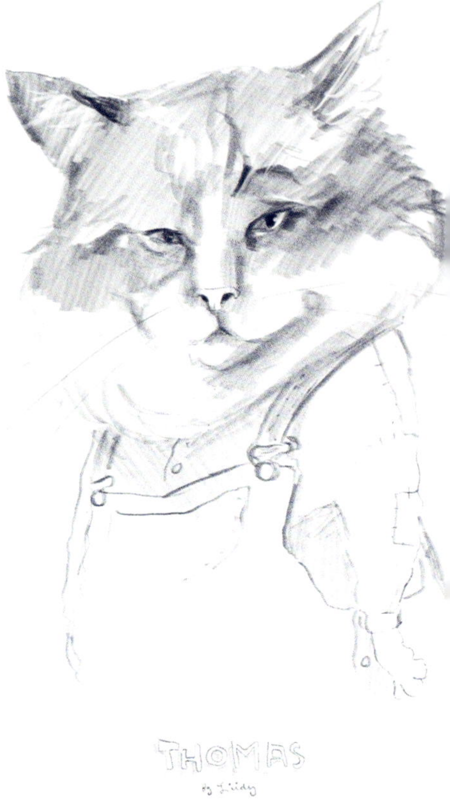
THOMAS

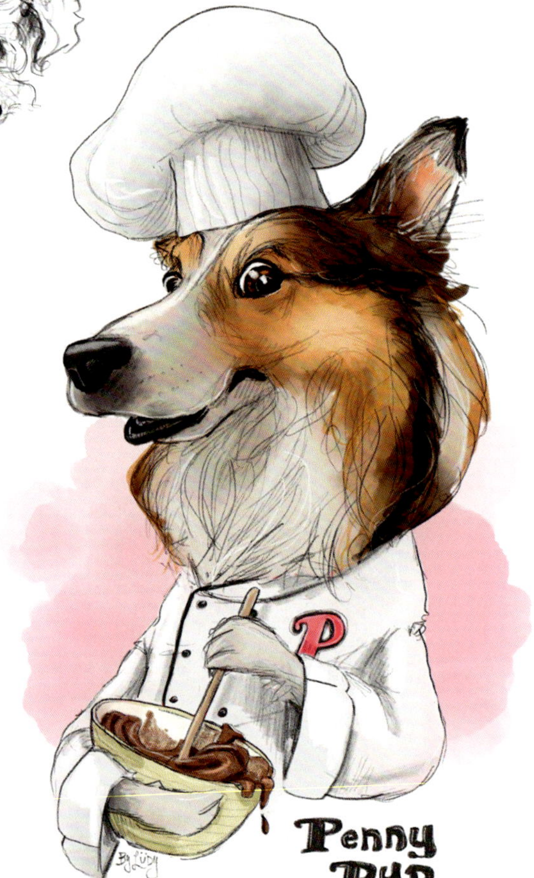
Penny Pup

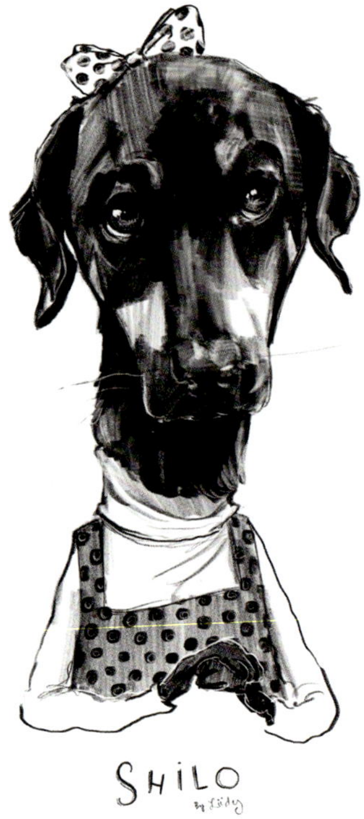
SHILO

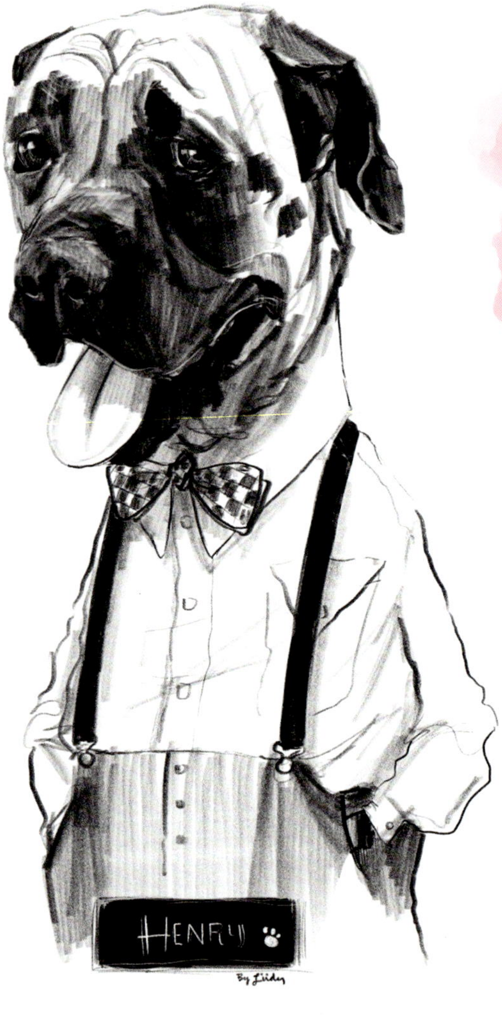
HENRY

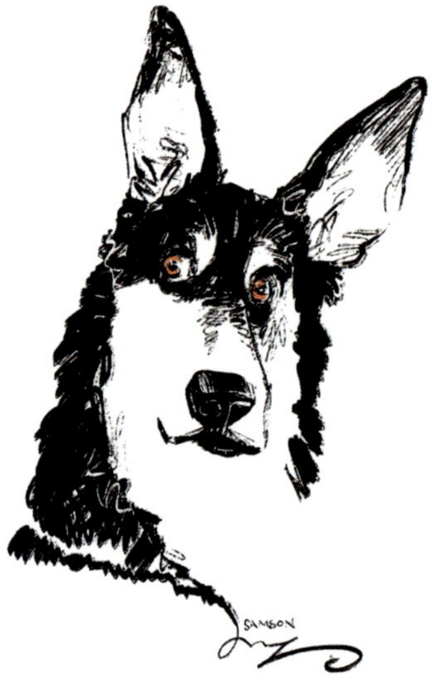
SAMSON

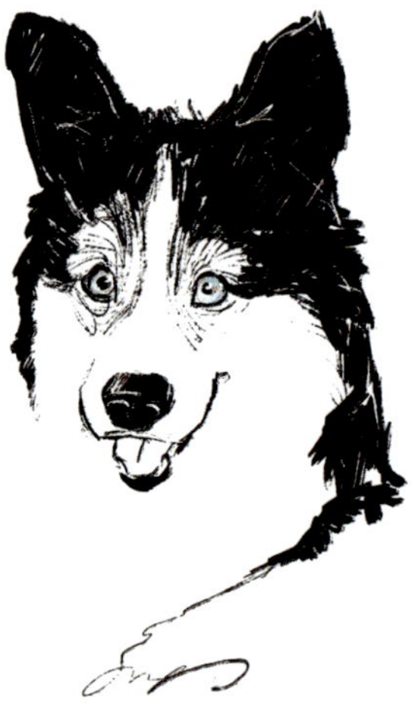

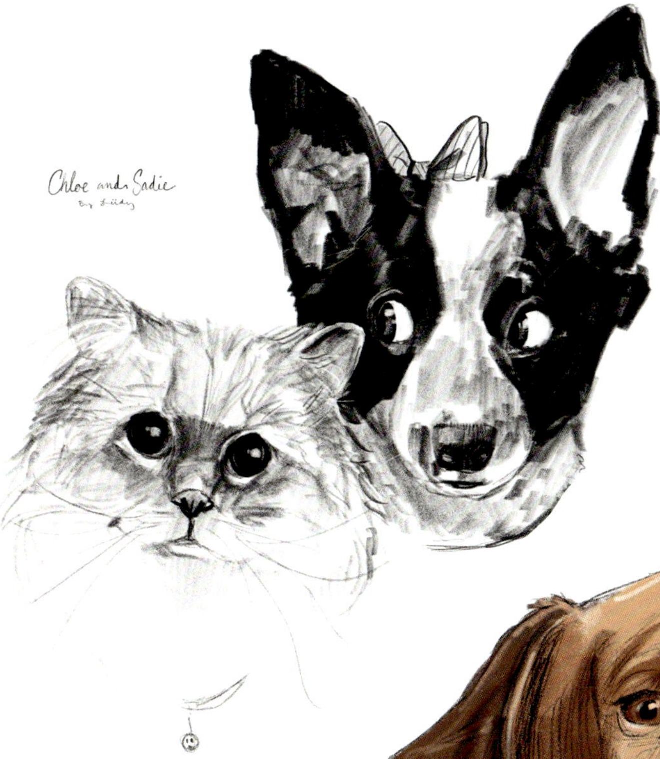

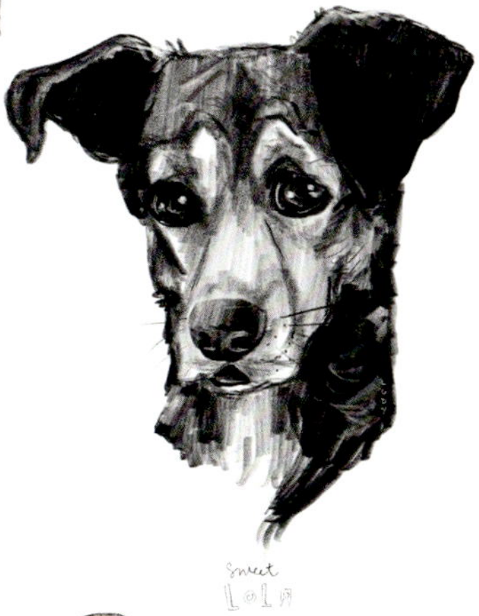

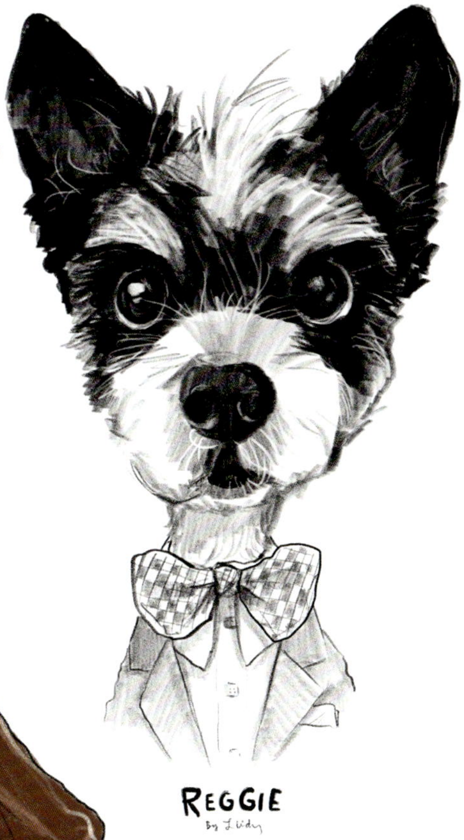

"Such short little lives our pets have to spend with us, and they spend most of it waiting for us to come home each day."

- John Grogan,
author of *Marley & Me*

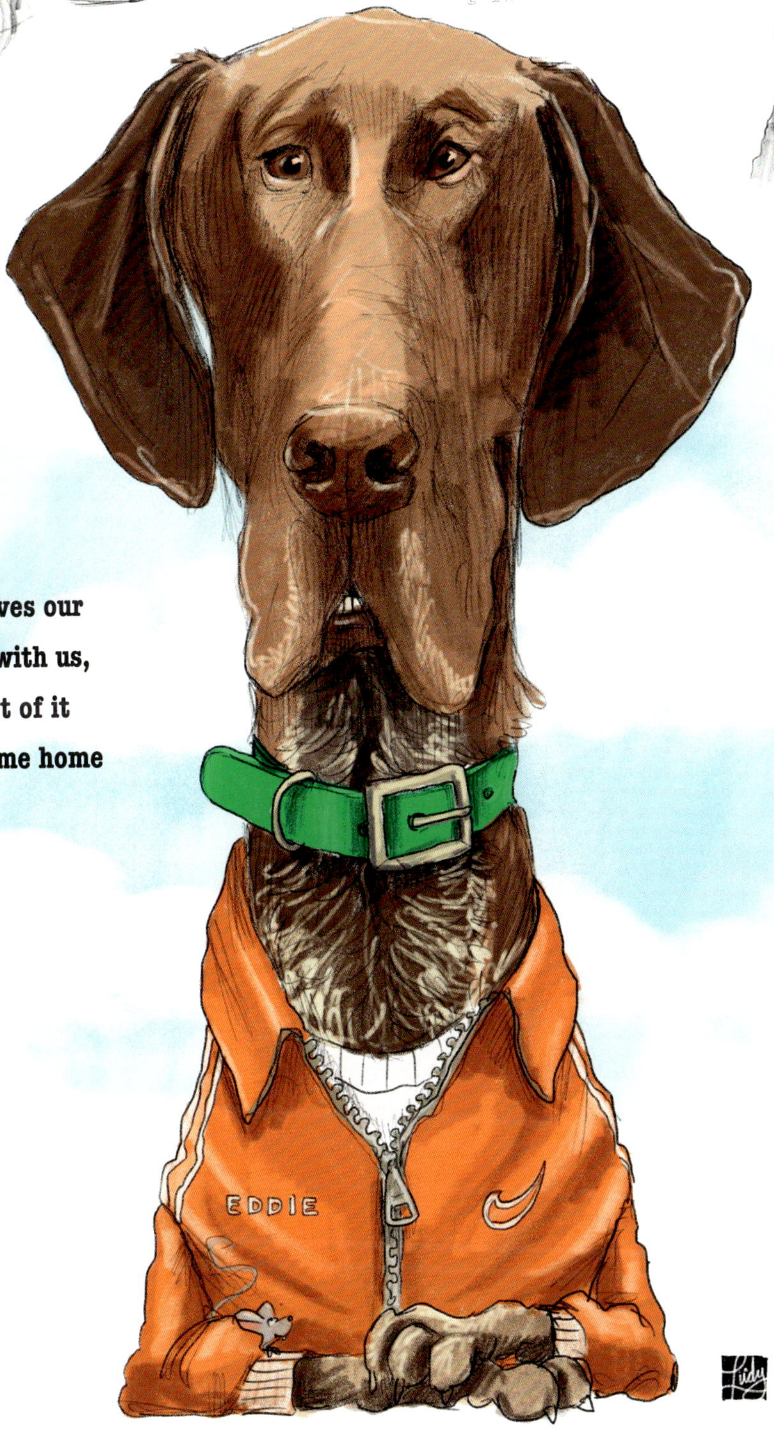

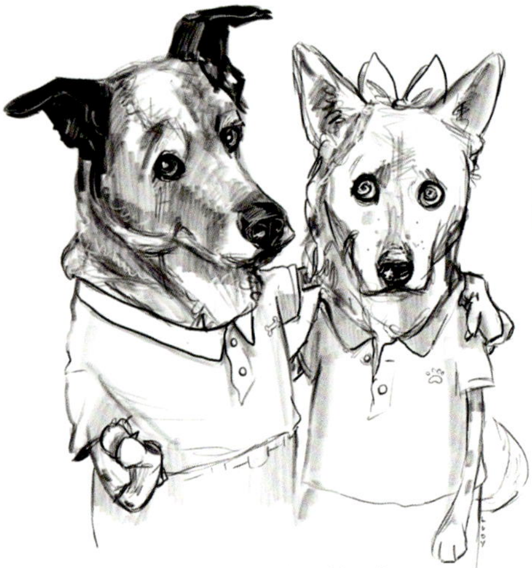

CHAYSE and SAYDE

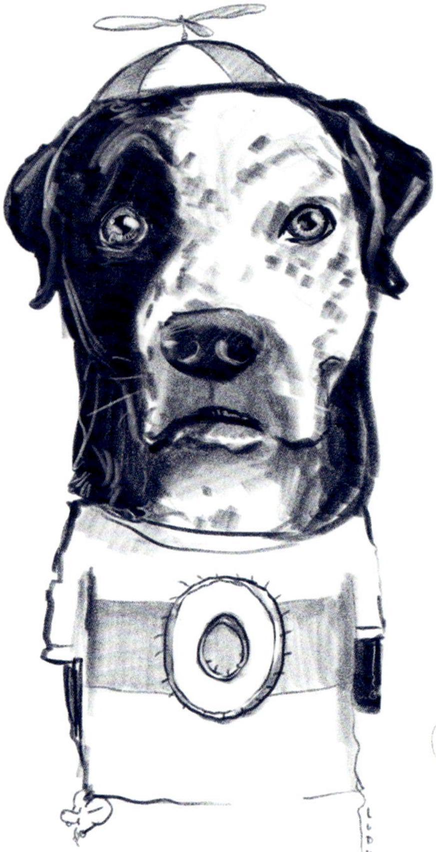

OLIVER

a good boy

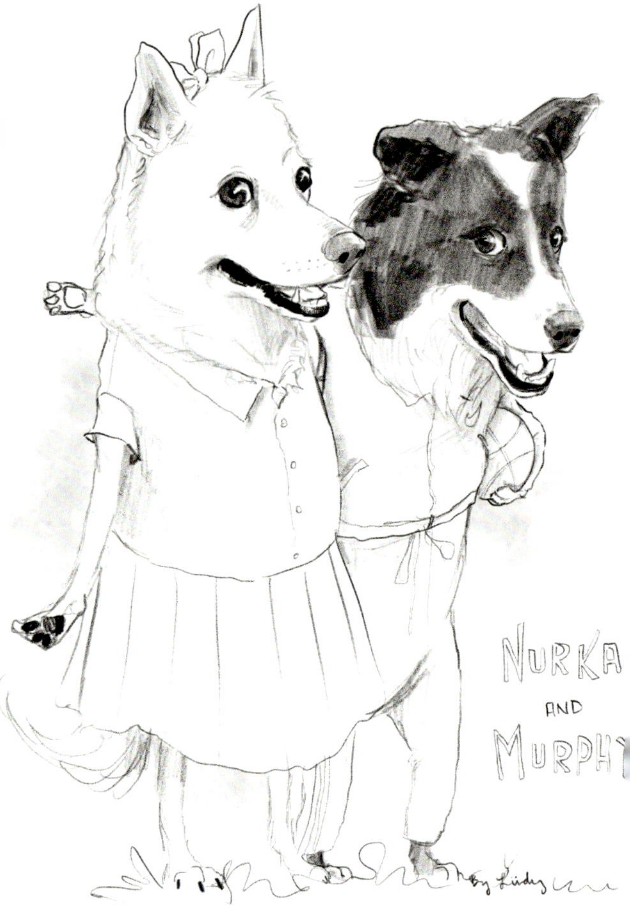

NURKA AND MURPHY

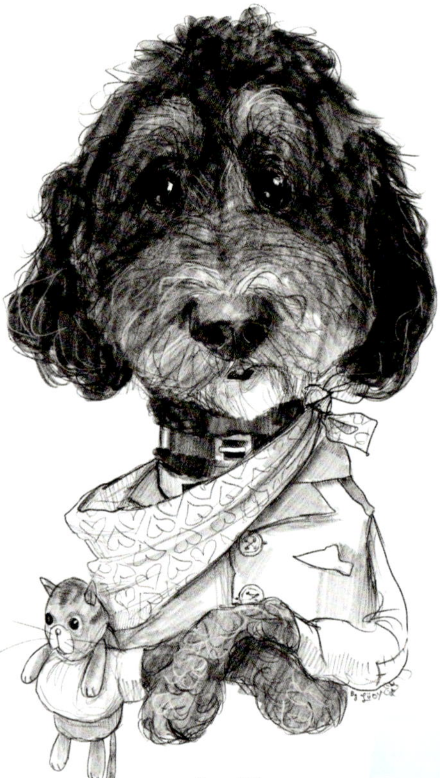

LoKi

snuggle buddy

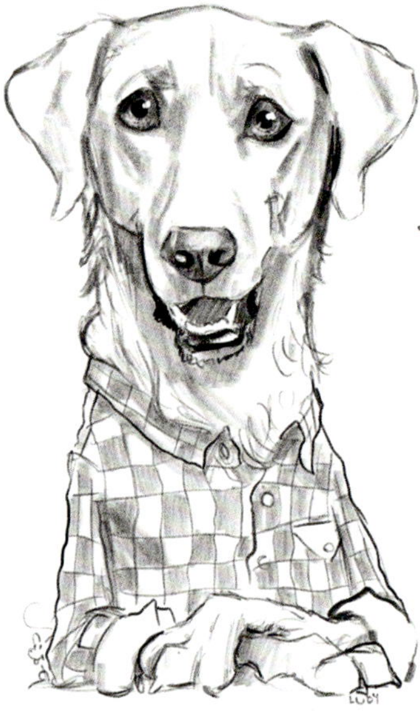

Charlie

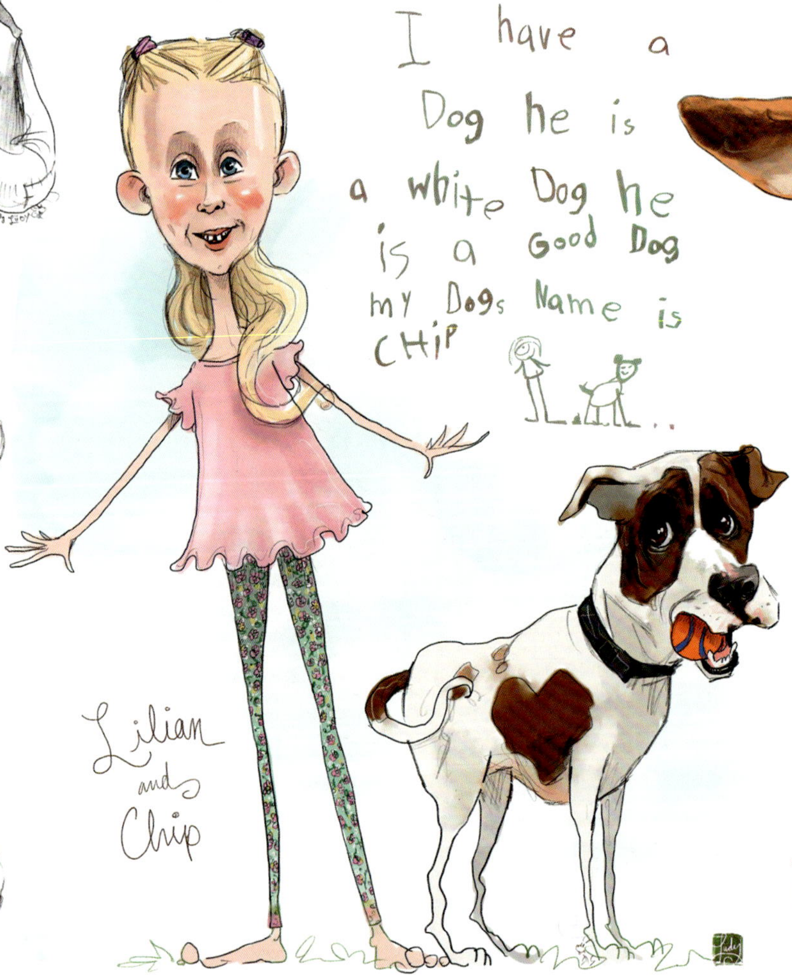

Lilian and Chip

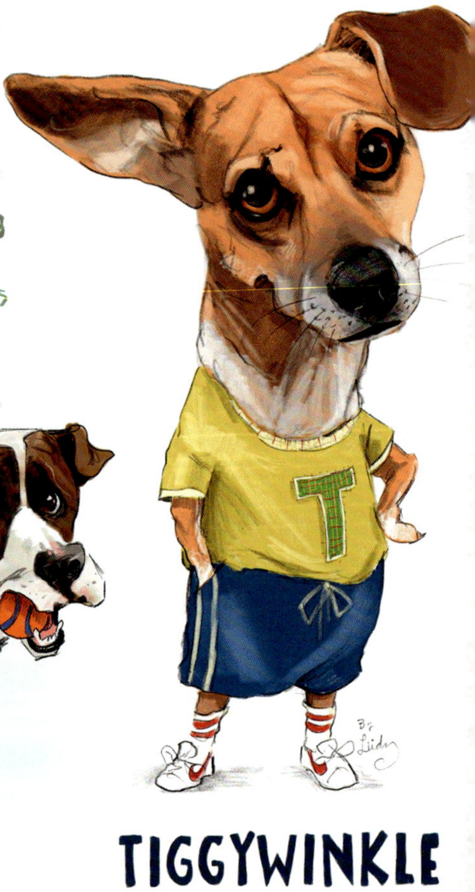

TIGGYWINKLE

T
U
C
K
E
R

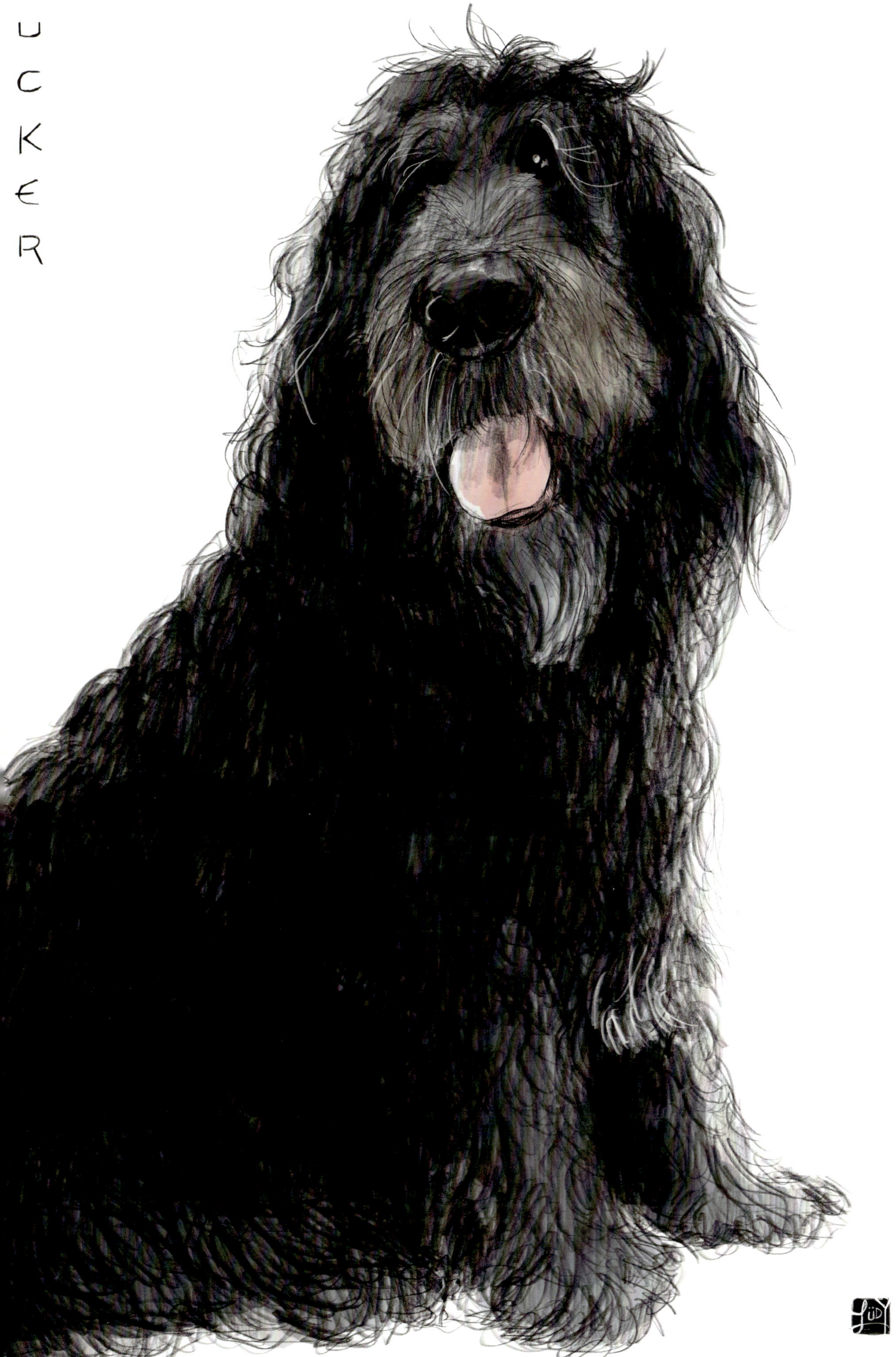

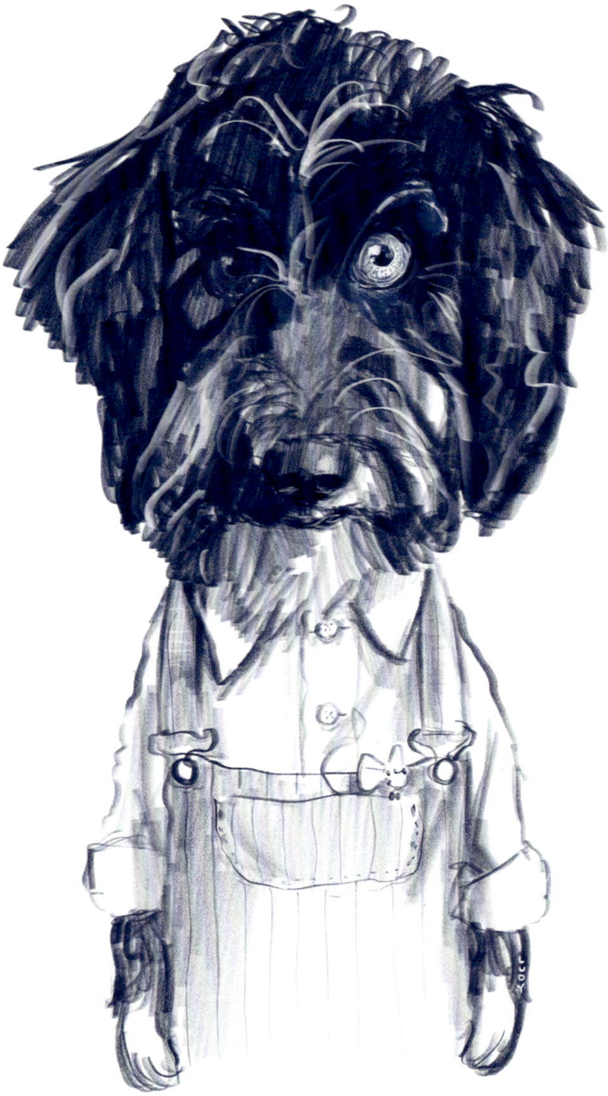

FLETCHER

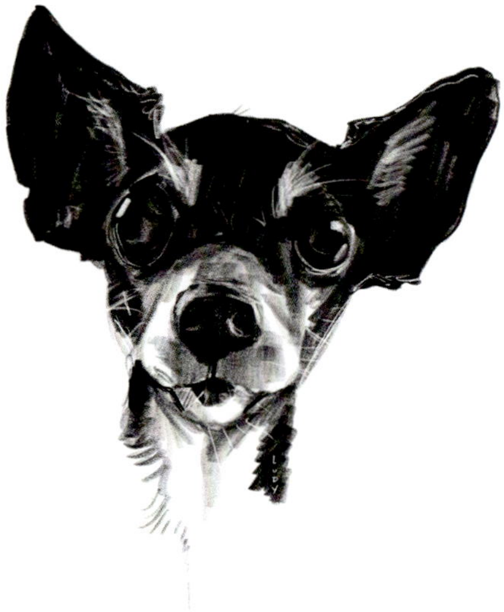

DILLA

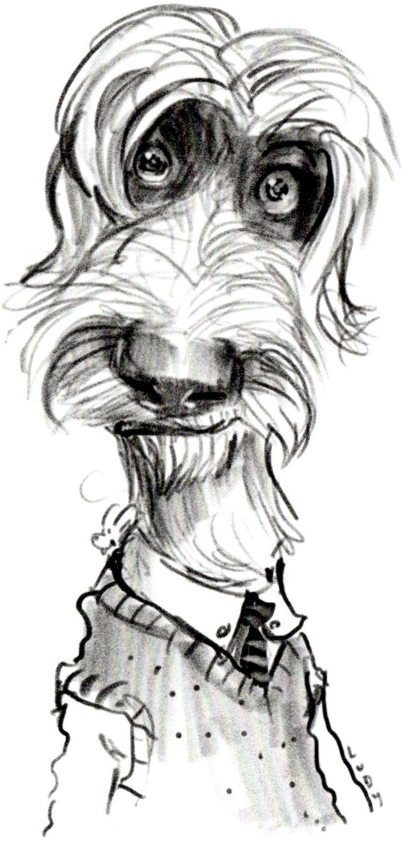

BRUNO

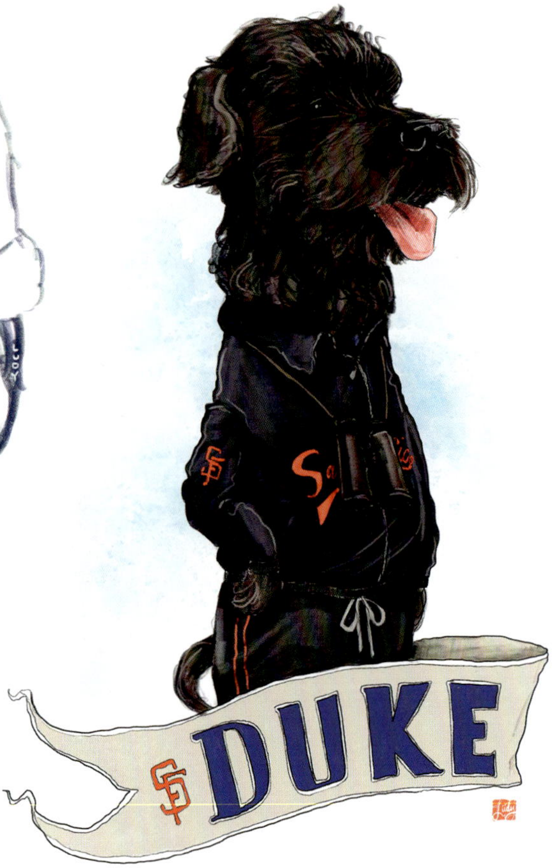

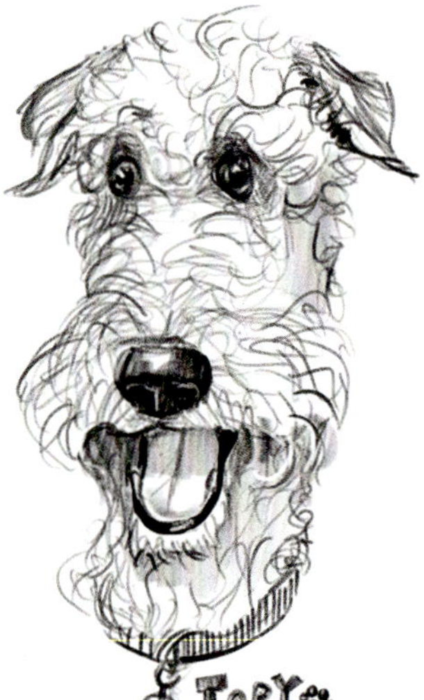

TOBY

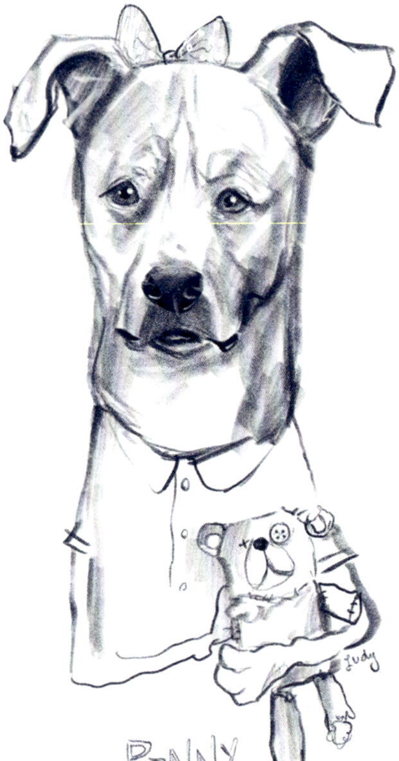

PENNY
The Toy
Assassin

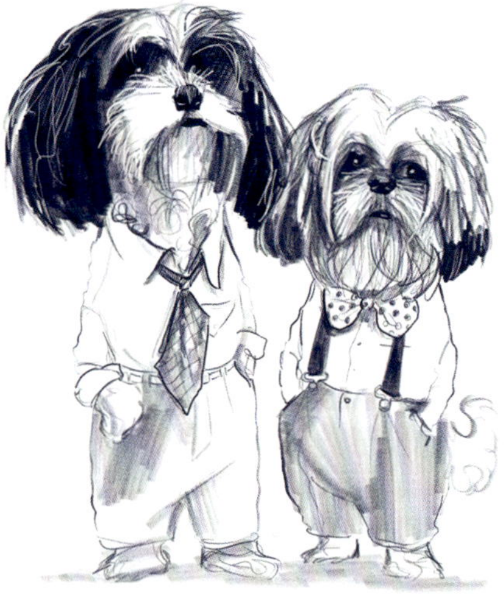

FRANKIE and KIPPER

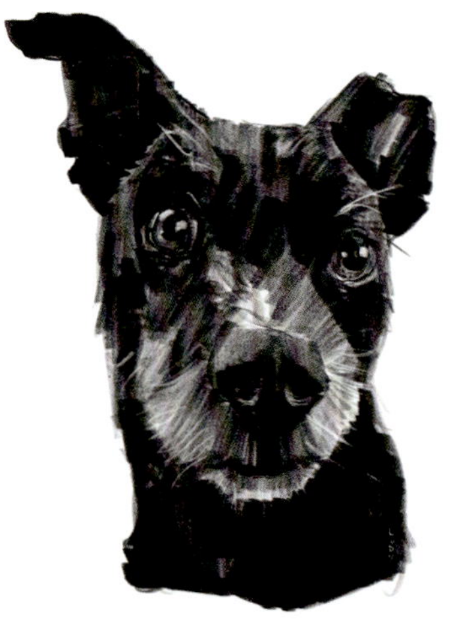

FANG

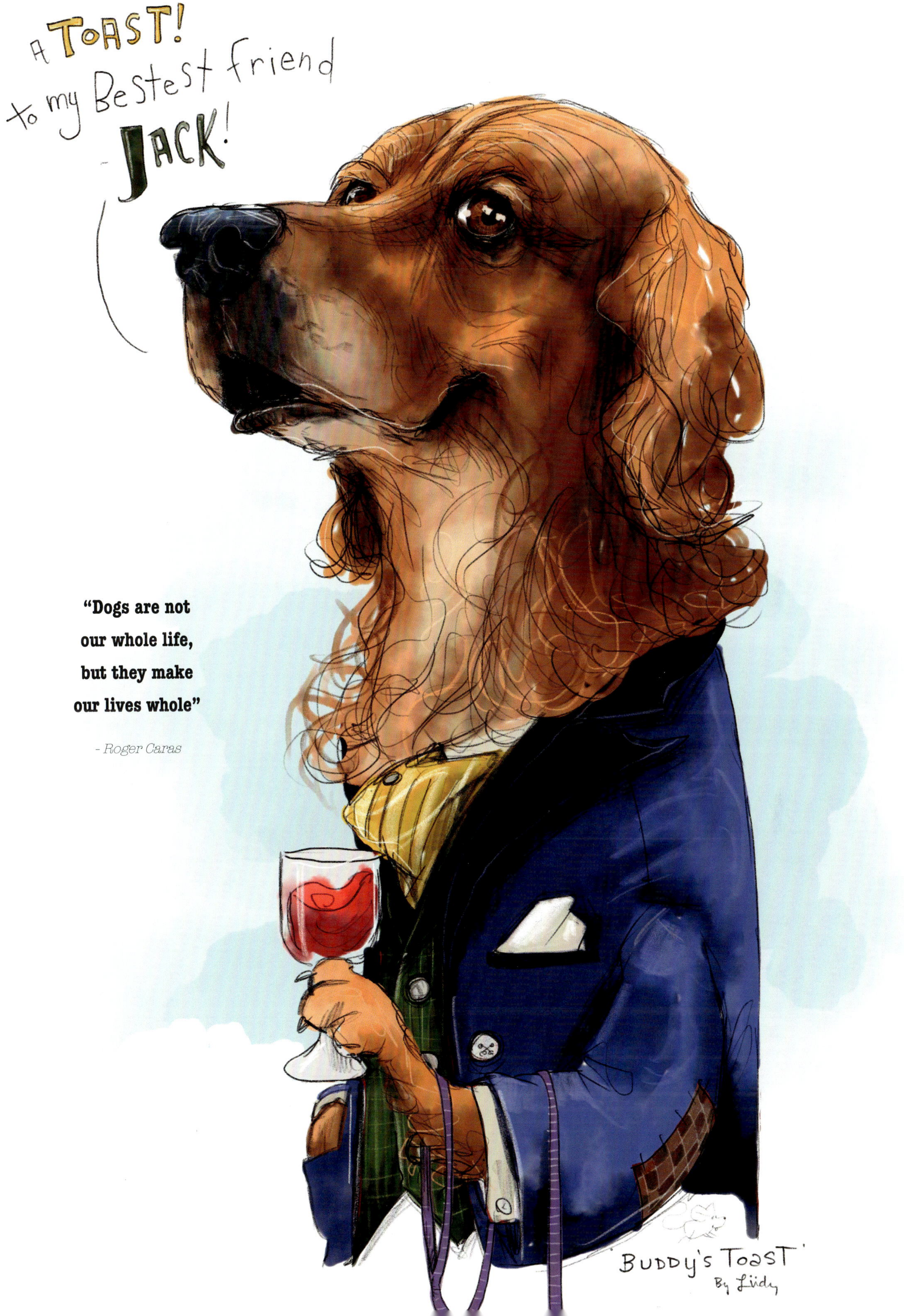

"Dogs are not our whole life, but they make our lives whole"

- Roger Caras

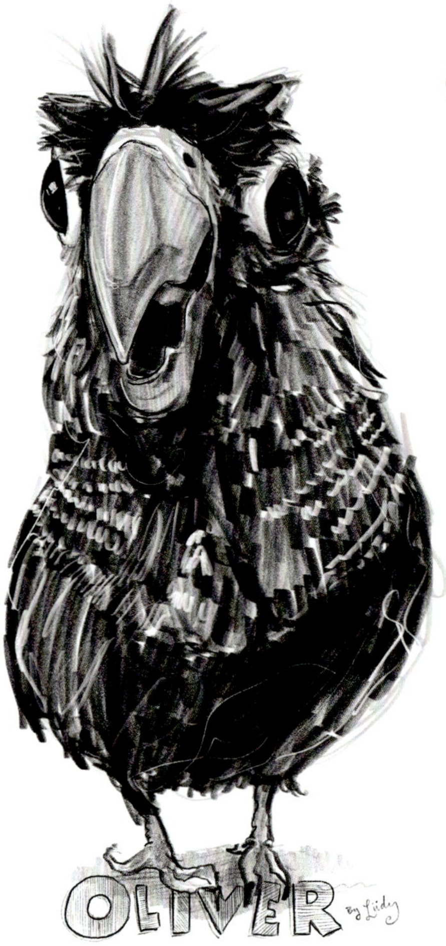
OLIVER
By Lüdy

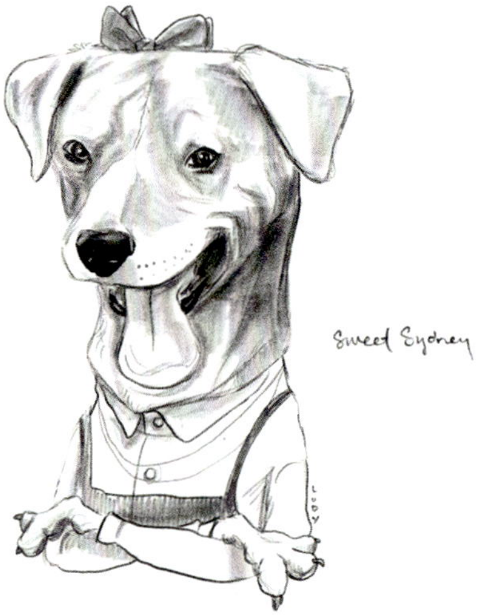
Sweet Sydney

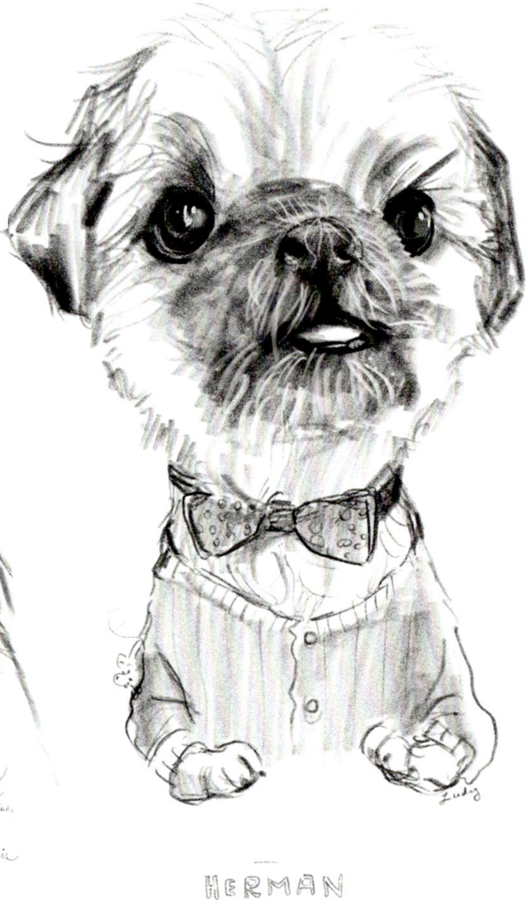
HERMAN

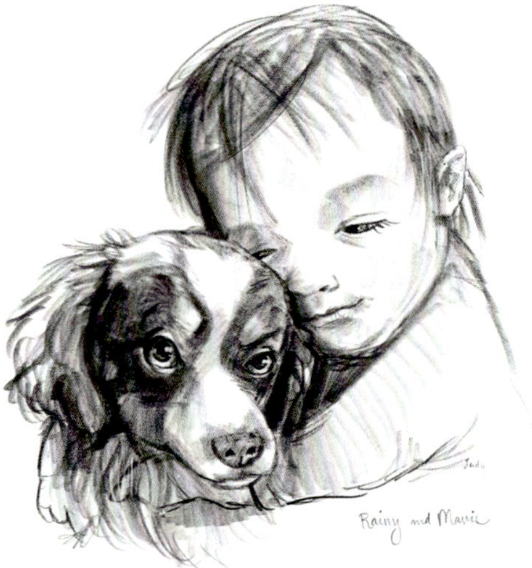
Rainy and Maxie

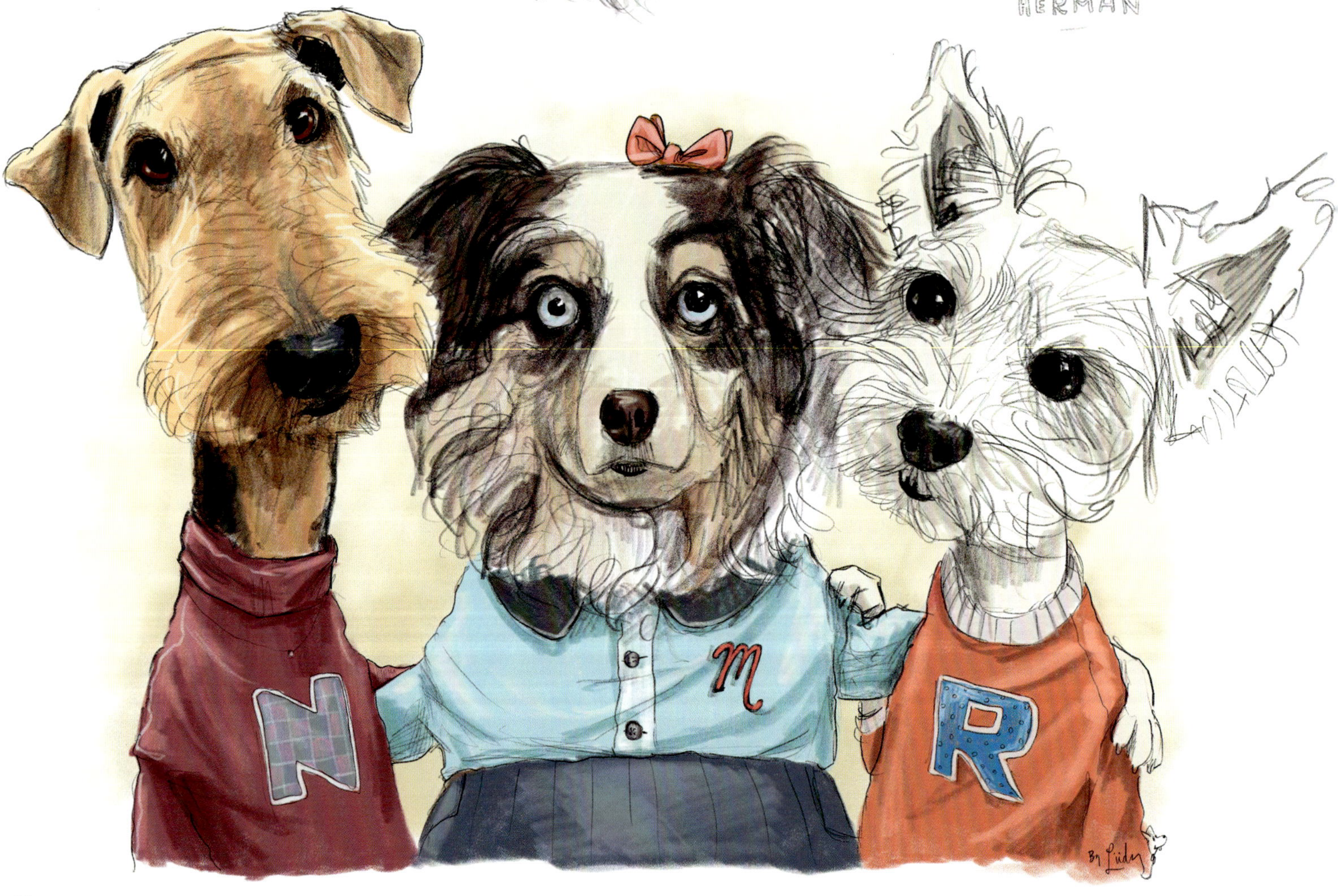
N
M
R
By Lüdy

She may not chase squirrels
or leap without thinking,
but she's a master
of the slow wag,
the cozy curl,
and being utterly,
beautifully loved.

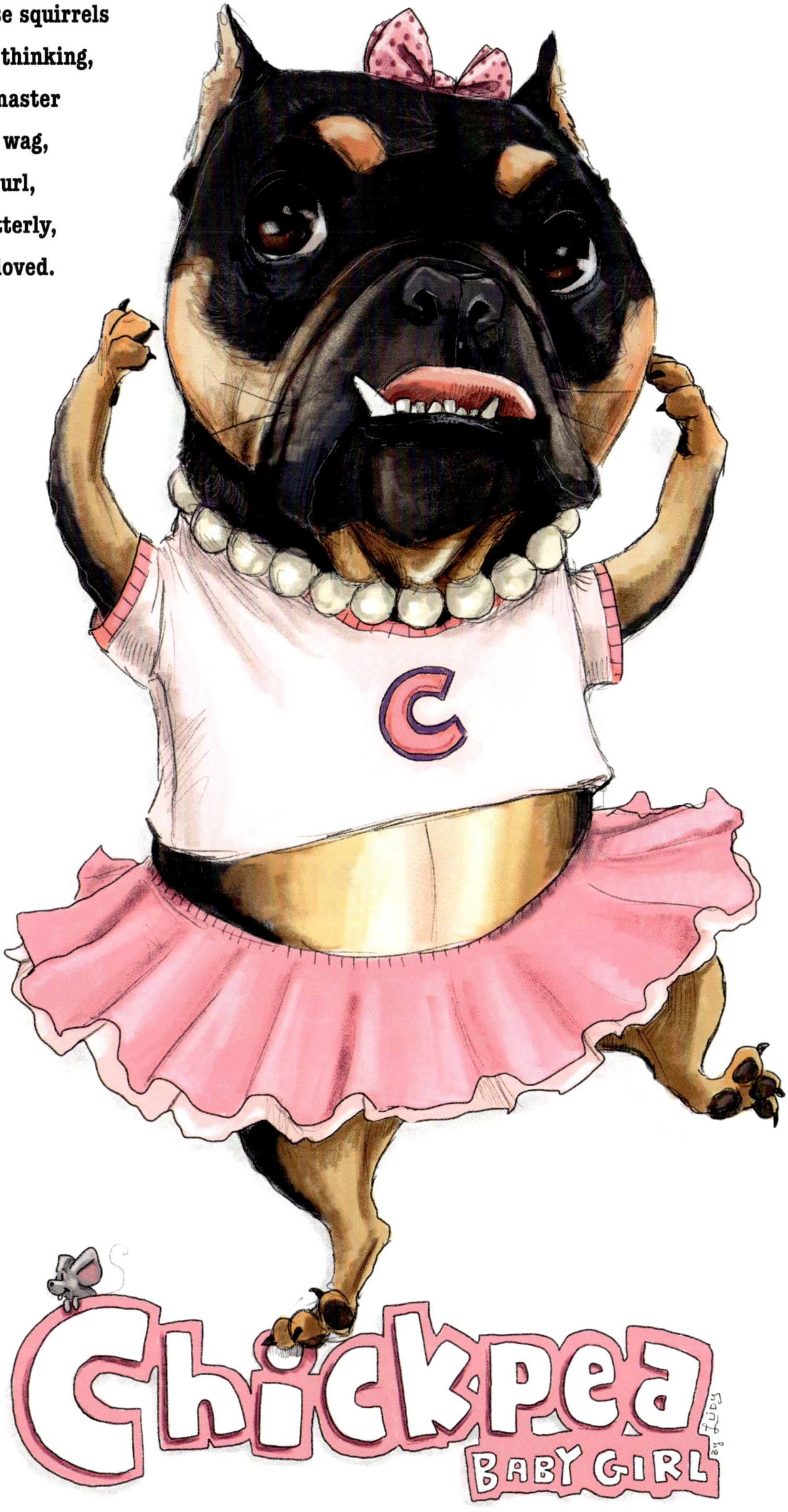

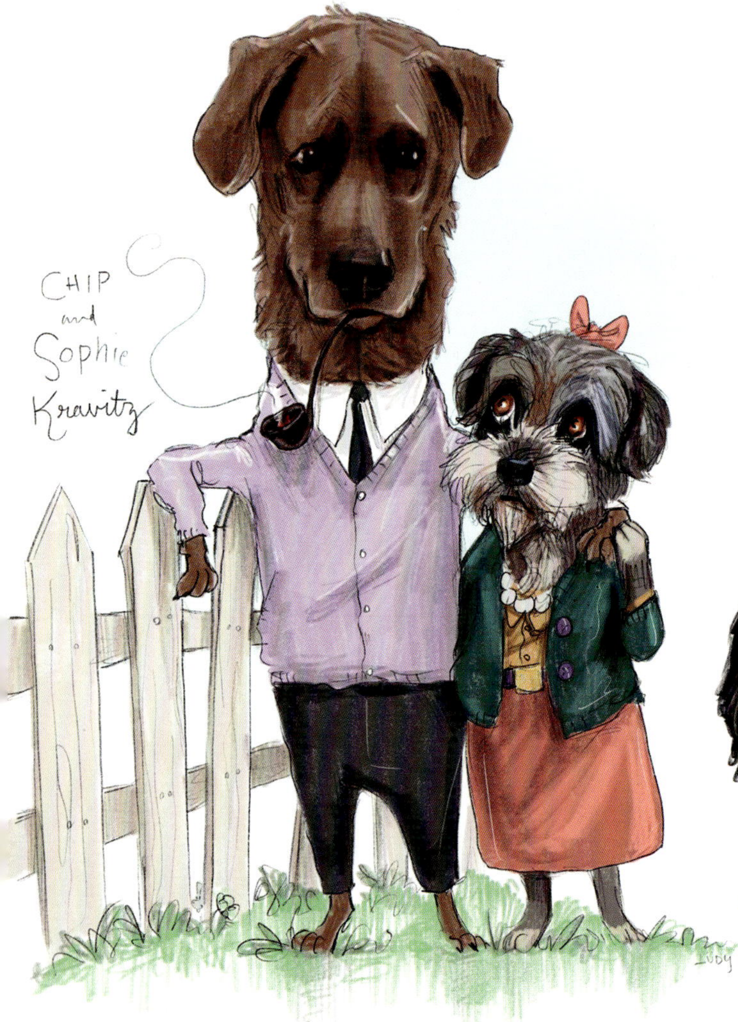
CHIP
and
Sophie
Kravitz

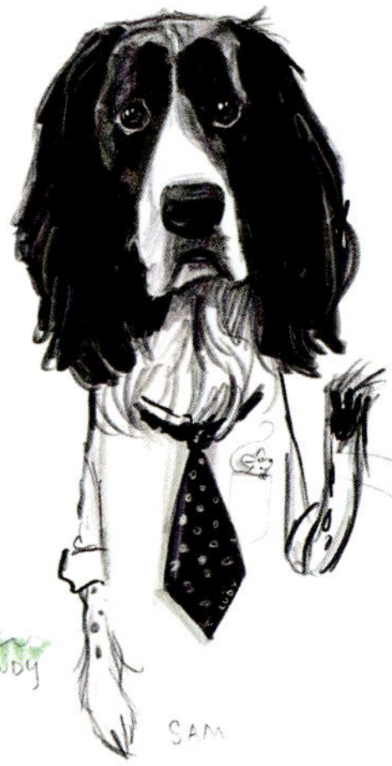
SAM

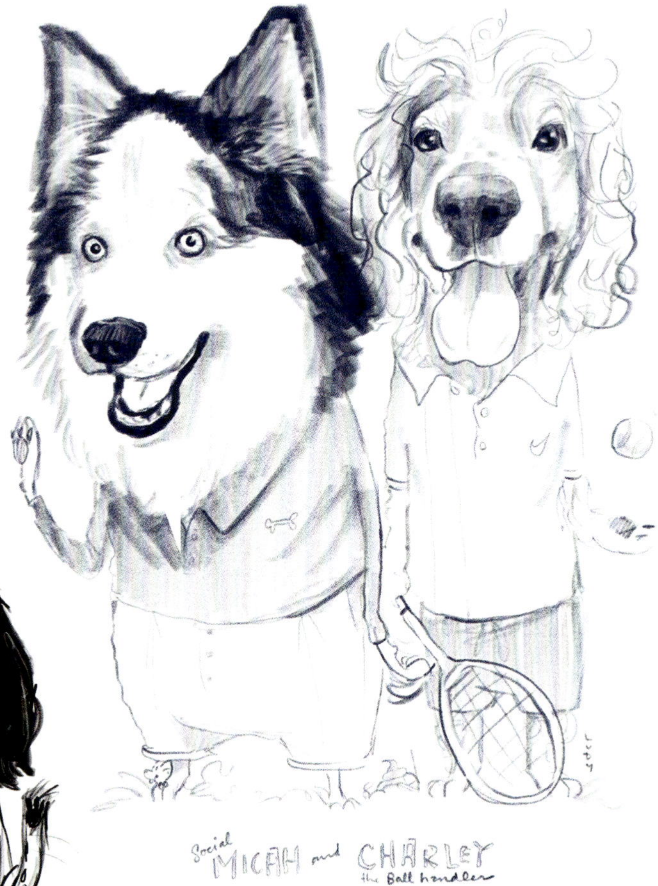
Social MICAH and CHARLEY
the Ball handler

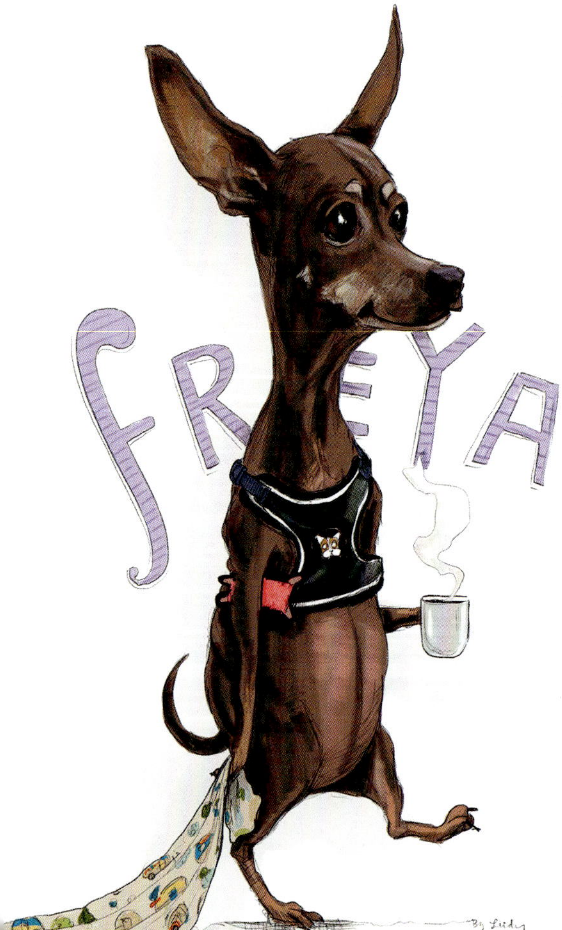
FREYA

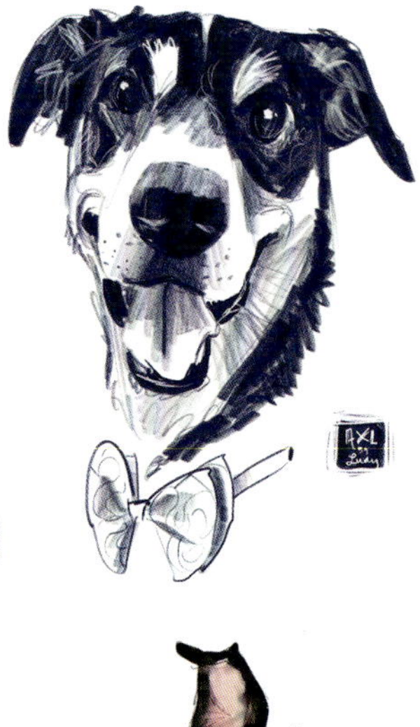

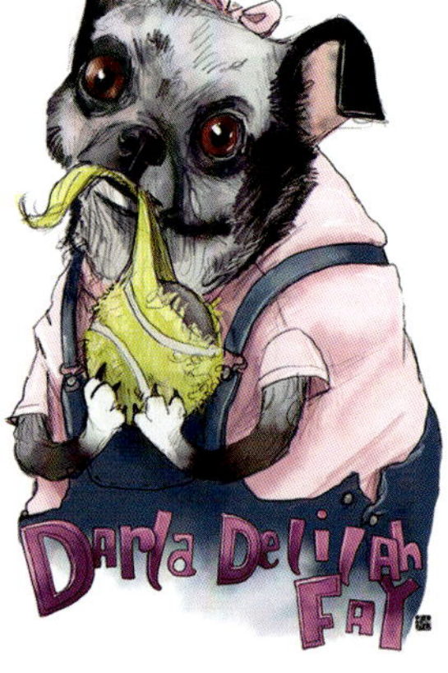
Darla Delilah
Fat

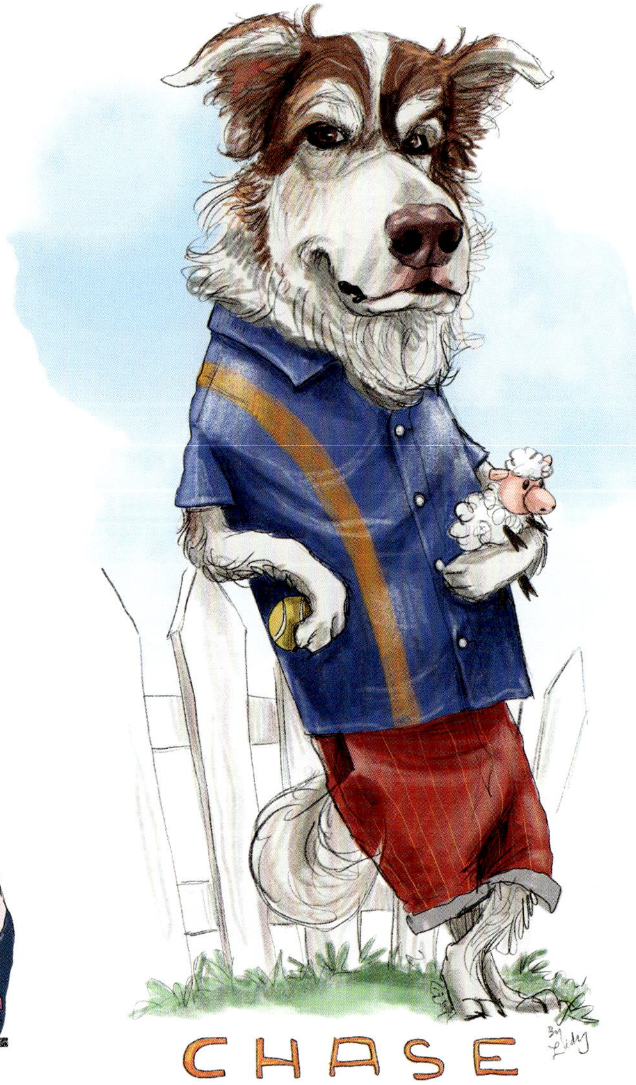
CHASE

“Dogs come when they’re called. Cats take a message and get back to you.”

– Mary Bly

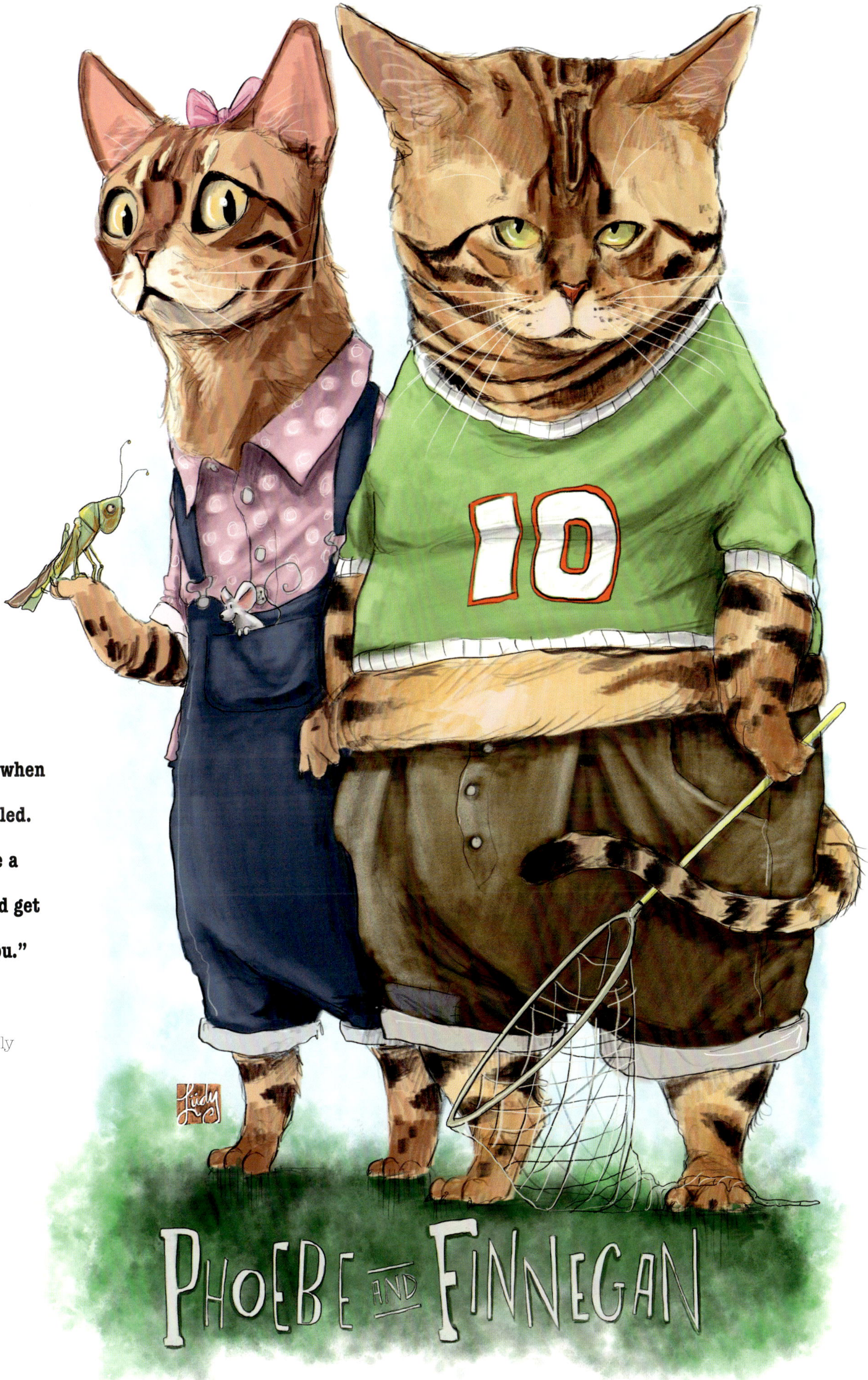

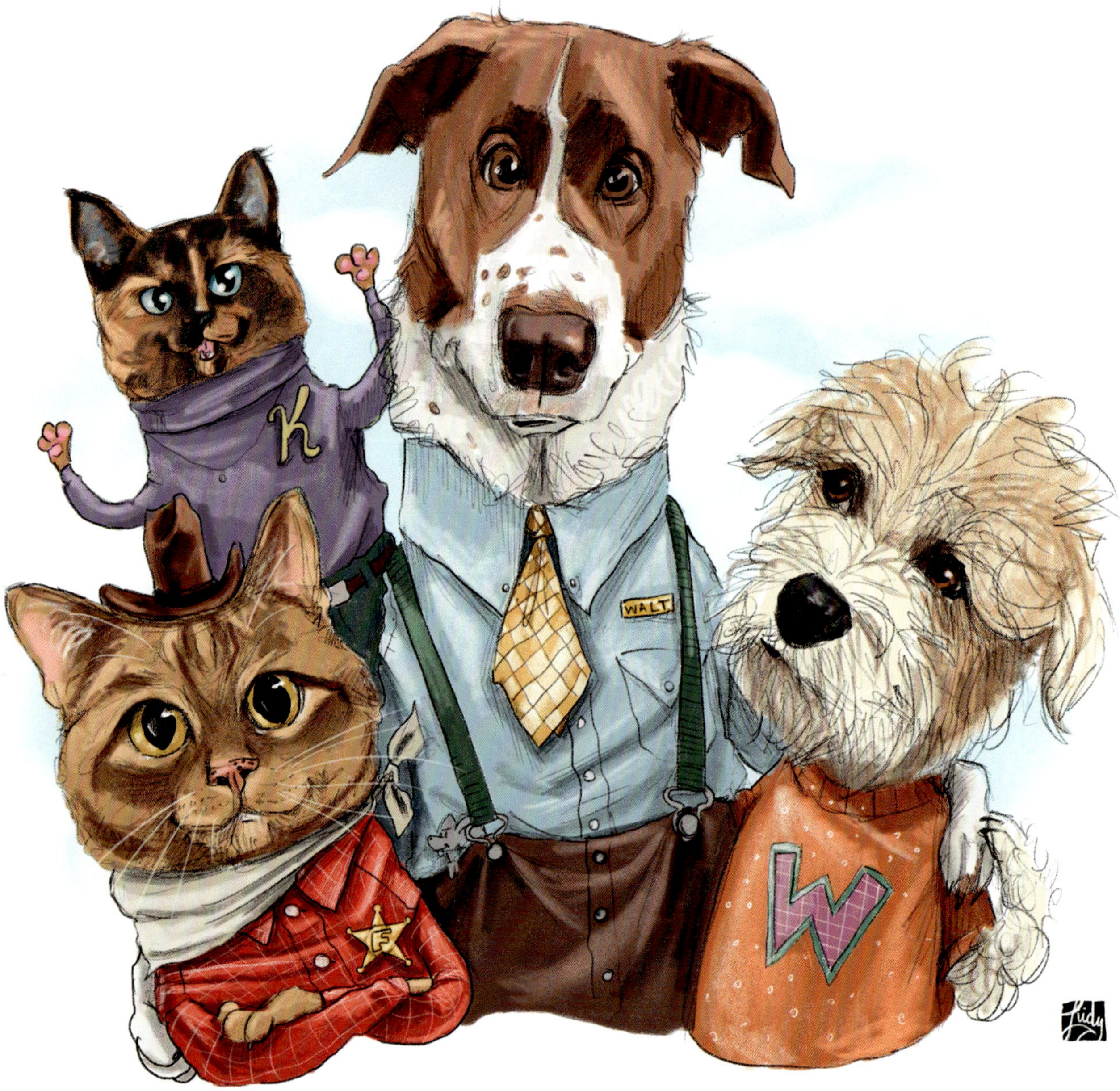

K
WALT
F
W
Judy

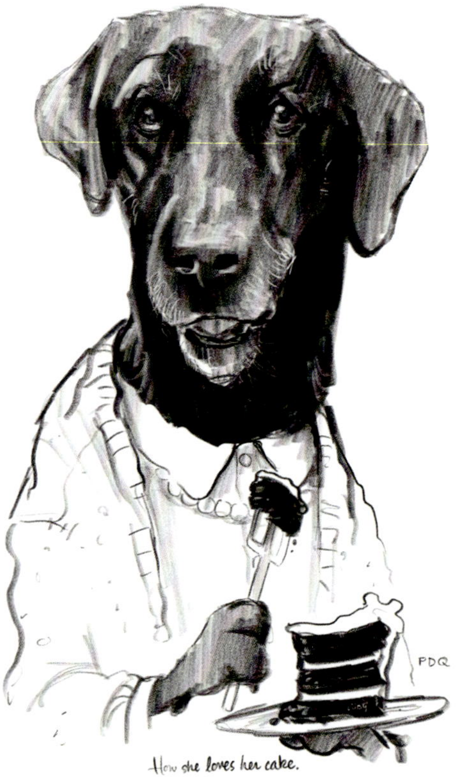

PDQ
How she loves her cake.

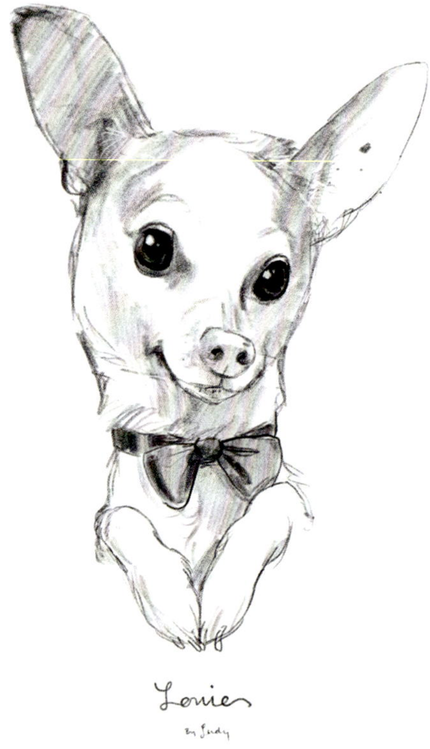

Lonie
By Judy

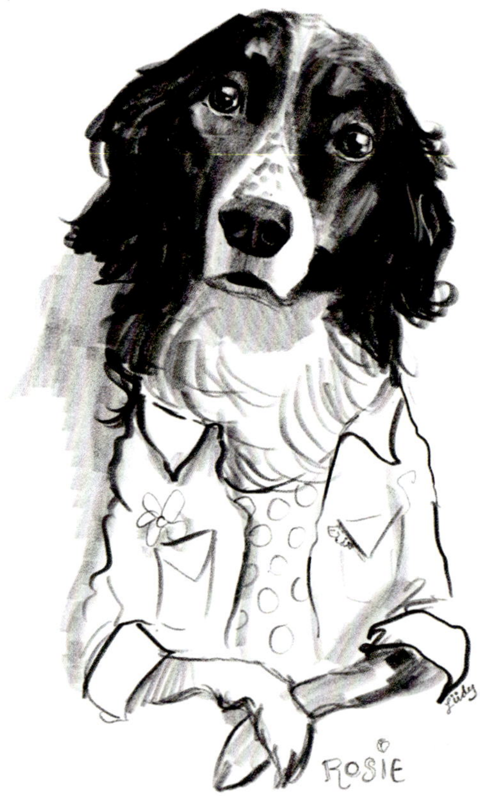

Judy
ROSIE

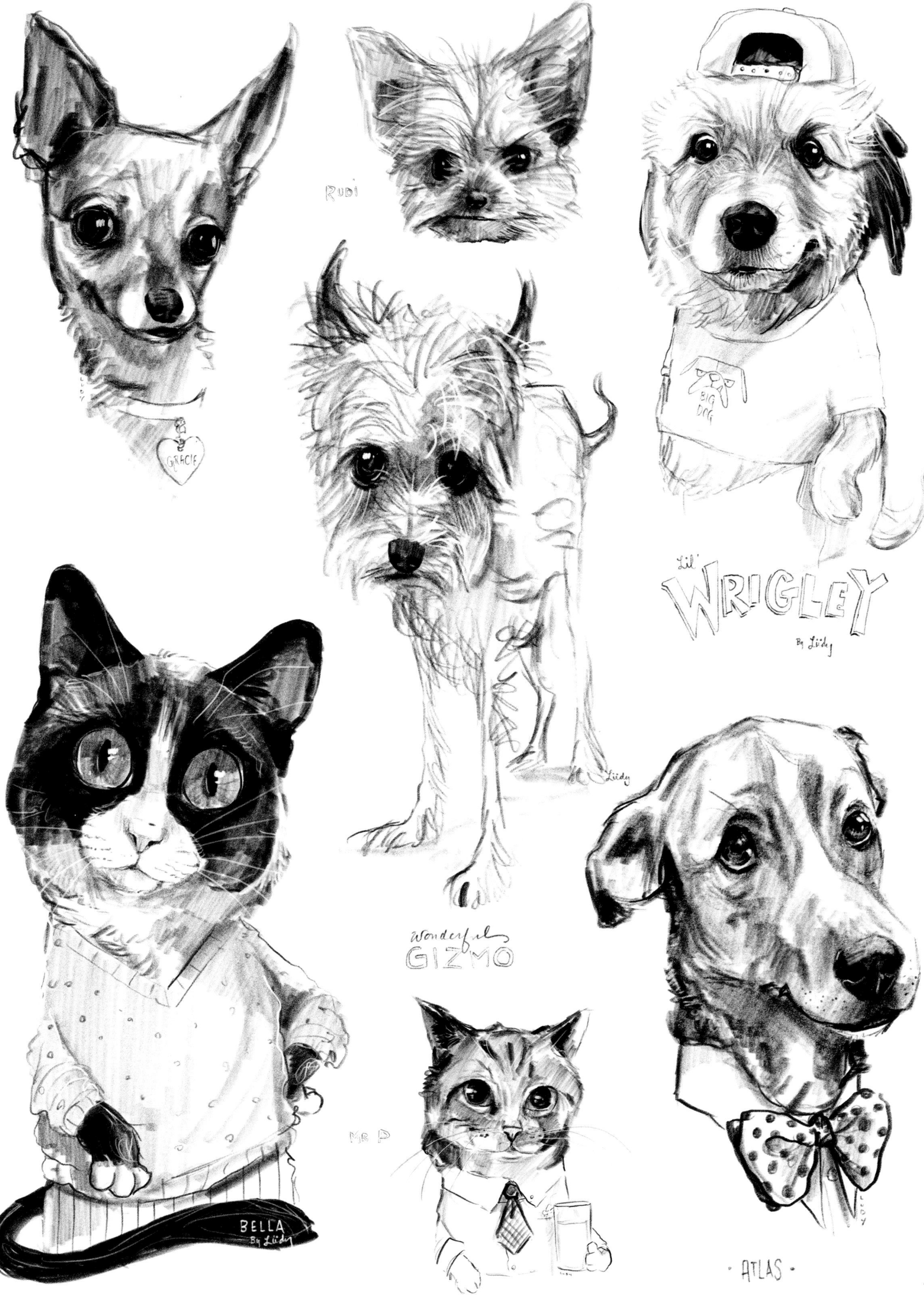
GRACIE
RUDI
Lil' WRIGLEY
By Lüdy
BIG DOG
Lüdy
Wonderful
GIZMO
BELLA
By Lüdy
MR P
ATLAS

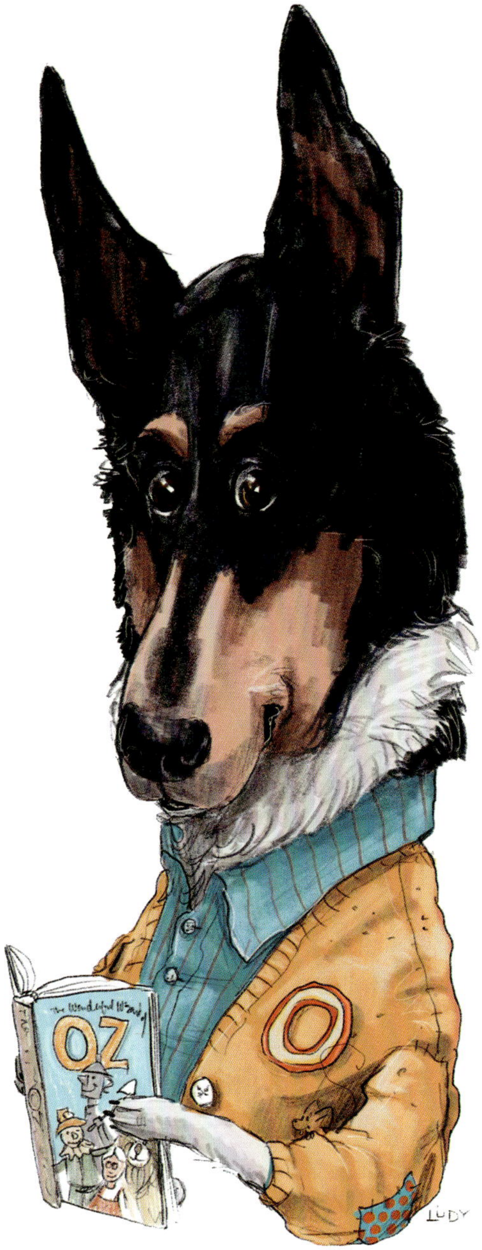
OZ
LIDY

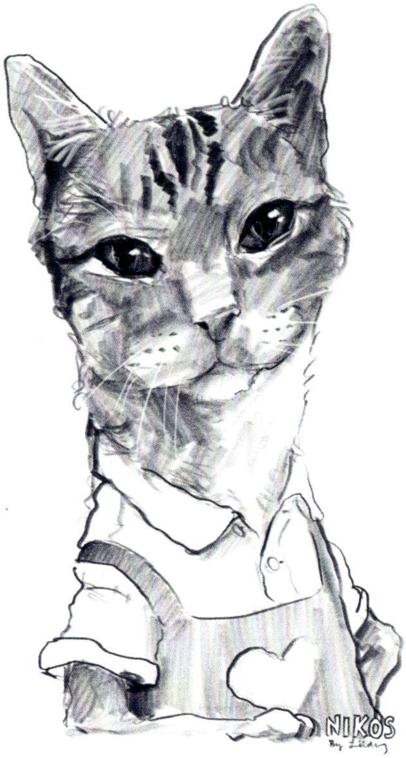
NIKOS
By Lidy

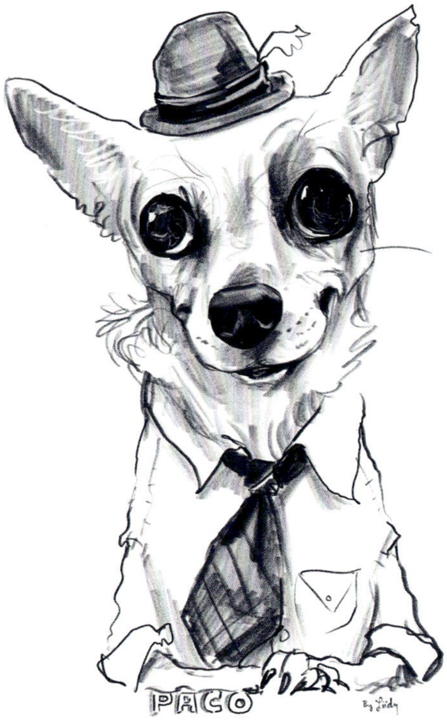
PACO
By Lidy

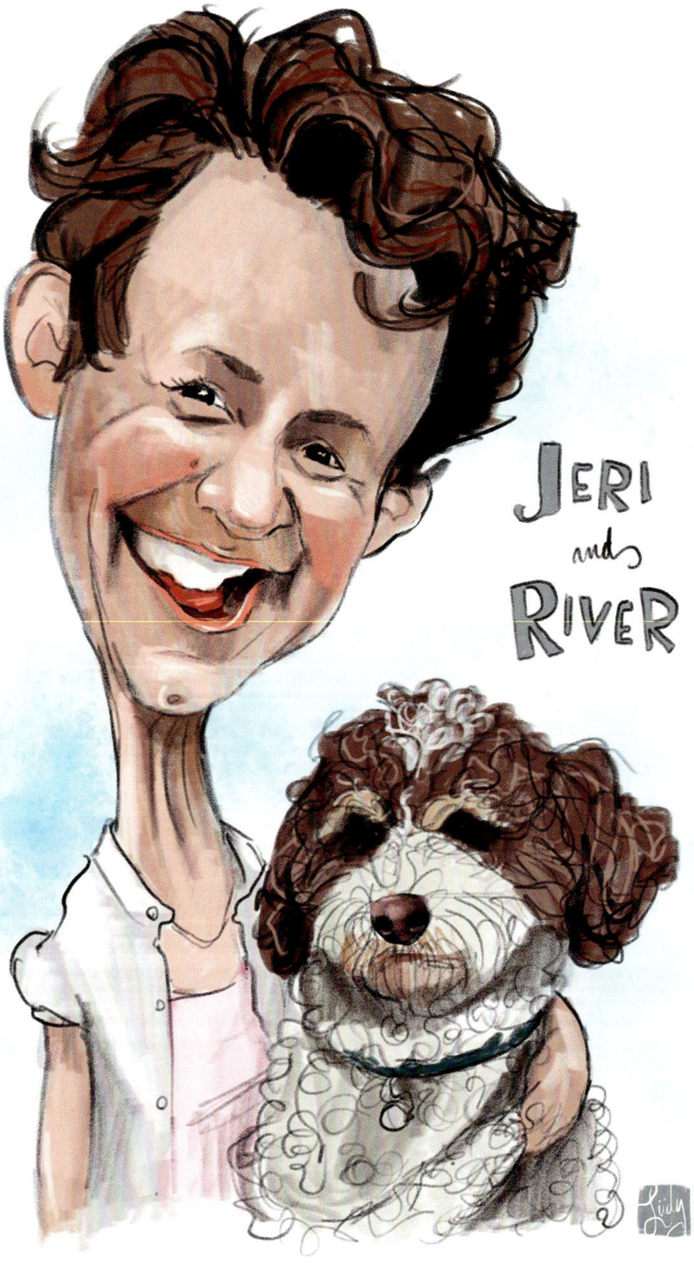
JERI
and
RIVER
Lidy

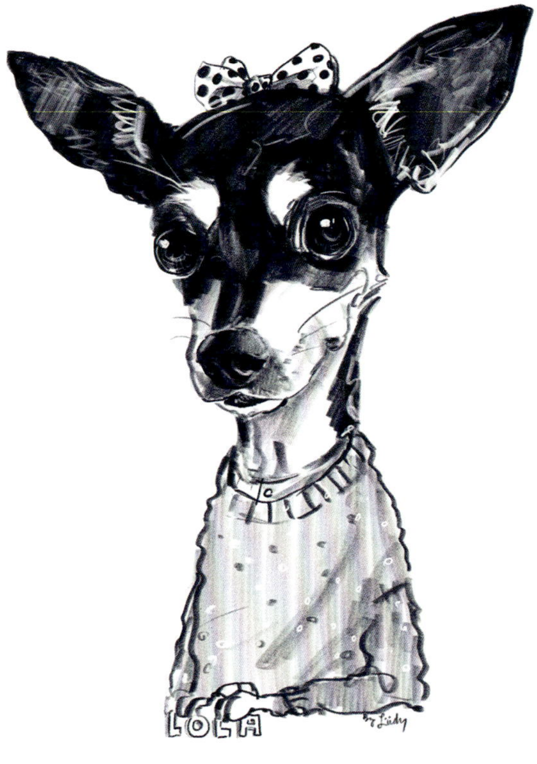
LOLA
By Lidy

We bring the snacks.
They bring the serotonin.

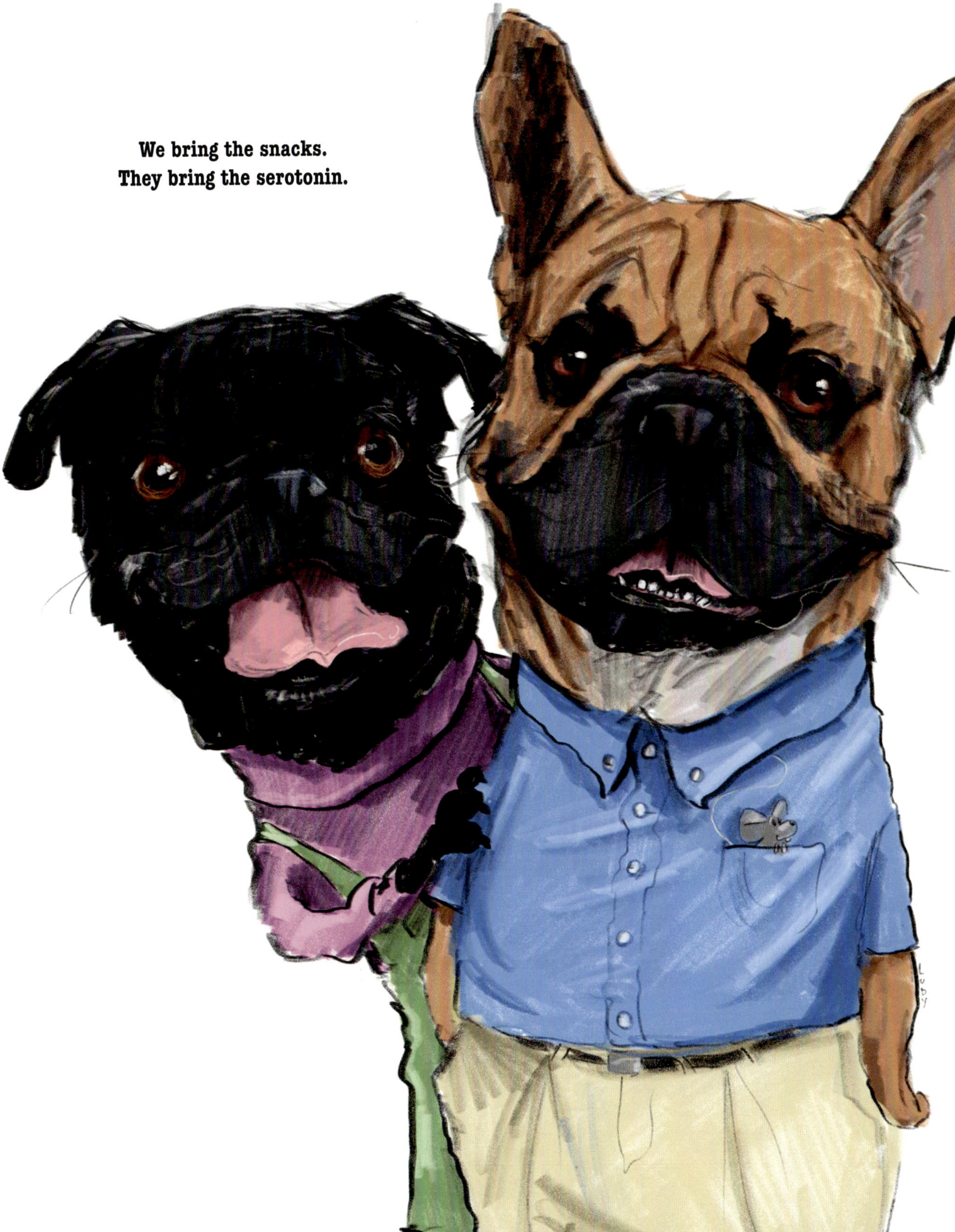

STAR and THOR

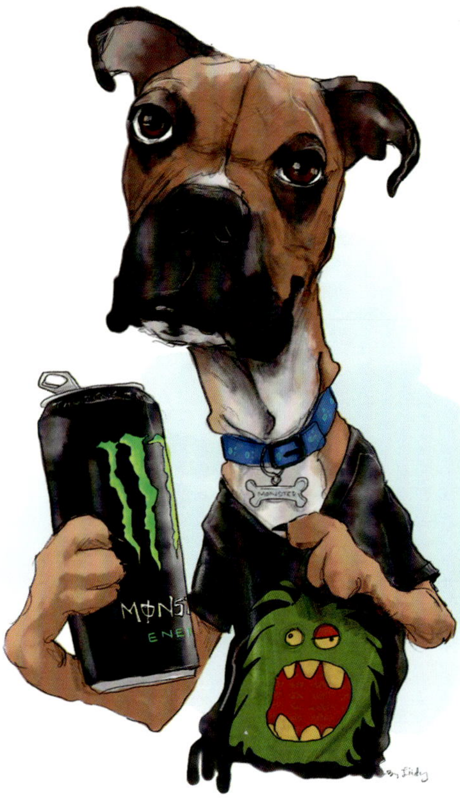

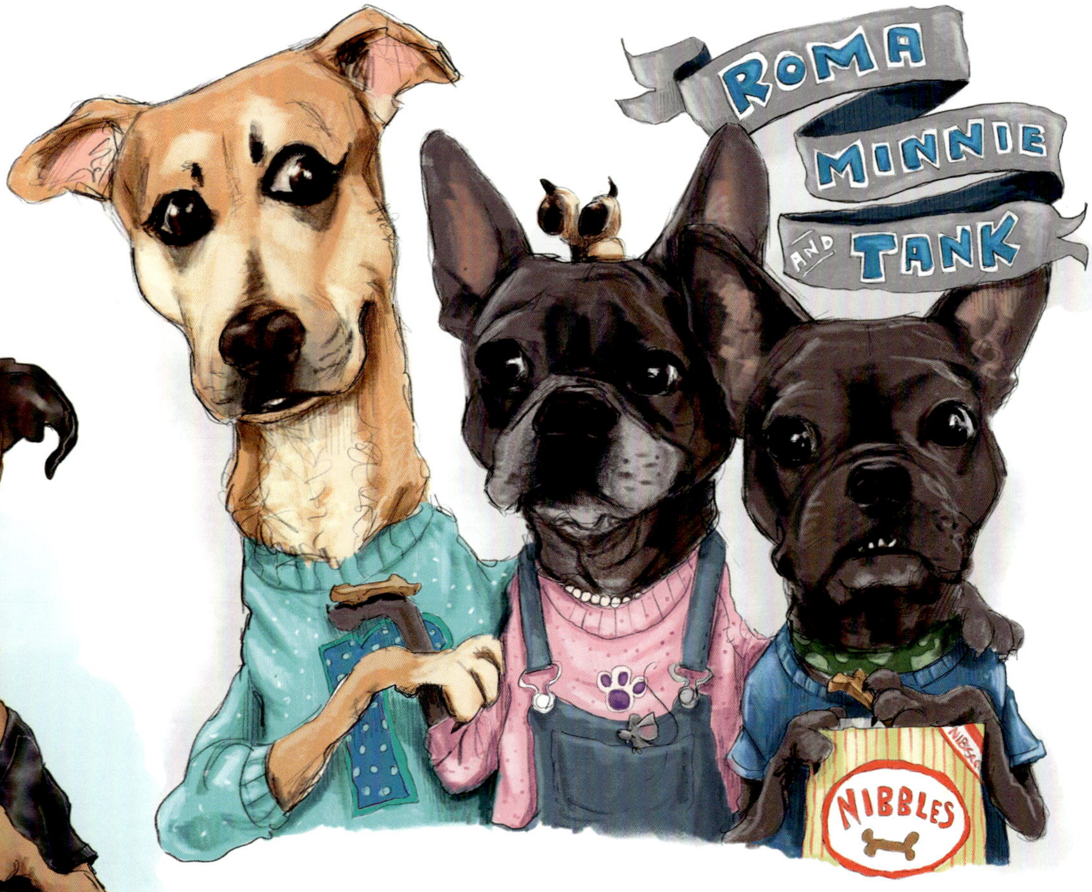
ROMA
MINNIE
AND TANK
NIBBLES

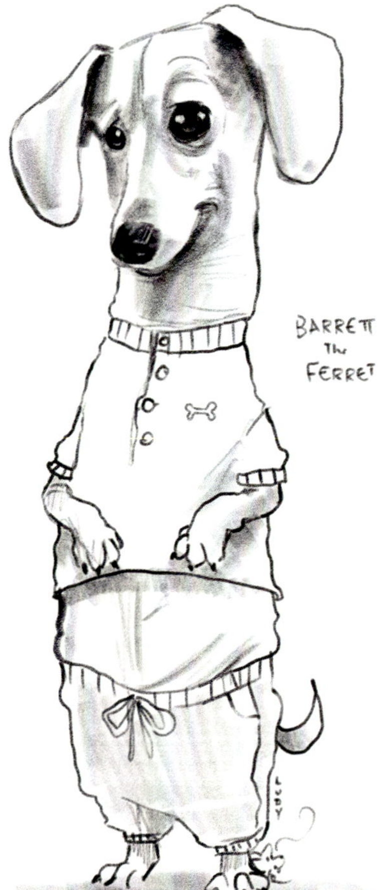
BARRETT
the
FERRET

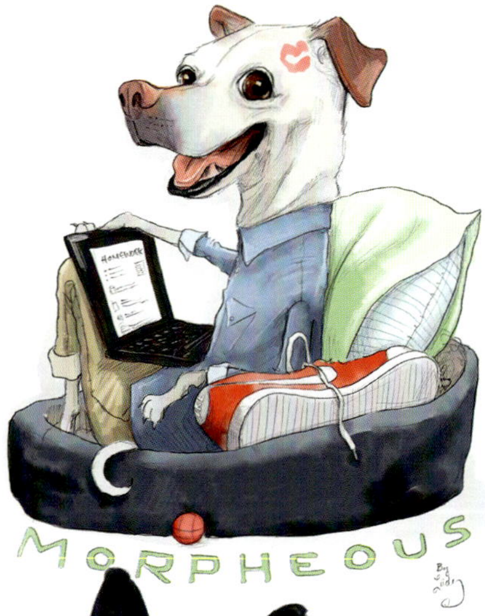
MORPHEOUS

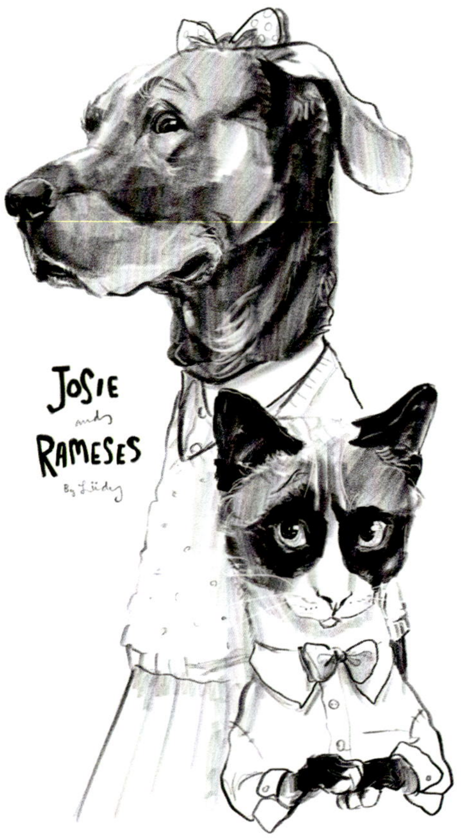
JOSIE
and
RAMESES

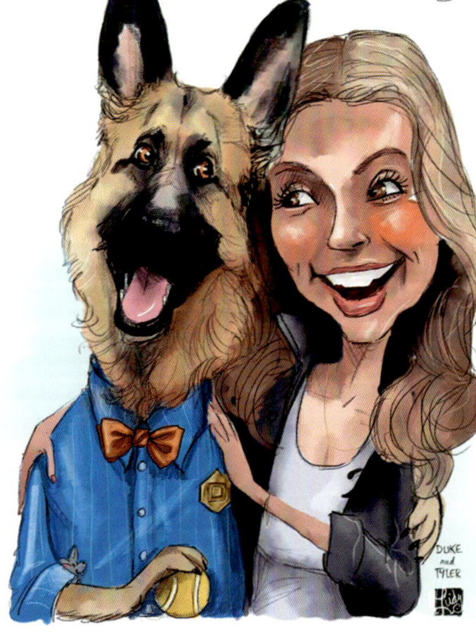
DUKE
and
TYLER

"Ever consider what our dogs must think of us?"

— Anne Tyler
("We come back from a grocery store with the most amazing haul: chicken, pork, half a cow. They must think we're the greatest hunters on earth!")

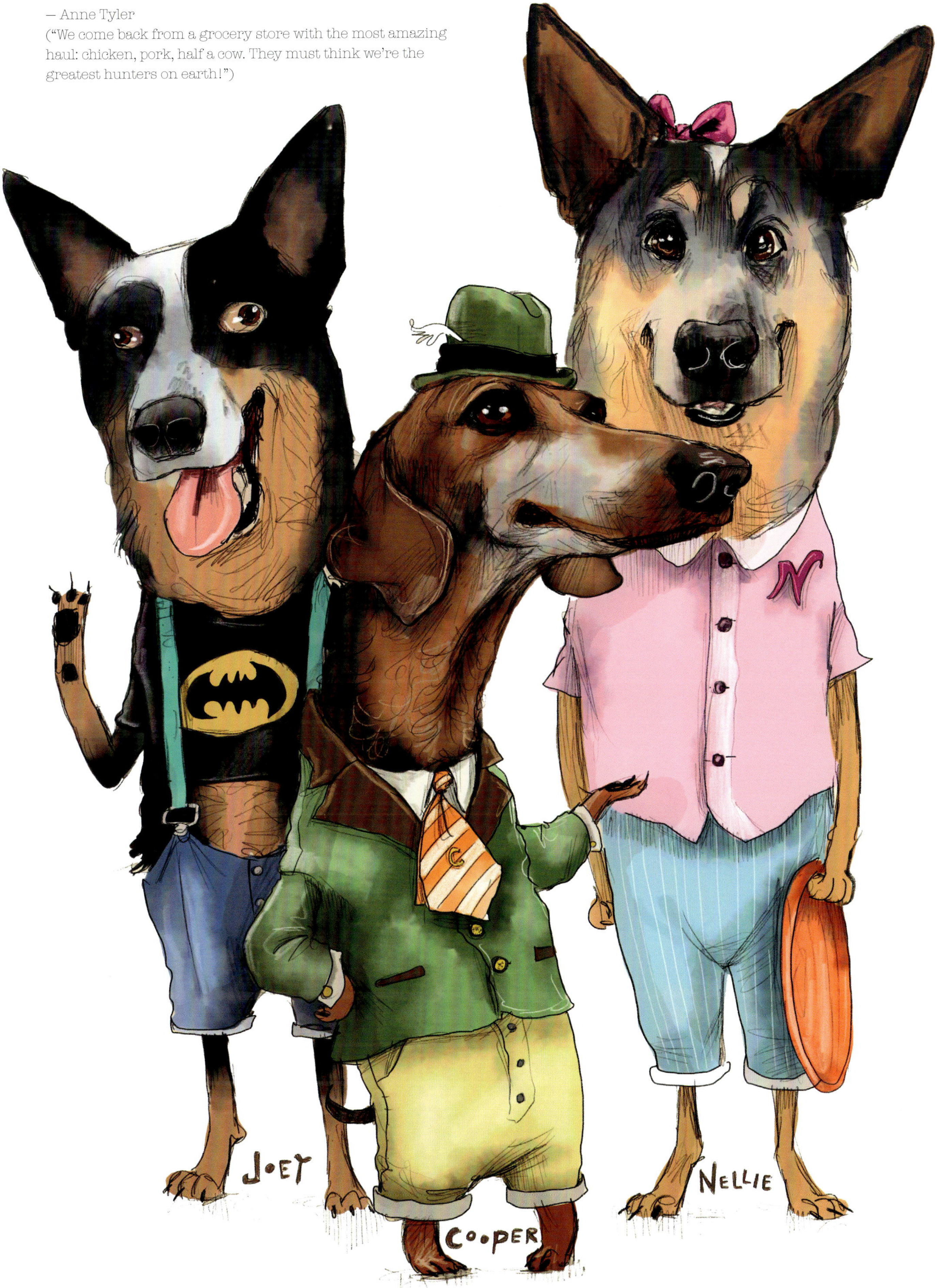

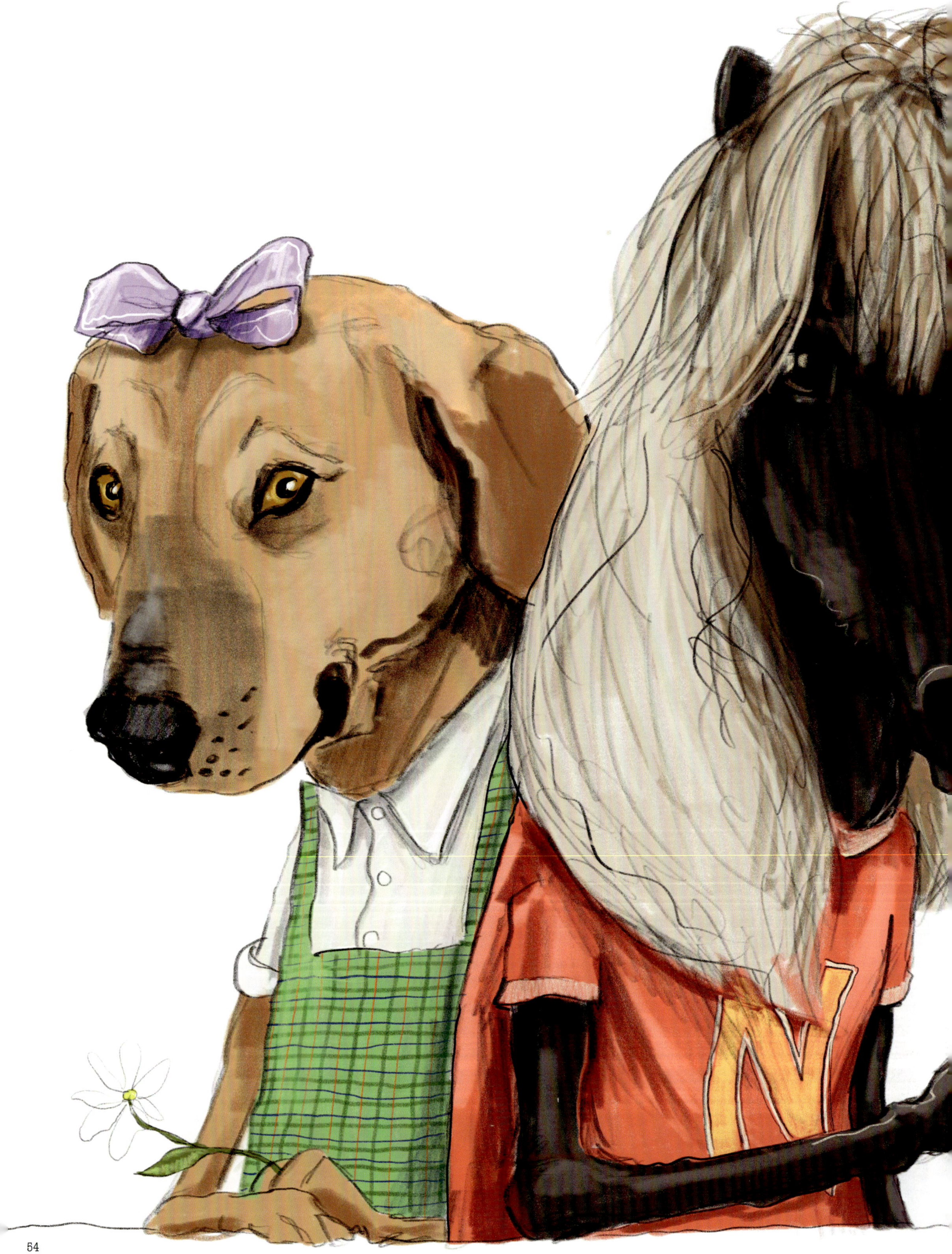
N

No one knew what brought them together–

but somehow, it worked.

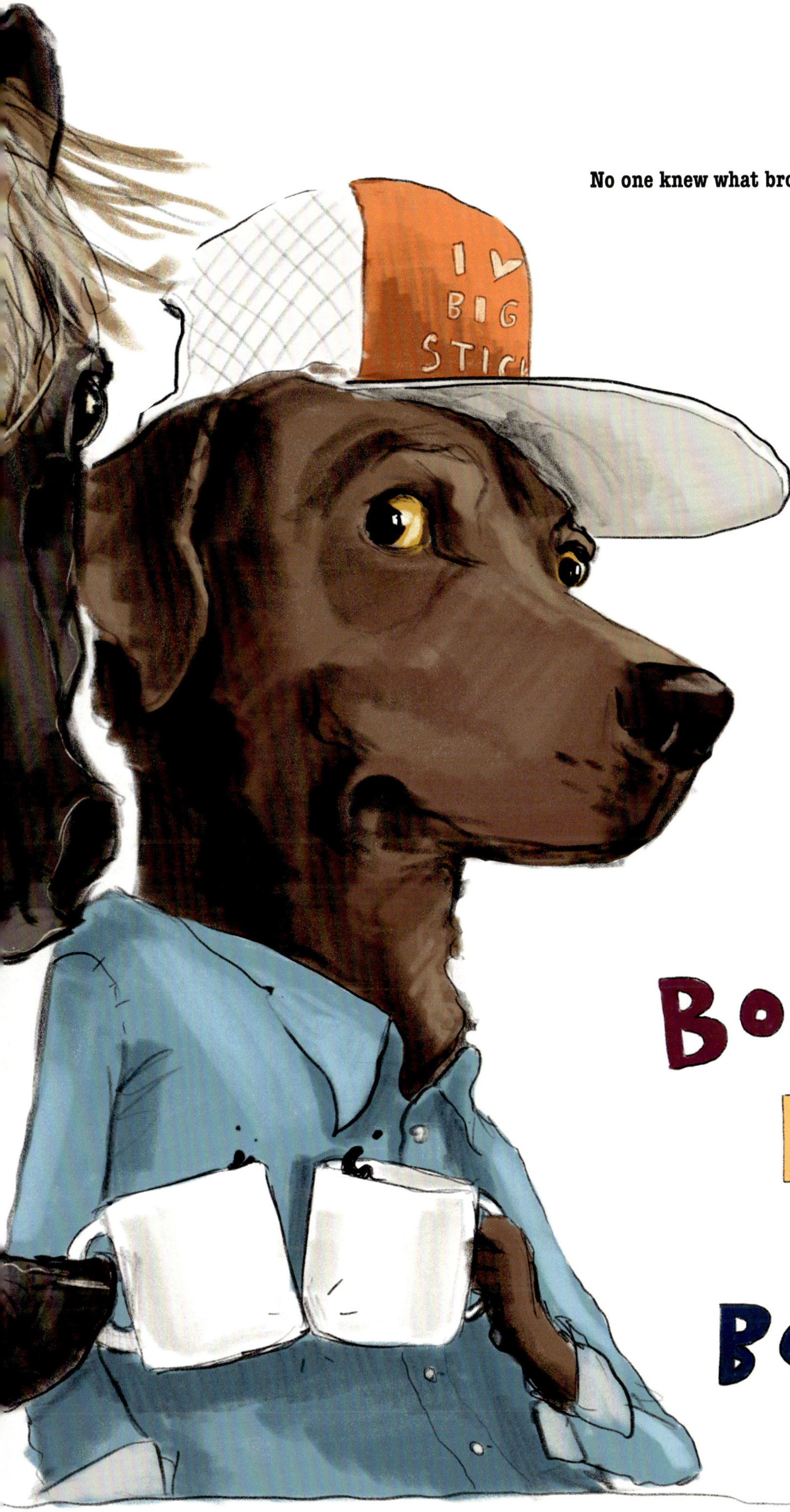

BONNIE NED -AND- BODHI

By Lüdy

GUS GUS

By Lüdy

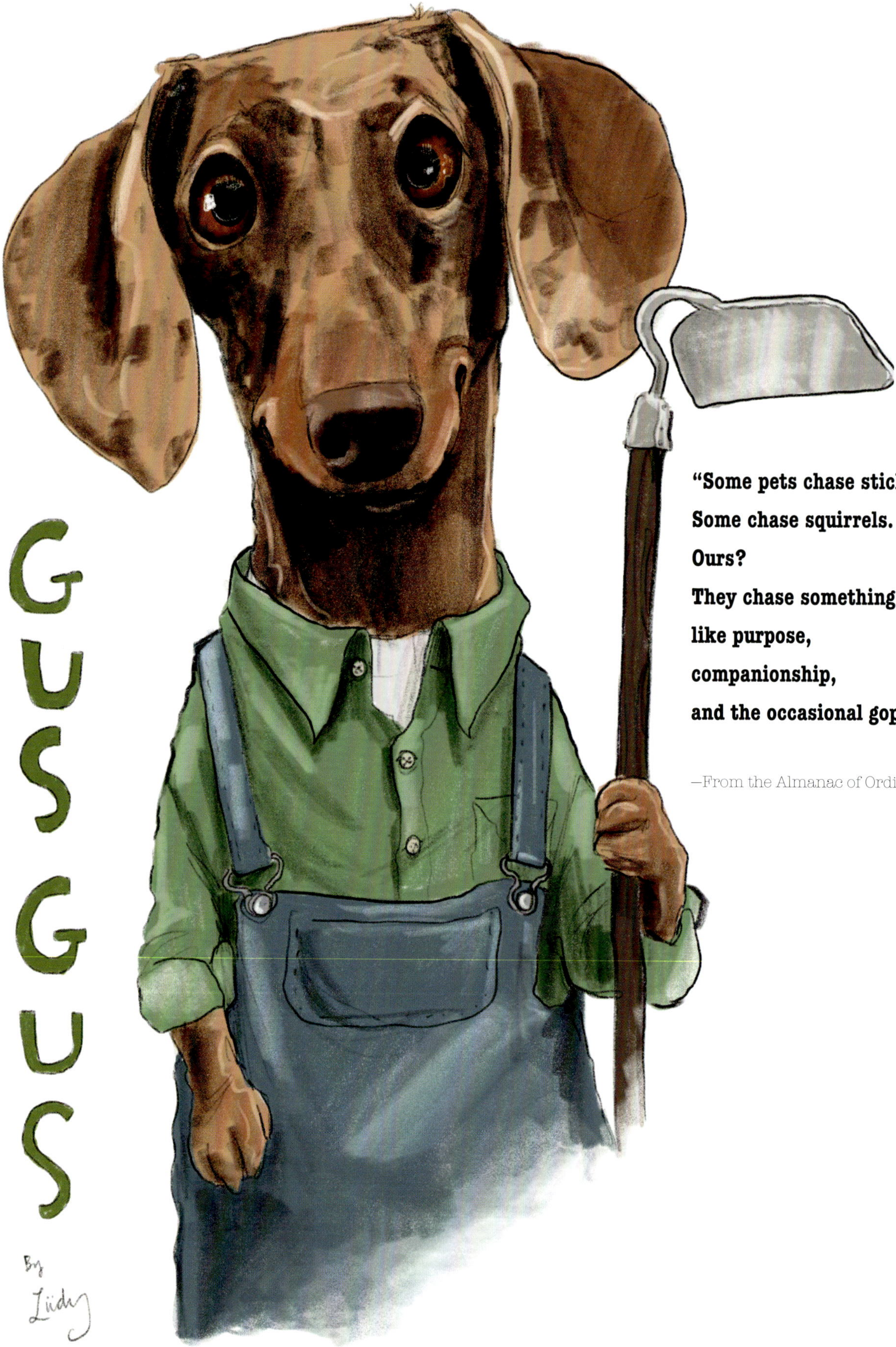

"Some pets chase sticks.
Some chase squirrels.
Ours?
They chase something truer—
like purpose,
companionship,
and the occasional gopher."

—From the Almanac of Ordinary Miracles

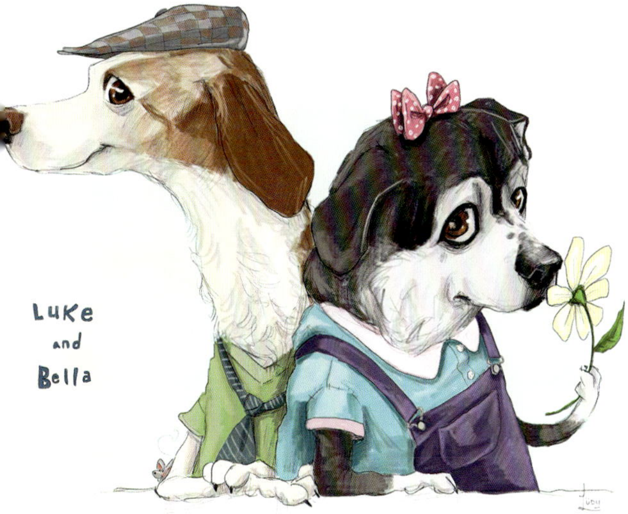
Luke
and
Bella

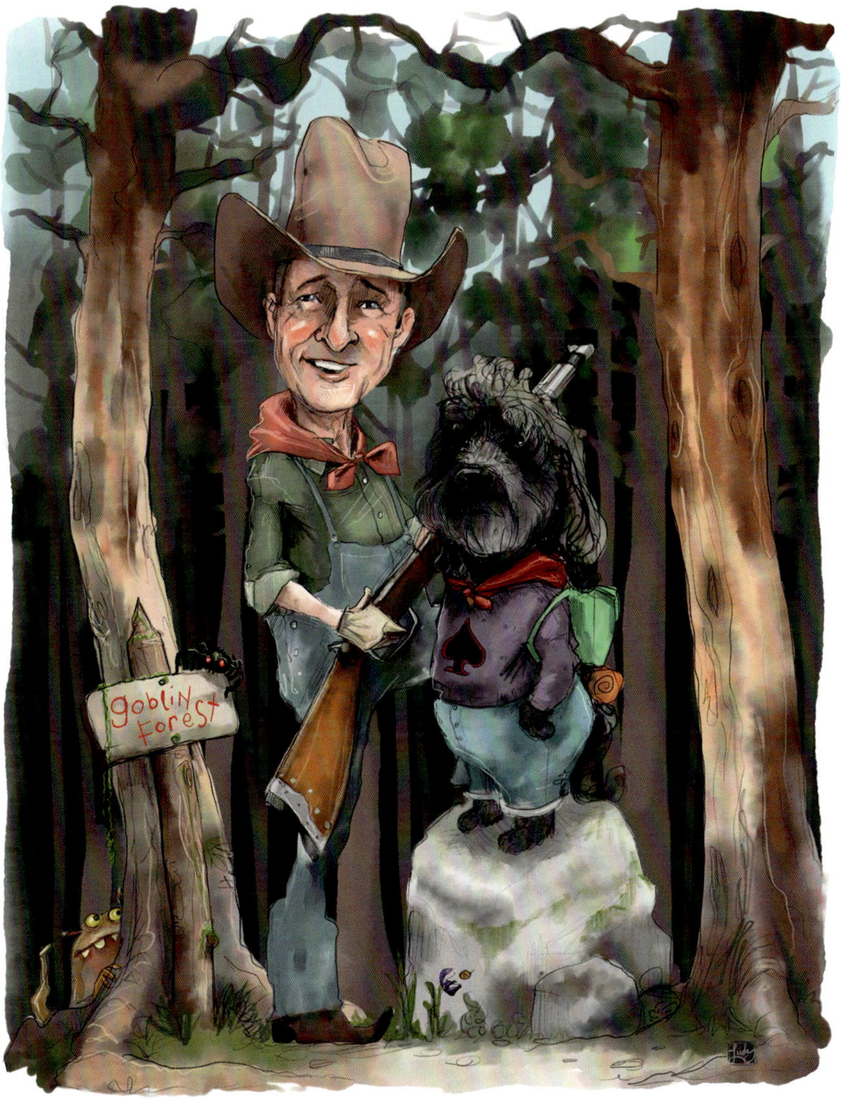
goblin
Forest

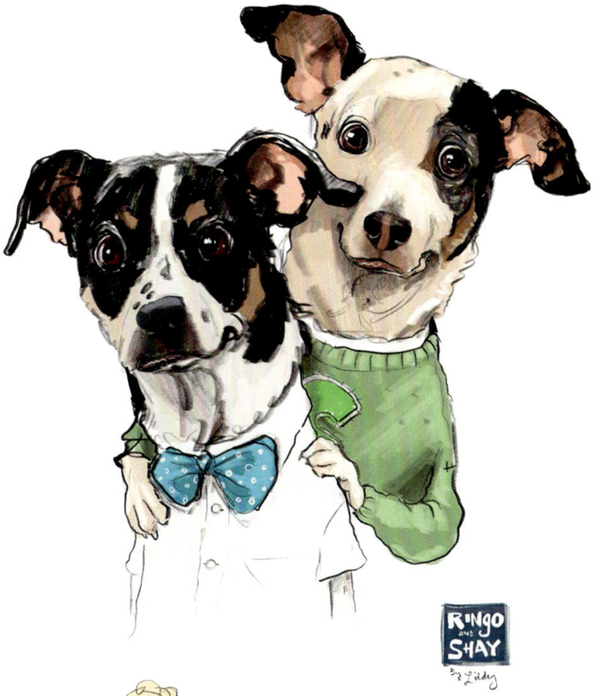
Ringo
SHAY

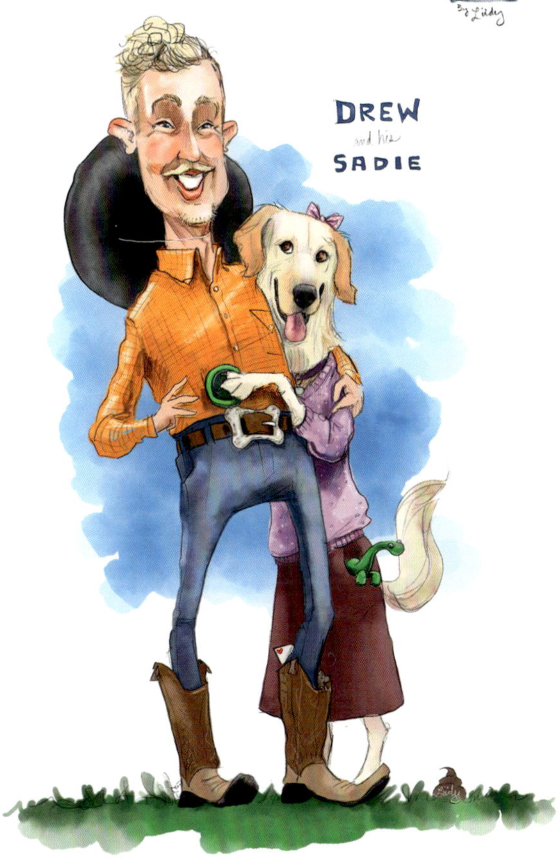
DREW
SADIE

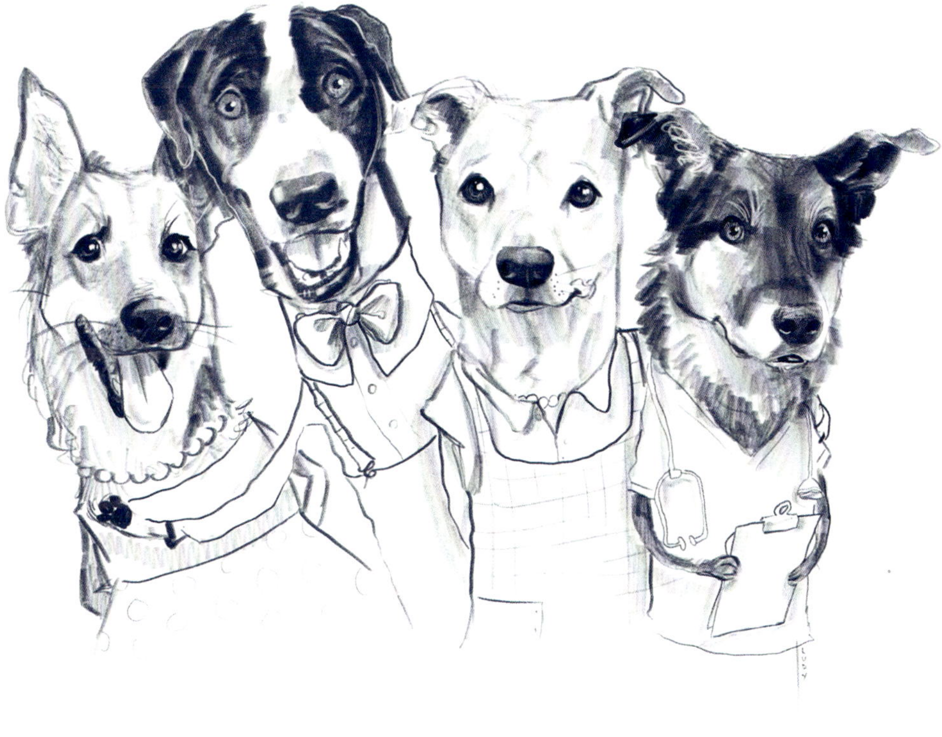
CHEYANNE GEORGE MAGGIE BEAUTY

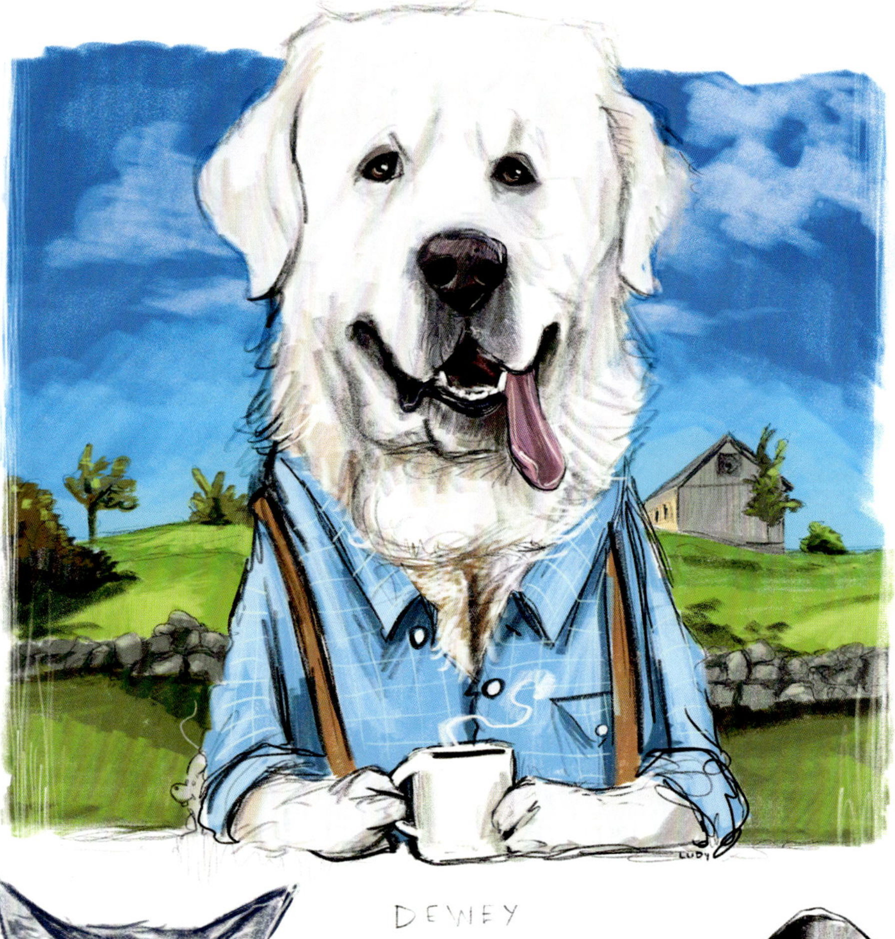
DEWEY

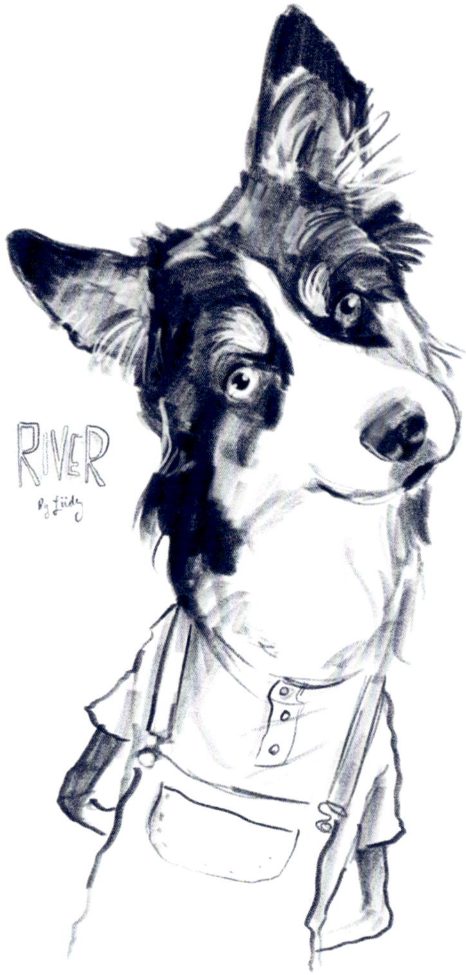
RIVER

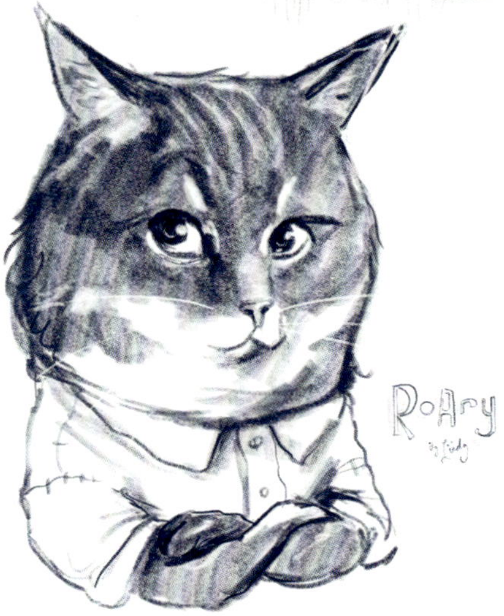
ROARY

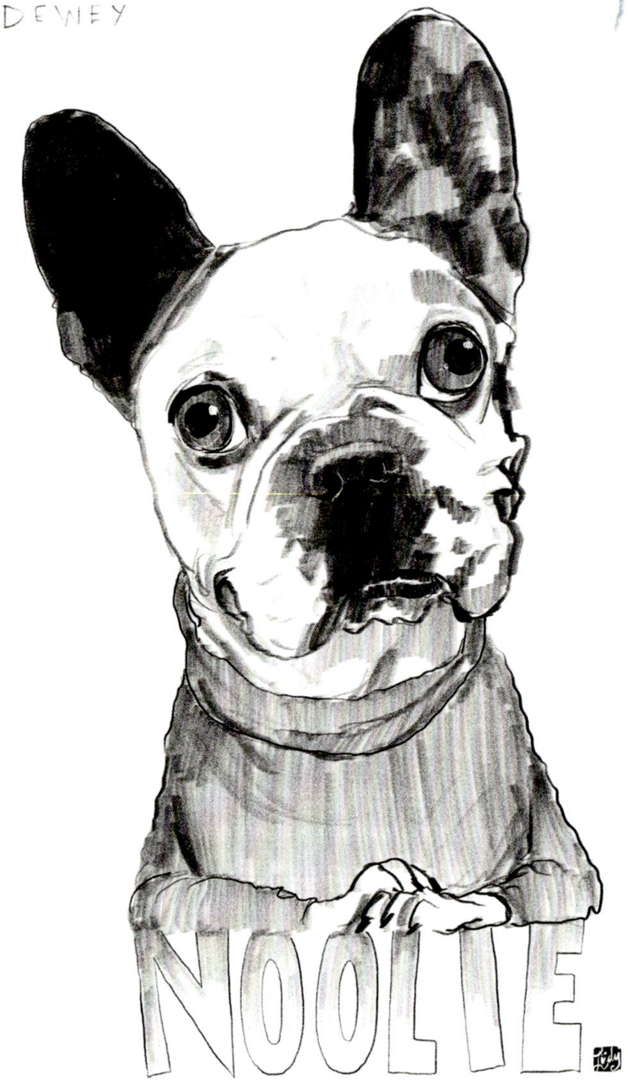
NOOLIE

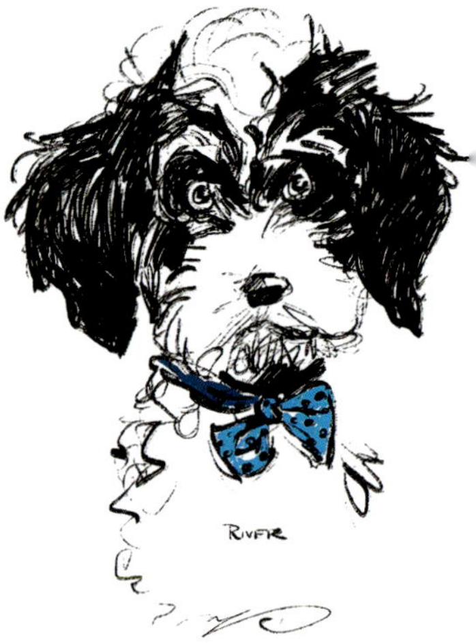

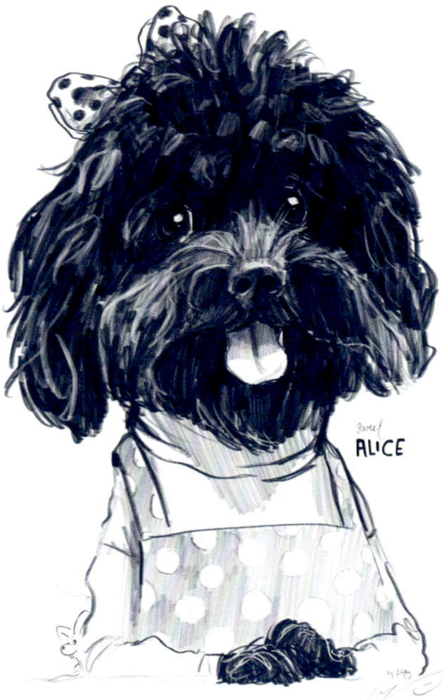
ALICE

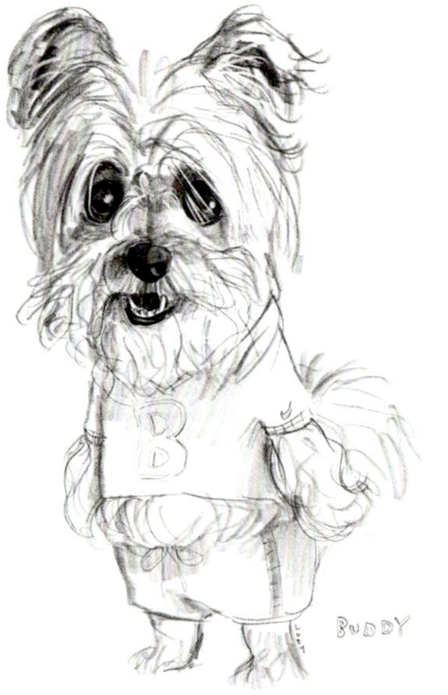
BUDDY

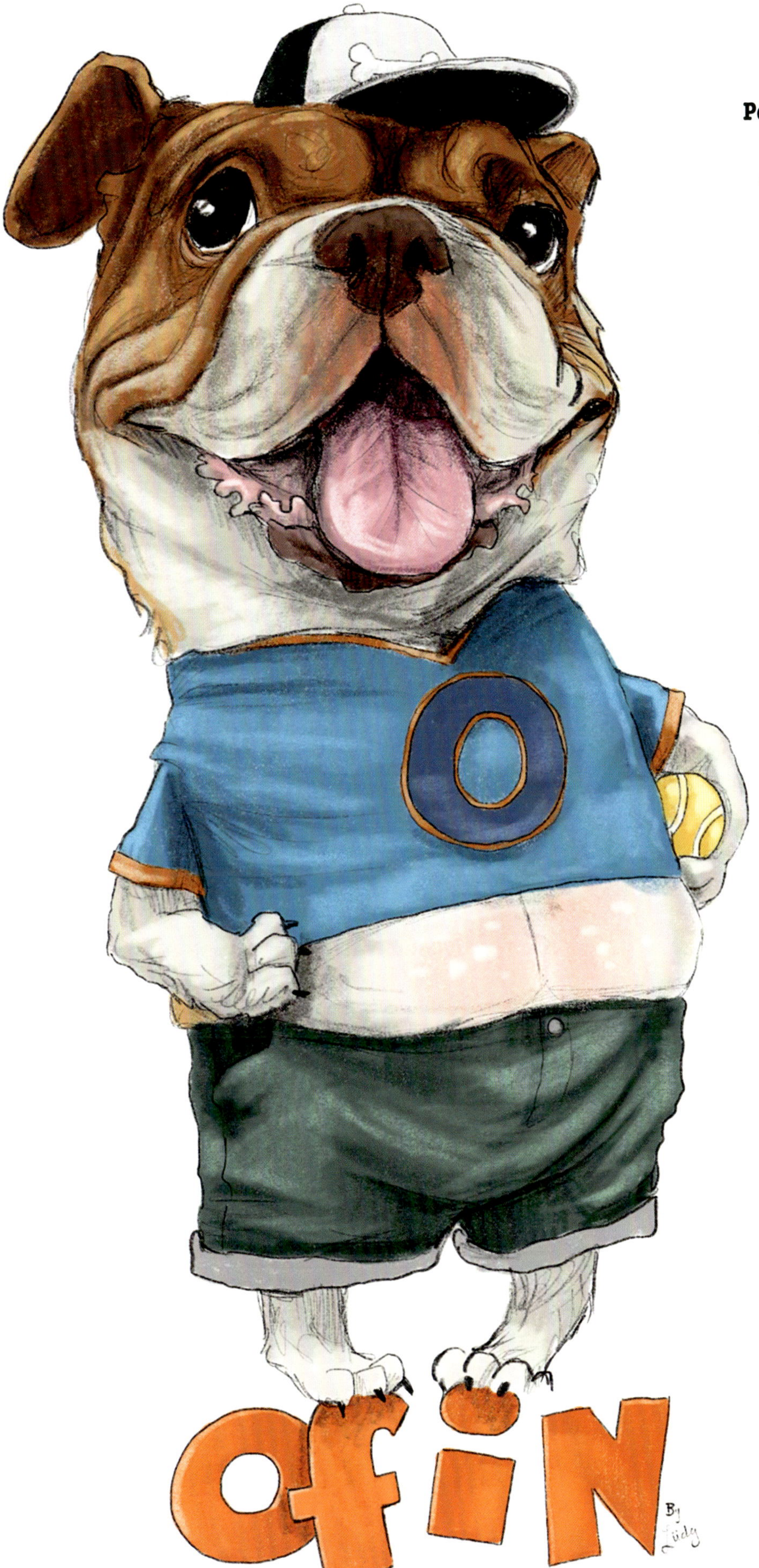

Pets see the world

as it could be—

full of play,

full of love,

and worth

wagging about.

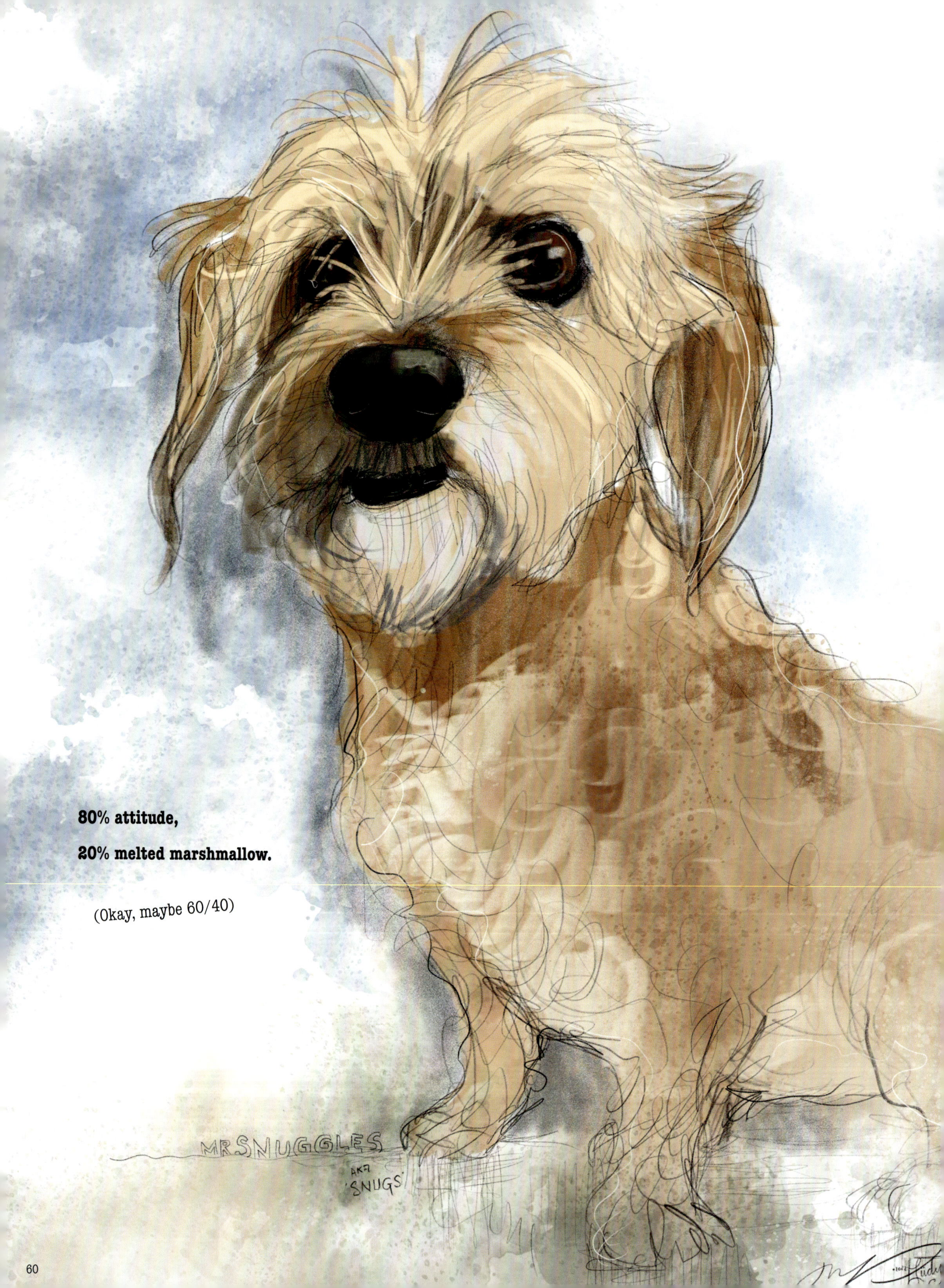

80% attitude,

20% melted marshmallow.

(Okay, maybe 60/40)

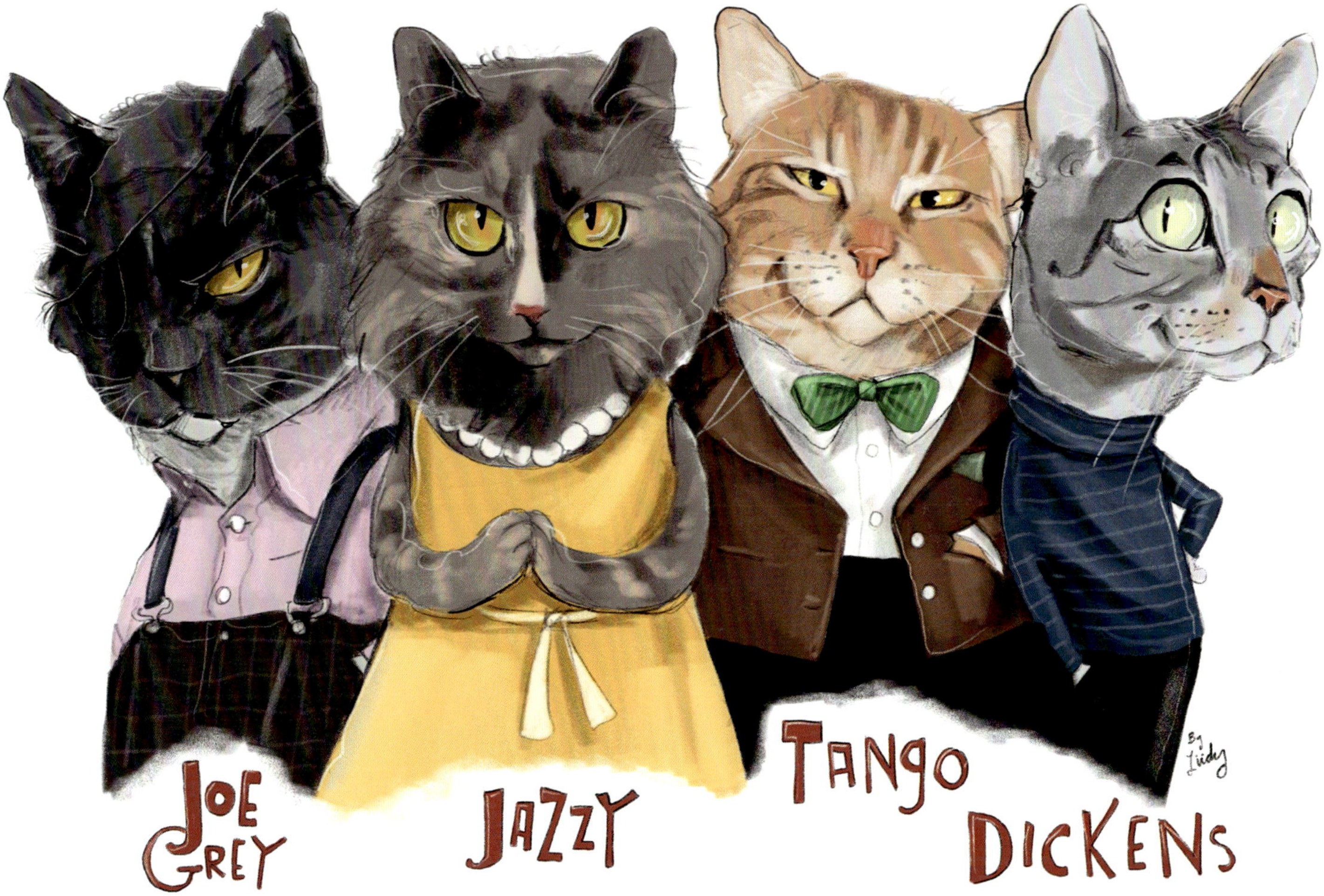
JOE GREY
JAZZY
TANGO
DICKENS

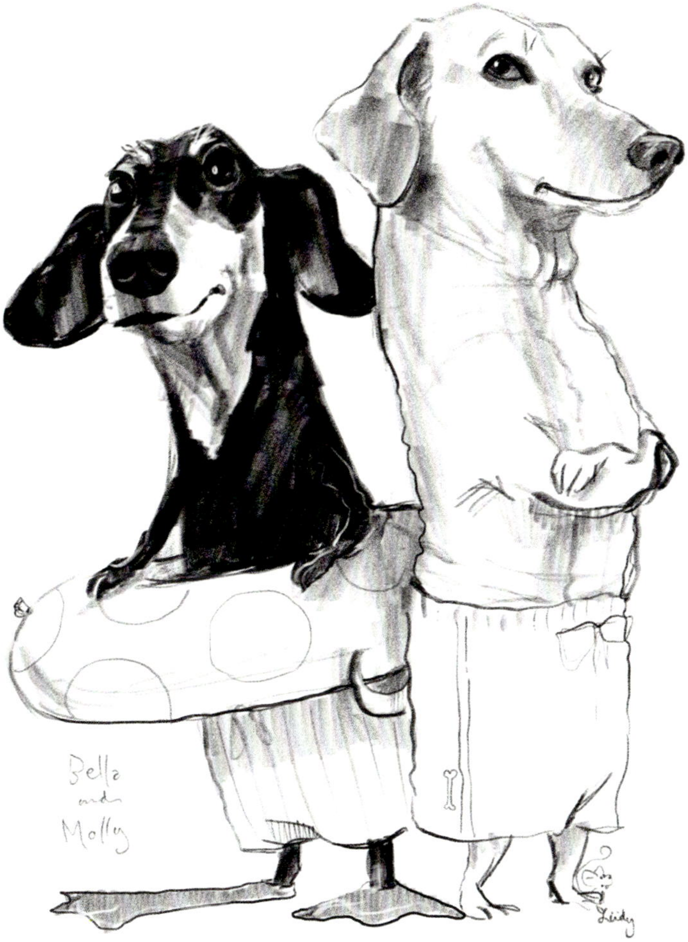
Bella and Molly

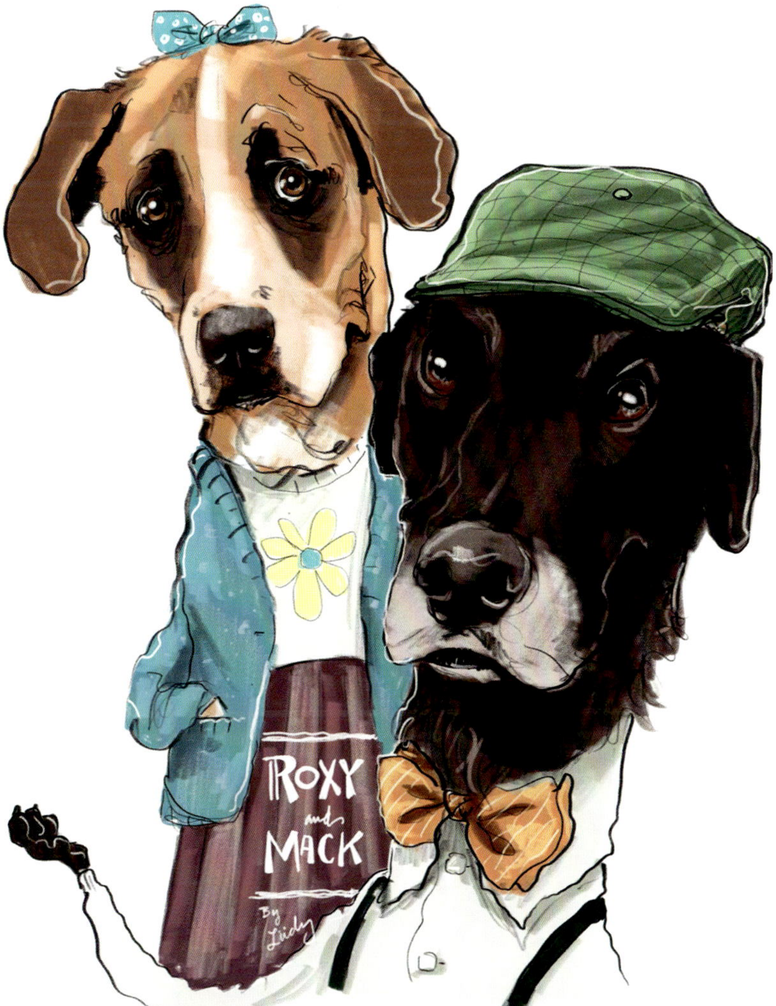
ROXY and MACK

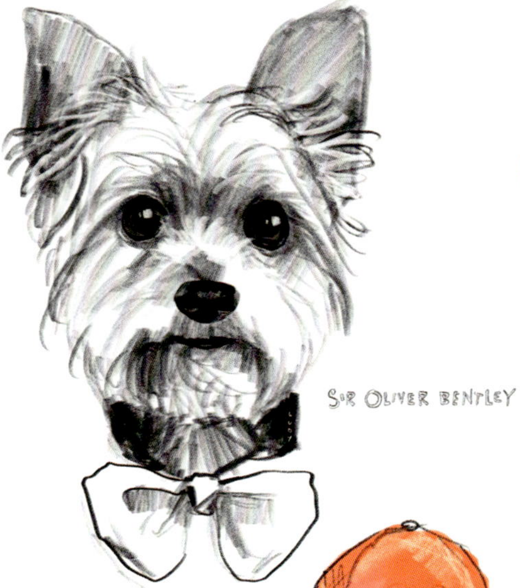
SIR OLIVER BENTLEY

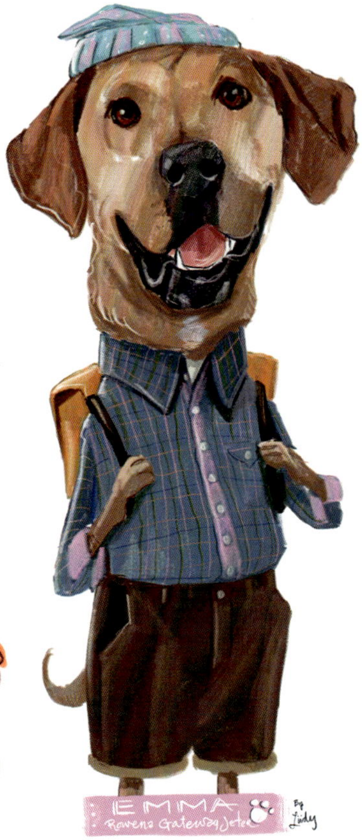
EMMA

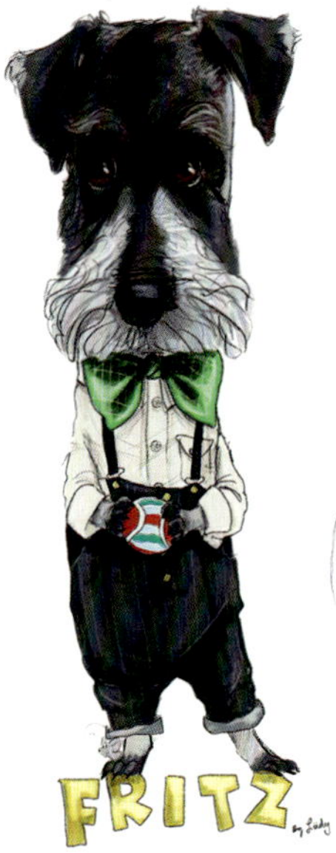
FRITZ

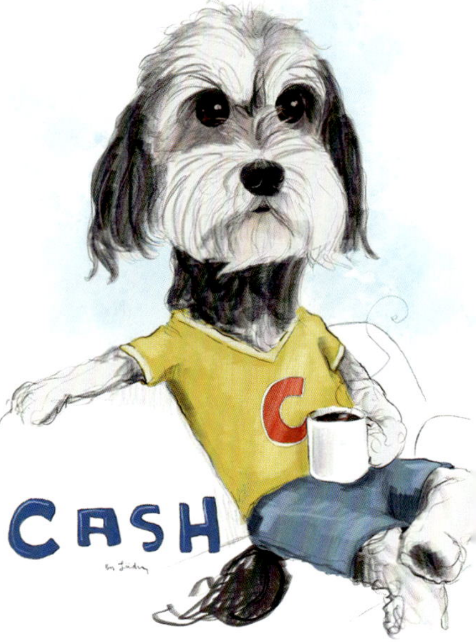
CASH

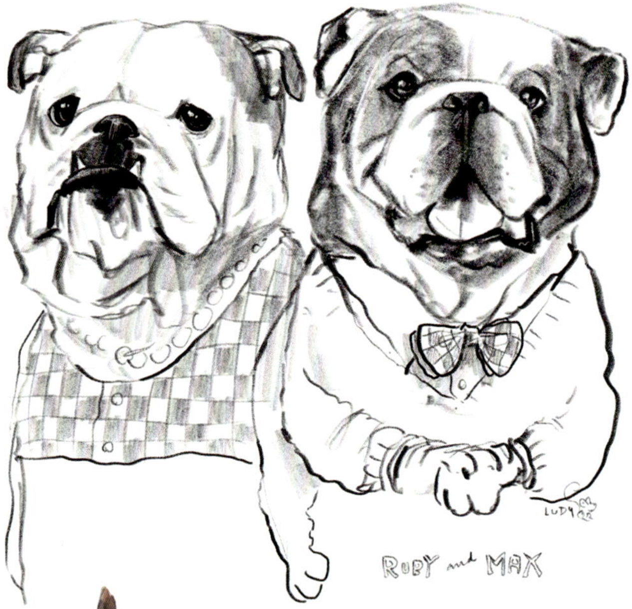
RUBY and MAX

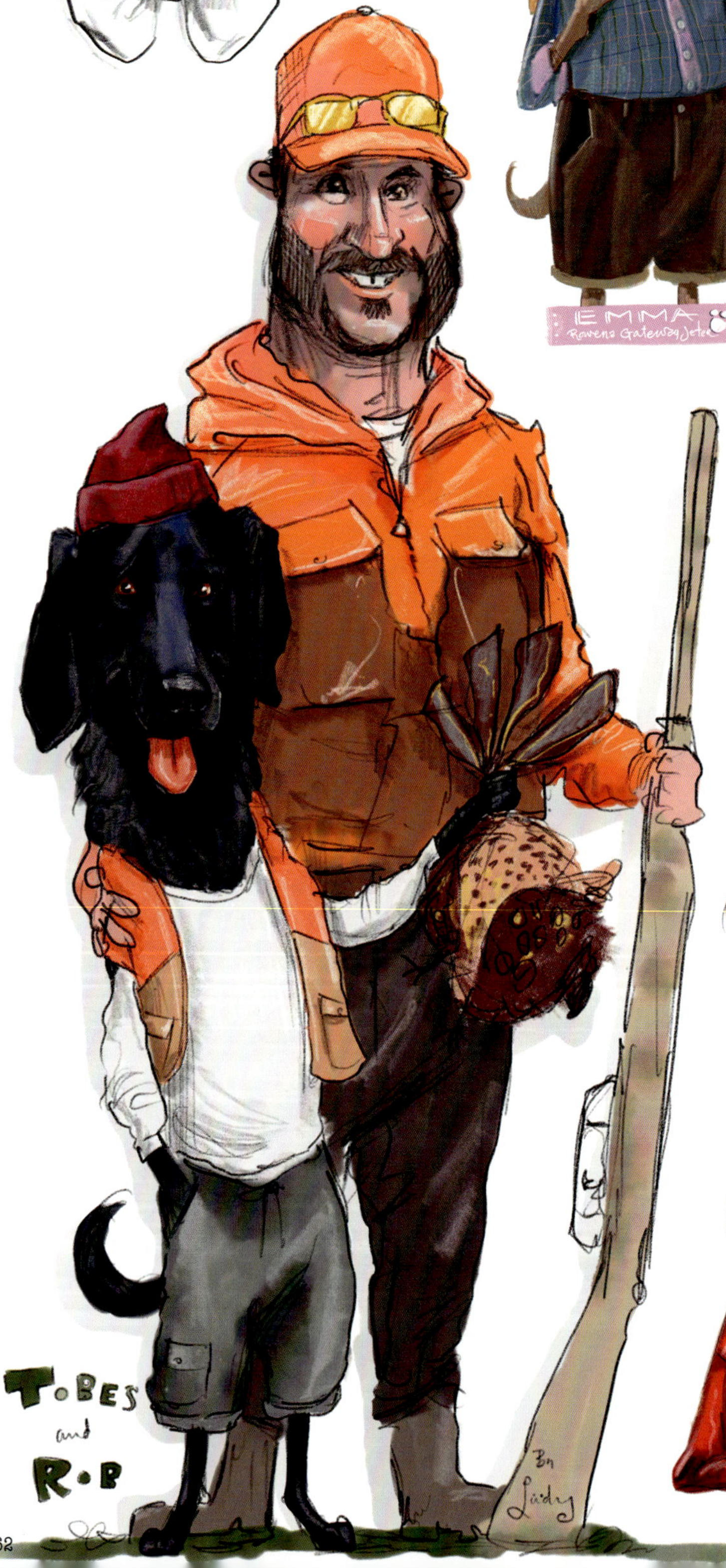
TOBES
and
ROB
By Lüdy

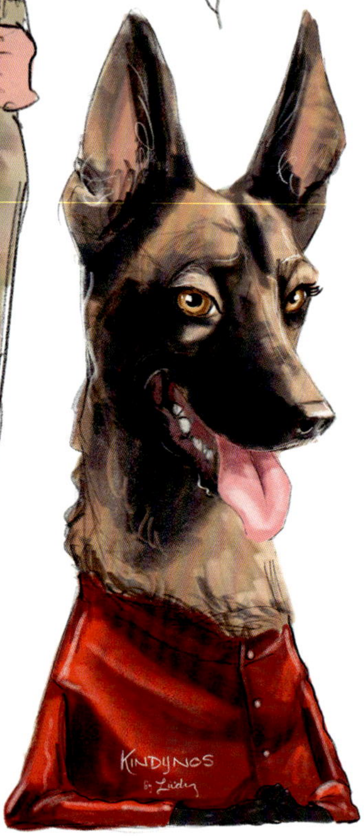
KINDYNOS

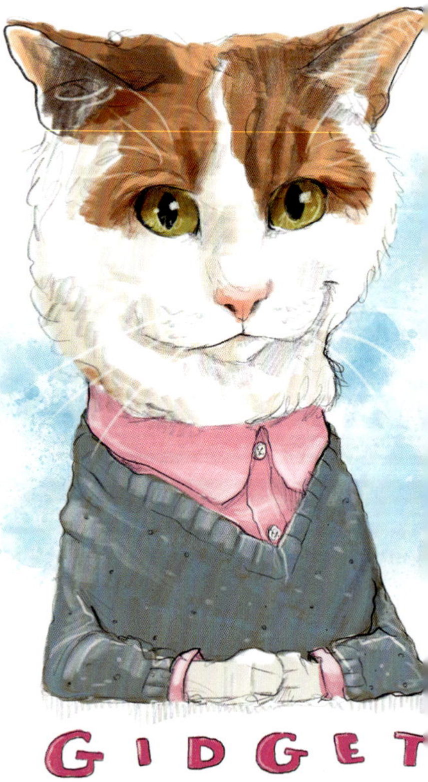
GIDGET

Together, they make just enough sense to keep the world spinning.

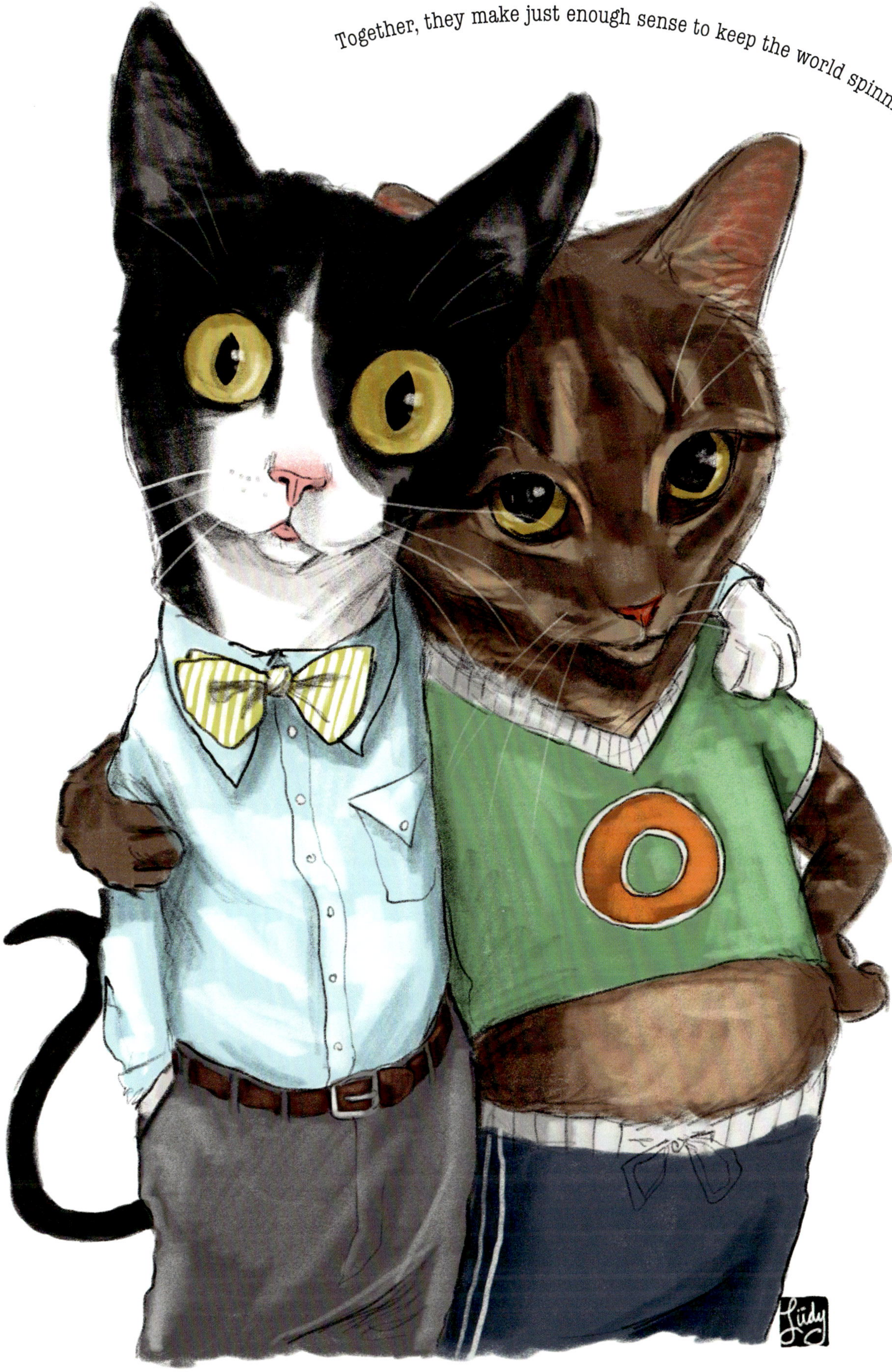

BRINKLEY AND OPIE

March
to
your
own
drum.
Even
if
it's
slightly
offbeat.

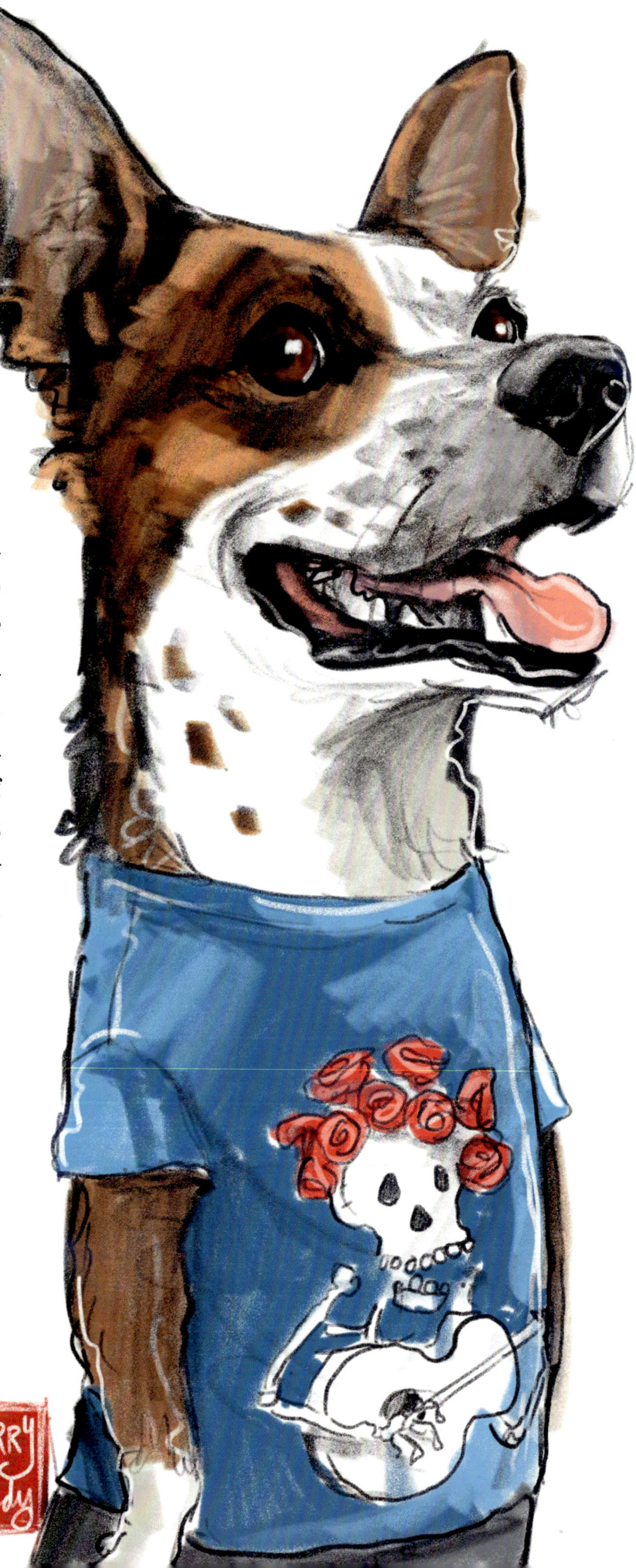

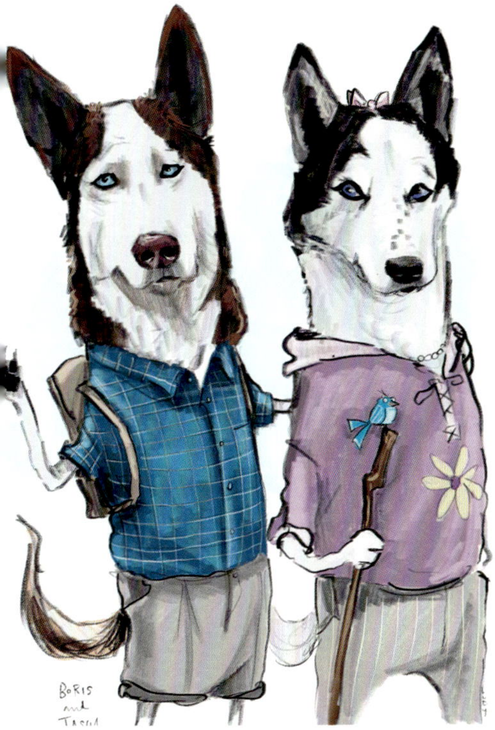

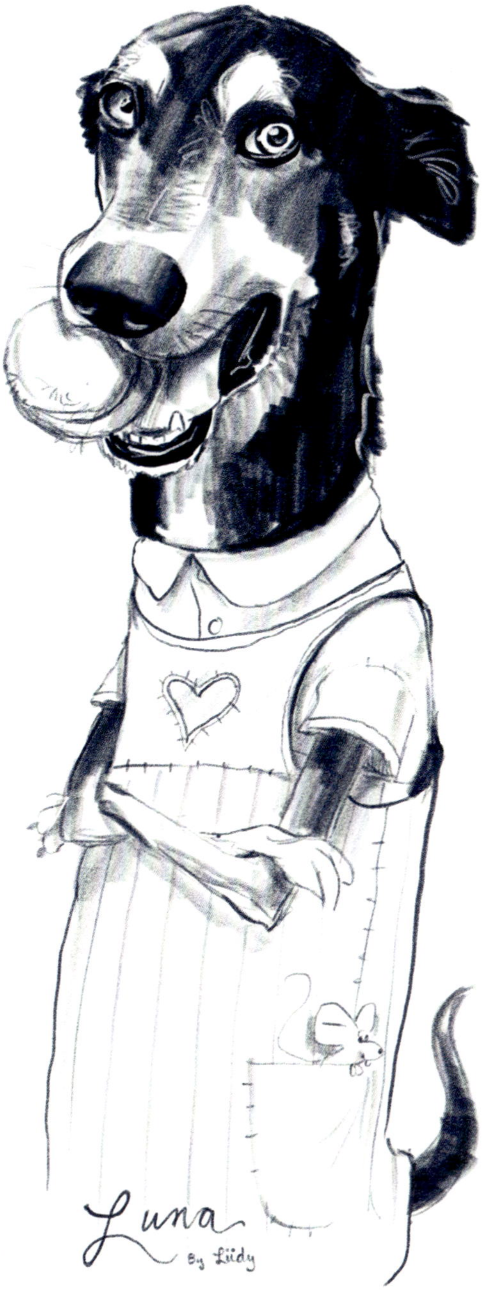
Luna

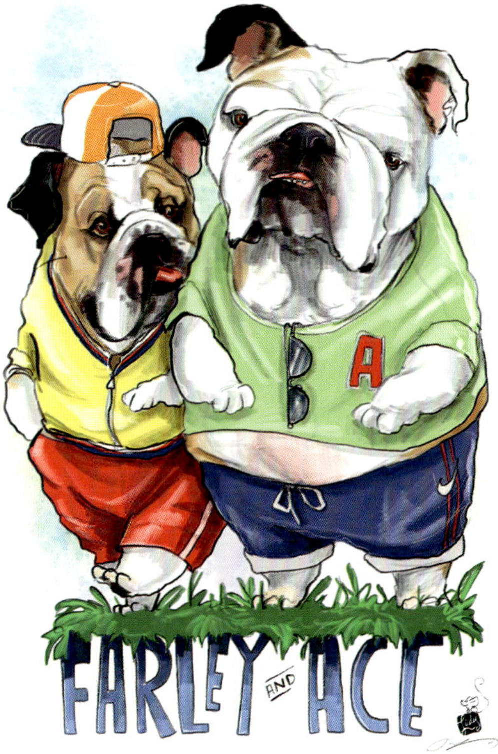
FARLEY AND ACE

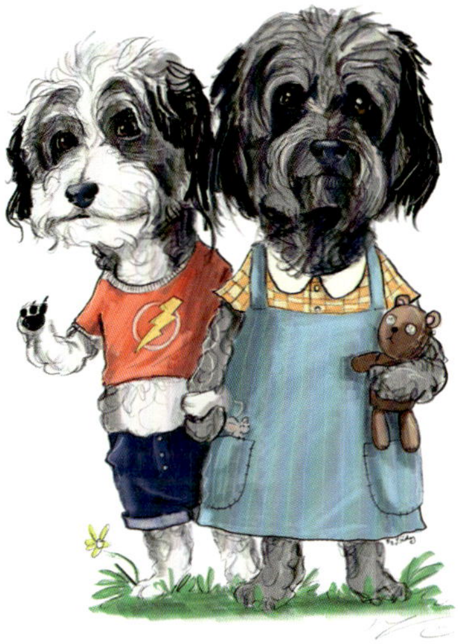

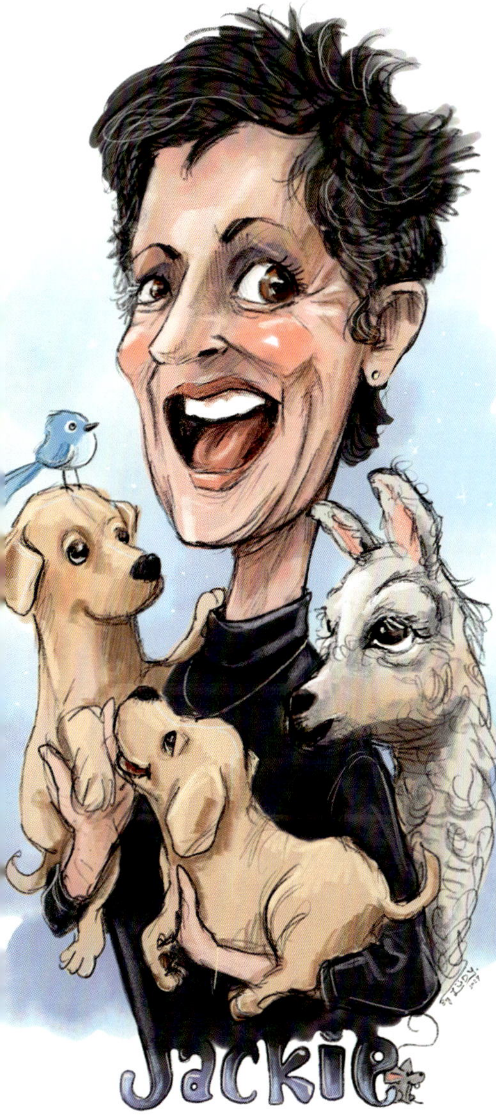
Jackie

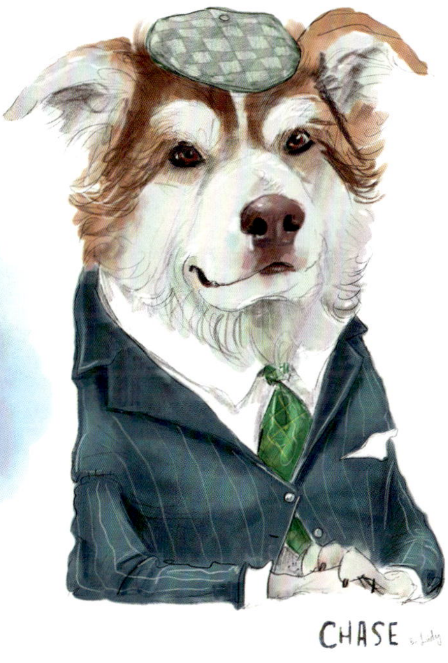
CHASE

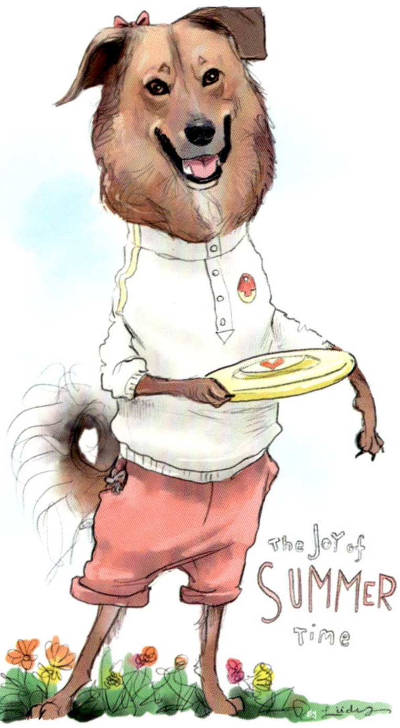
The Joy of
SUMMER
Time

They ruin the furniture. And completely renovate your heart.

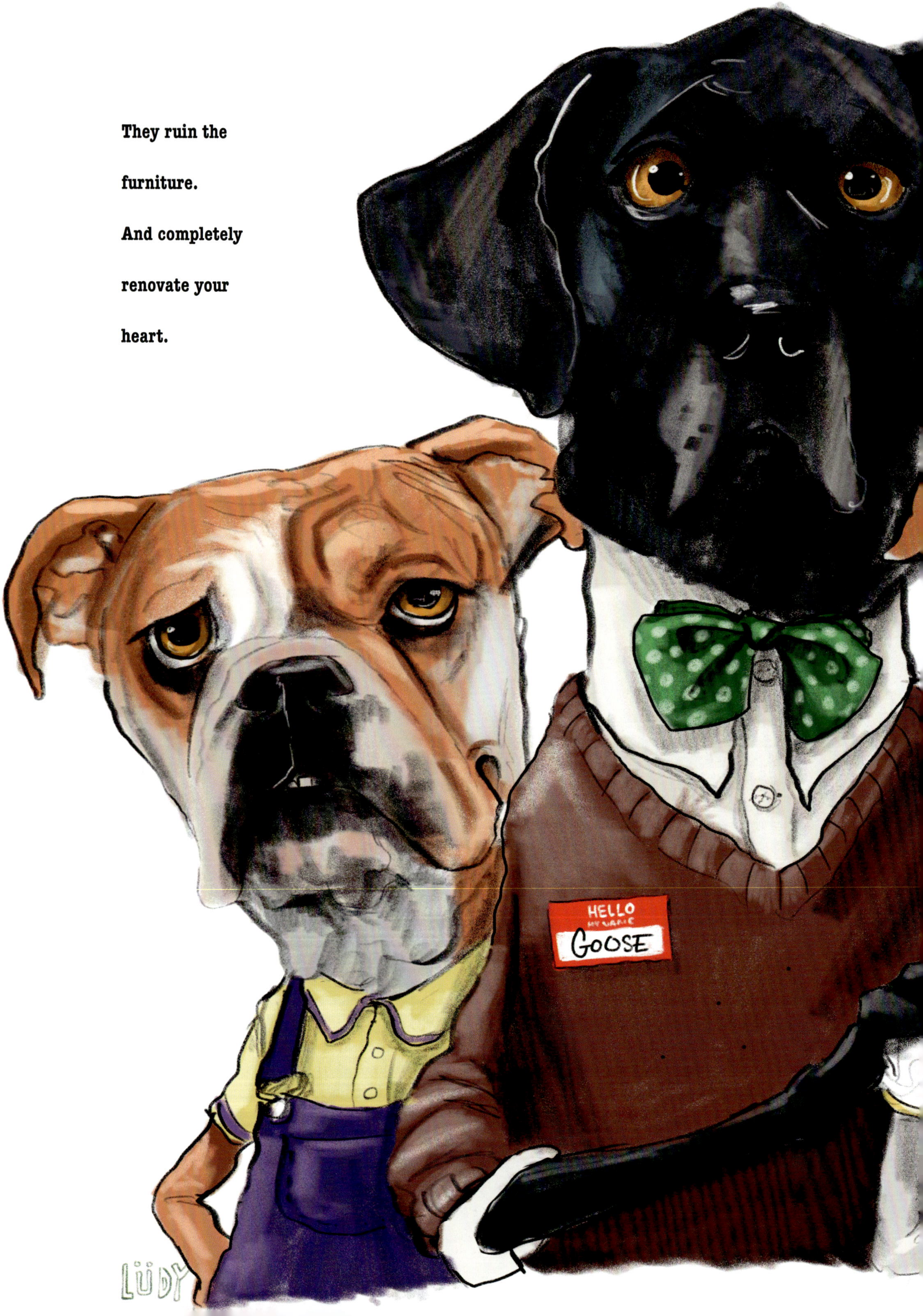

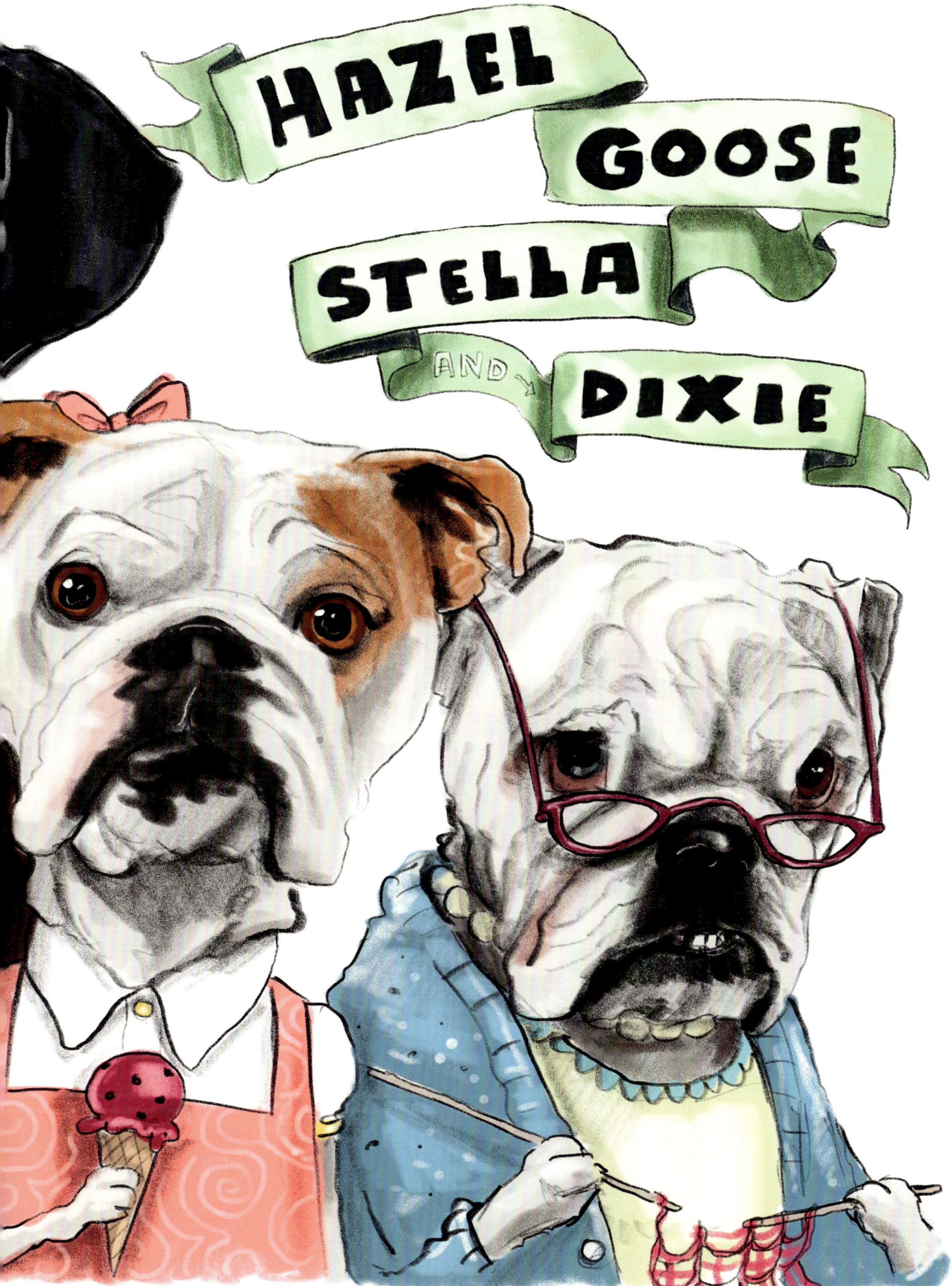
HAZEL
GOOSE
STELLA
AND
DIXIE

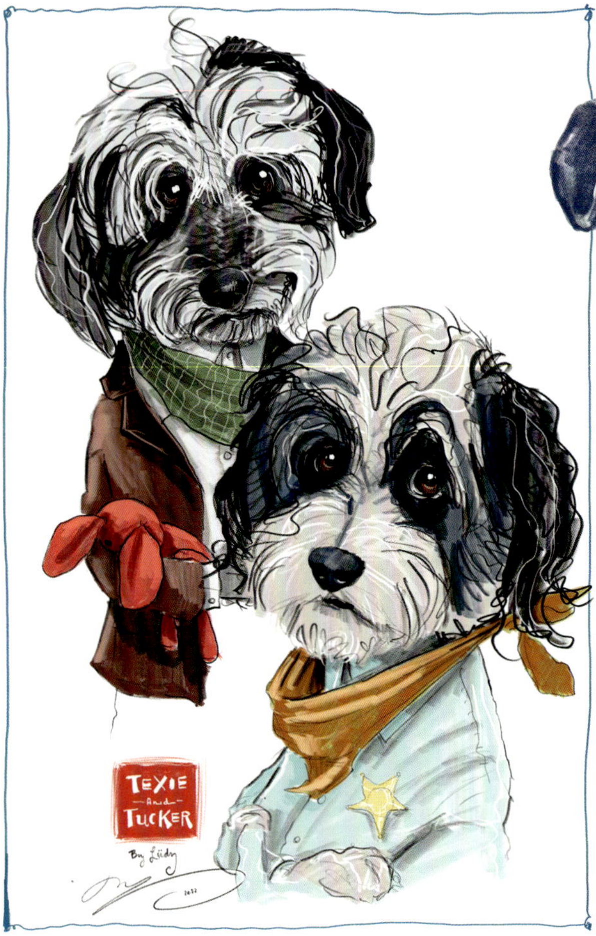
TEXIE AND TUCKER
By Lüdy

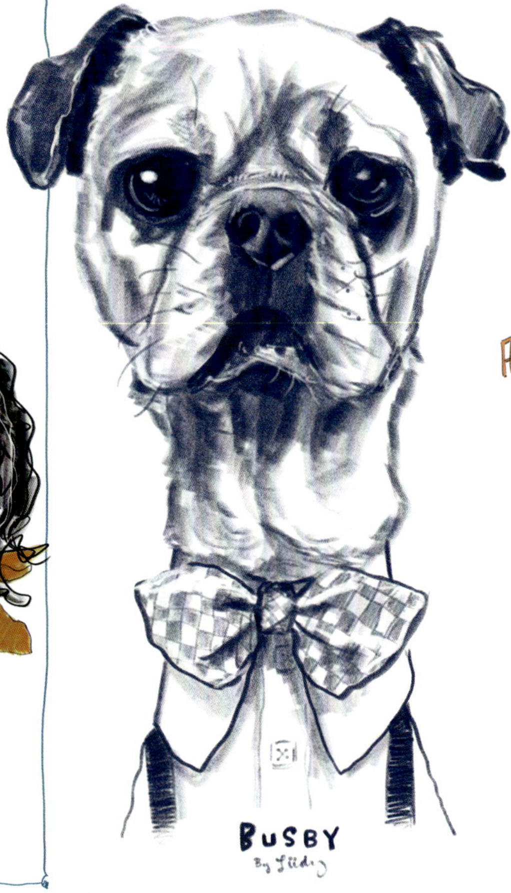
BUSBY
By Lüdy

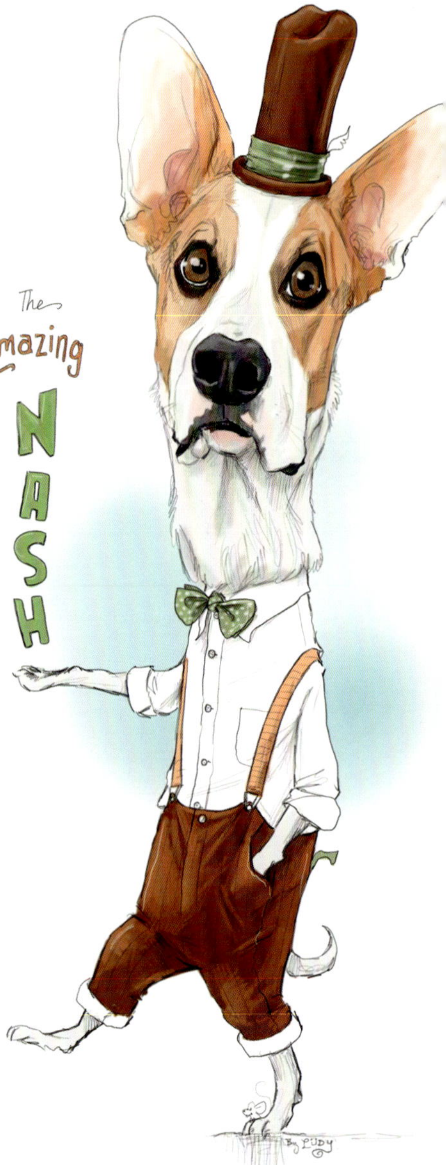
The Amazing NASH
By Lüdy

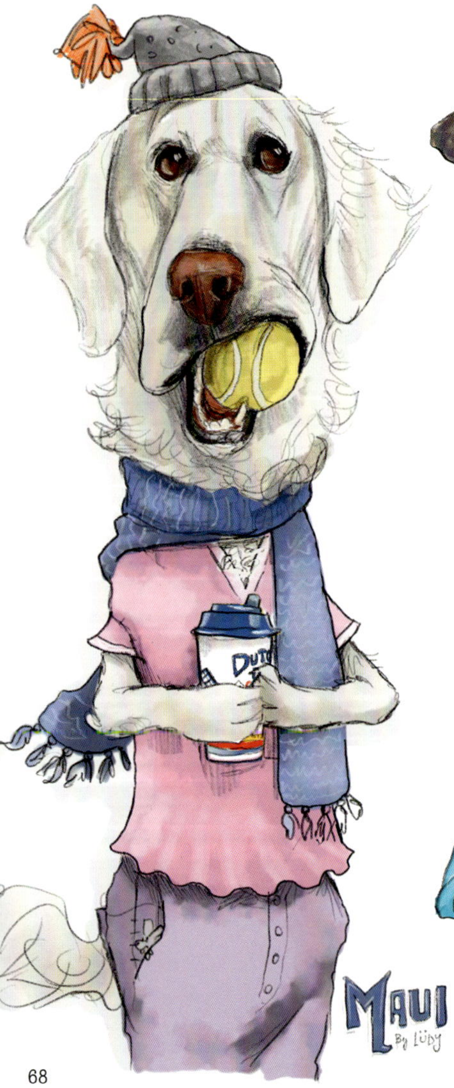
MAUI
By Lüdy

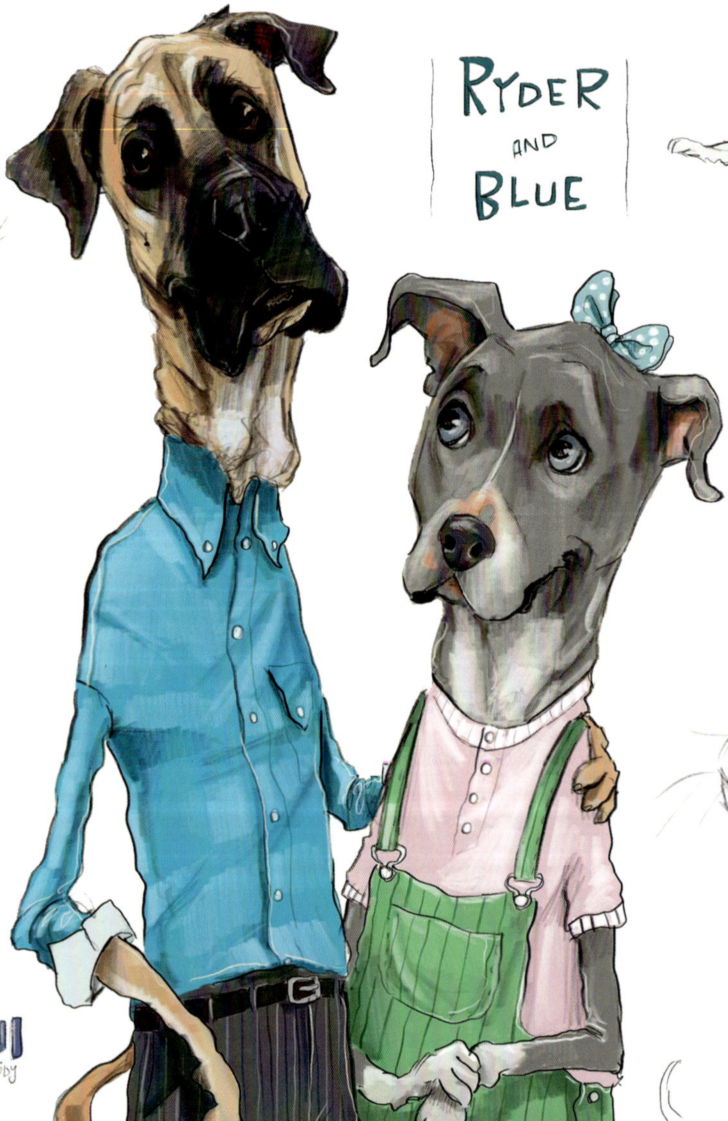
RYDER AND BLUE

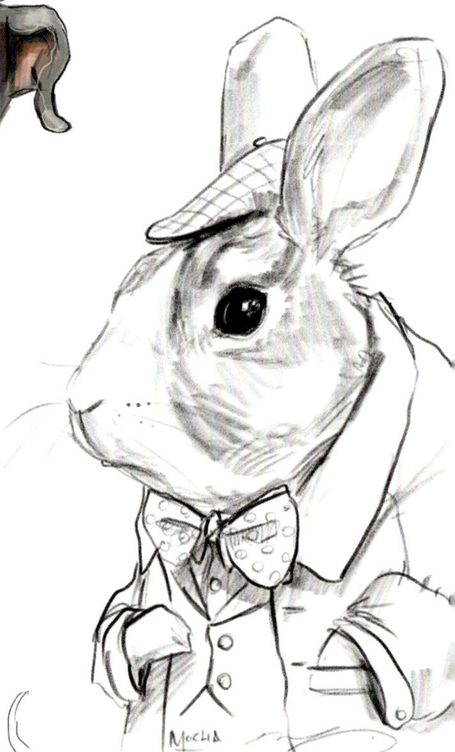
MOCHA

They may not win medals,

but they always steal the show.

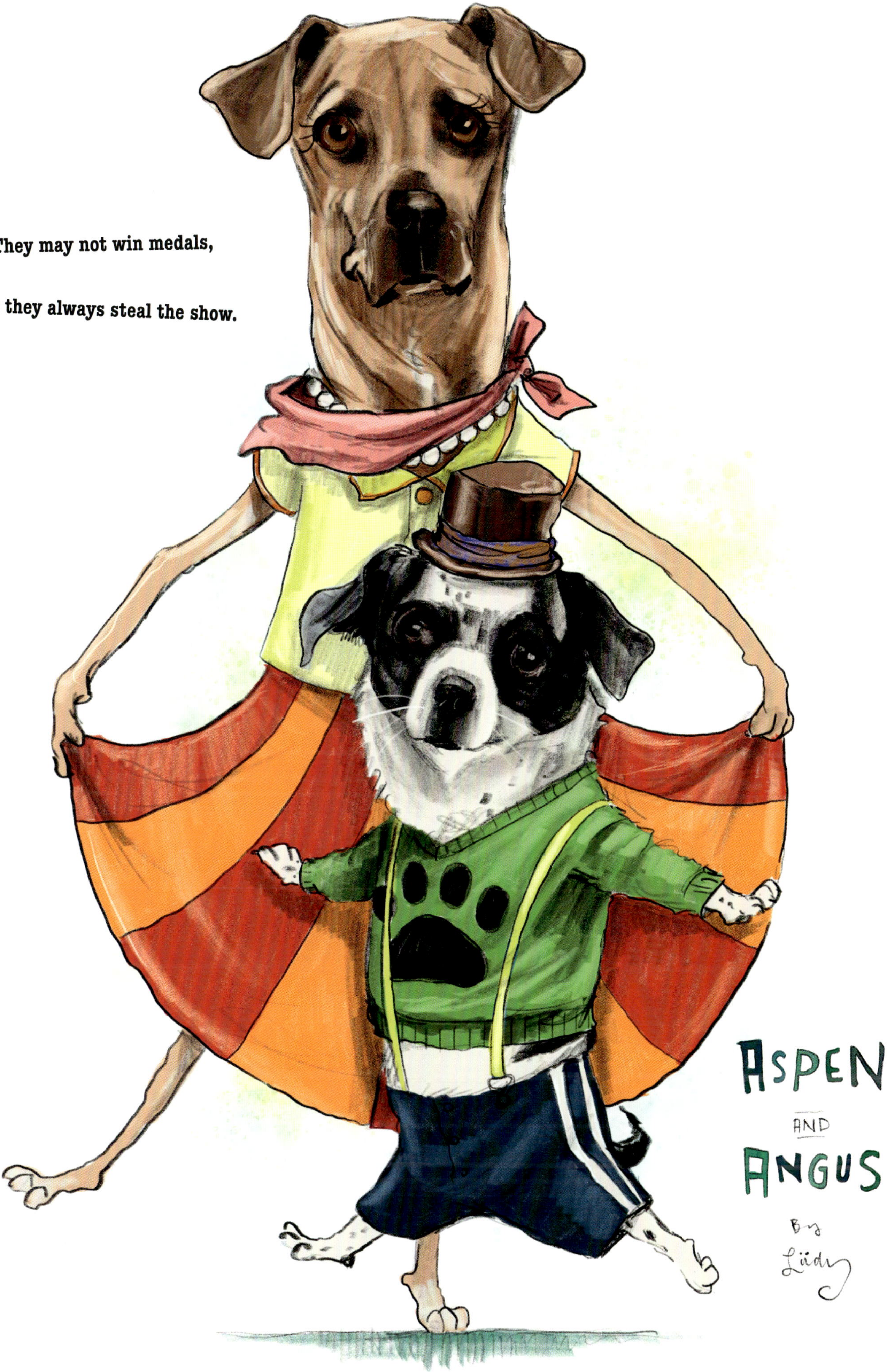

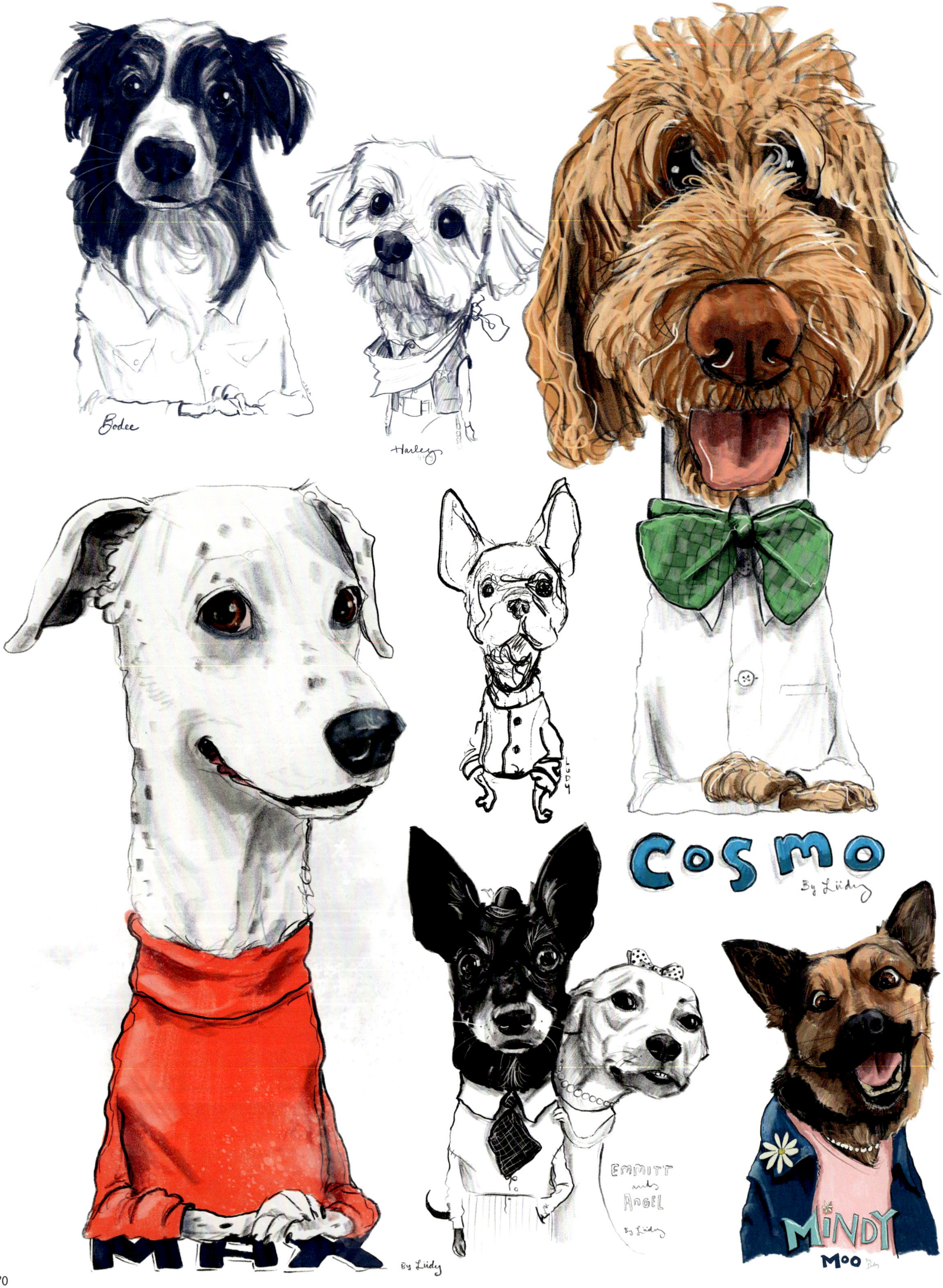
Bodee
Harley
COSMO
By Lüdy
EMMITT
and
ANGEL
By Lüdy
By Lüdy
MINDY
MOO

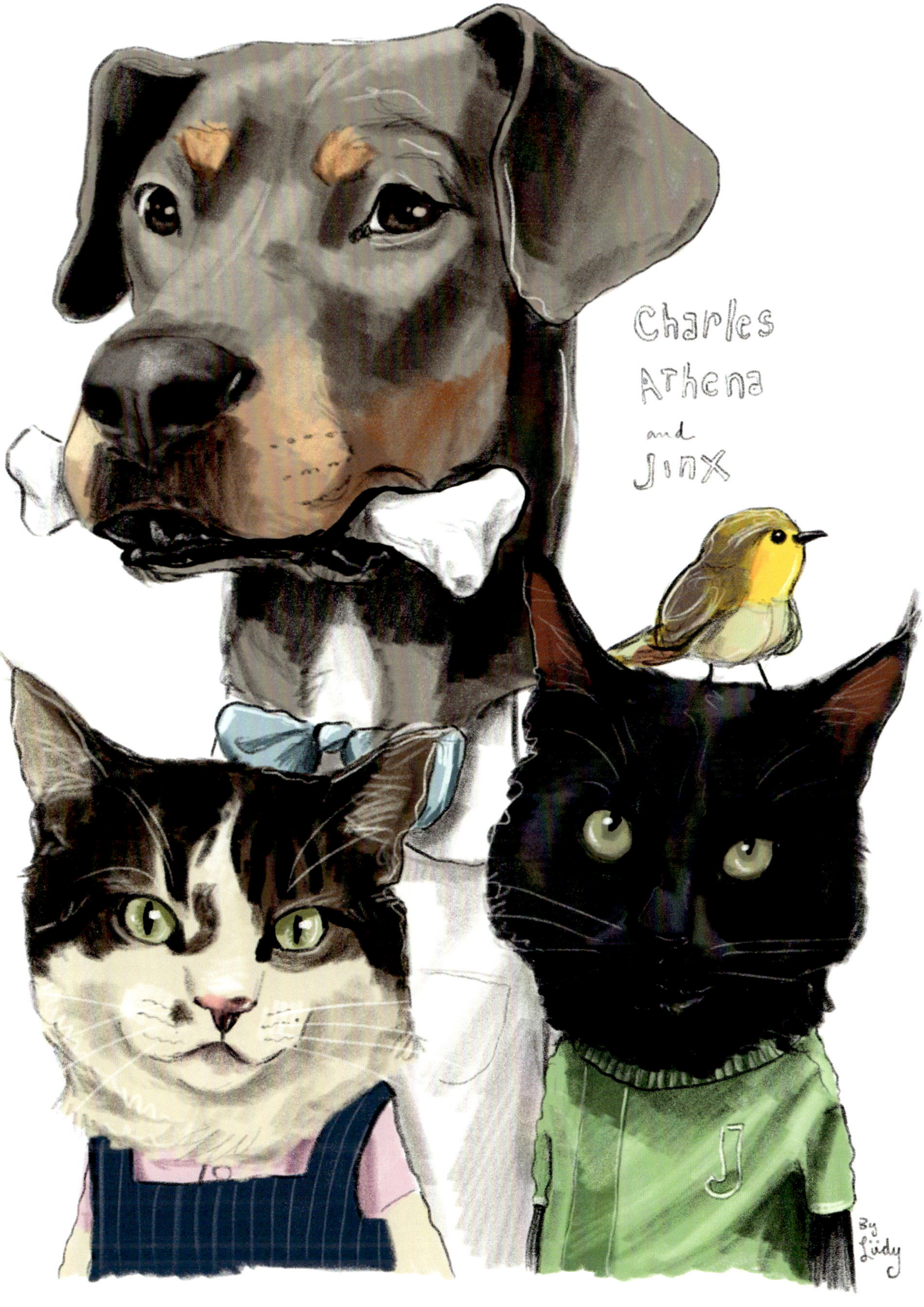

Together, they make one very full heart.

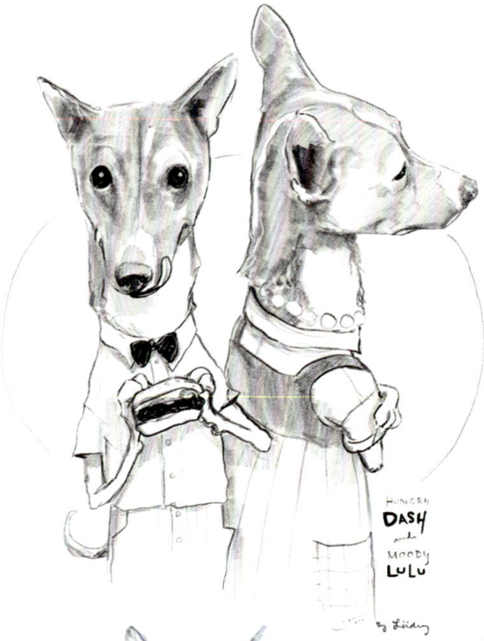
HUNGRY
DASH
MOODY
LULU

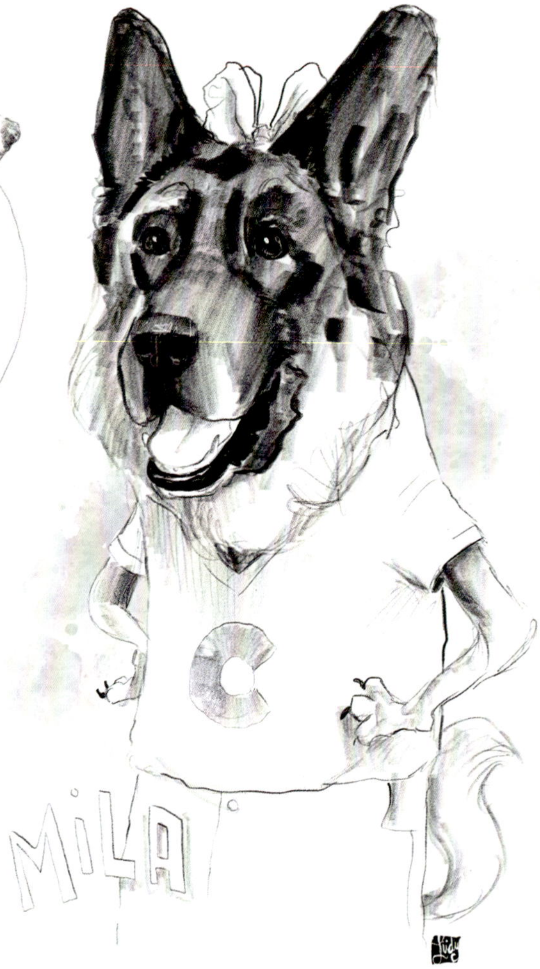
MILA

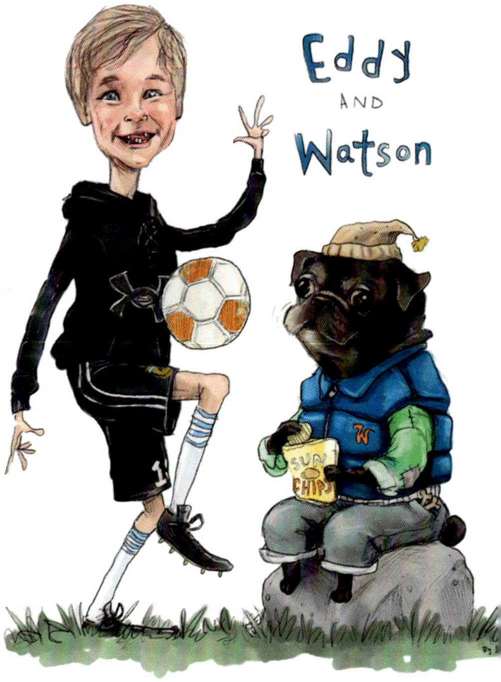
Eddy
AND
Watson

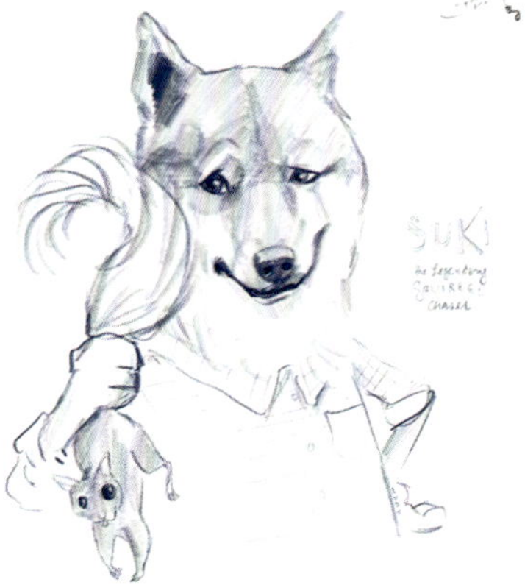
SUKI

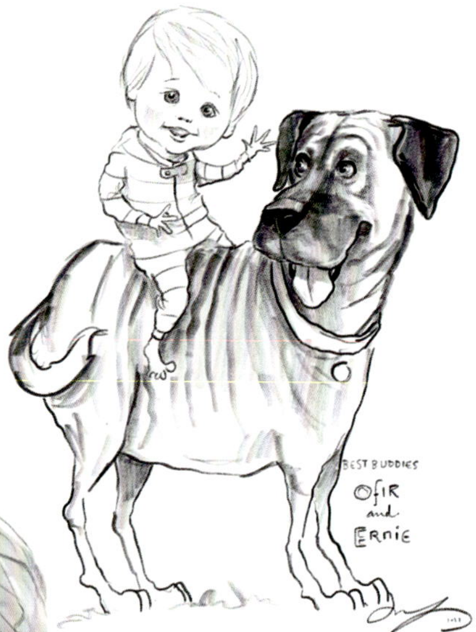
BEST BUDDIES
OFIR
and
ERNIE

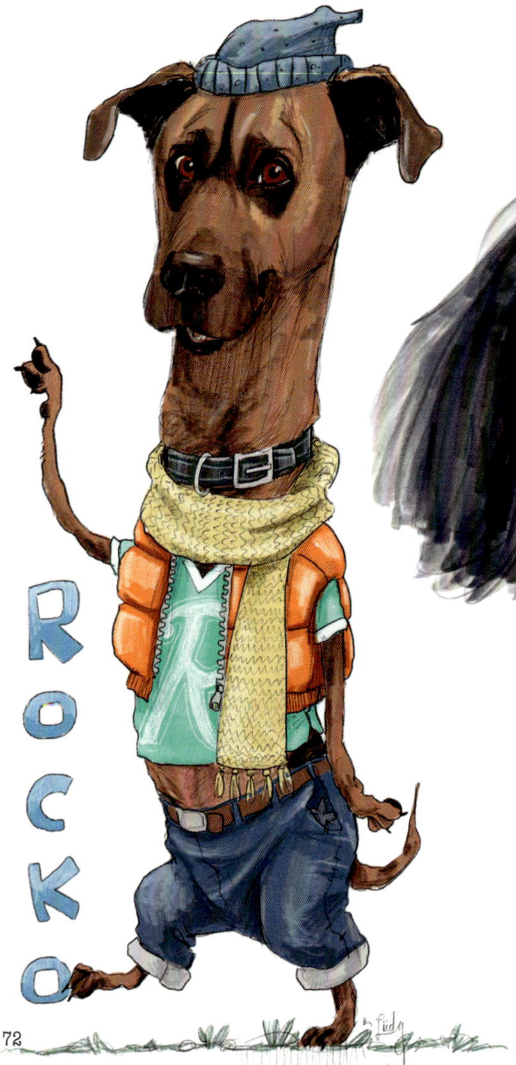
ROCKO

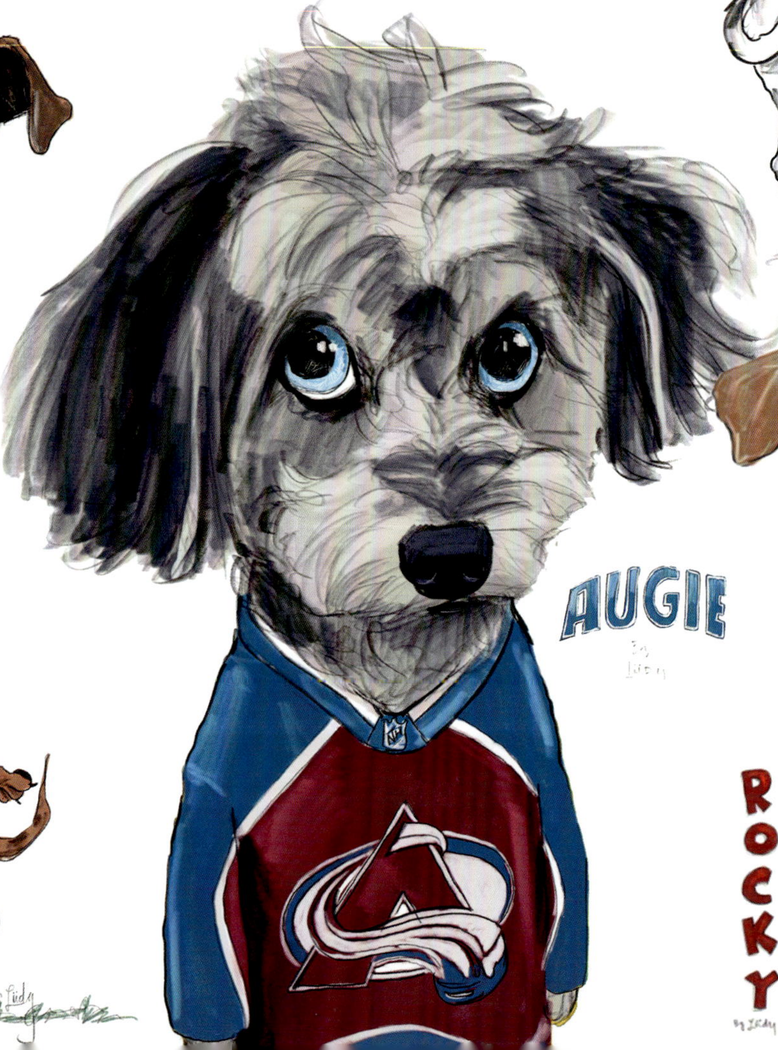
AUGIE

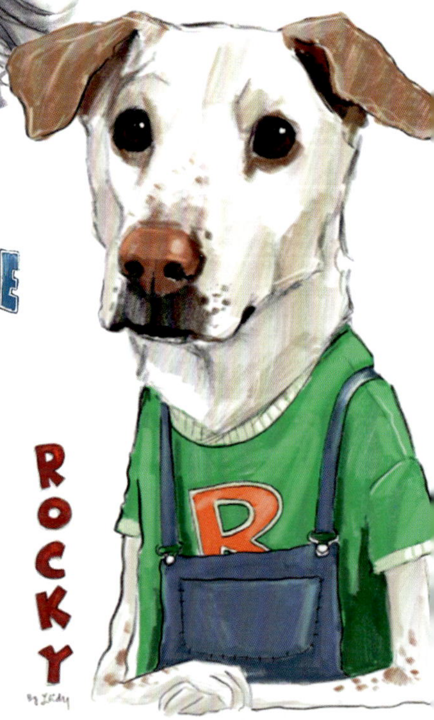
ROCKY

MOOSE

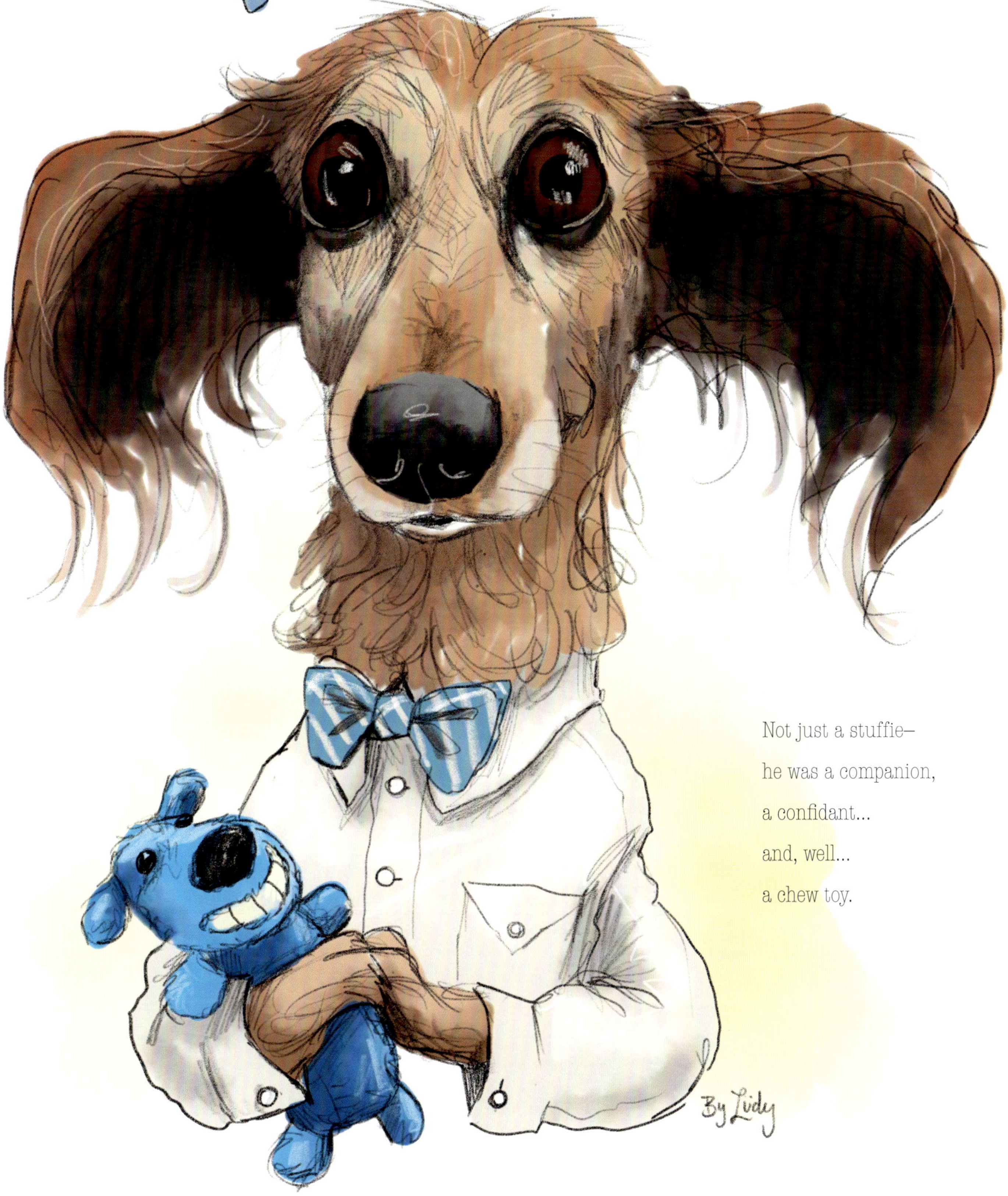

Not just a stuffie–

he was a companion,

a confidant...

and, well...

a chew toy.

They may outgrow the shoes,
but never the dog who walked
beside them.

- Some who's been there

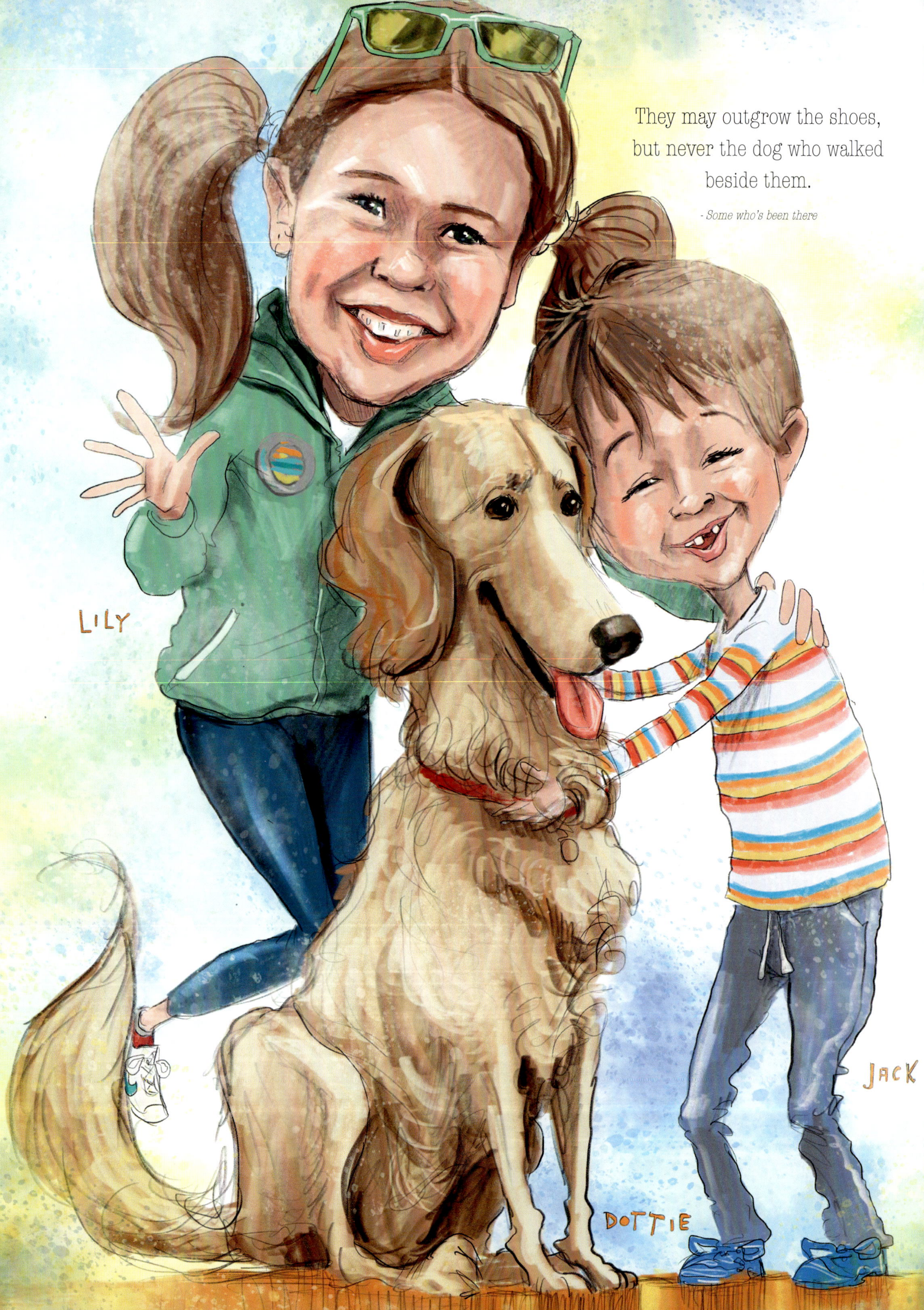

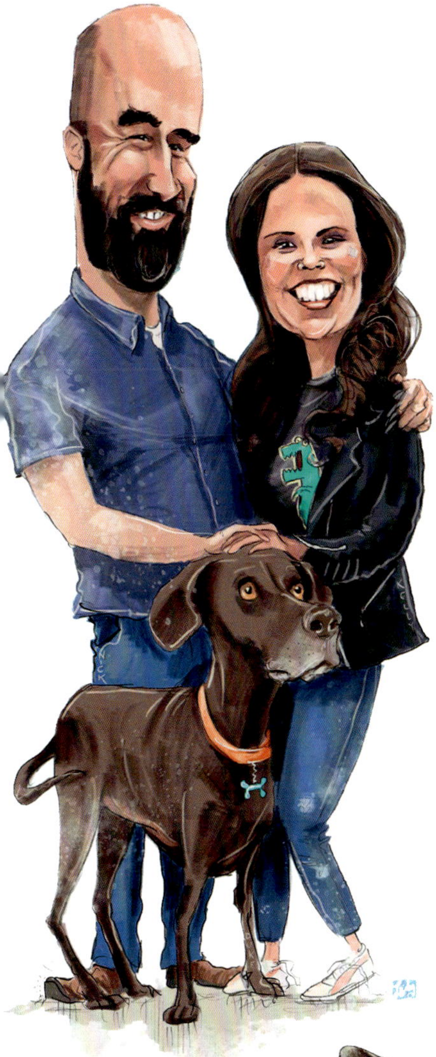

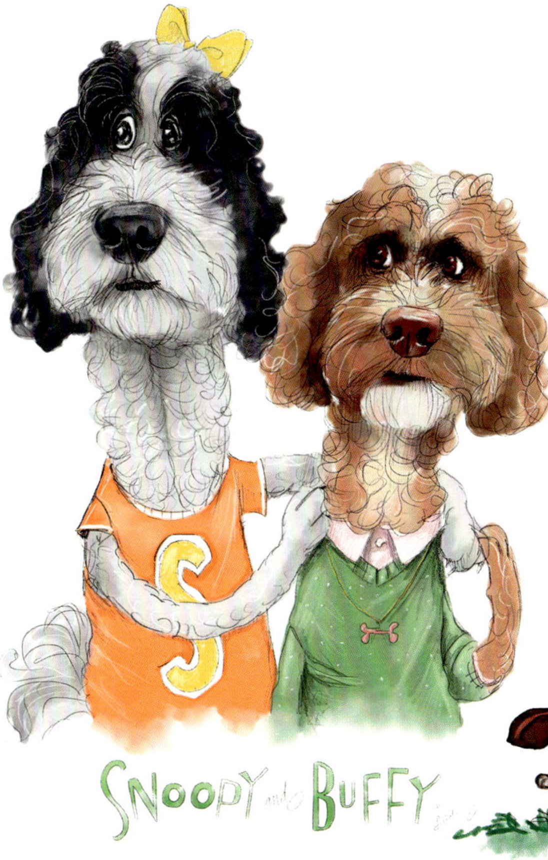
SNOOPY and BUFFY

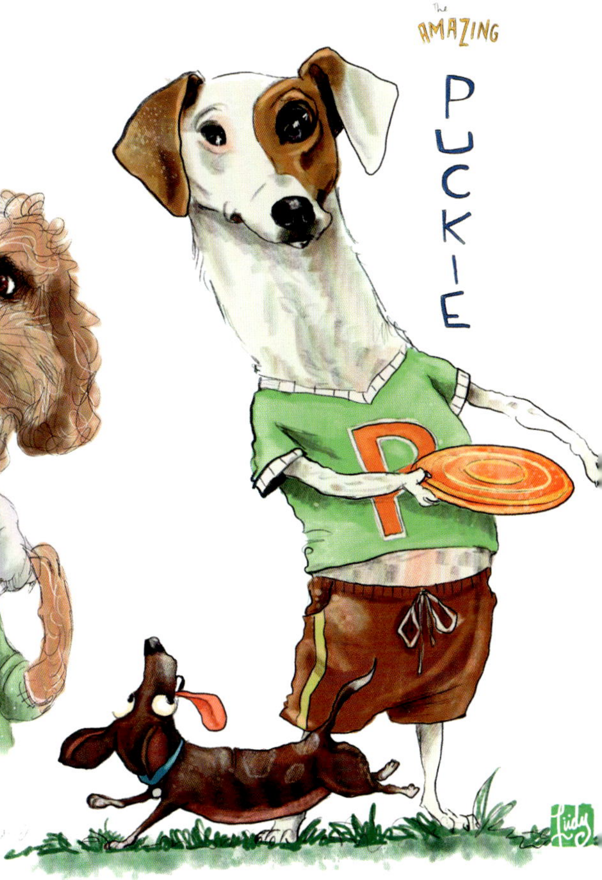
The AMAZING
PUCKIE

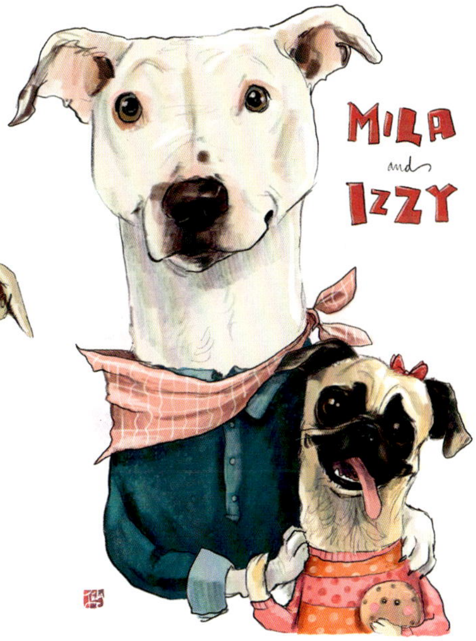
MILA
and
IZZY

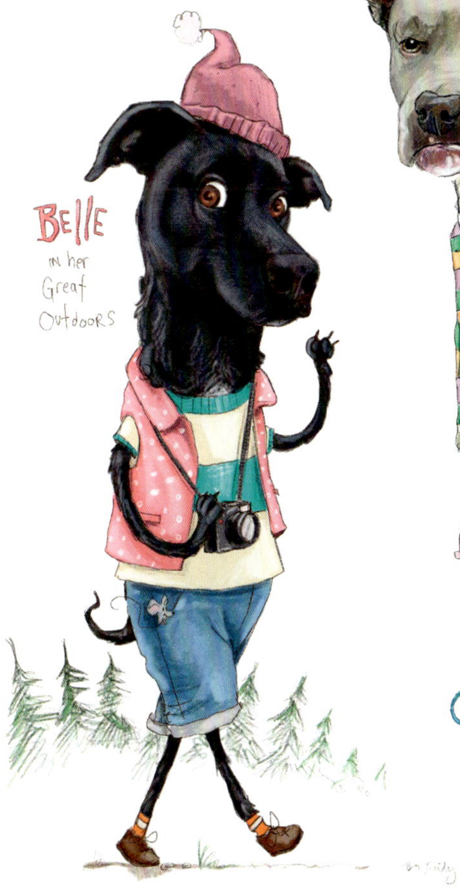
BELLE
in her
Great
Outdoors

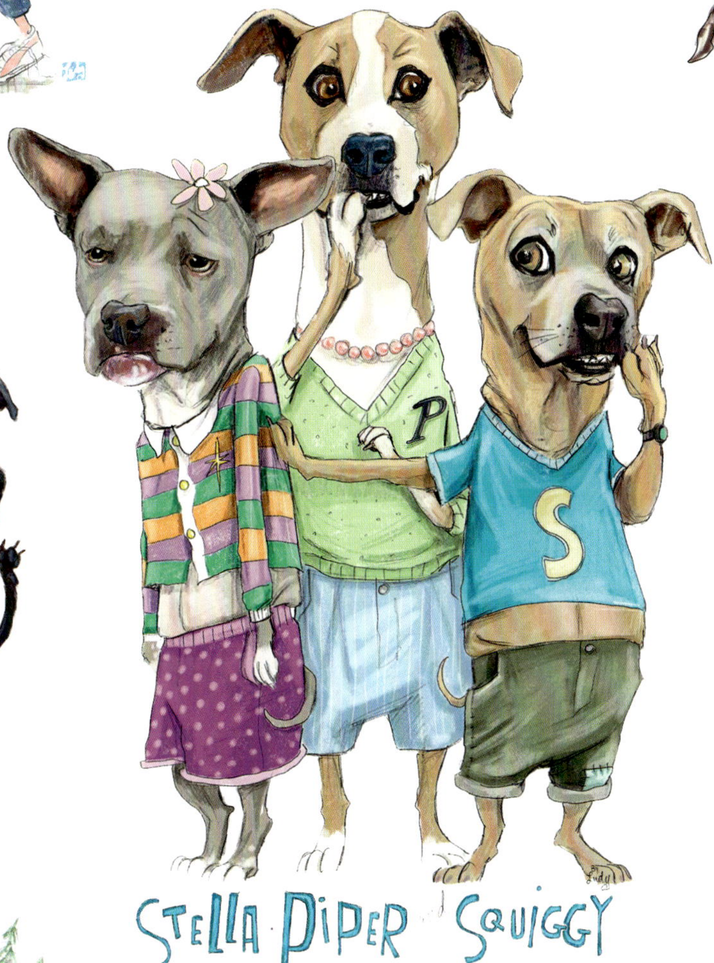
STELLA PIPER and SQUIGGY

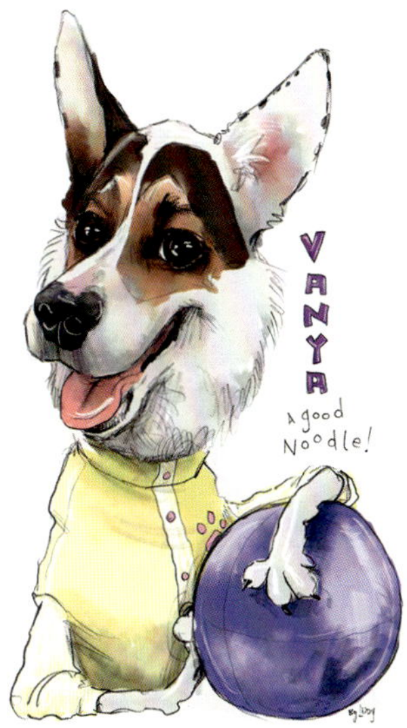
VANYA
a good
Noodle!

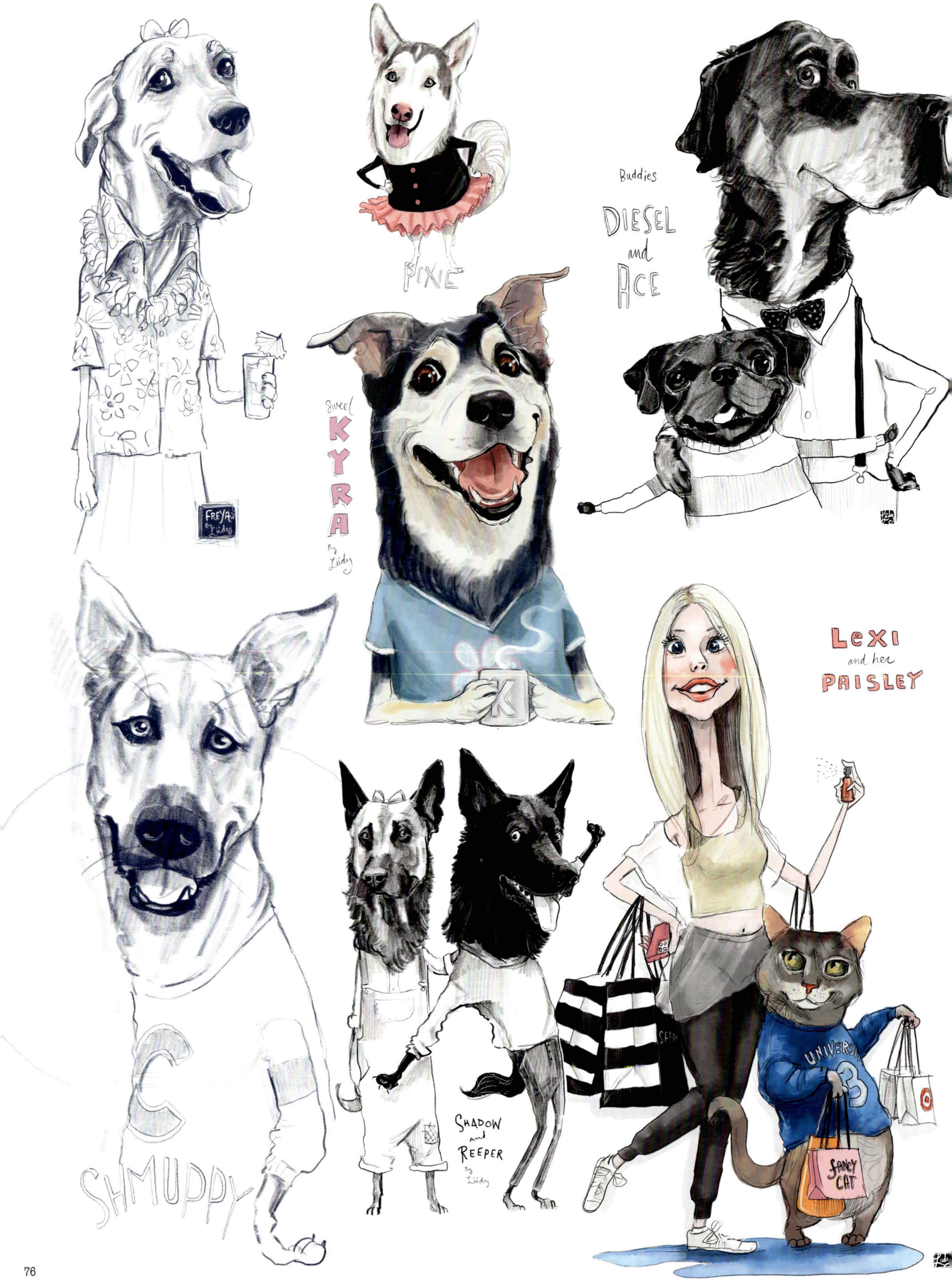
FREYA
By Liidy
PIXIE
Buddies
DIESEL
and
ACE
Sweet
KYRA
By
Liidy
Lexi
and her
PAISLEY
SHADOW
and
REEPER
By
Liidy
SHMUPPY
fancy
CAT

He wasn't

showing off.

He simply

couldn't help

being

fabulous.

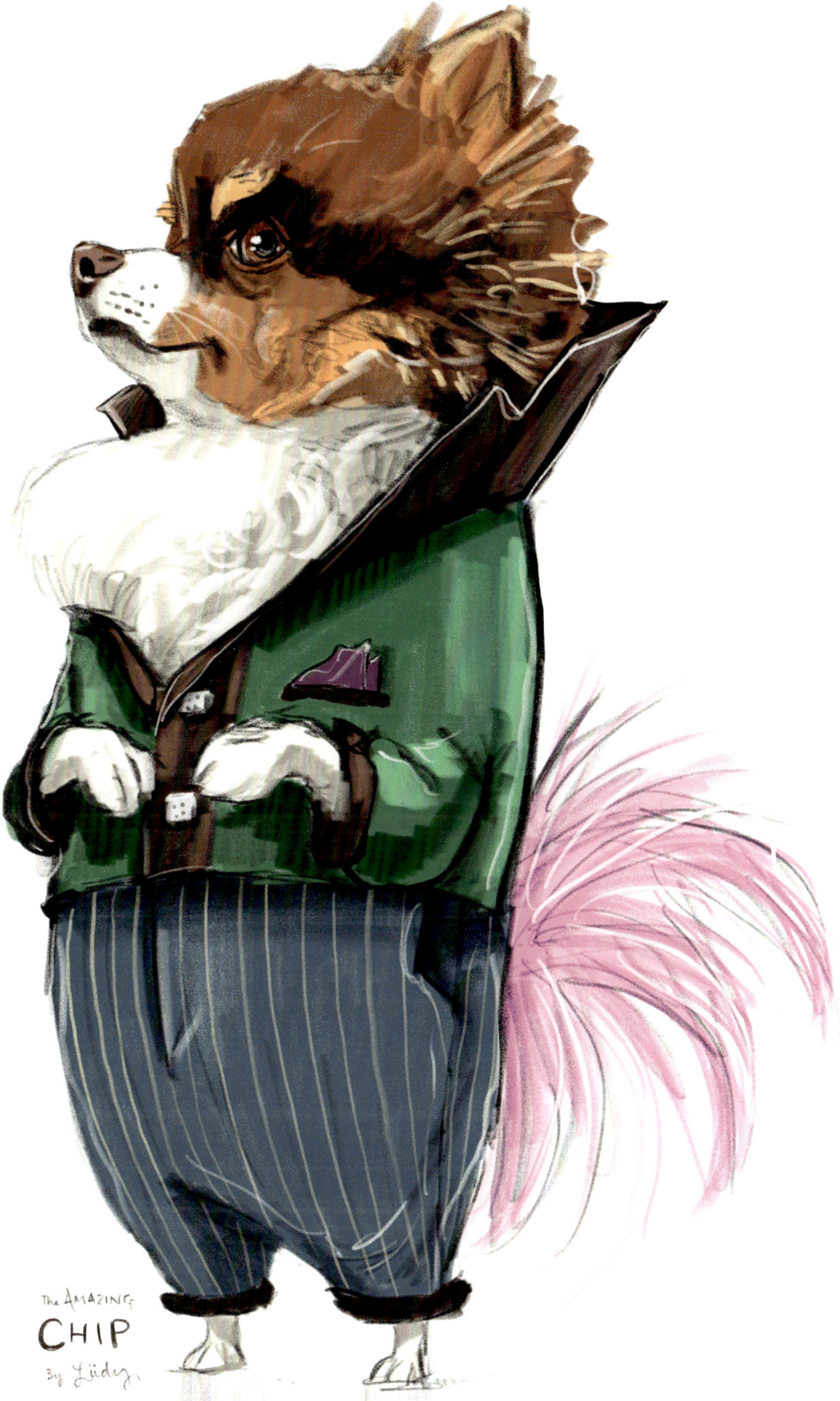

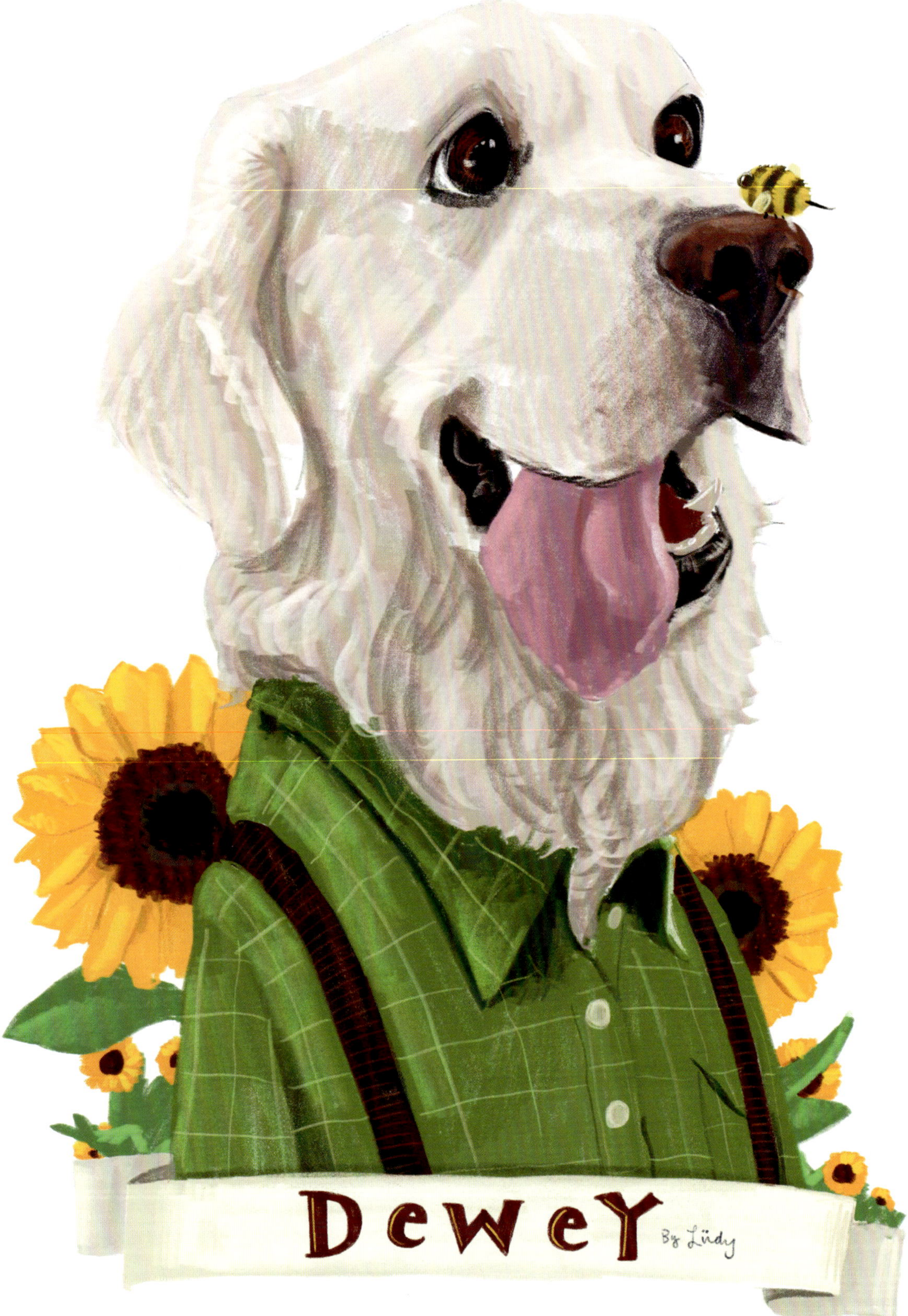

The secret to happiness?

Chase butterflies. Befriend bees. Smile for no reason at all.

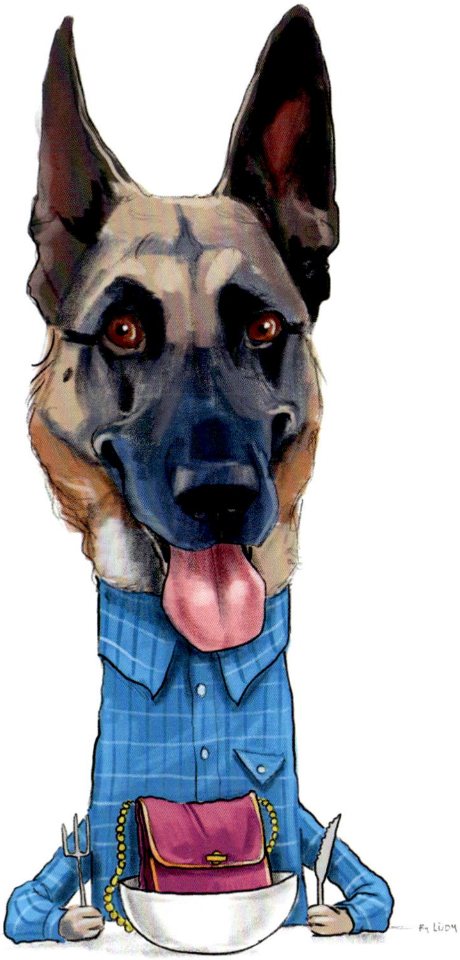

Rio

loves Mom's handbag

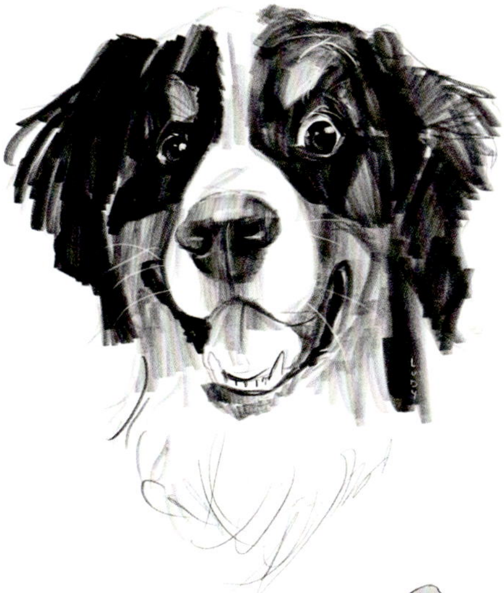

OTTO

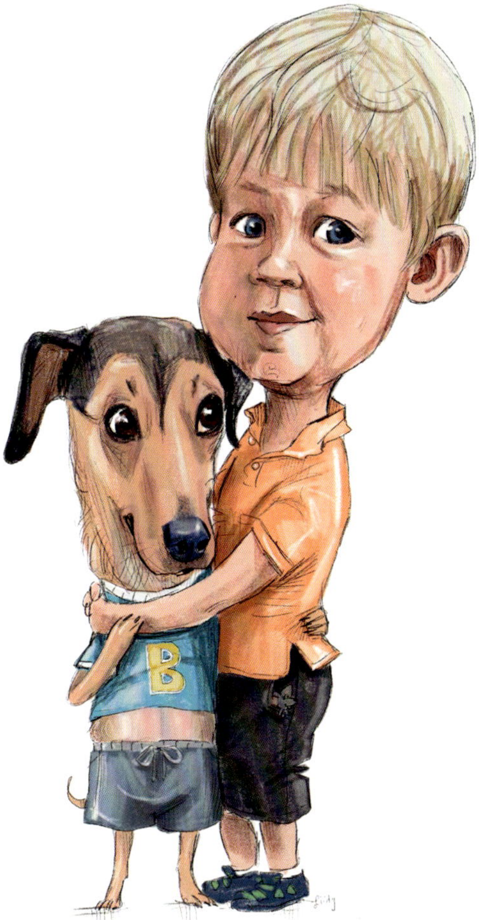

Jackson and his Buddy

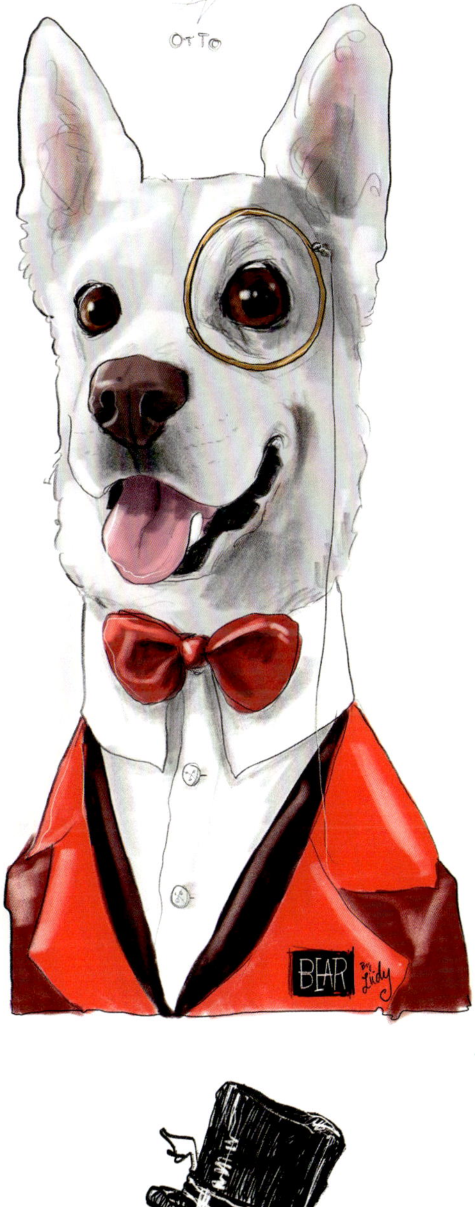

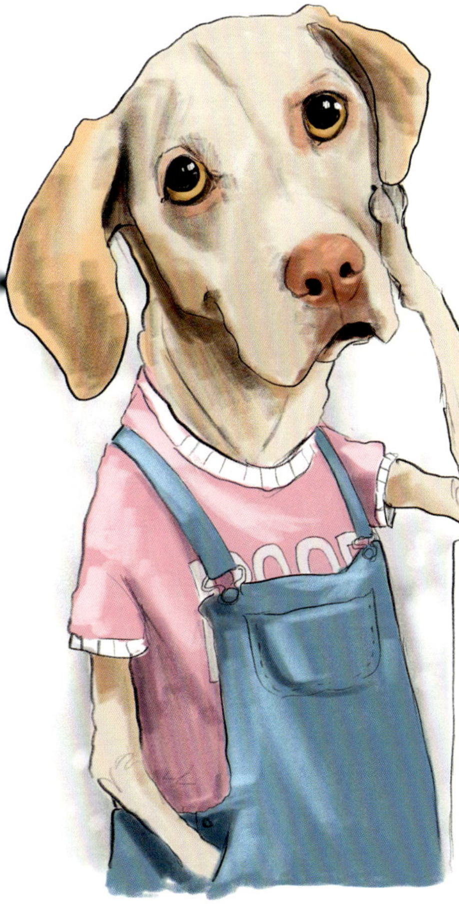

HALLOW

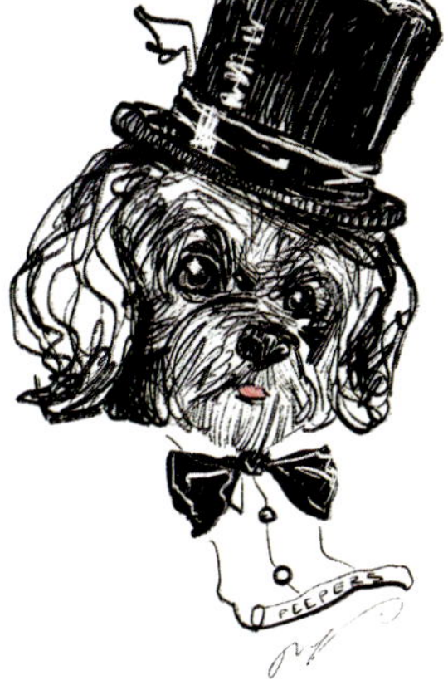

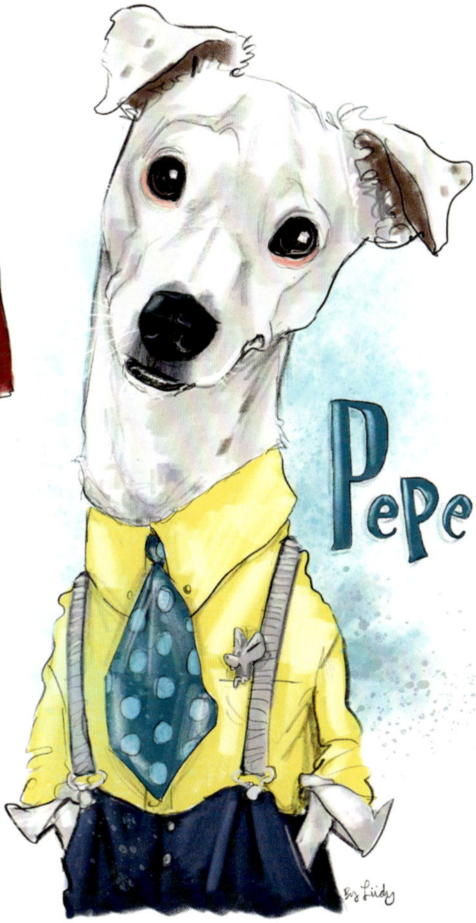

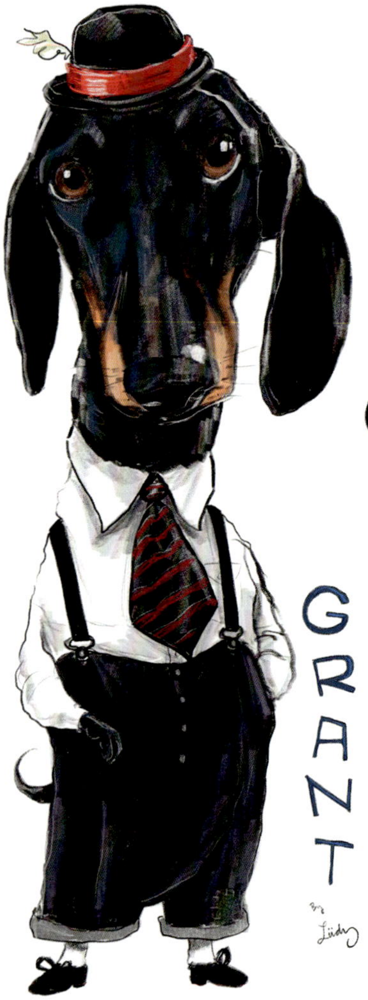

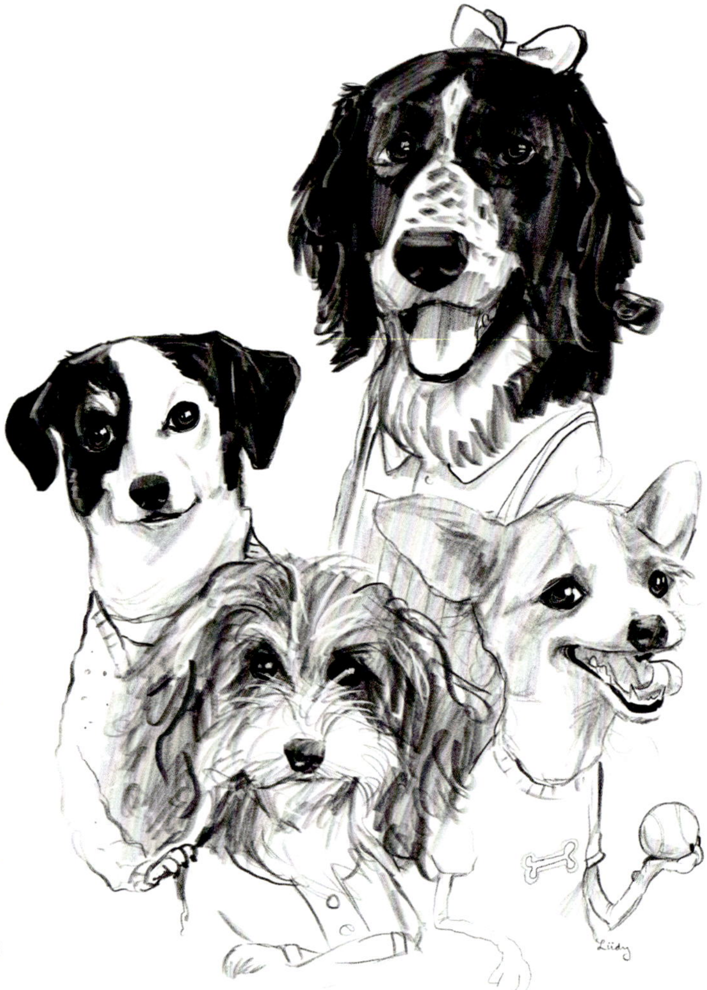

KAUAI HAZEL CHARA and HENRY

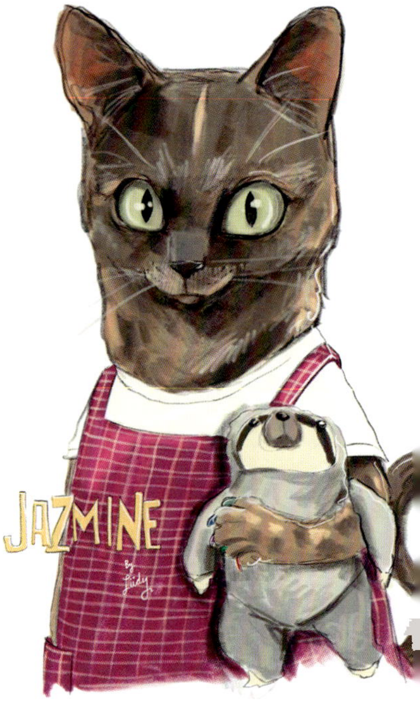

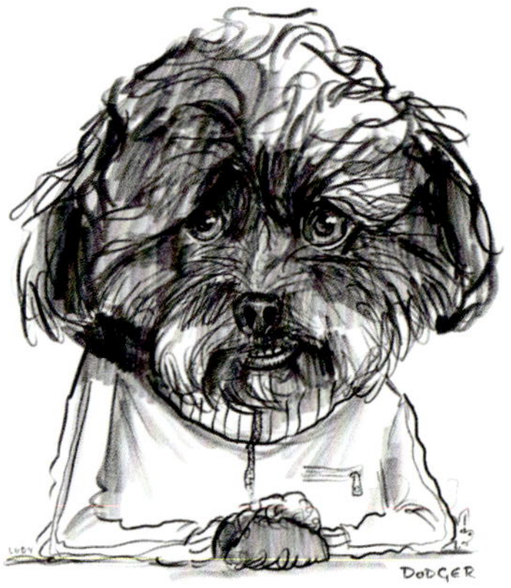

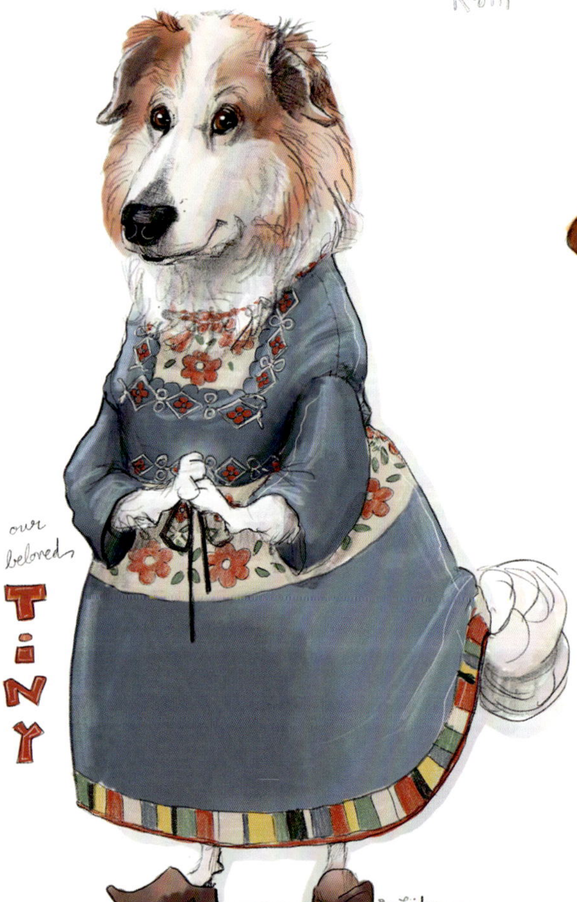

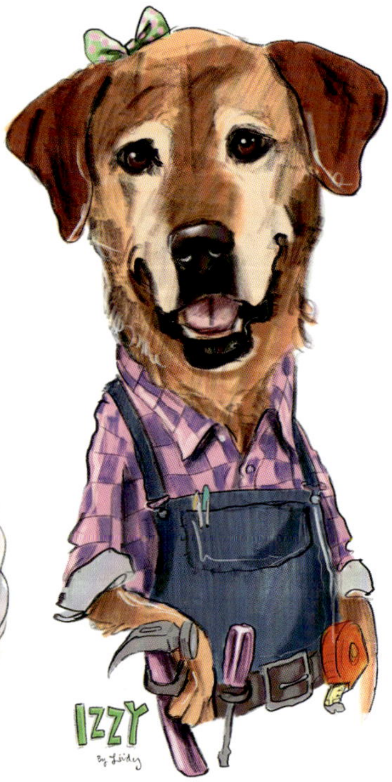

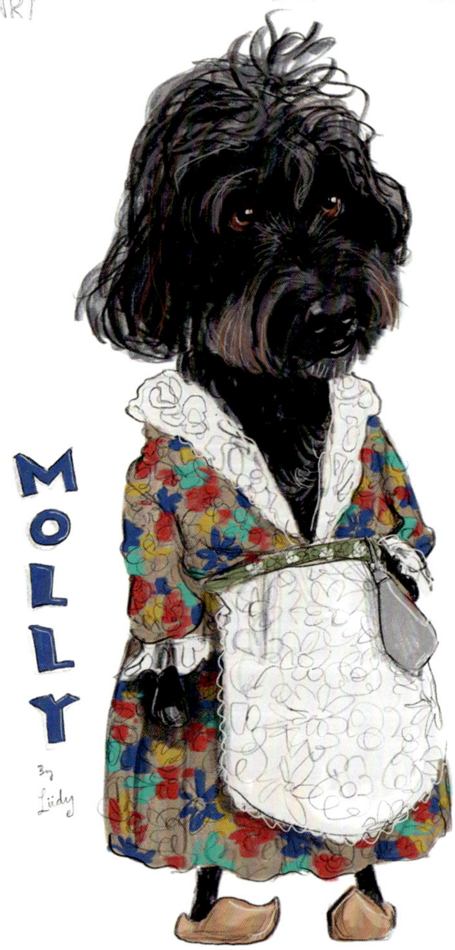

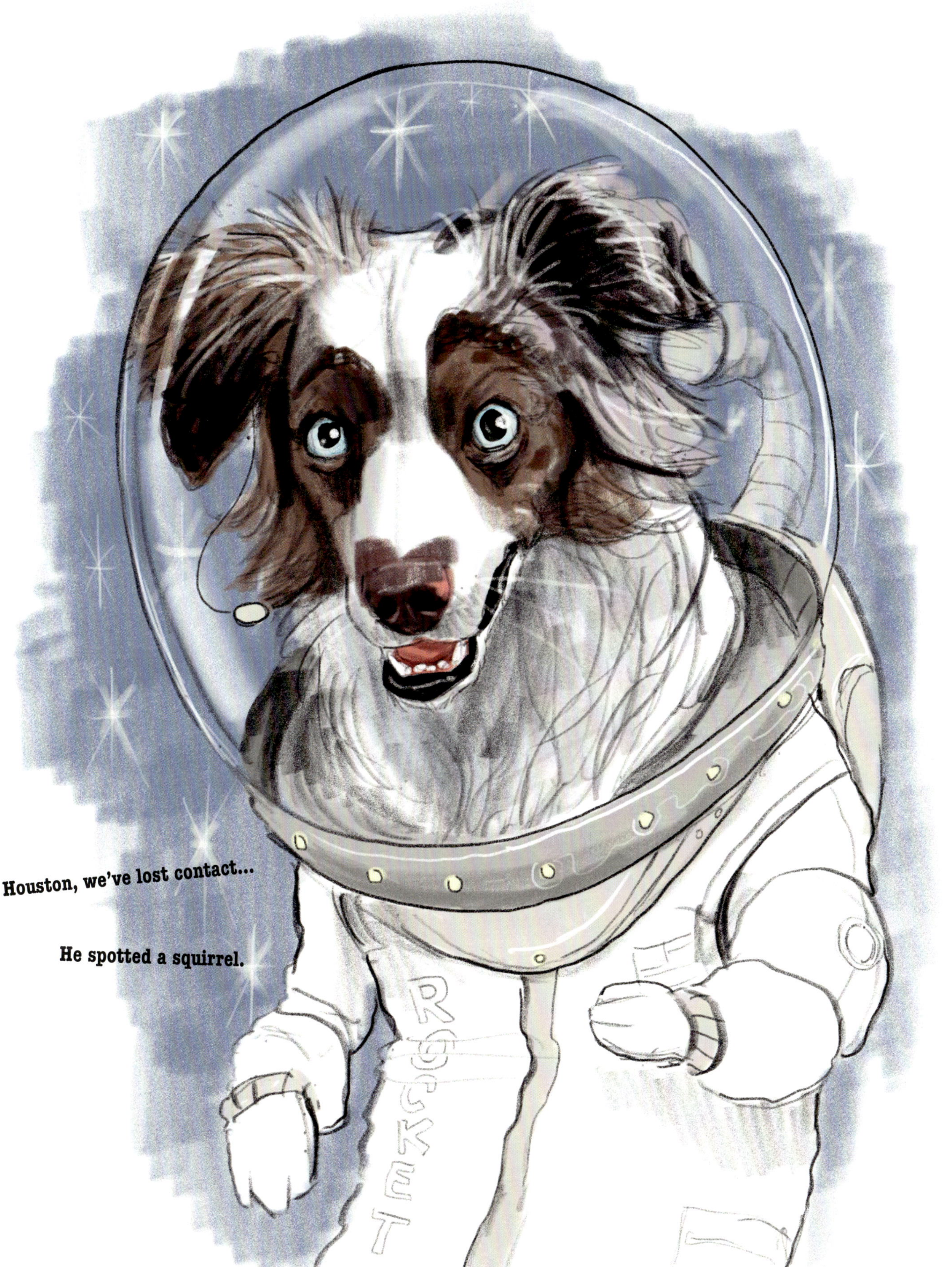
Houston, we've lost contact...
He spotted a squirrel.
ROCKET

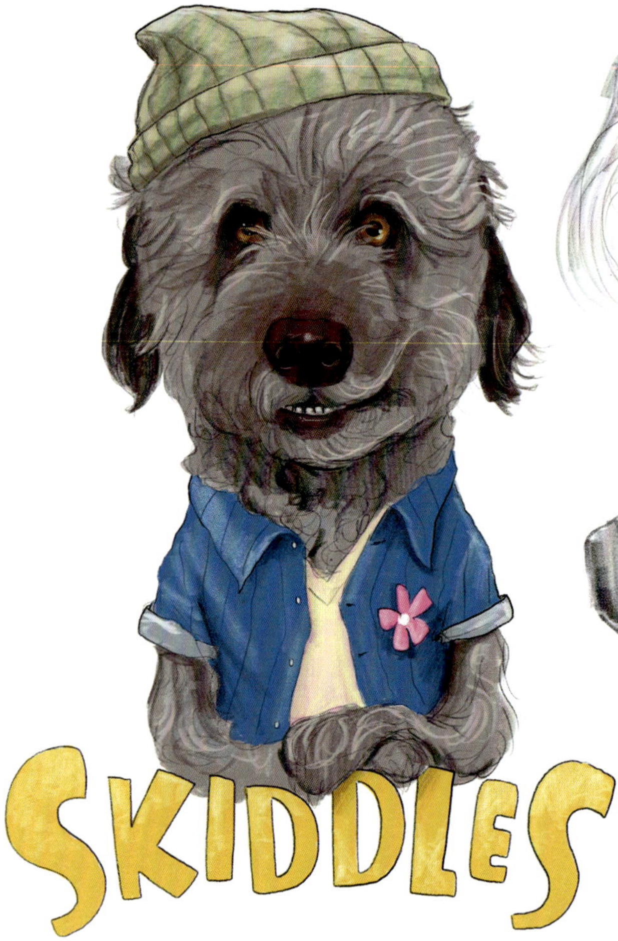
SKIDDLES

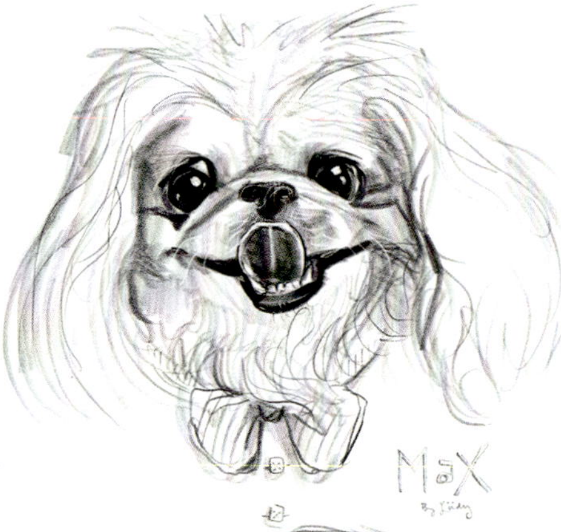
MAX

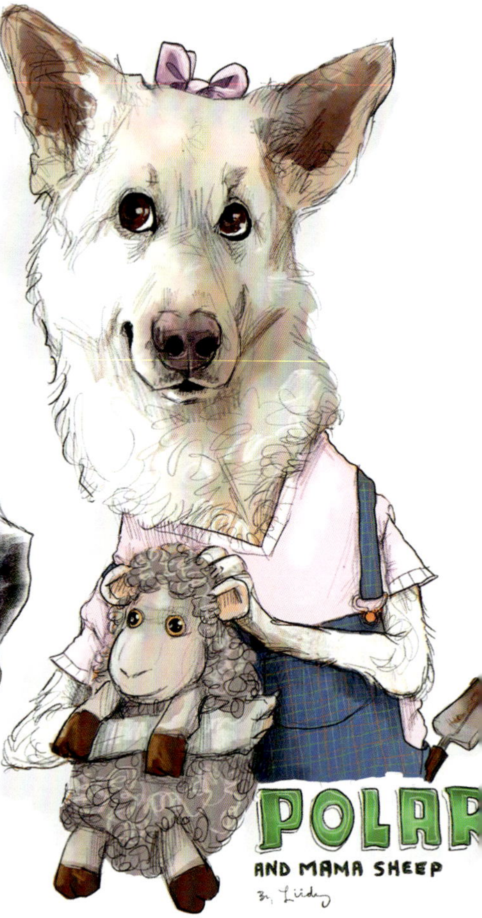
POLAR
AND MAMA SHEEP
By Lüdy

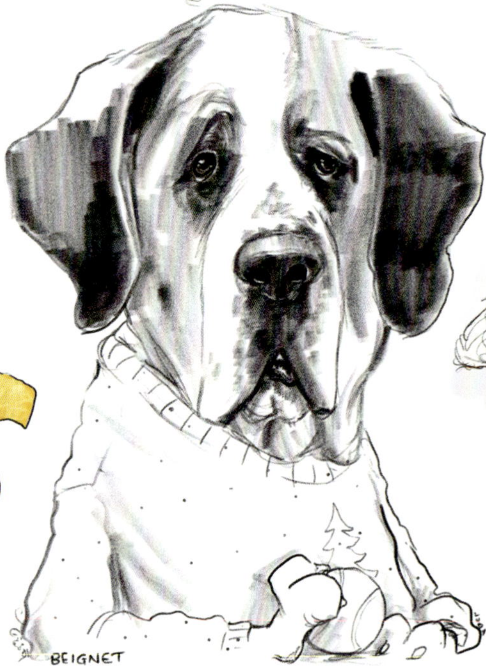
BEIGNET

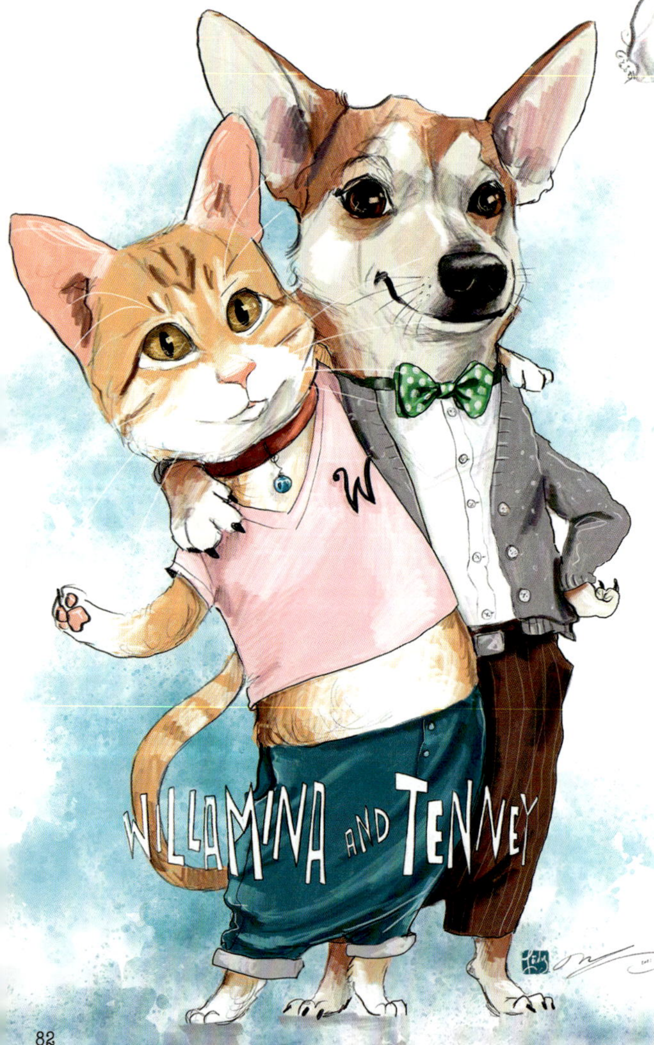
WILLAMINA AND TENNEY

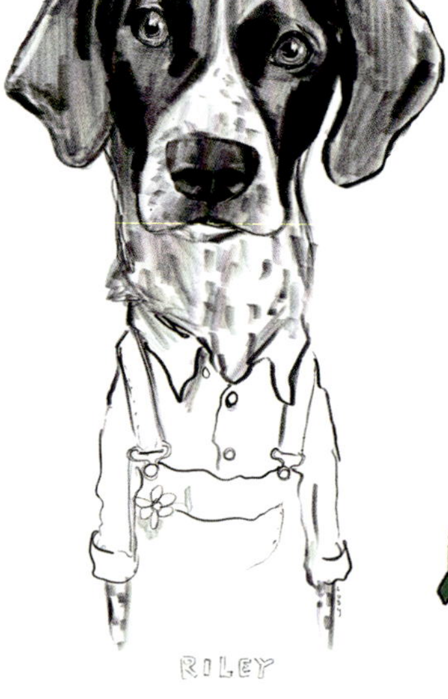
RILEY

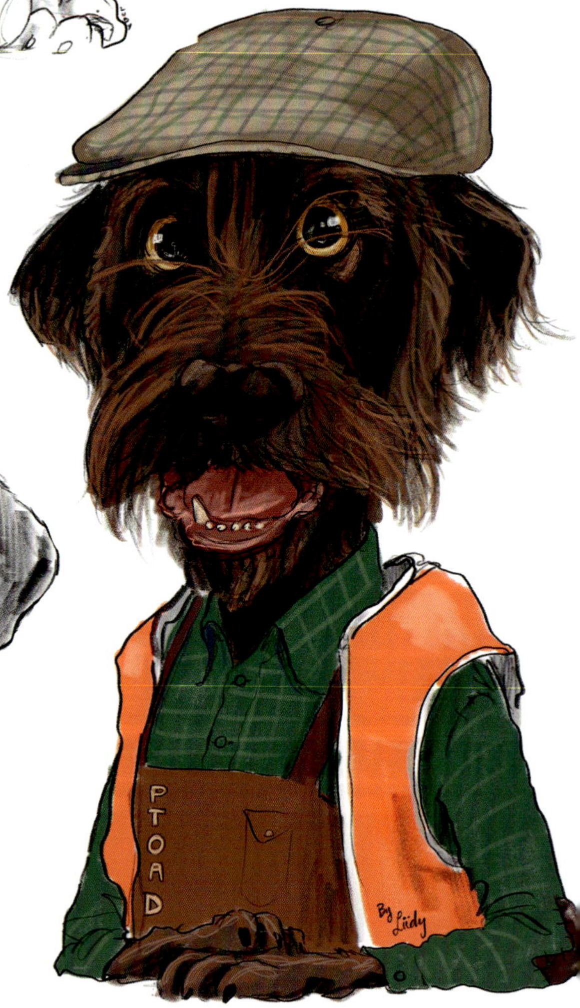
PTOAD
By Lüdy

"Sometimes, the smallest things take up the most room in your heart."

—A.A. Milne (Winnie the Pooh)

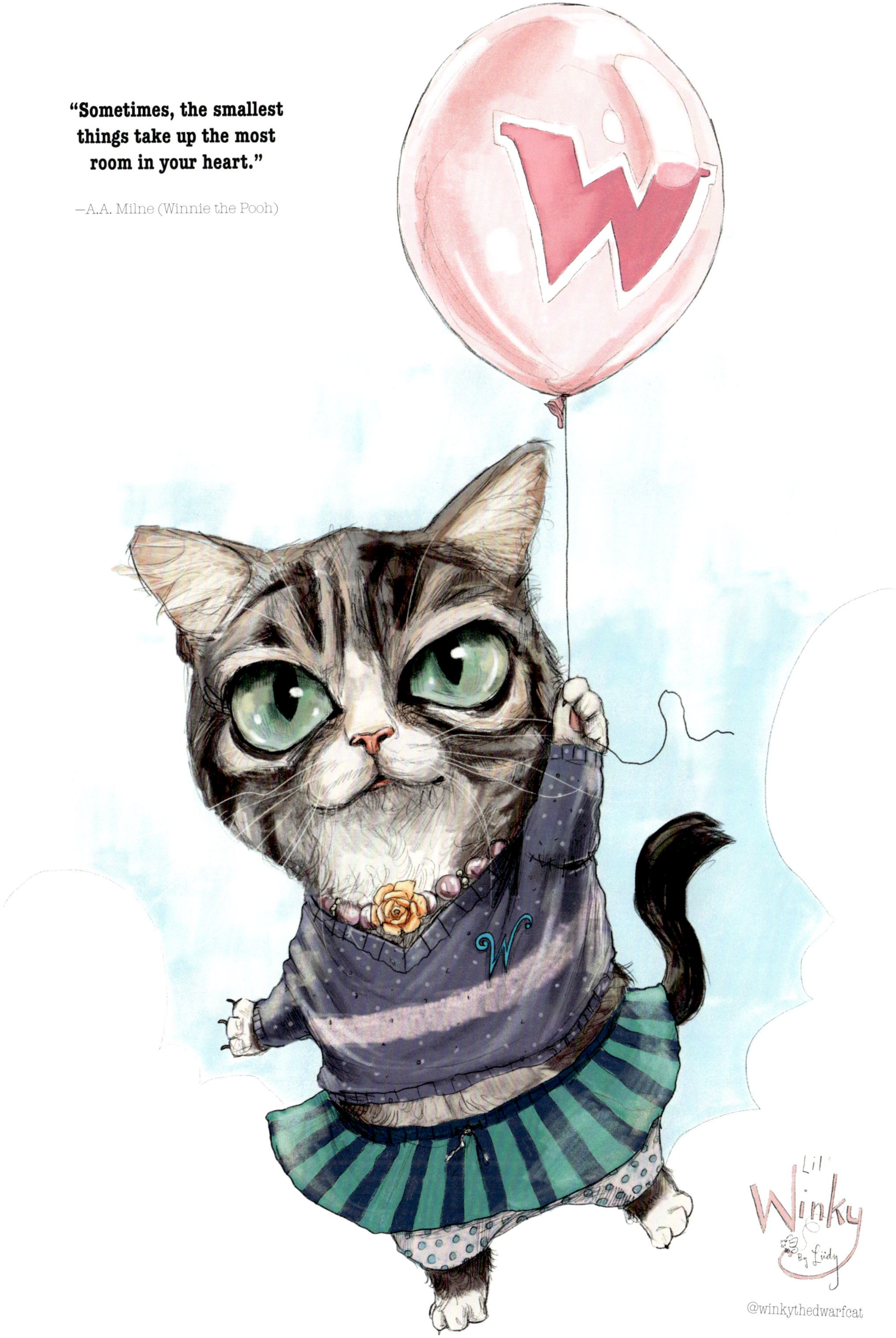

"Until one has loved an animal, a part of one's soul remains unawakened."

—Anatole France

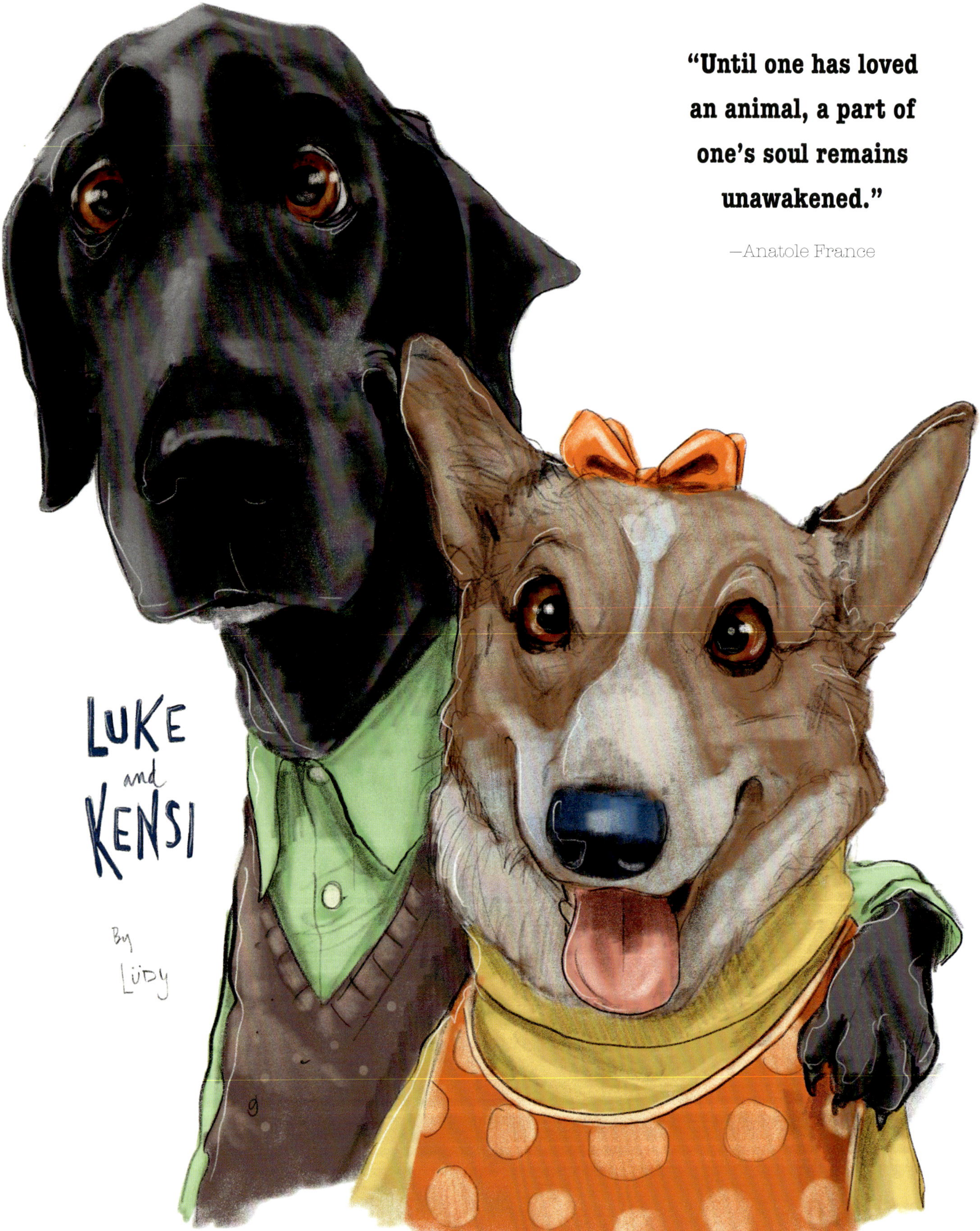

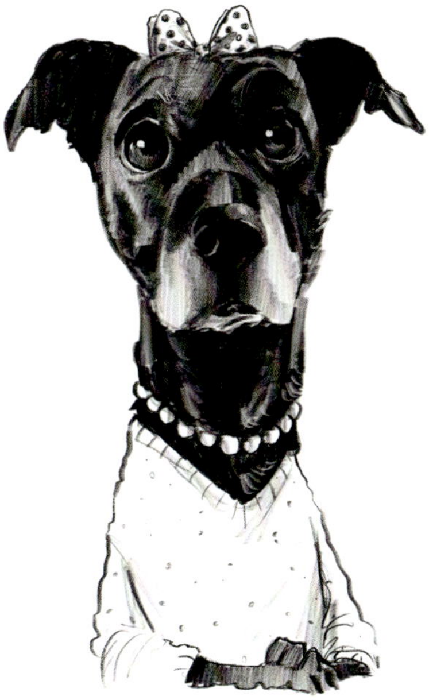

MOLLY WOBBLES

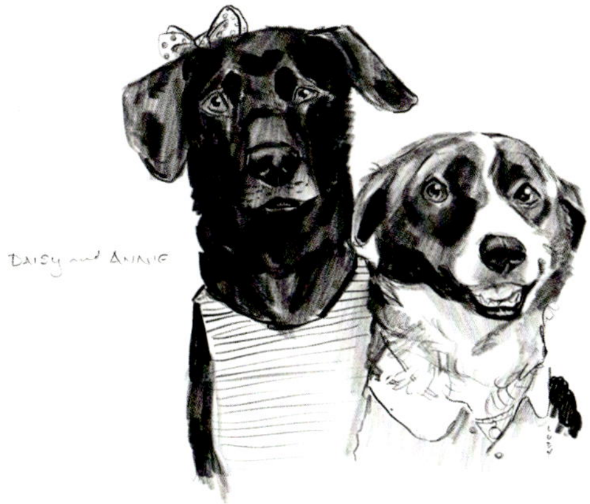

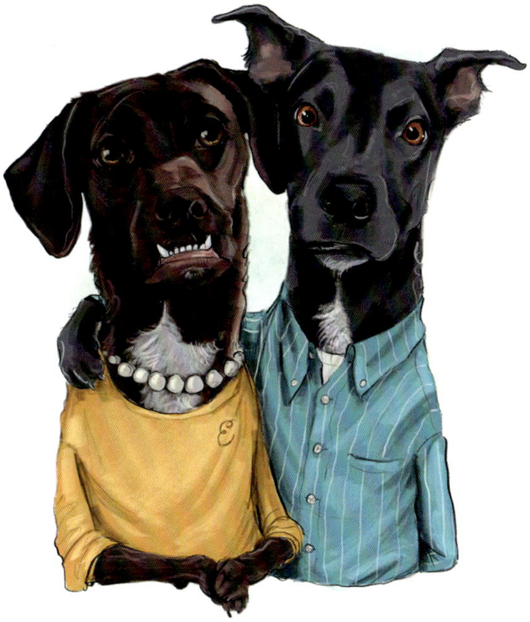

ELEANOR AND ASHTON

They bark at nothing.
Snore like freight trains.
Track every snack within
a six-mile radius.

And still—
they steal our hearts.
They know when to nuzzle close,
and when to do zoomies across
freshly mopped floors.

They wear bow ties or tutus,
but never pretend to be anything
but themselves.
They remind us to live wide-eyed,
tail-wagging,
and to never,
ever skip second breakfast.

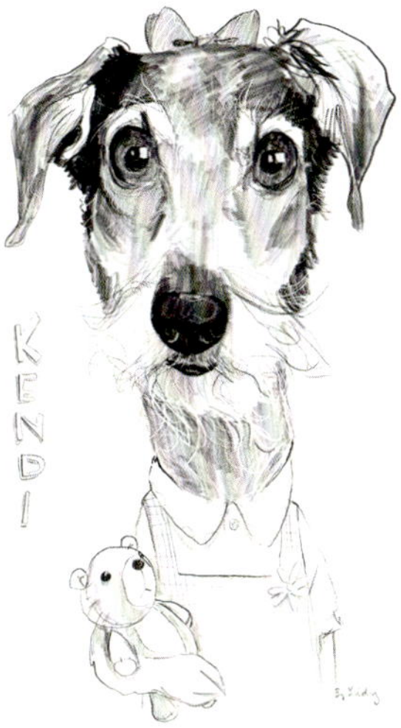

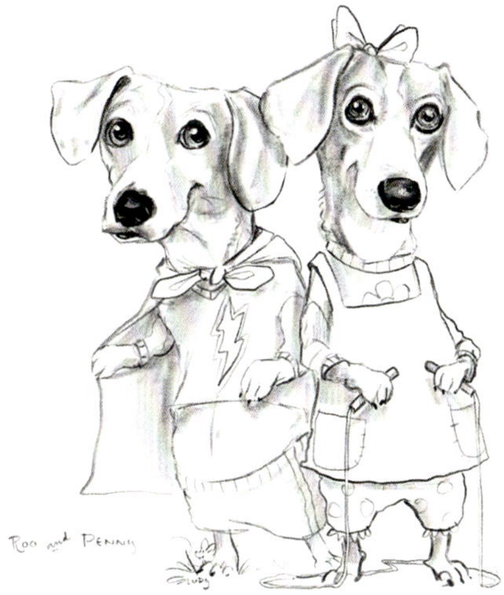

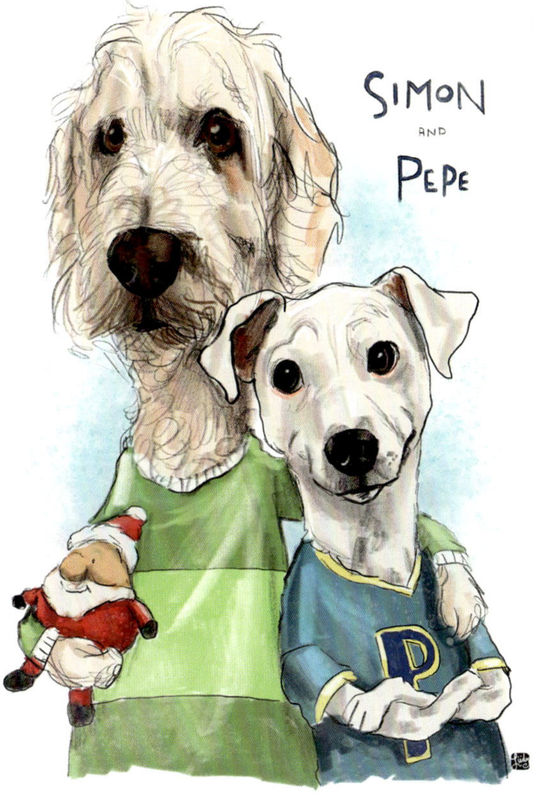

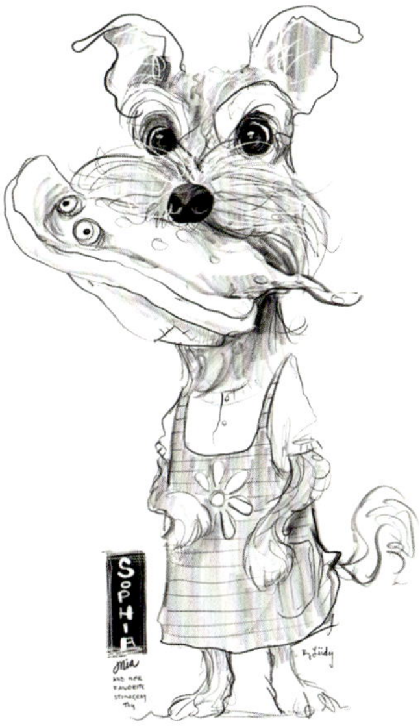

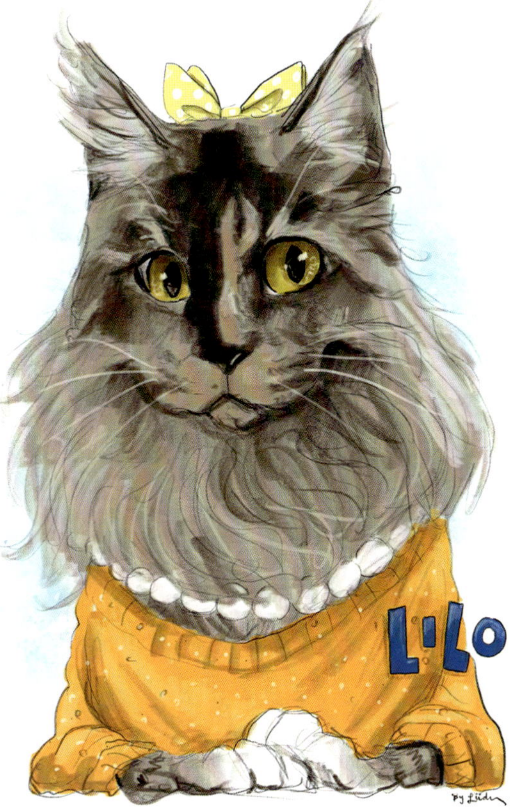

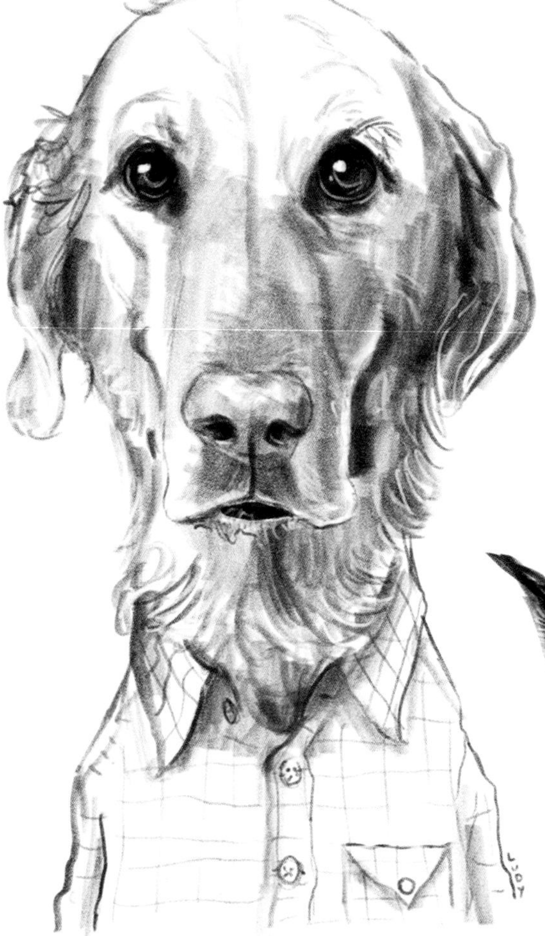

Remington

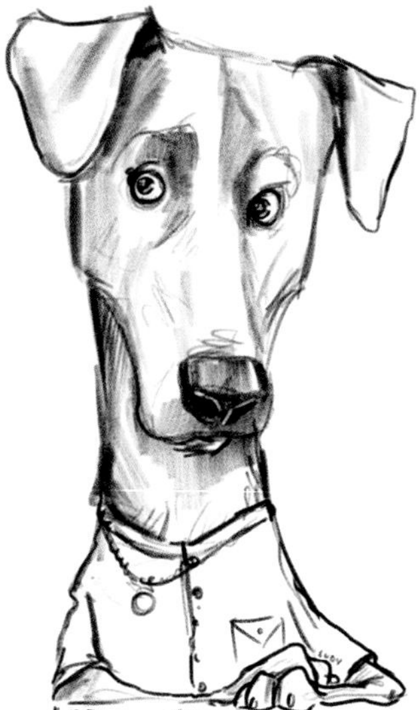

LEO

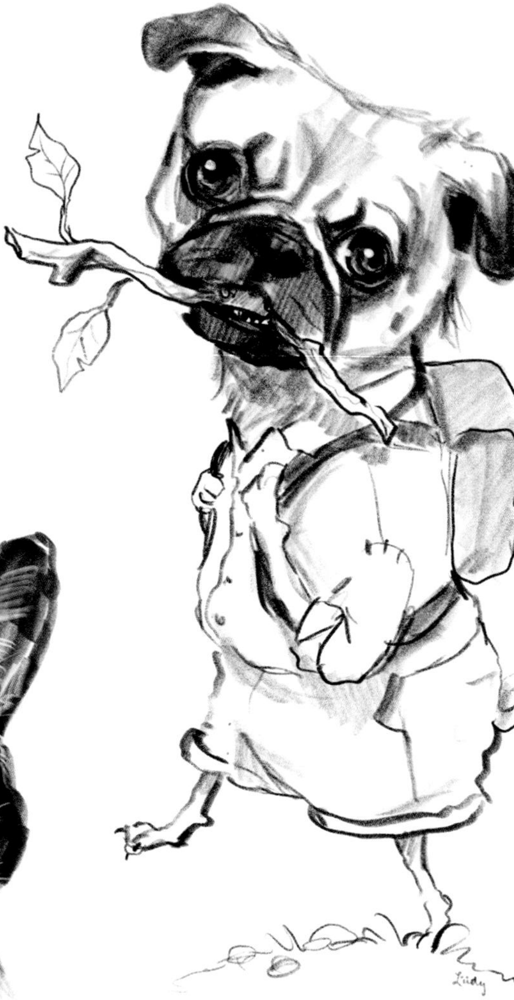

JB

loves to pick up things on his walks

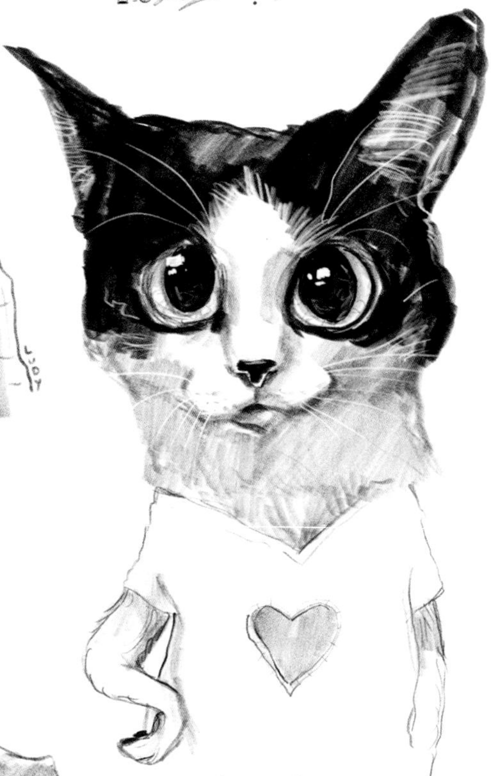

CLIO

By Liidy

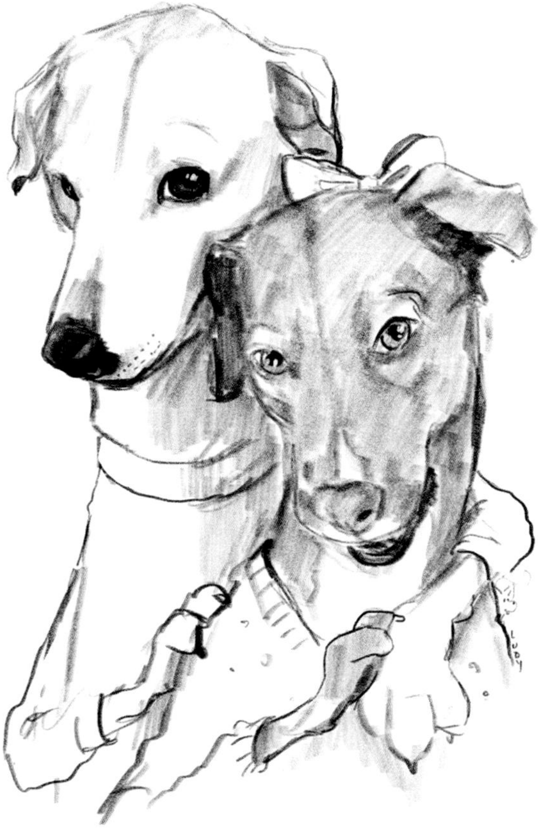

SI and PIPER

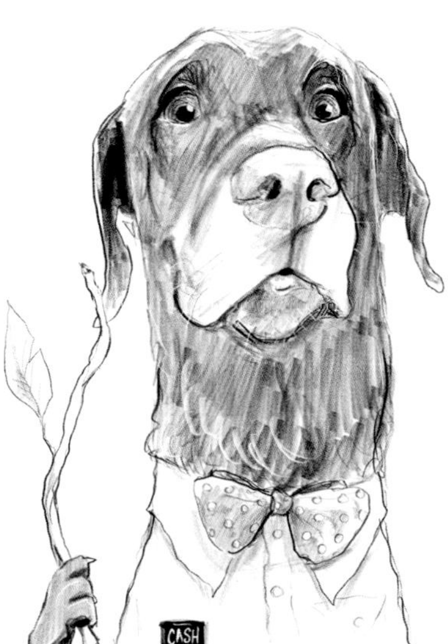

CASH

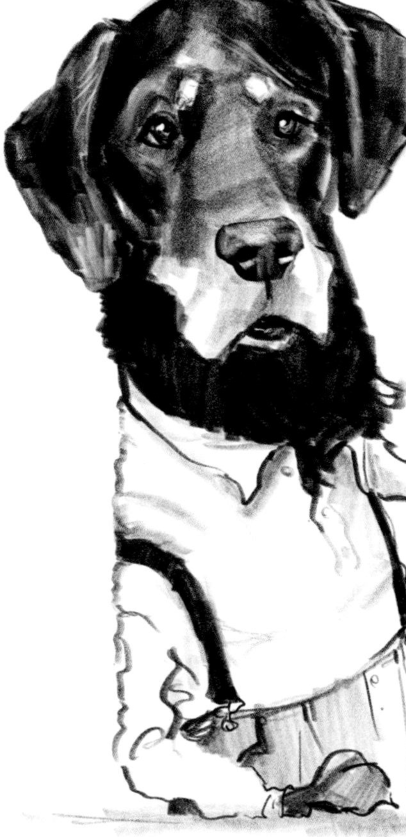

BRIDGER

By Liidy

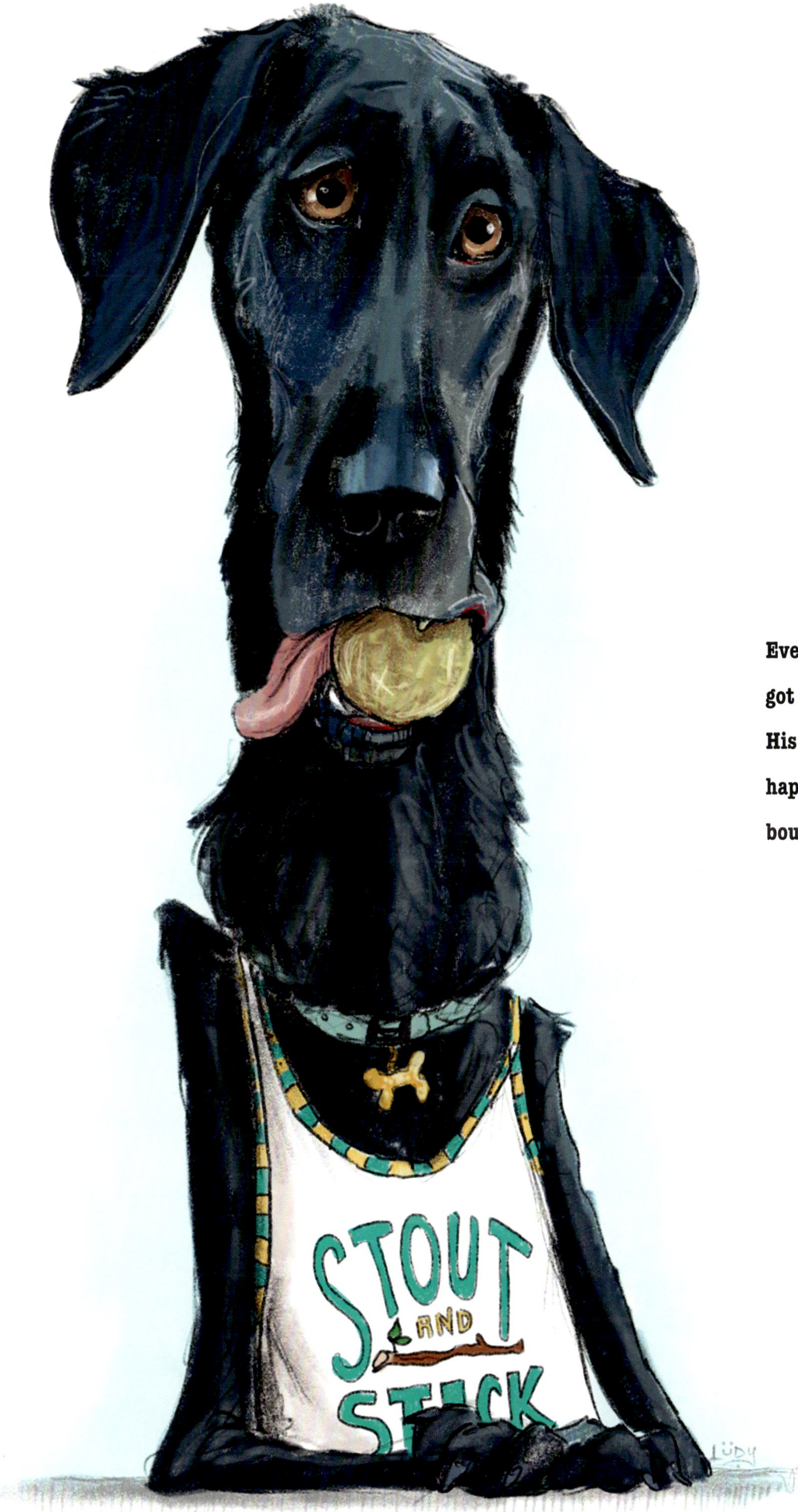

Everyone's
got a calling.
His just
happens to
bounce.

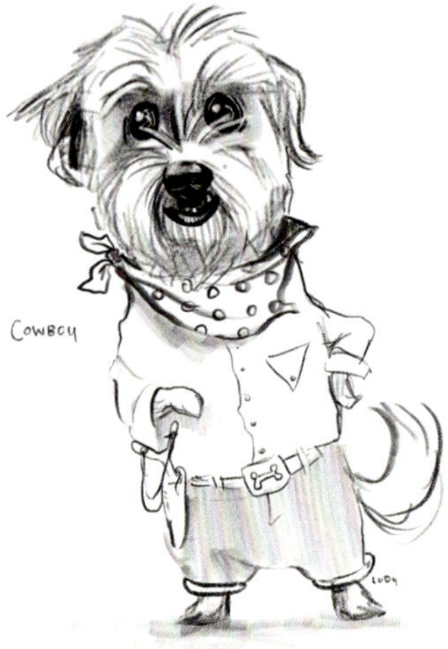
Cowboy

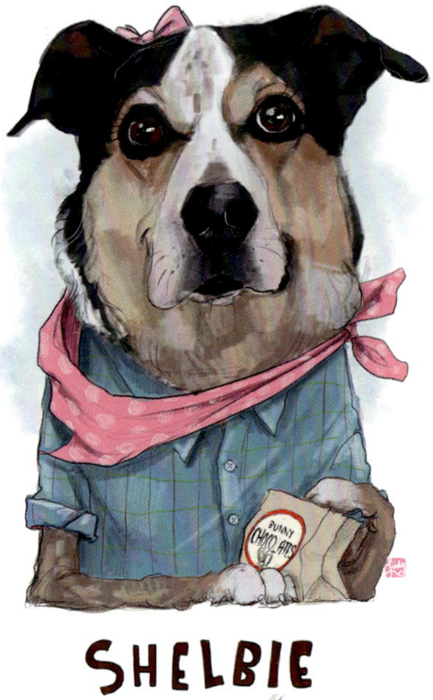
SHELBIE

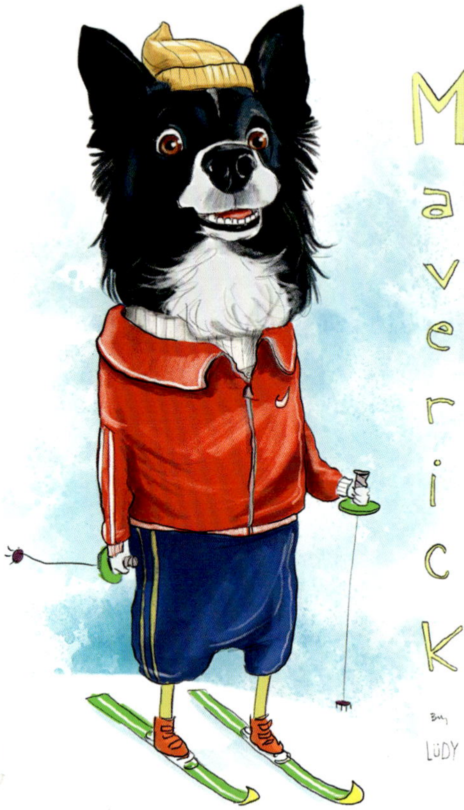
Maverick
By
LÜDY

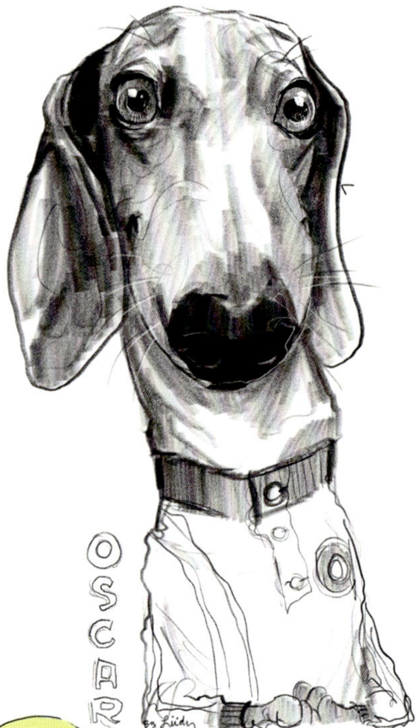
OSCAR
By Lüdy

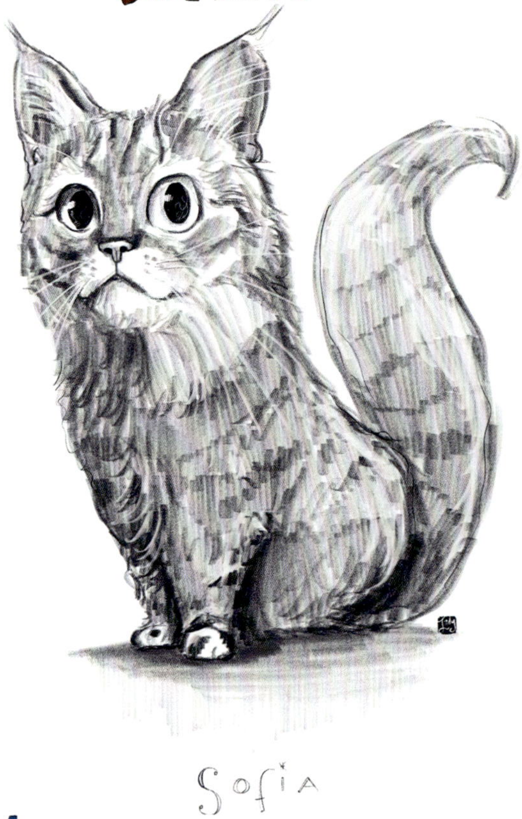
Sofia

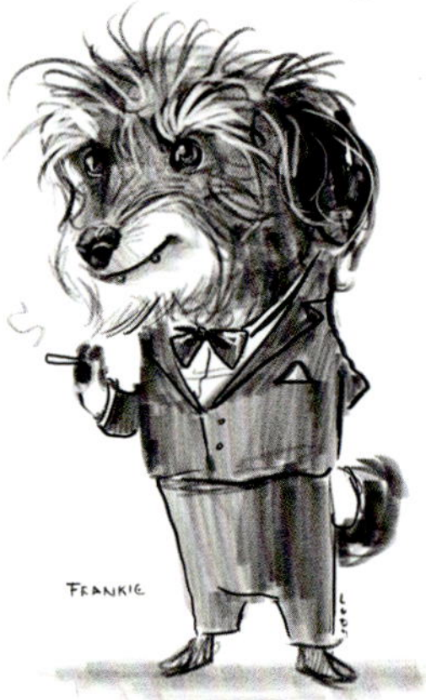
FRANKIE

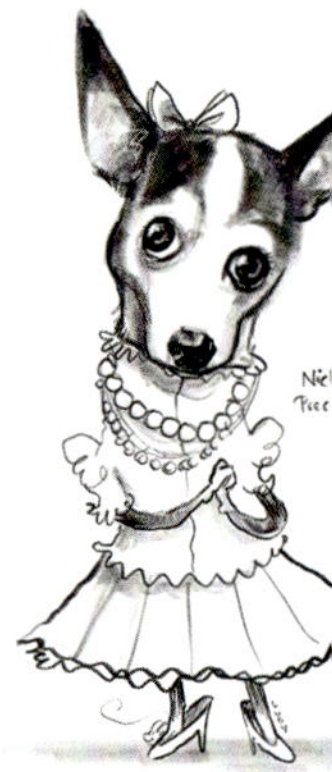

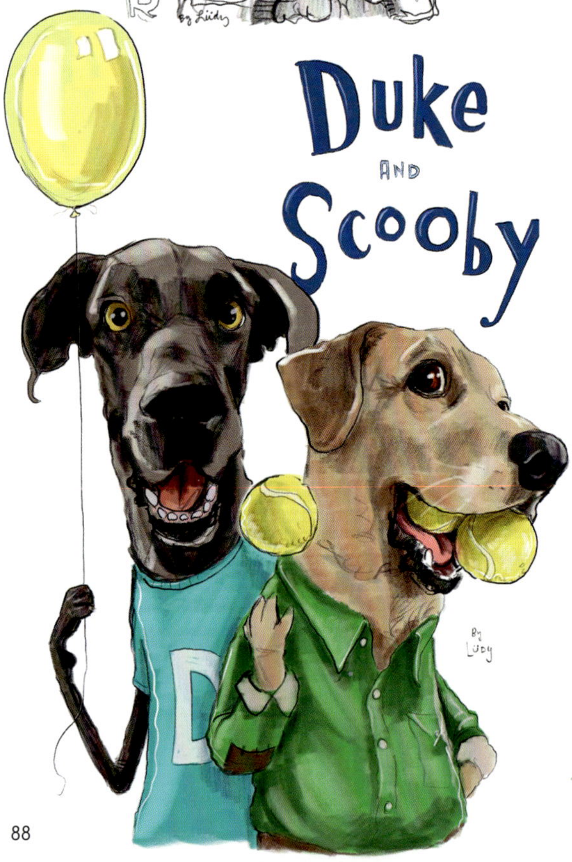
Duke
AND
Scooby
By
Lüdy

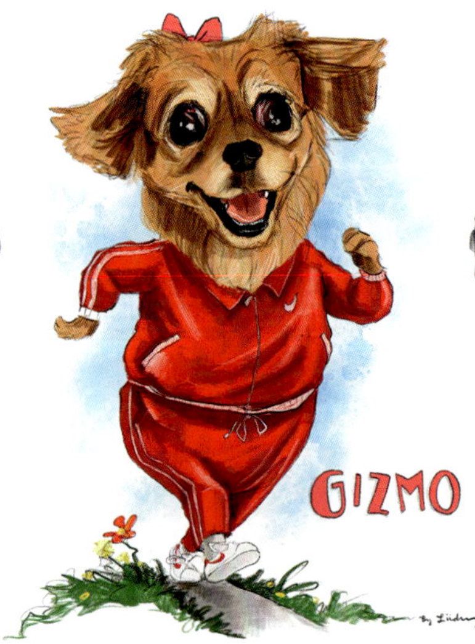
GIZMO
By Lüdy

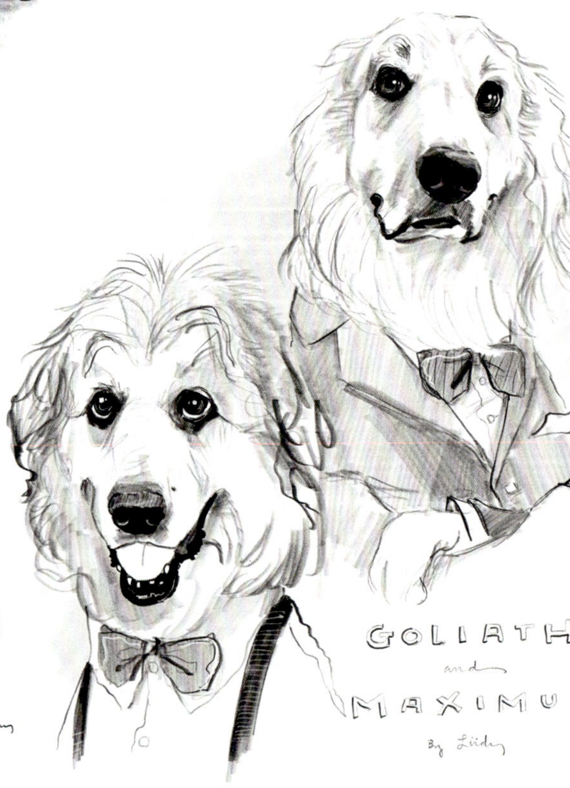
GOLIATH
and
MAXIMU
By Lüdy

Each one's a one-of-a-kind – never mass produced, always a masterpiece.

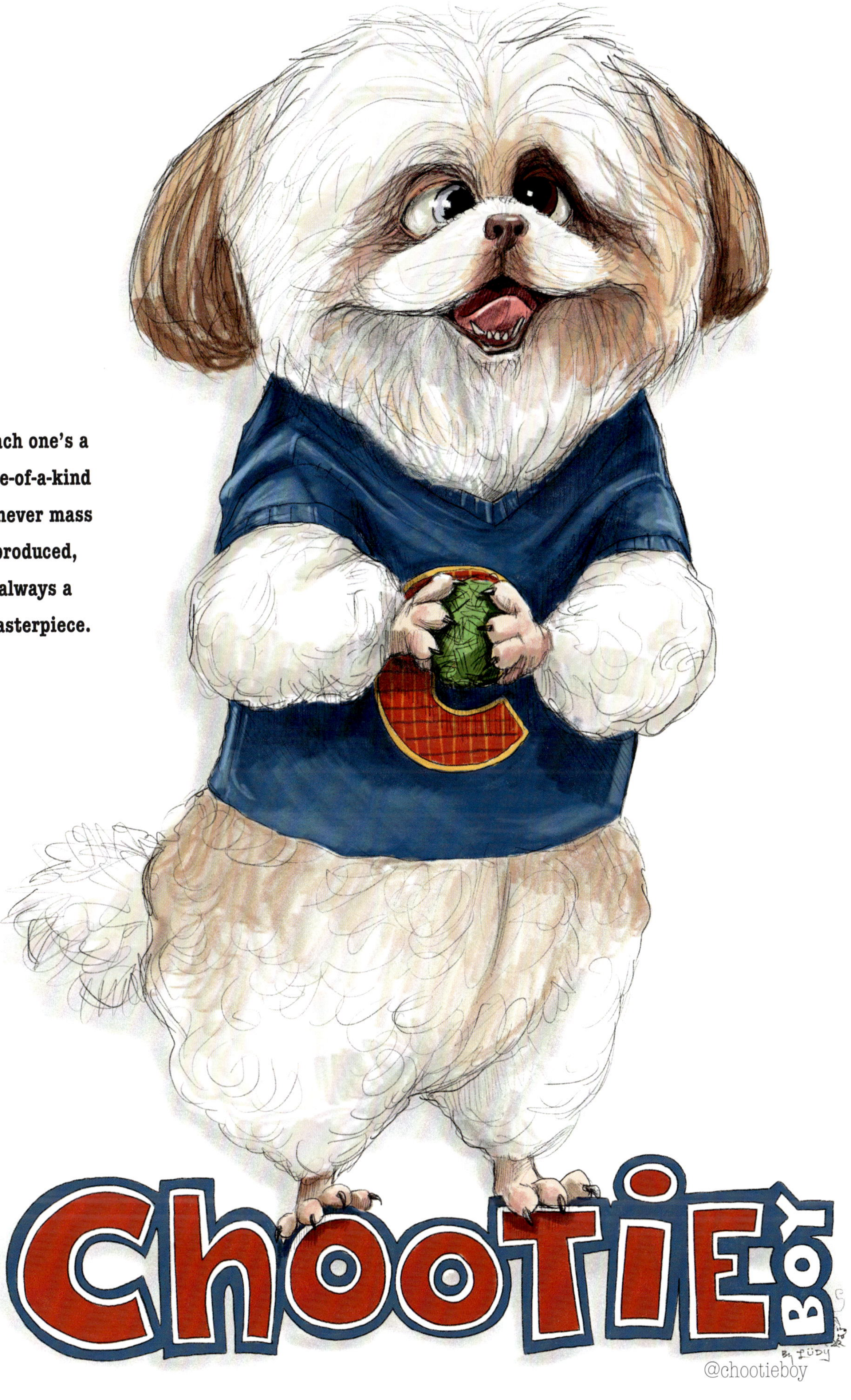

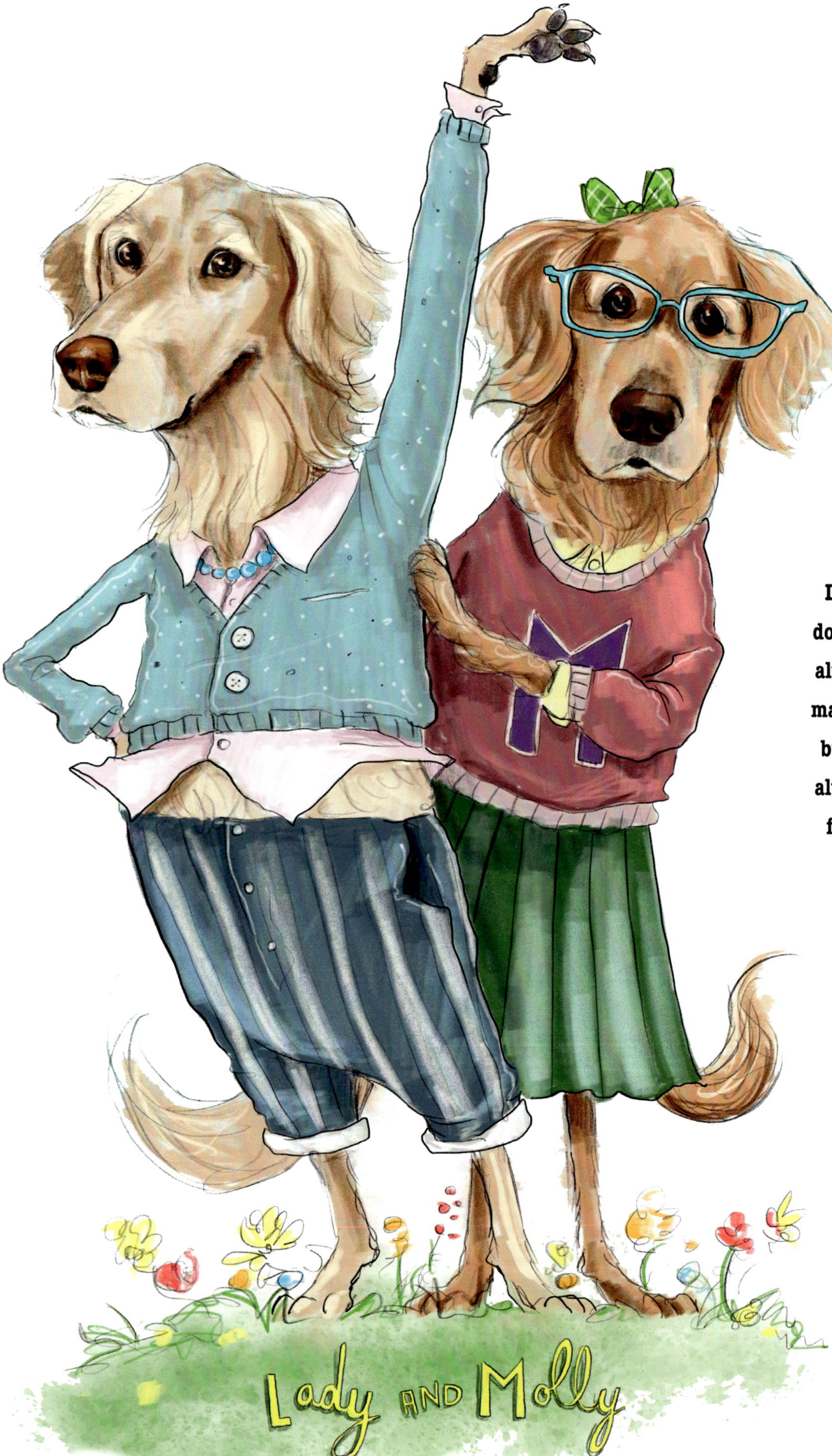

Love doesn't always match— but it always fits.

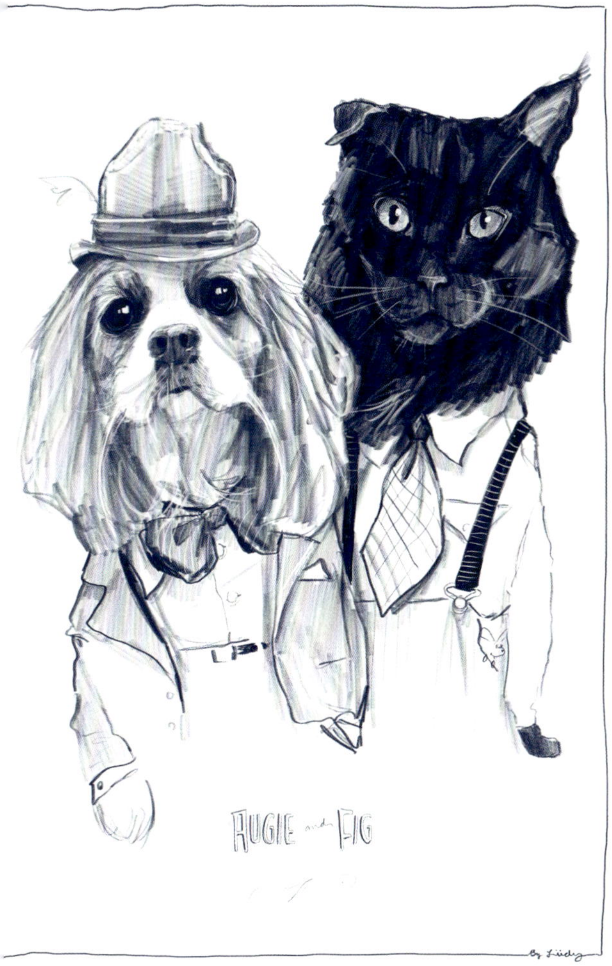
AUGIE and FIG

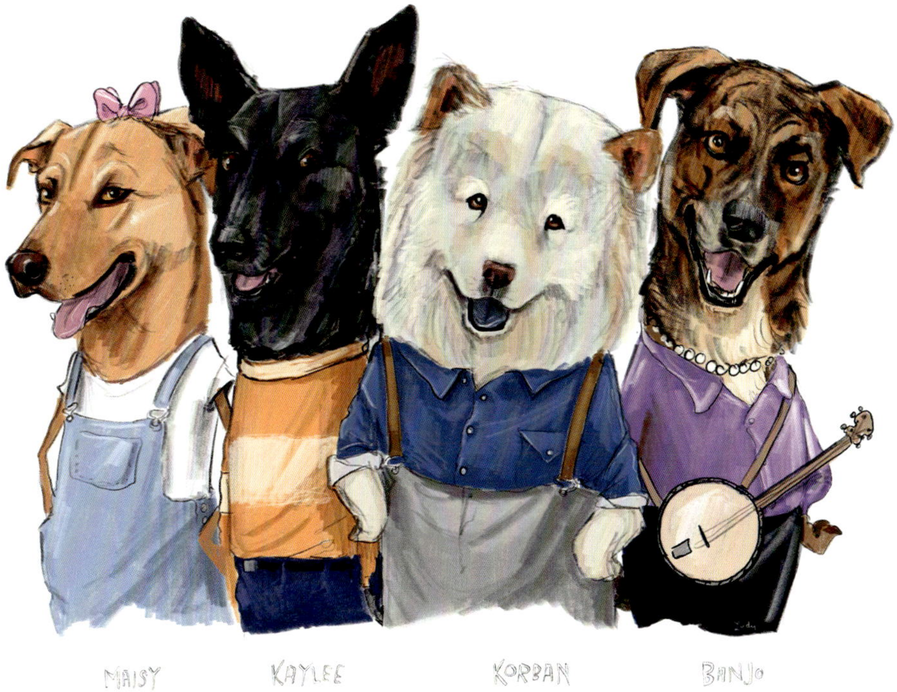
MAISY
KAYLEE
KORBAN
BANJO

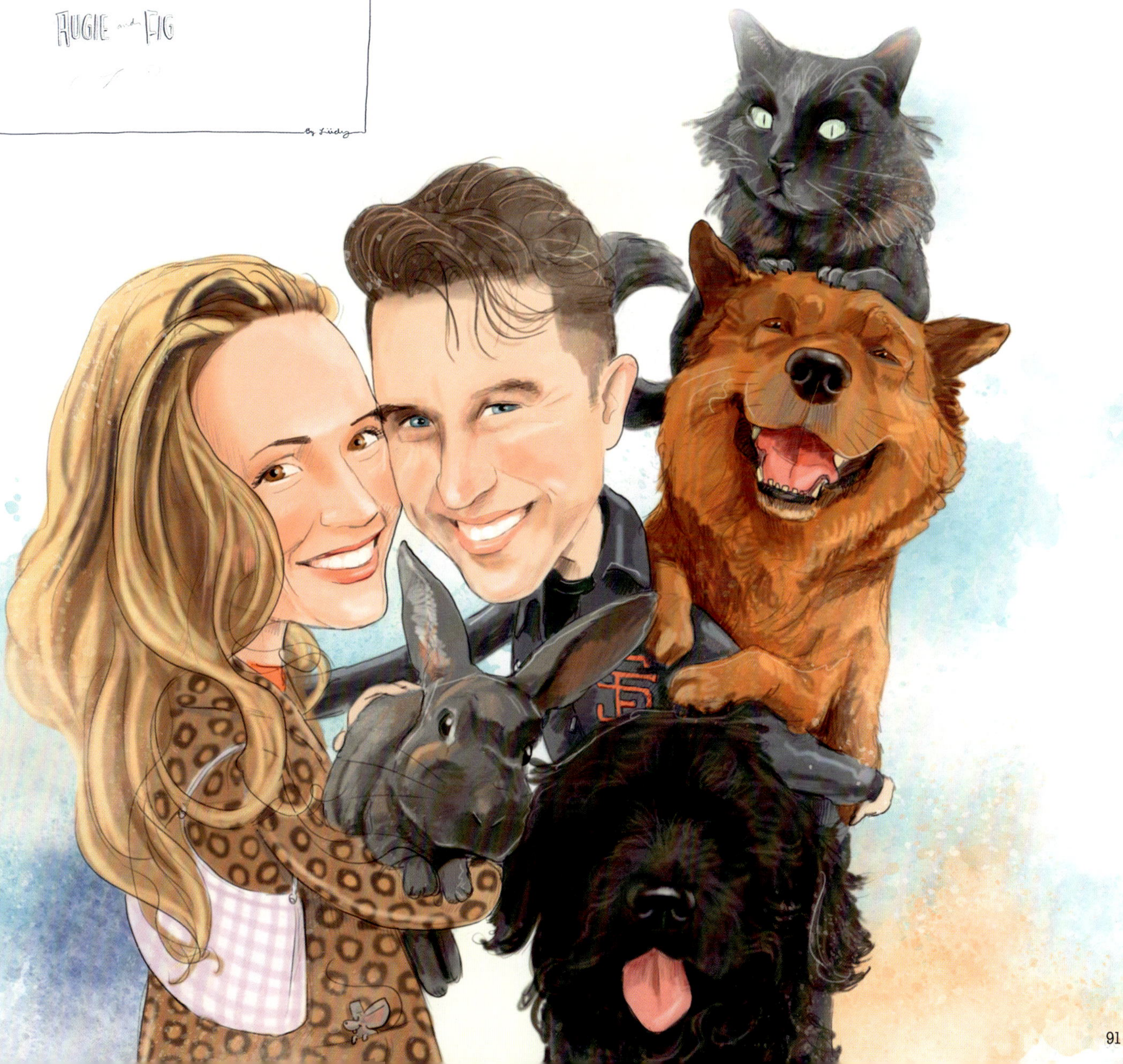

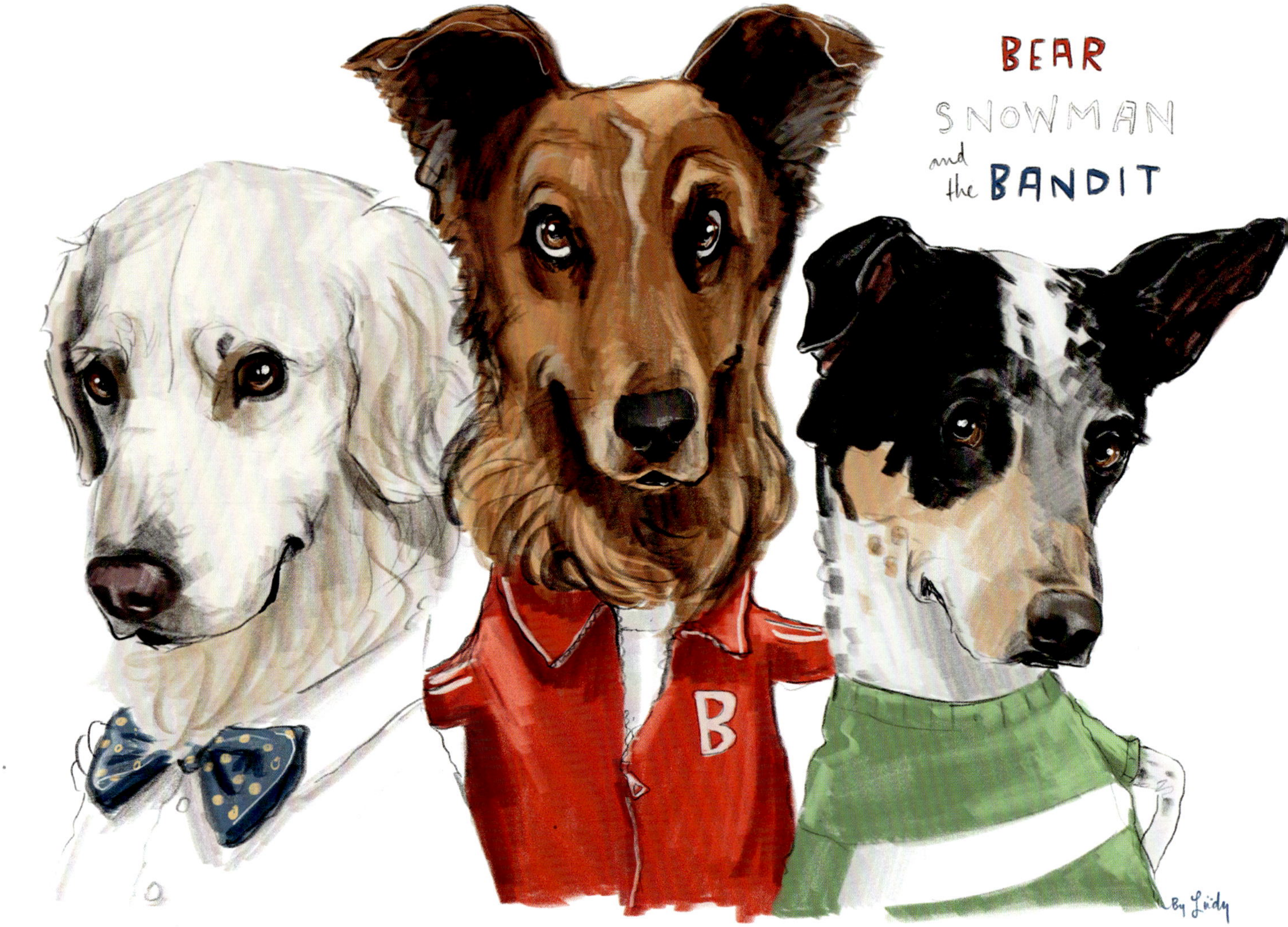
BEAR
SNOWMAN
and the BANDIT
B

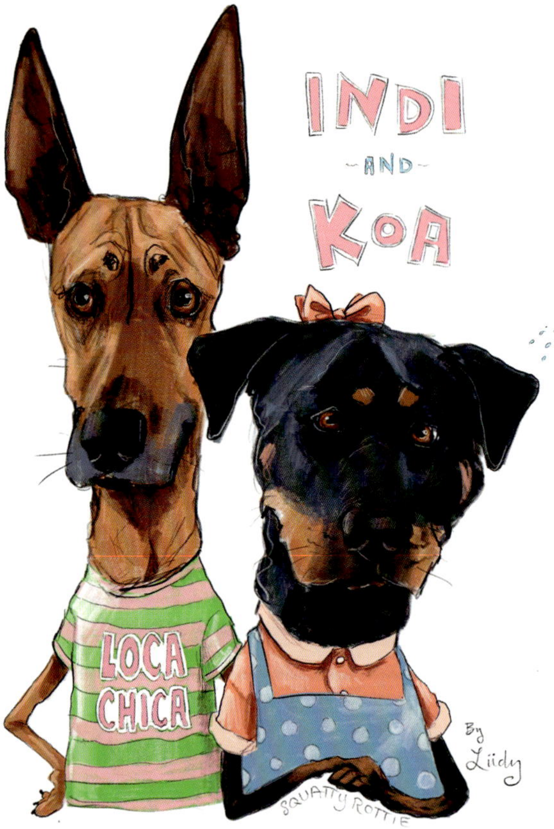
INDI
-AND-
KOA
LOCA CHICA
SQUATTY ROTTIE

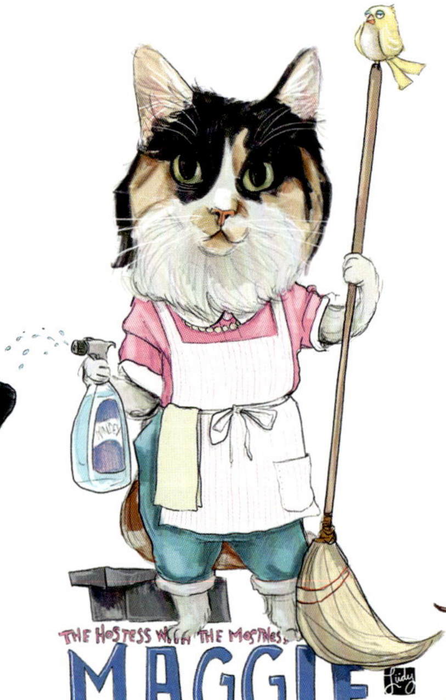
MAGGIE

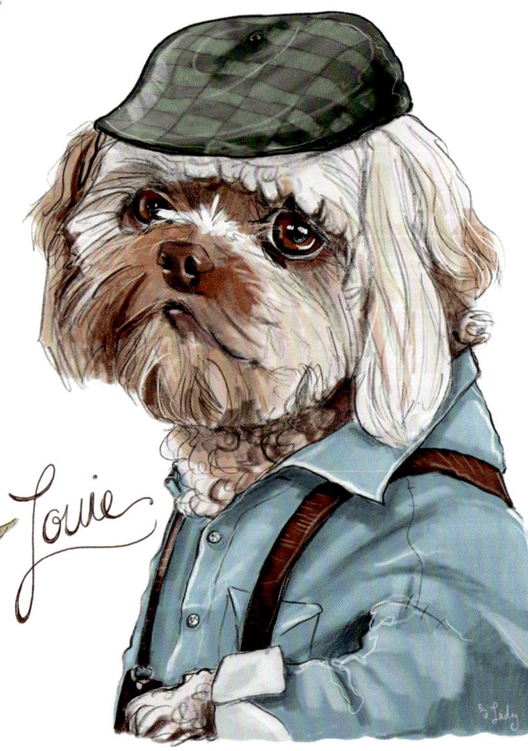
Louie

There are accidents you expect–

A chewed remote.

A stained rug.

The vanishing sock.

But take a man's Funyuns?

You've crossed the line.

– Ancient Pet Owner Proverb

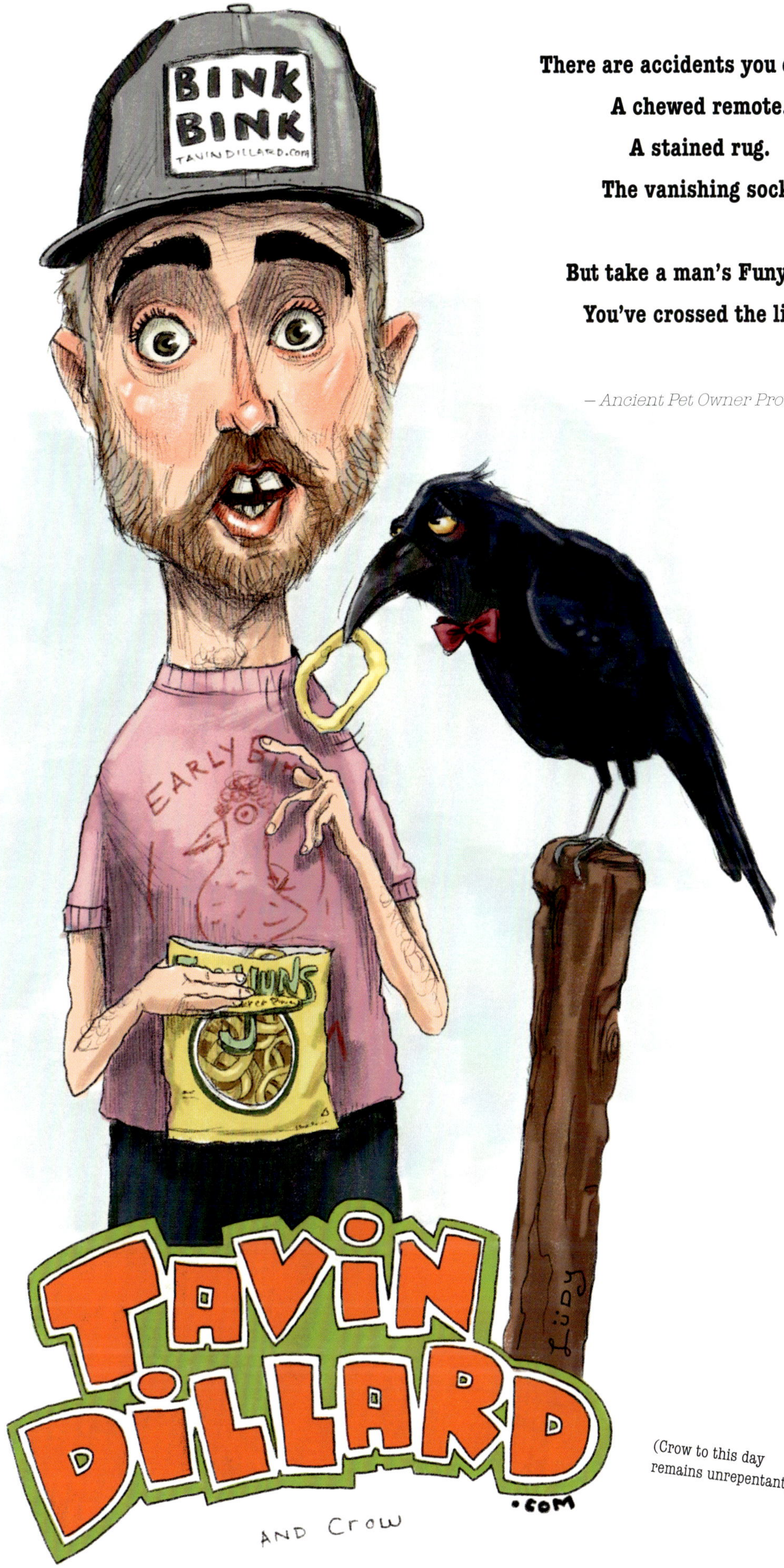

(Crow to this day remains unrepentant)

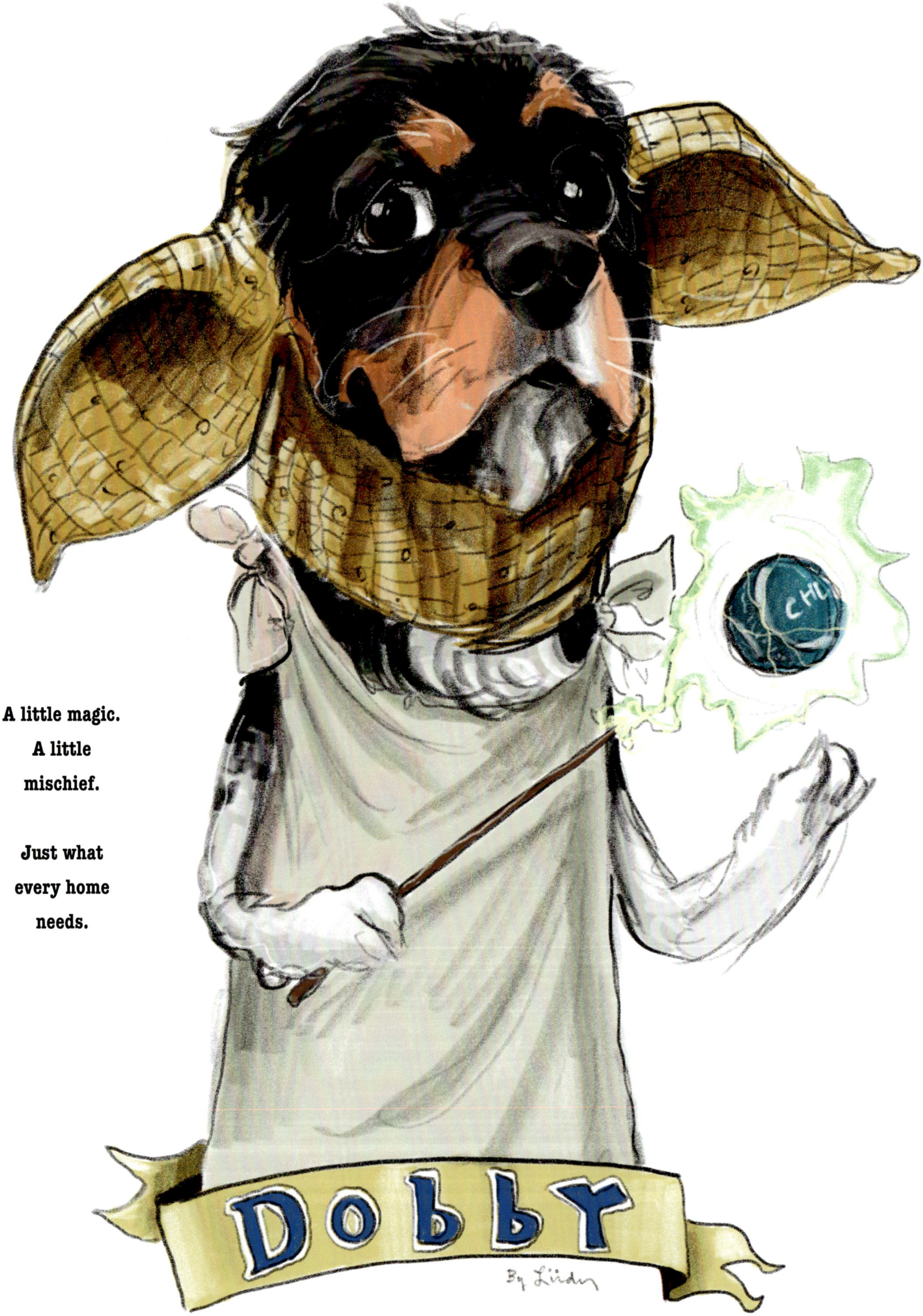

A little magic.
A little
mischief.

Just what
every home
needs.

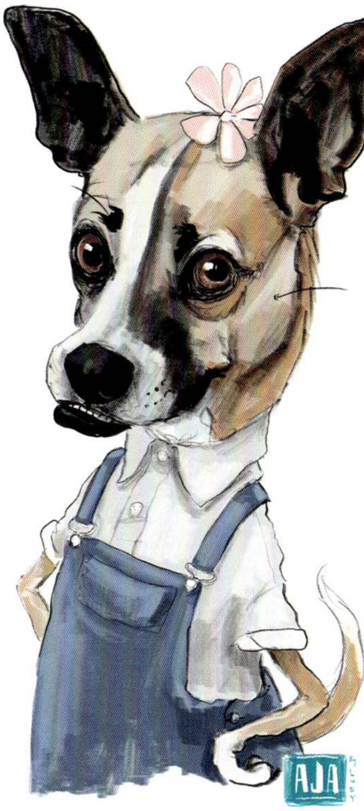
AJA

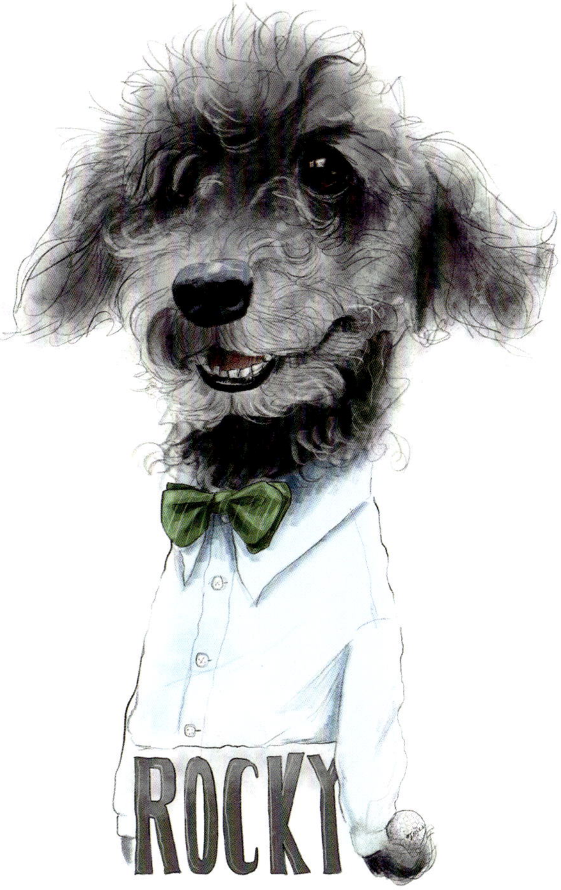
ROCKY

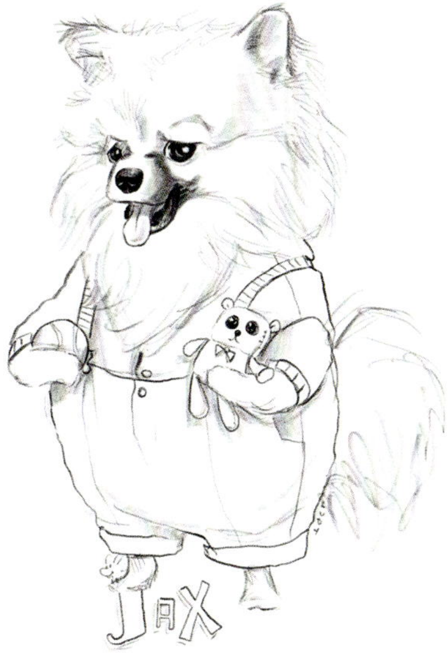
JAX

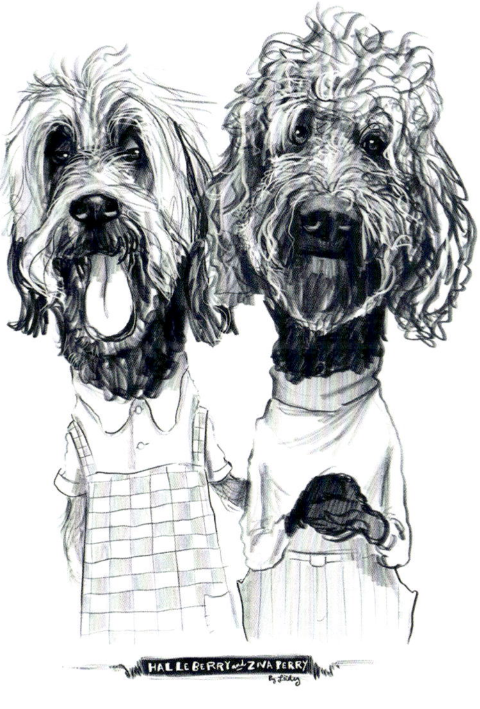
HALLE BERRY and ZIVA PERRY

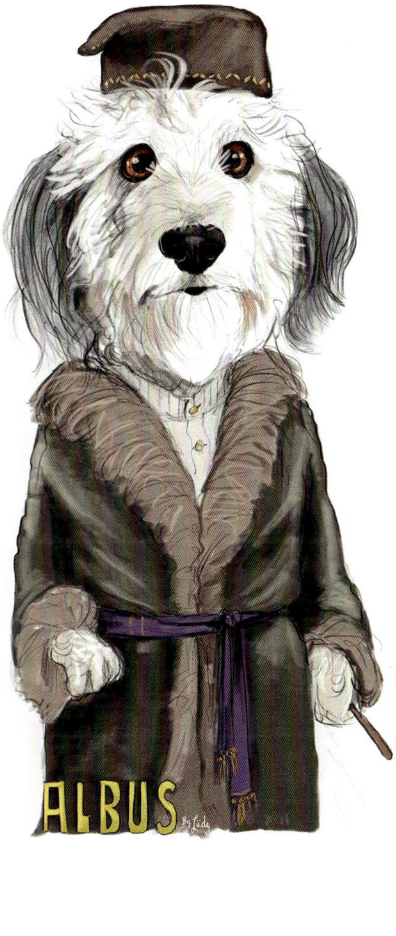
ALBUS

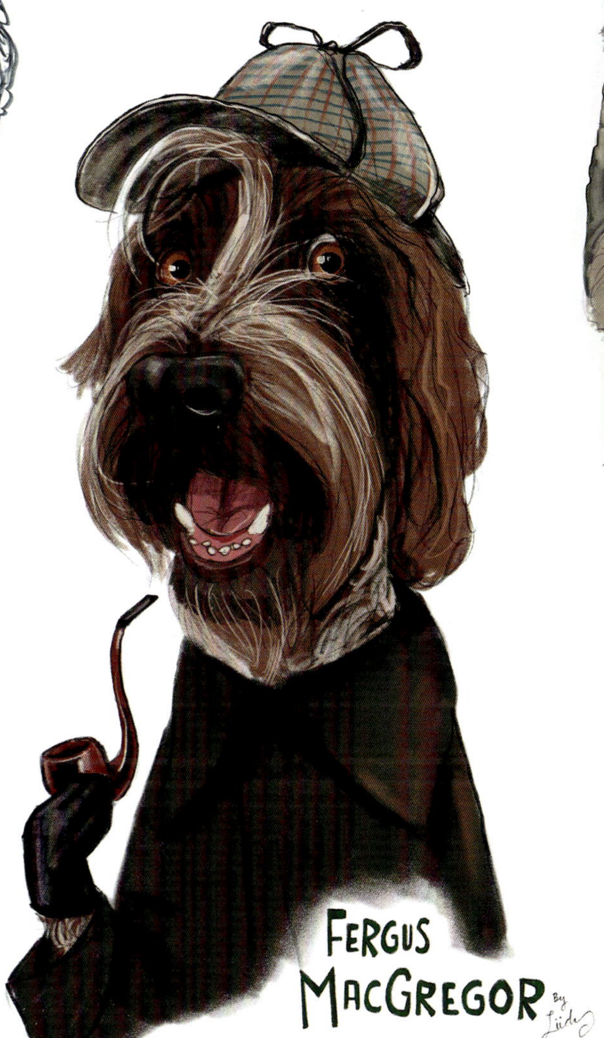
FERGUS
MACGREGOR

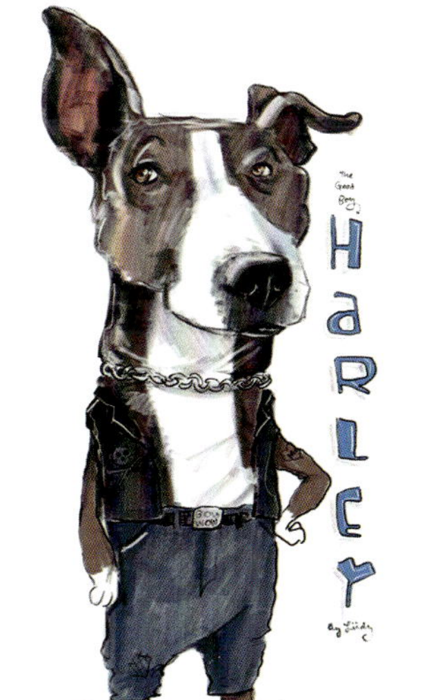
HARLEY

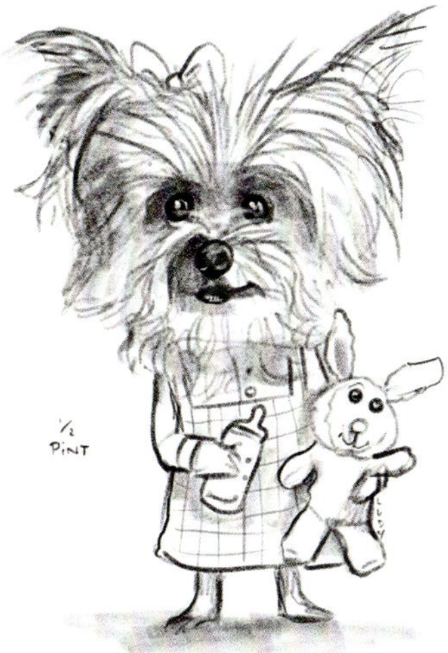
1/2
PINT

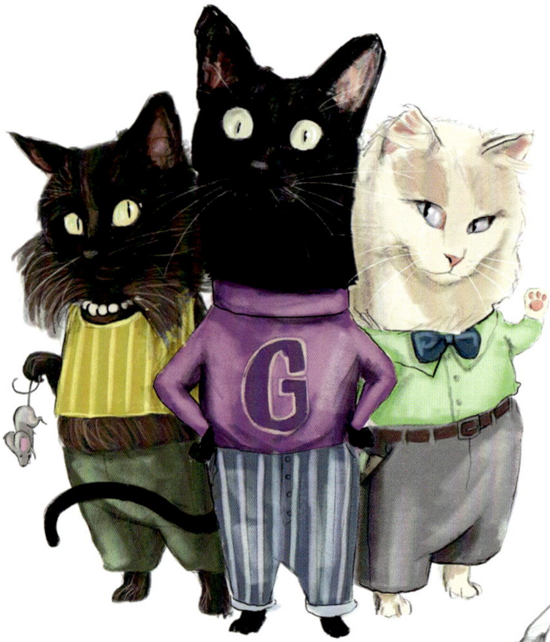

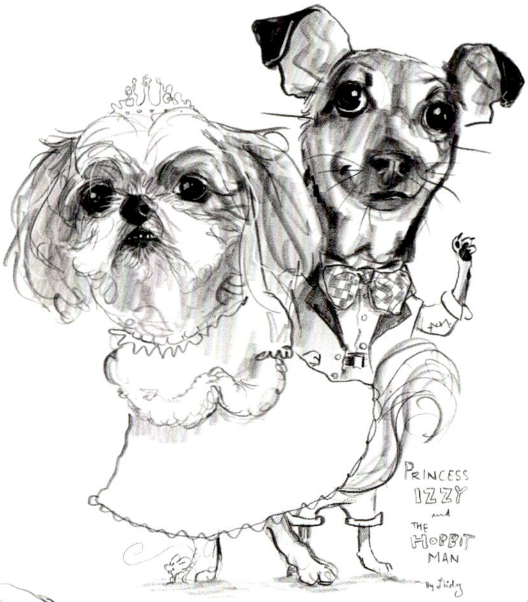
PRINCESS IZZY and THE HOBBIT MAN

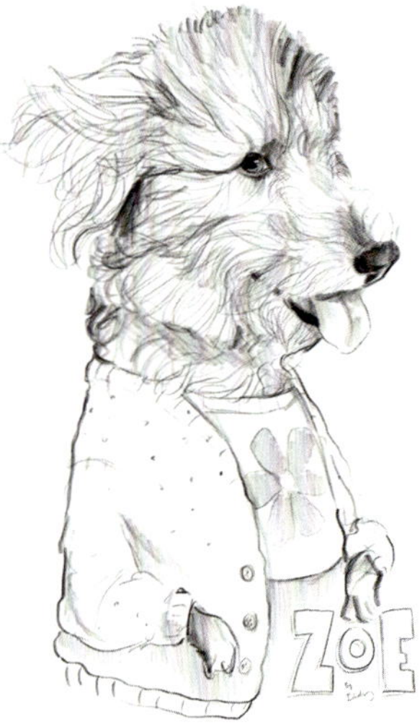
ZOE

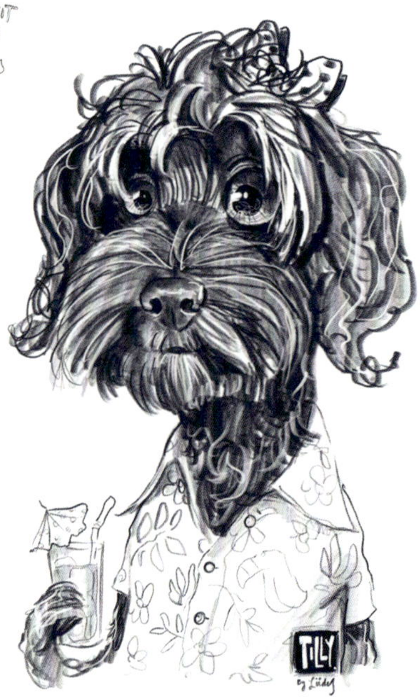
TILLY

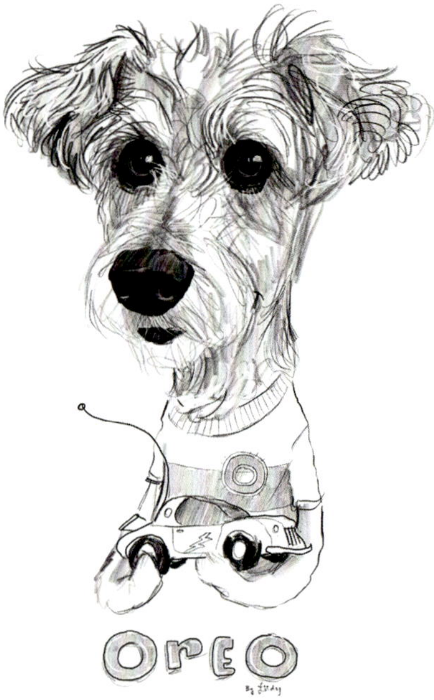
OrEO

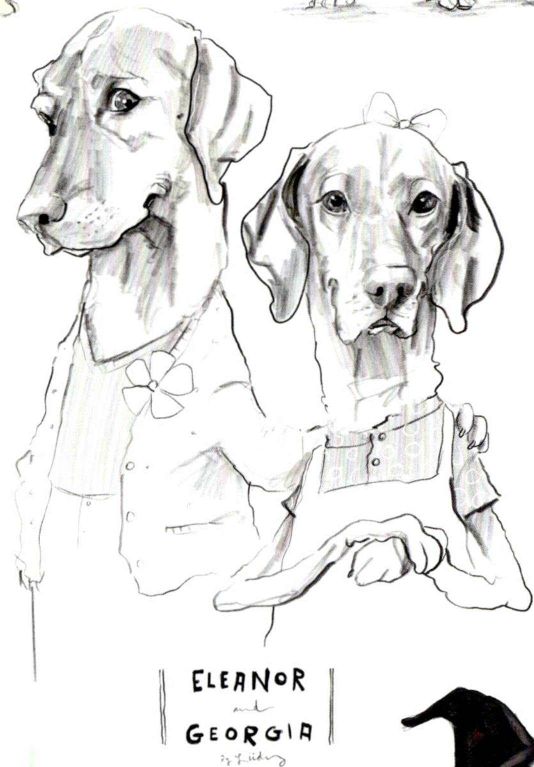
ELEANOR and GEORGIA

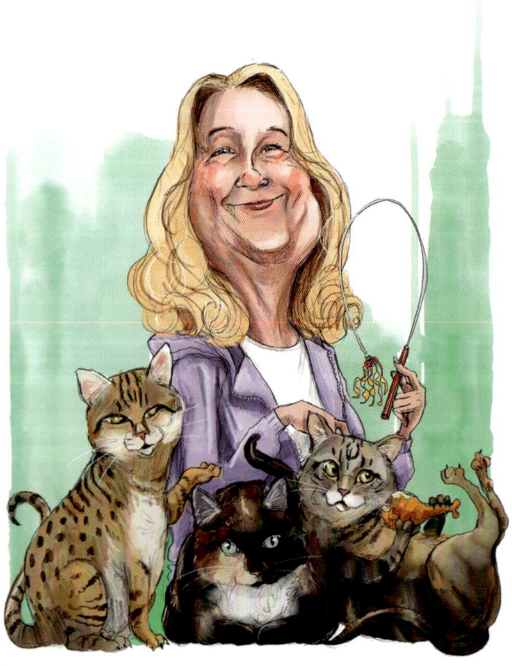

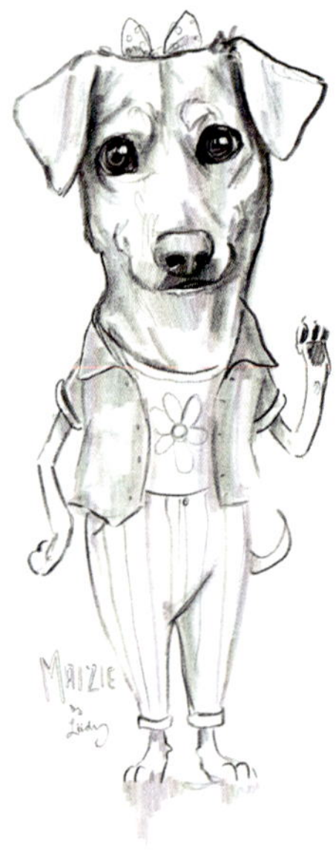
MAIZIE

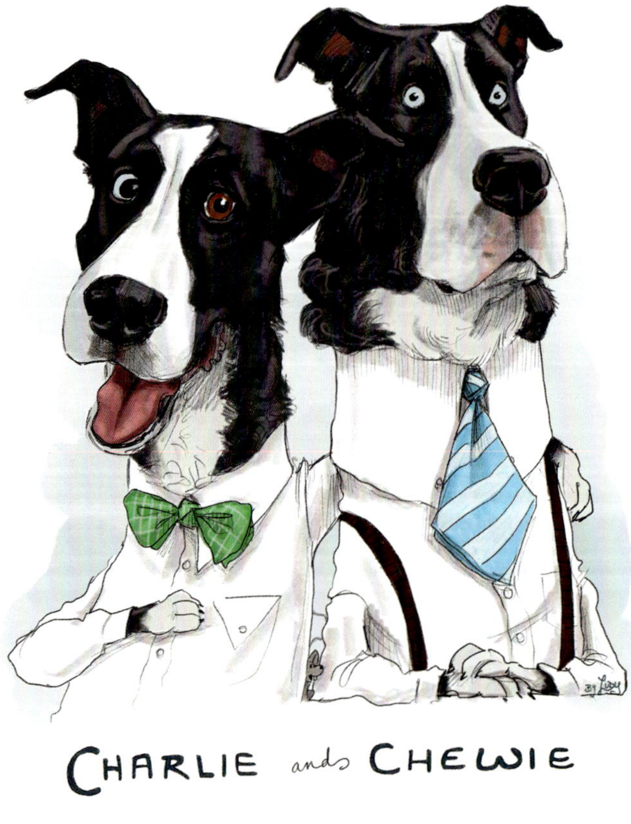
CHARLIE and CHEWIE

In a world
spinning too fast,
a pet will always
remind you to sit,
stay...
and maybe
sniff a flower.

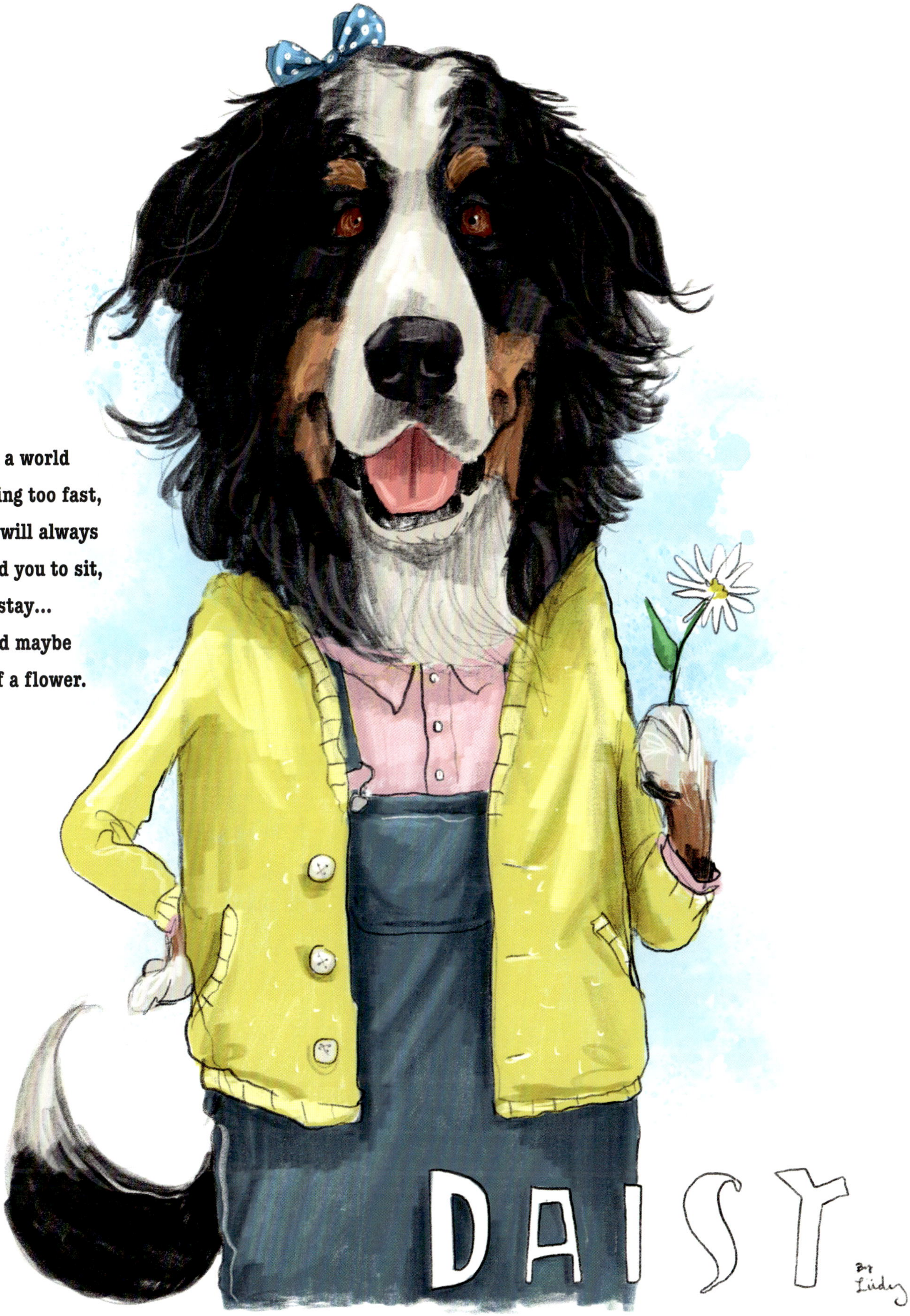

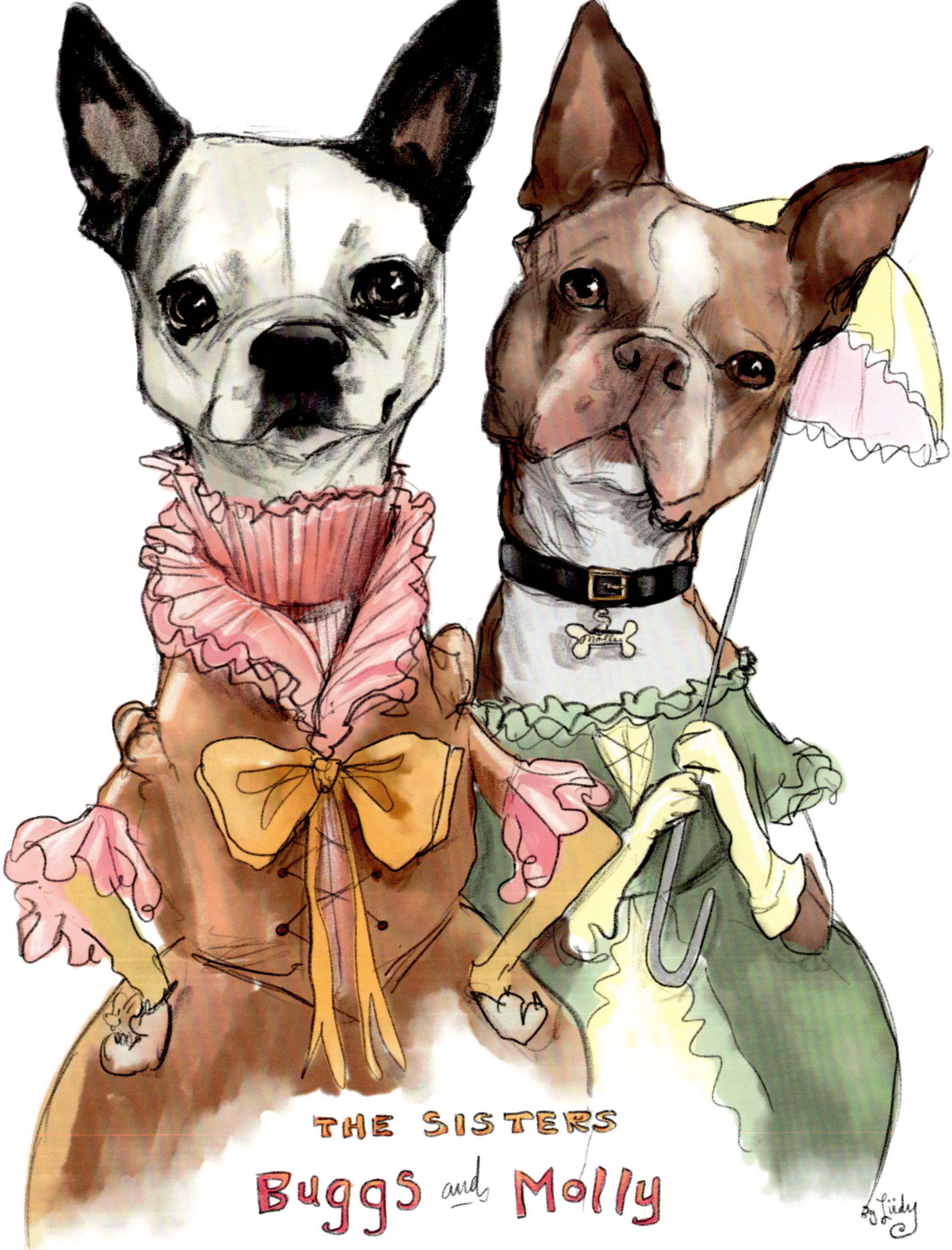

They may not agree on anything... except how fabulous they both are.

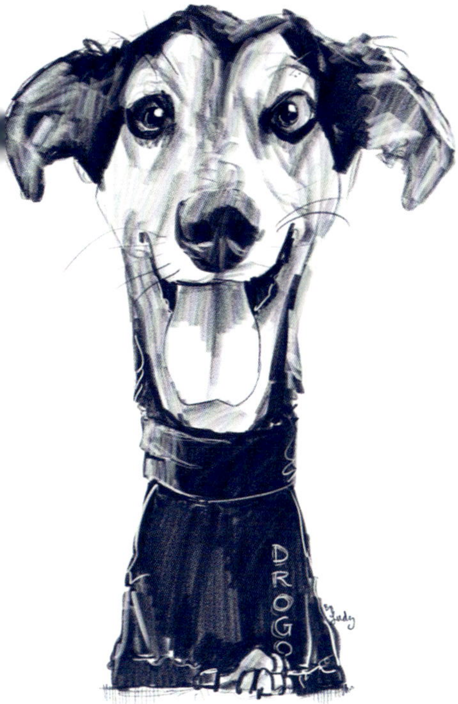
DROGO

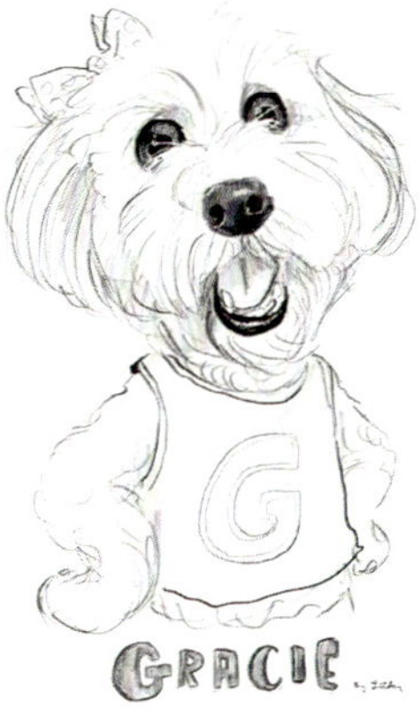
GRACIE

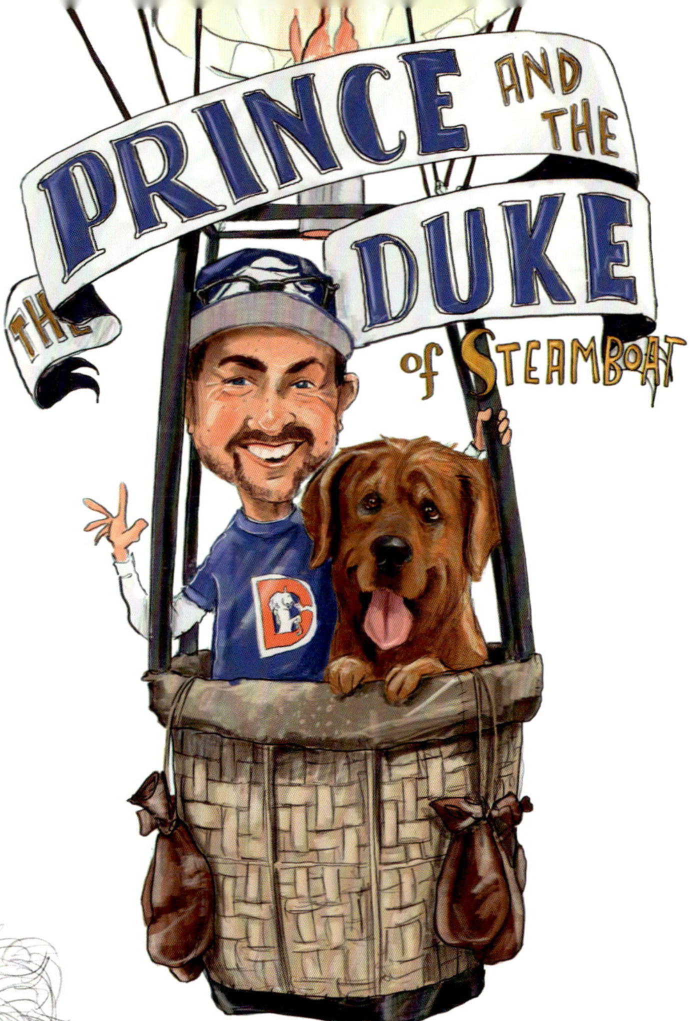
THE PRINCE AND THE DUKE
of STEAMBOAT

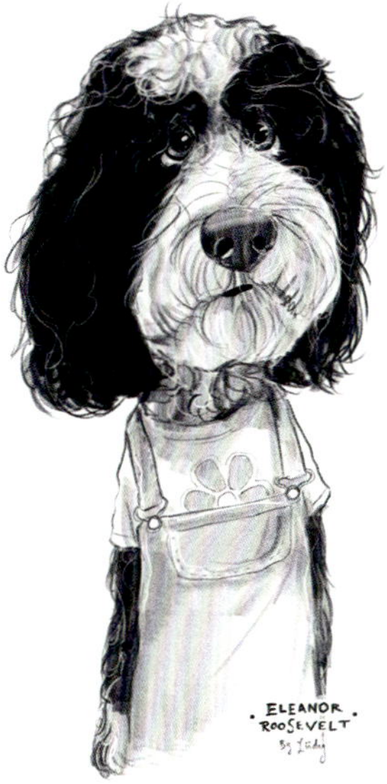
ELEANOR ROOSEVELT

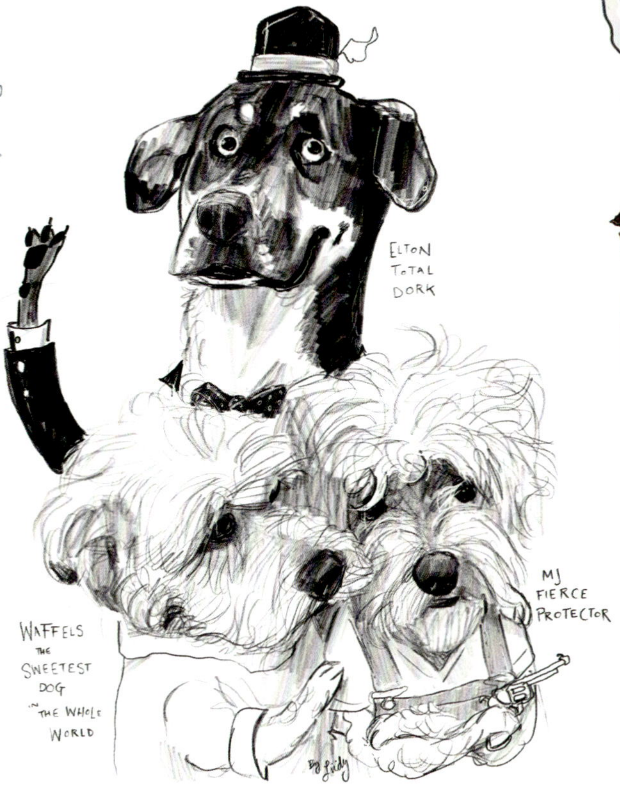
ELTON
TOTAL
DORK
WAFFELS
THE
SWEETEST
DOG
IN THE WHOLE
WORLD
MJ
FIERCE
PROTECTOR

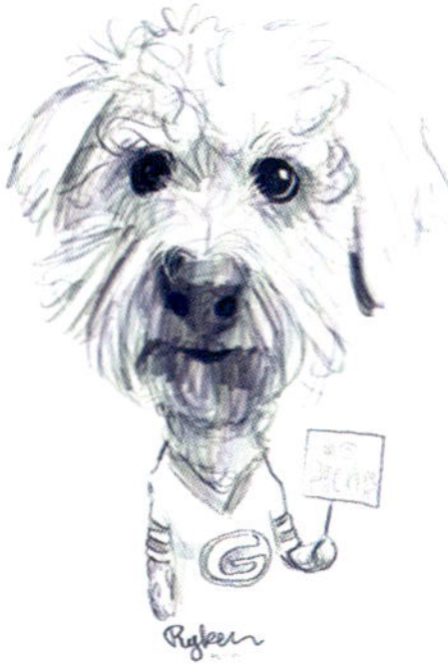
Ryker

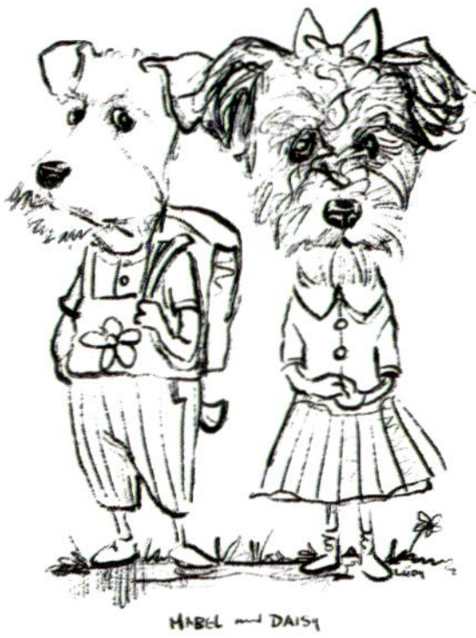
MABEL and DAISY

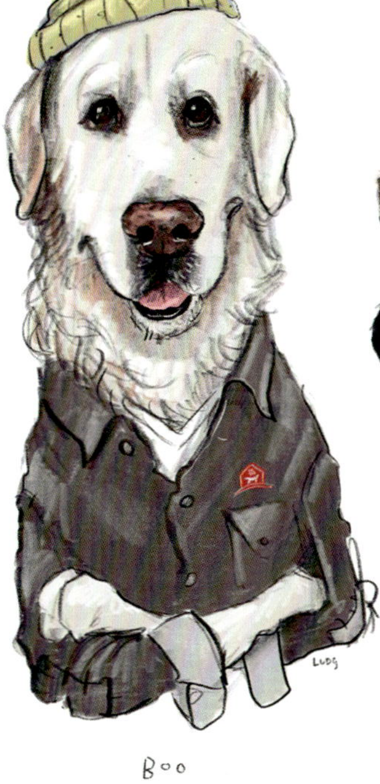
Boo

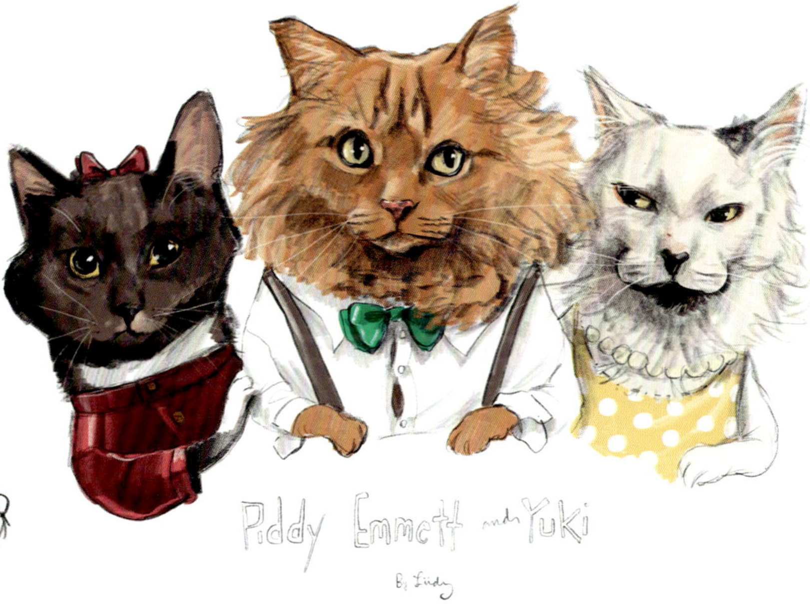
Piddy Emmett and Yuki

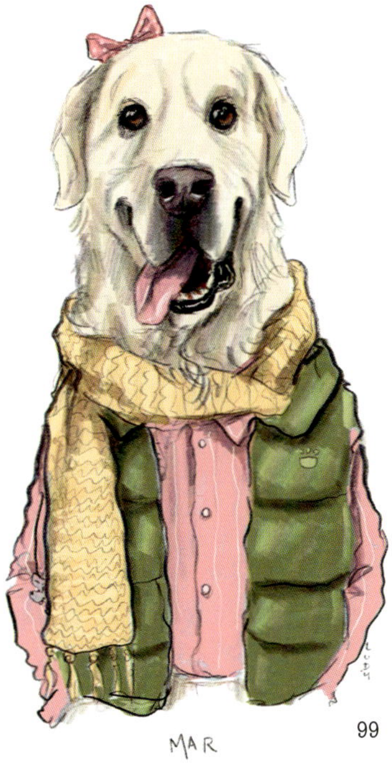
MAR

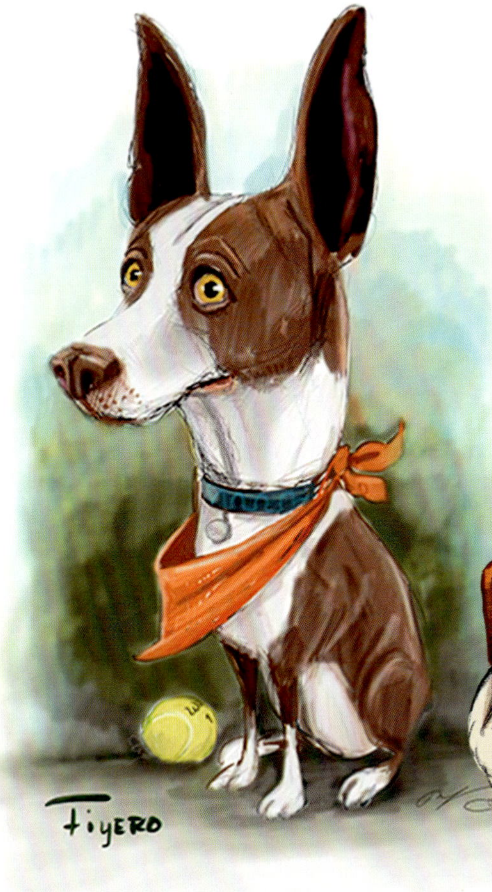
Fiyero

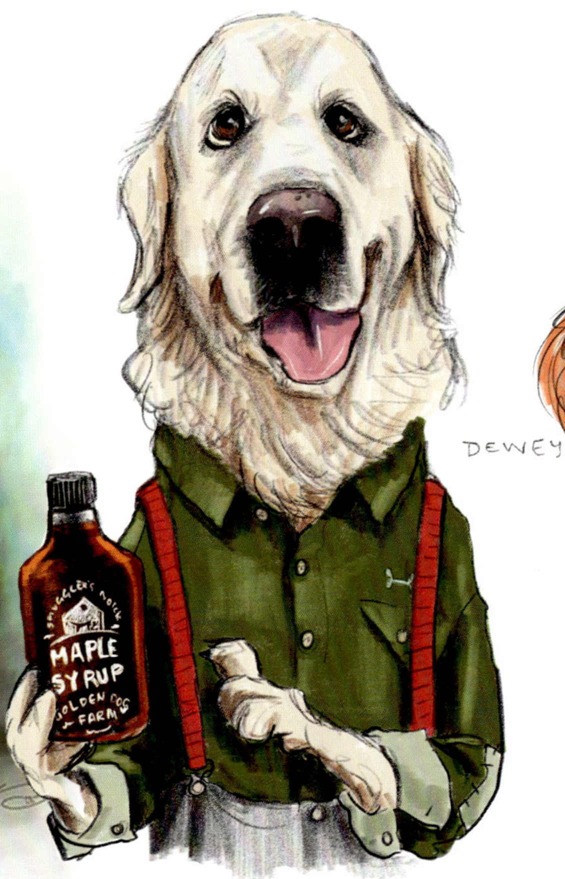
MAPLE
SYRUP
GOLDEN DOG
FARM
DEWEY

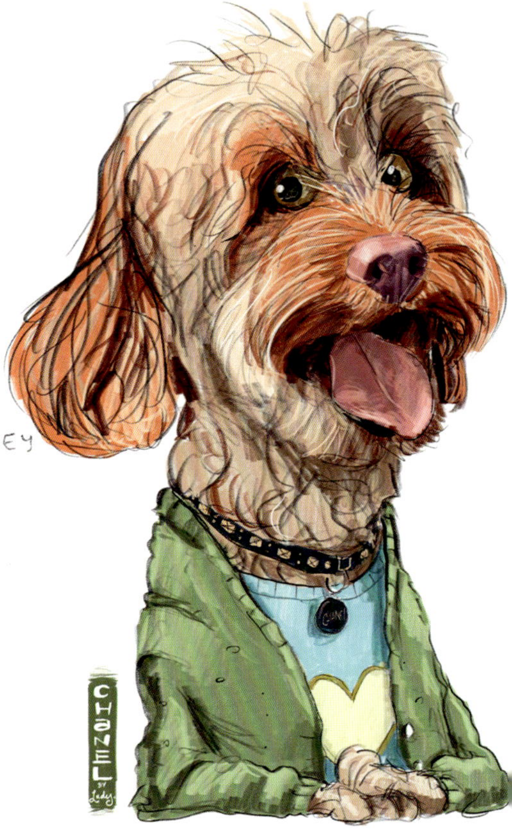
CHANEL

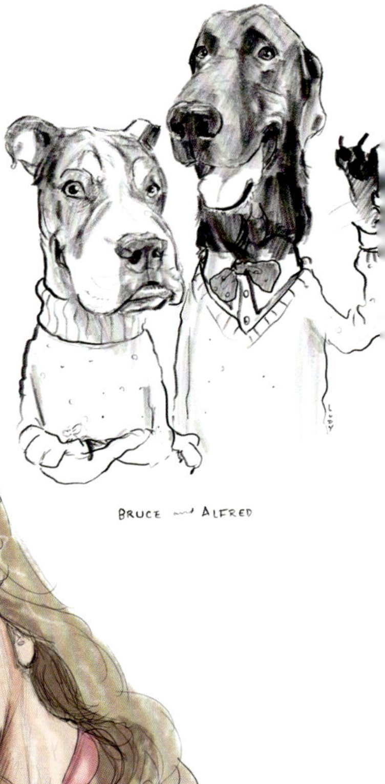
BRUCE ~ ALFRED

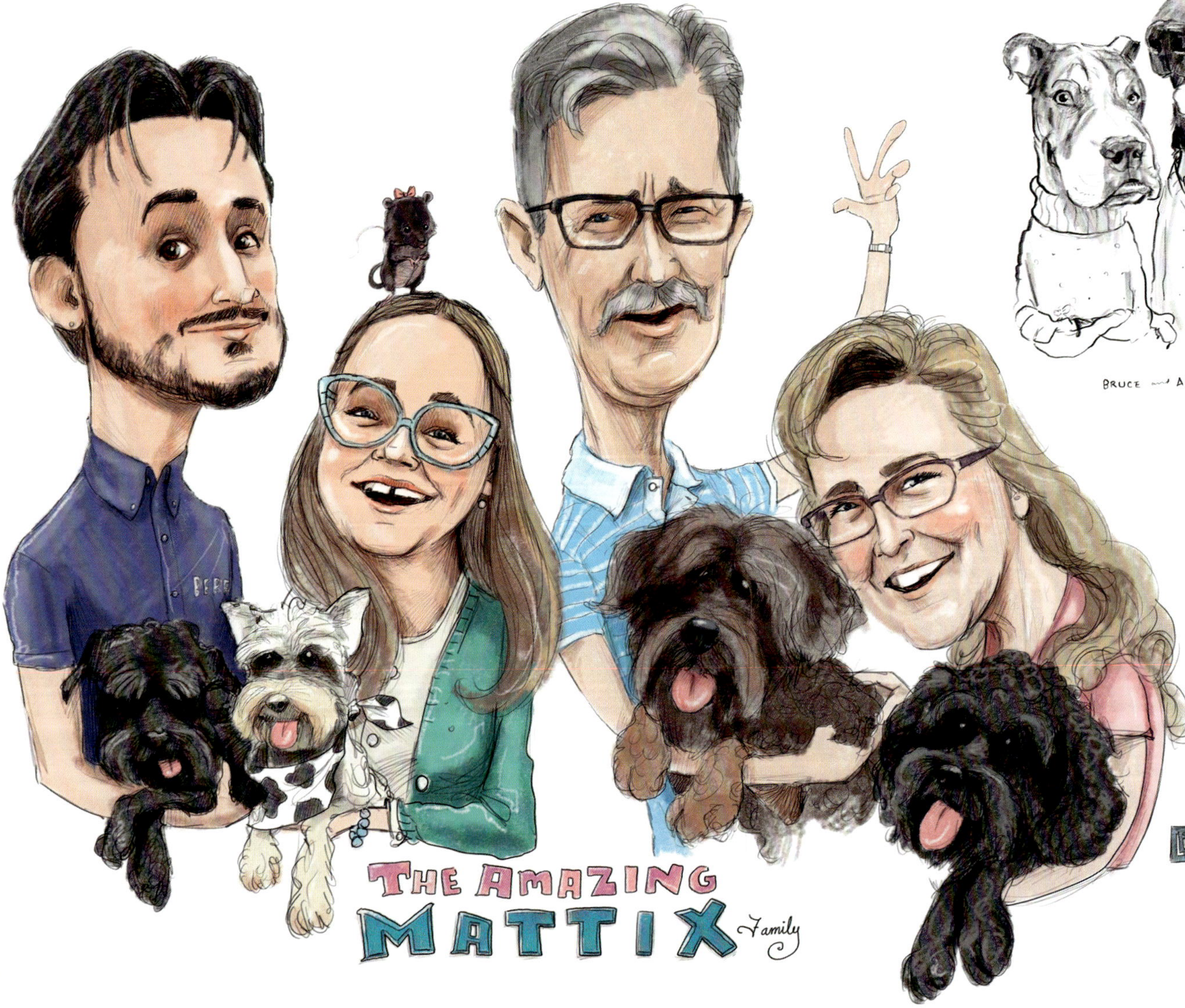
THE AMAZING
MATTIX
Family
LUDY.

“Saving one dog won’t change the world, but surely, for that one dog, the world will change forever.”

—Karen Davison

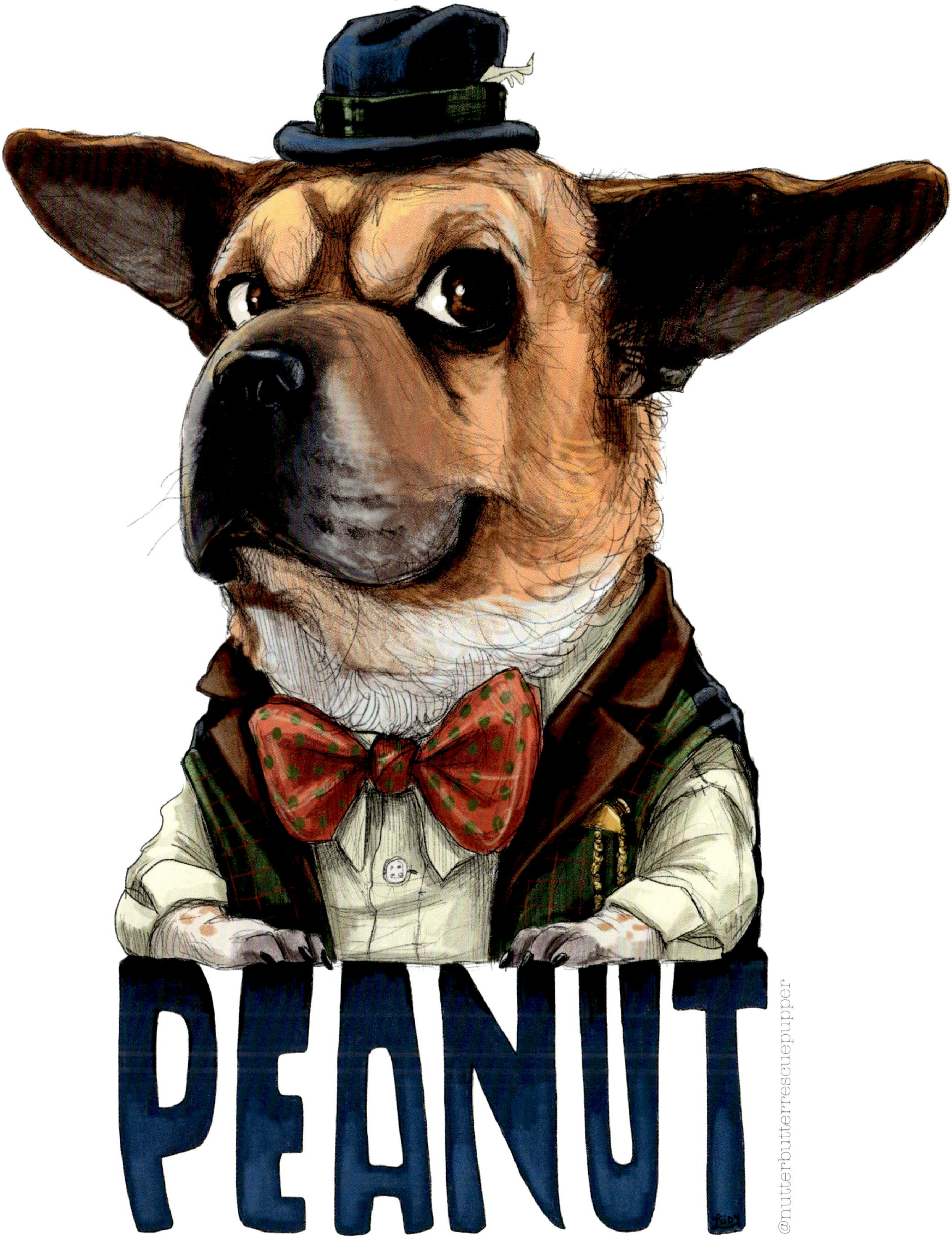

"You can't help respecting anybody who can spell TUESDAY, even if he doesn't spell it right."

– A.A. Milne (Winnie-the-Pooh)

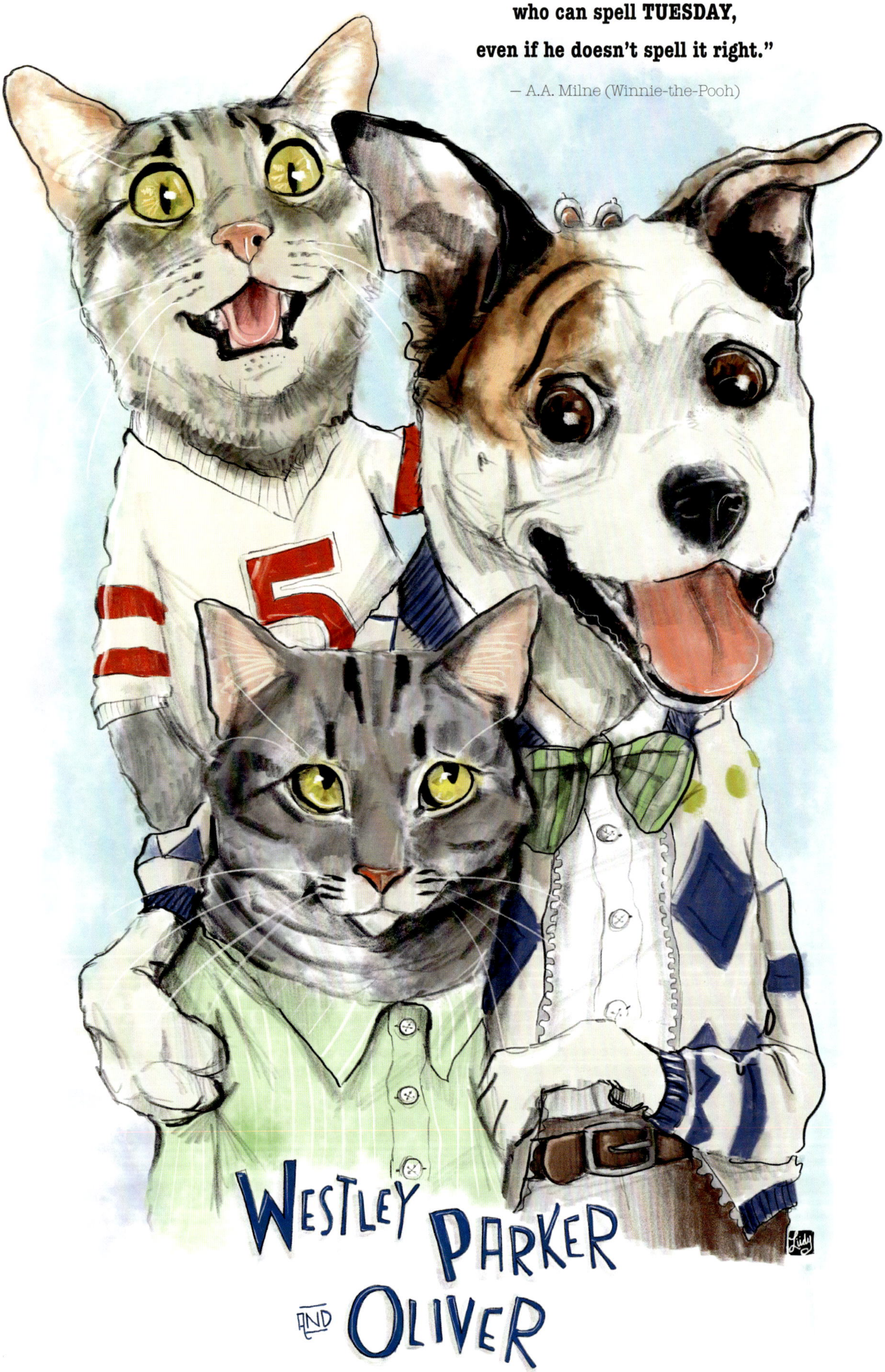

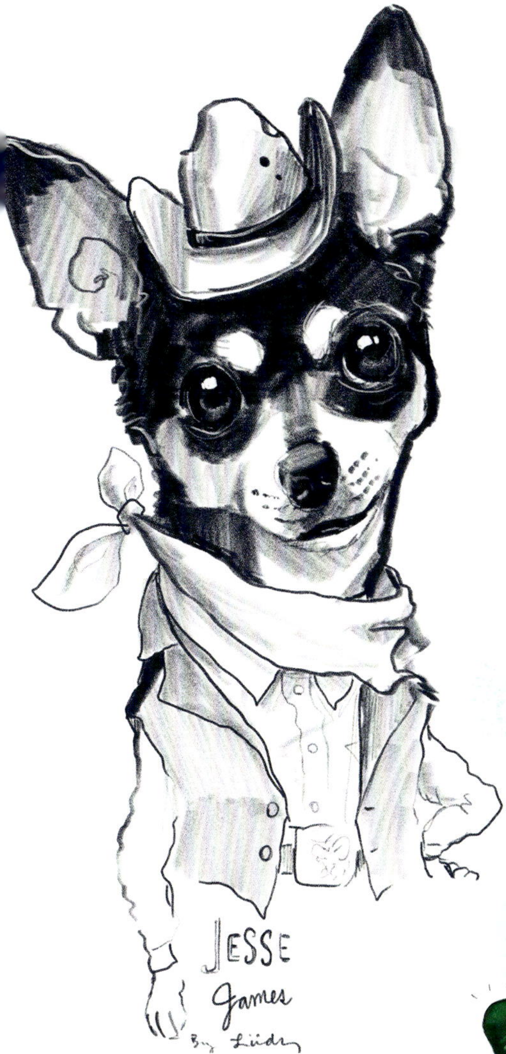
JESSE
James
By Lüdy
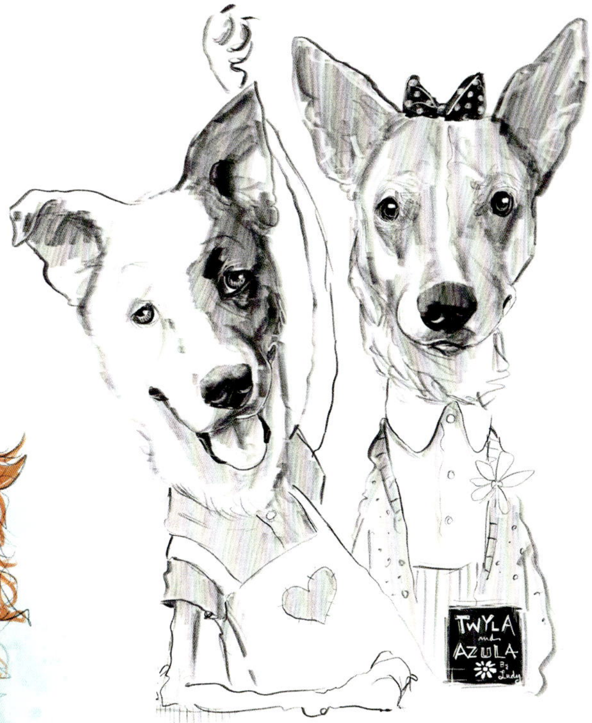
TWYLA and AZULA
By Lüdy
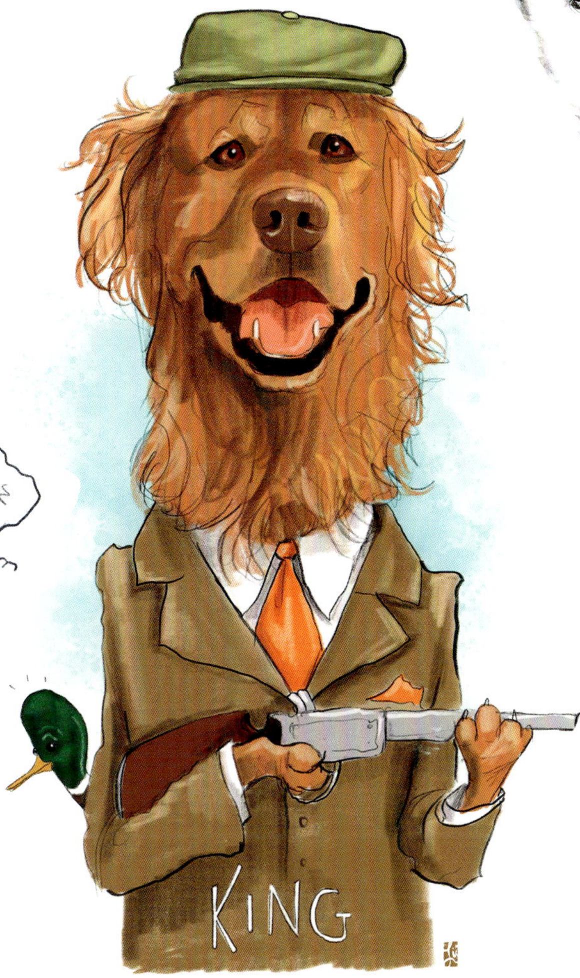
KING
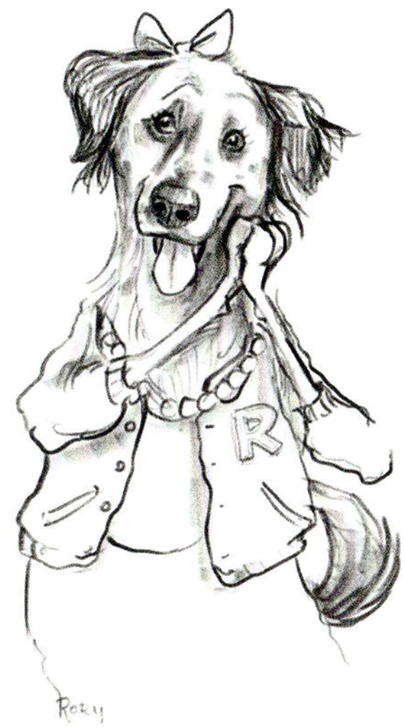
Rory
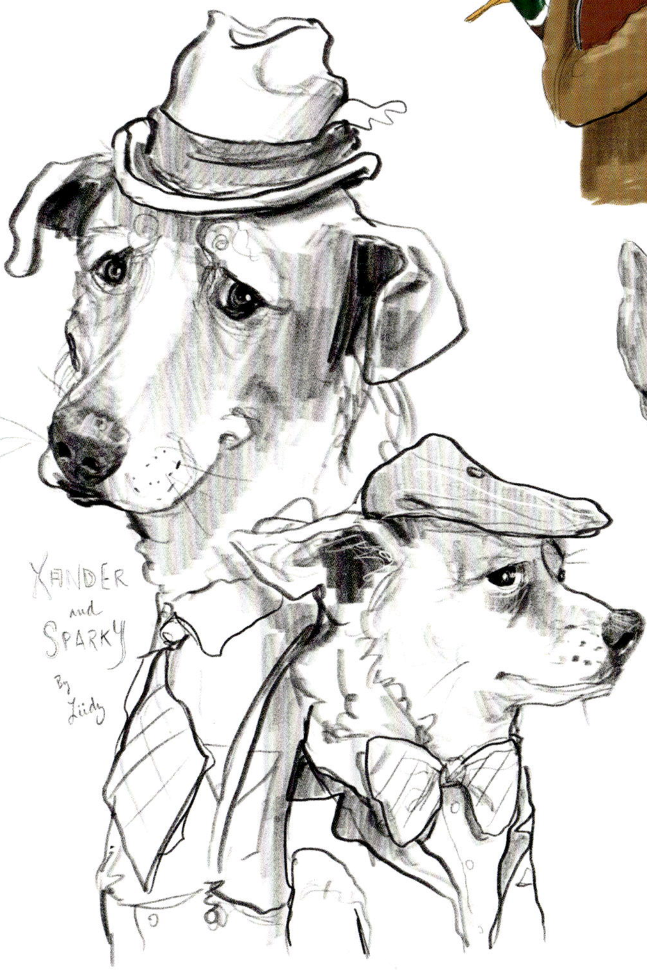
XANDER
and
SPARKY
By
Lüdy
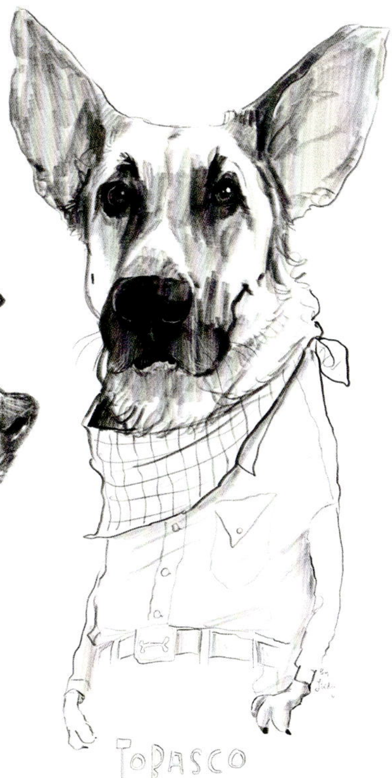
TOBASCO
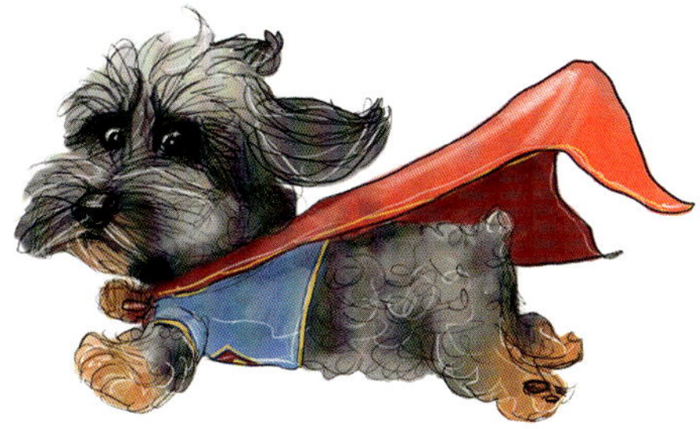
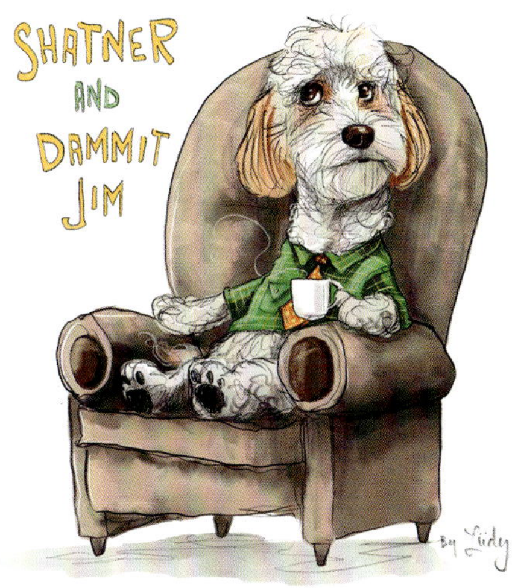
SHATNER
AND
DAMMIT
JIM
By Lüdy

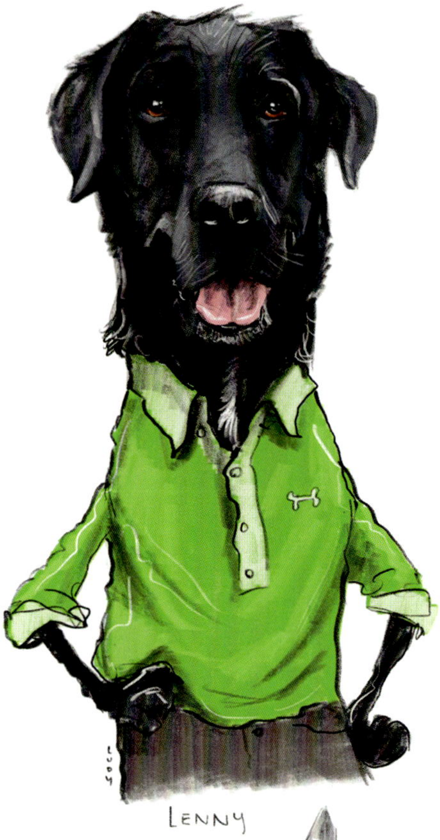
LENNY

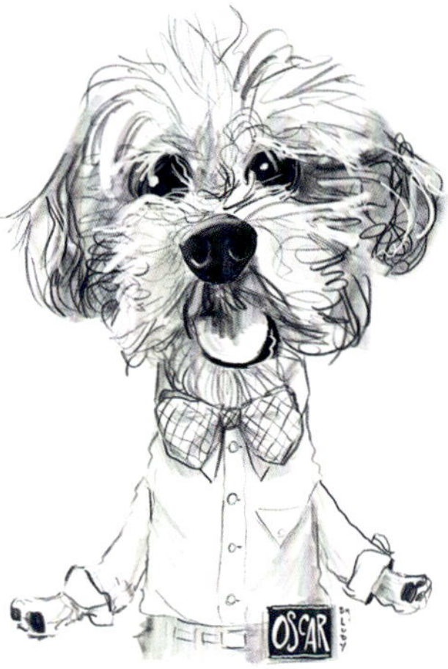
OSCAR

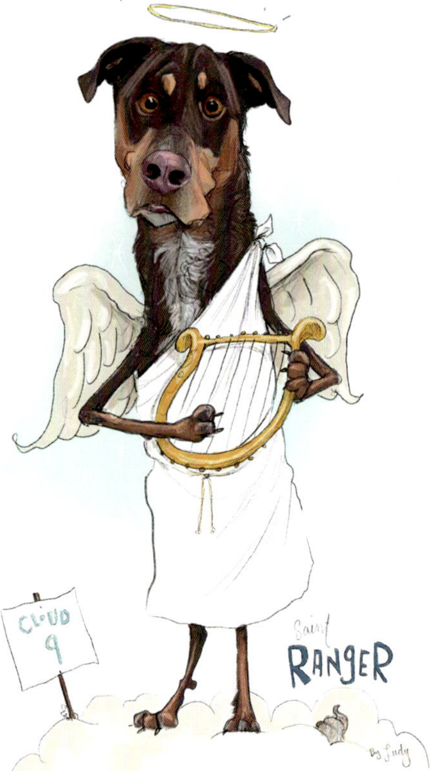
CLOUD 9
Saint
RANGER
By Lüdy

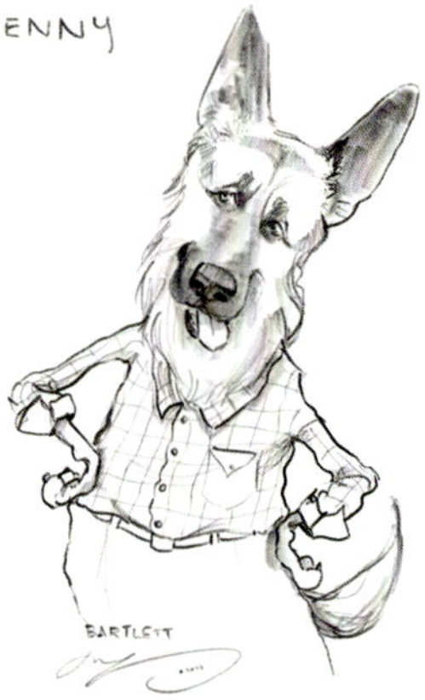
BARTLETT

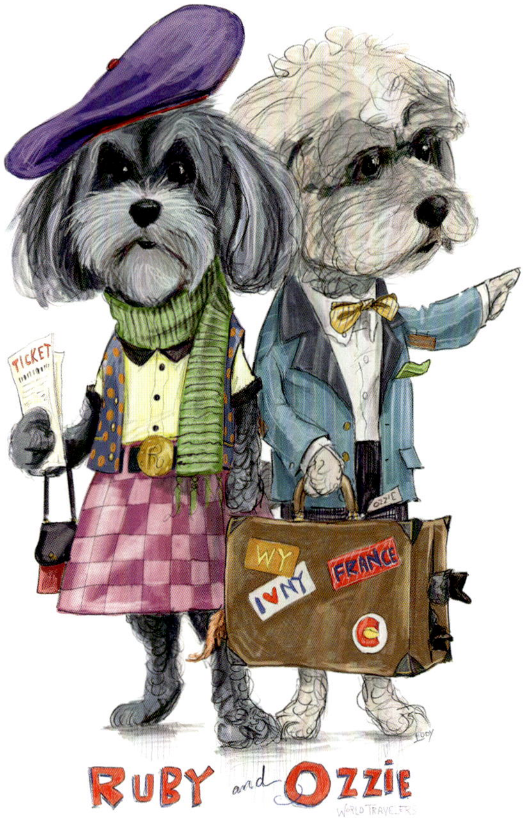
TICKET
WY
I ♥ NY
FRANCE
RUBY and OZZIE
WORLD TRAVELER

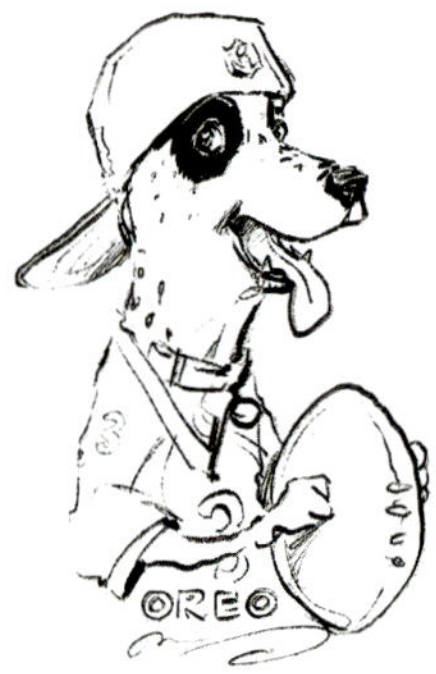
OREO

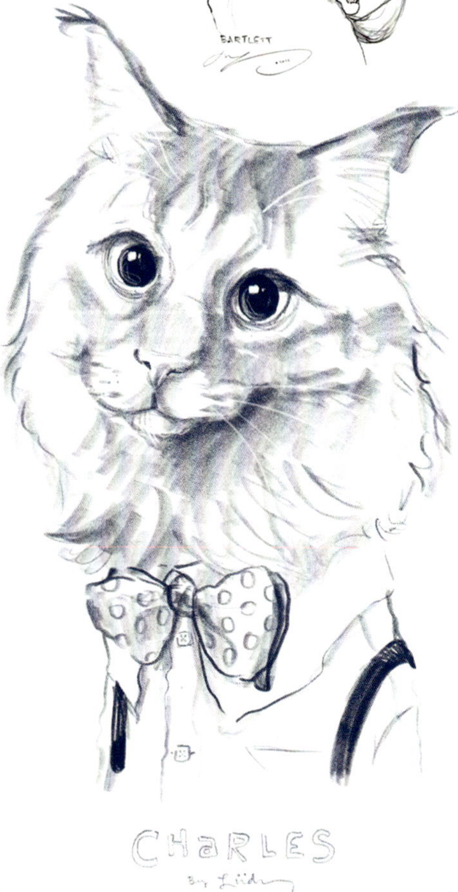
CHARLES
By Lüdy

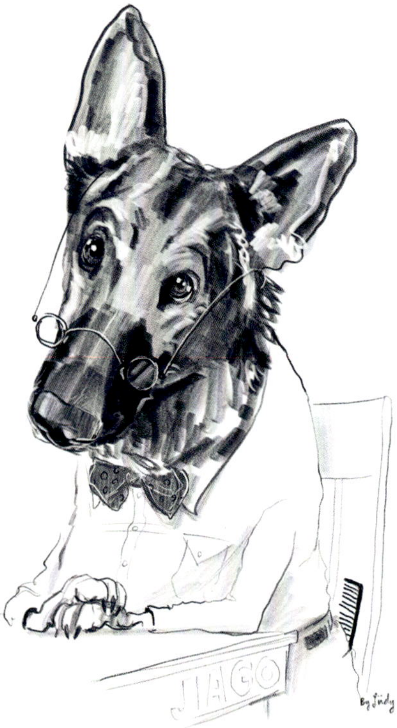
By Lüdy

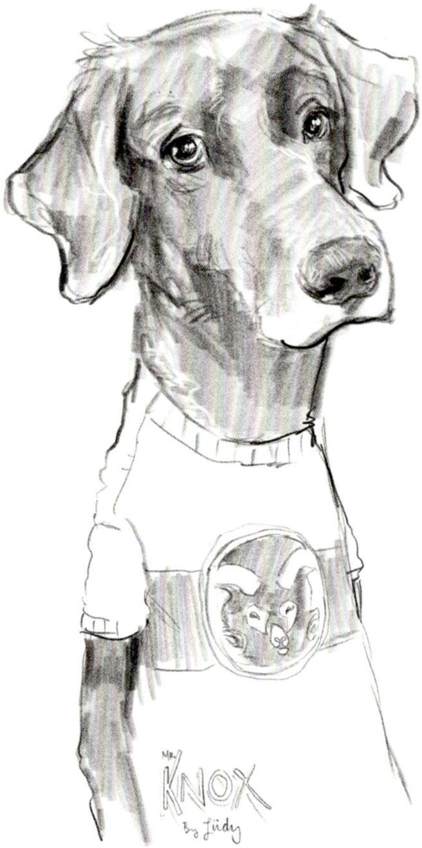
KNOX
By Lüdy

Nature's better with a buddy.

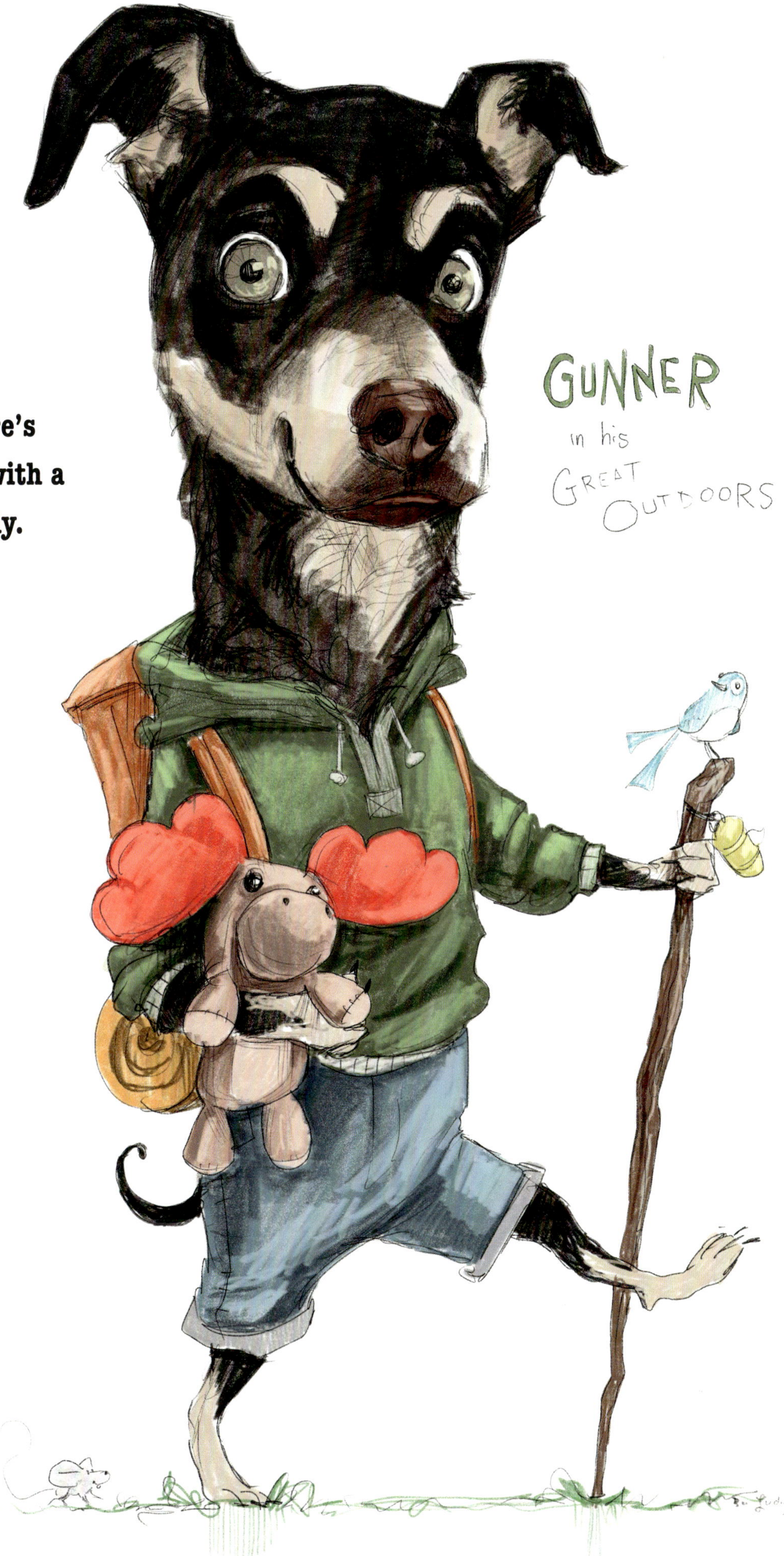

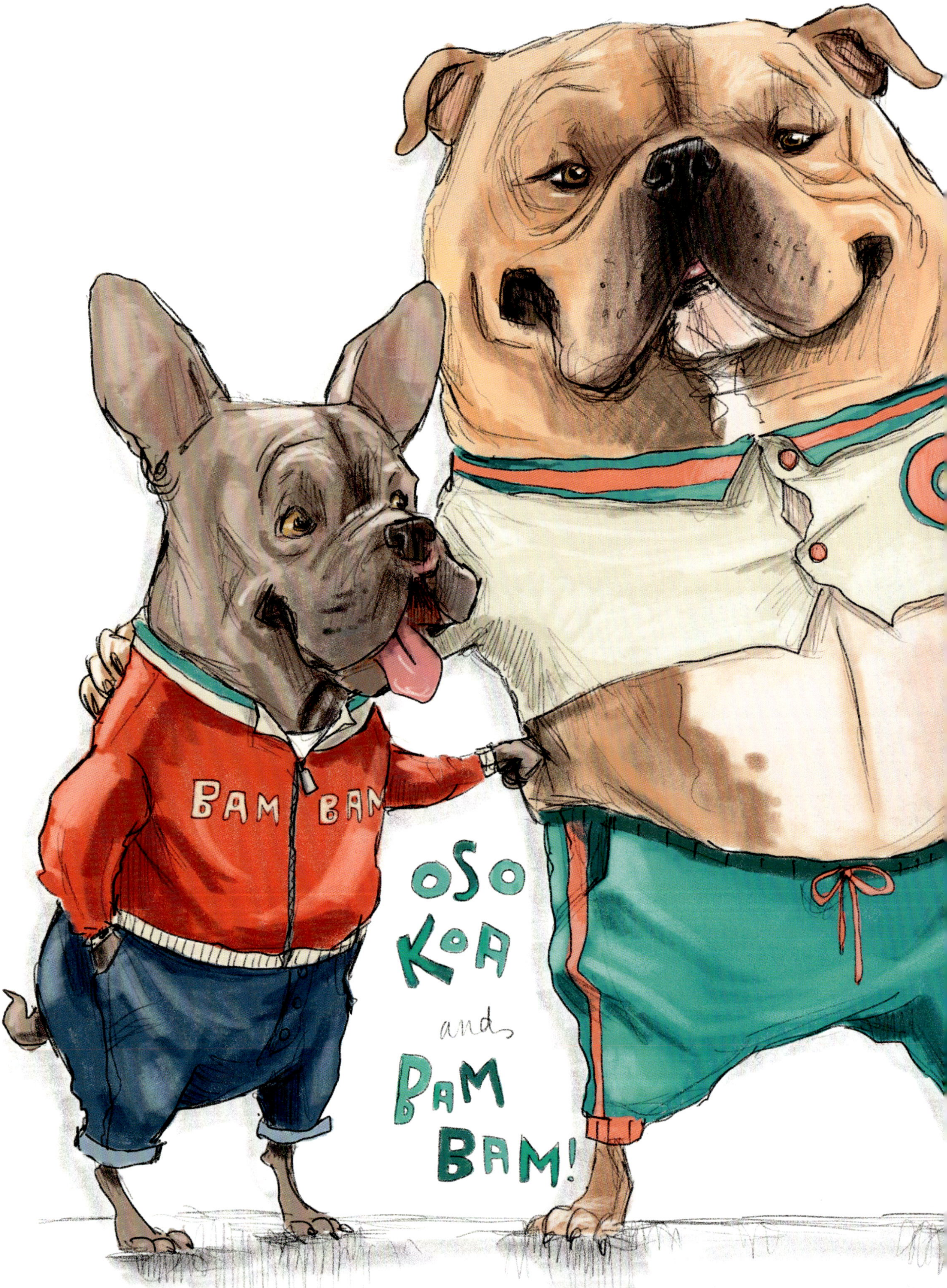
BAM BAM
OSO
KOA
and
BAM
BAM!

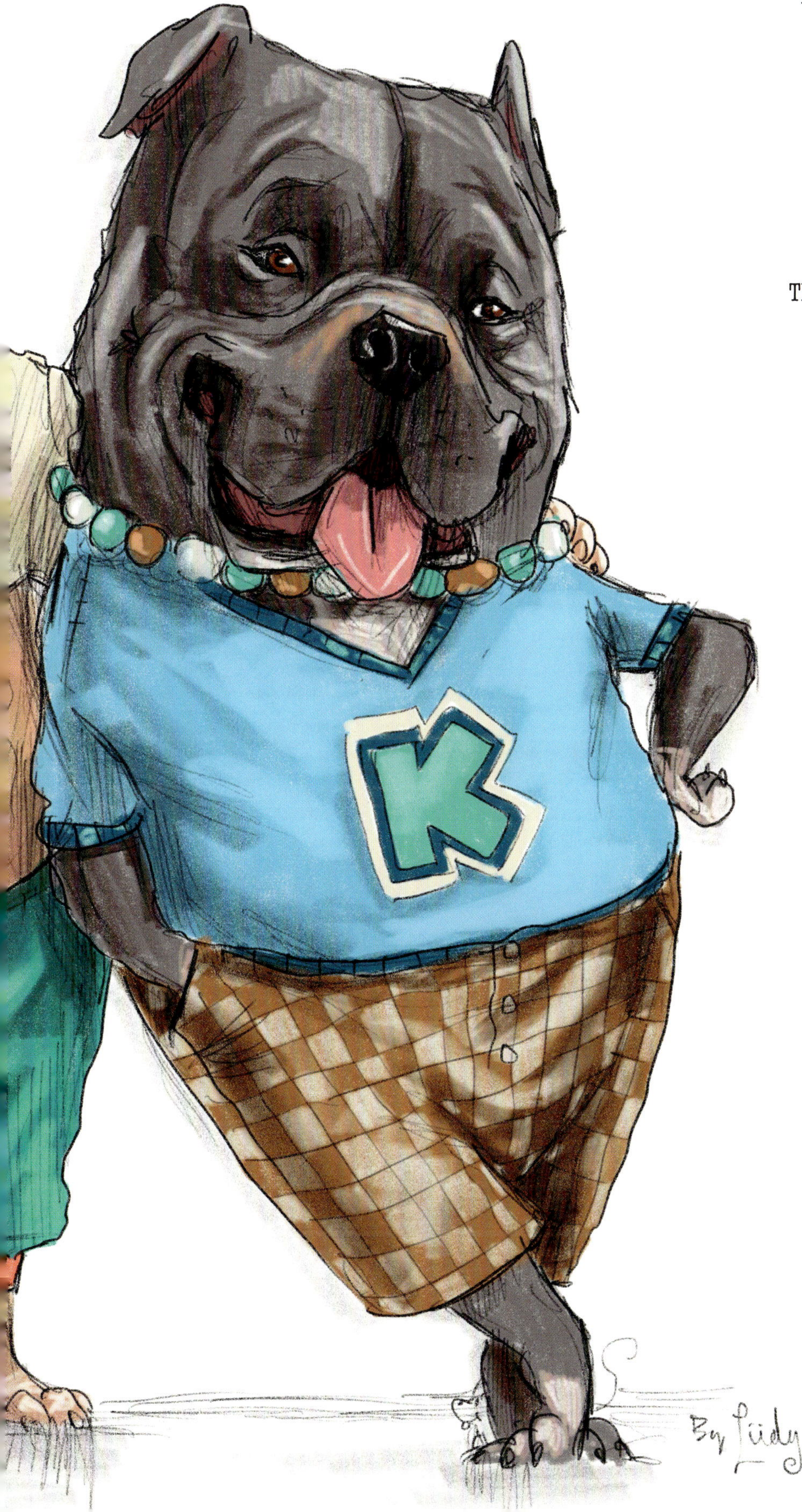

They enter our lives
Like they've always been there.

They steal every sock
And your side of the bed,
But give back tenfold
With a tilt of the head.

They're clowns and they're sages,
They're poets in paws,
They love without limits,
Without need for applause.

A trio, a team,
A thump-thump parade—
Joy in high volume,
Tail-waggin' brigade.

- Quill T Houndstone

@osa_n_koa

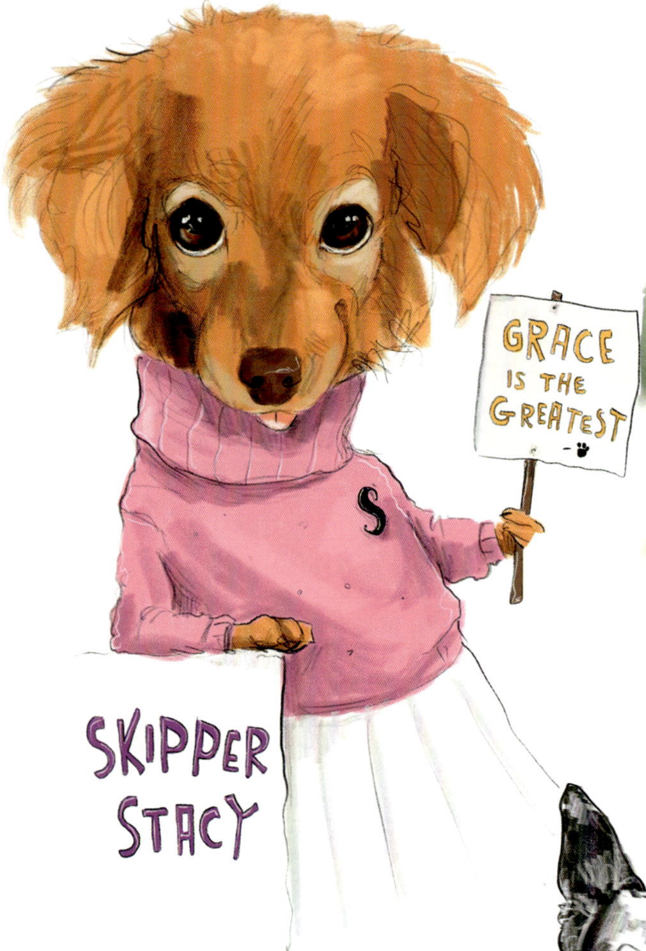
GRACE
IS THE
GREATEST
SKIPPER
STACY

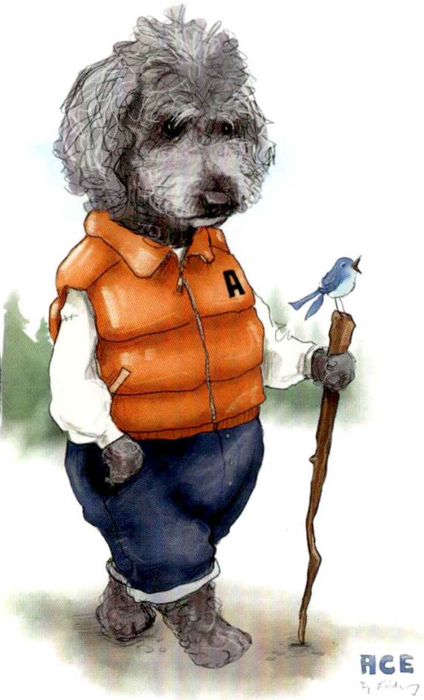
ACE

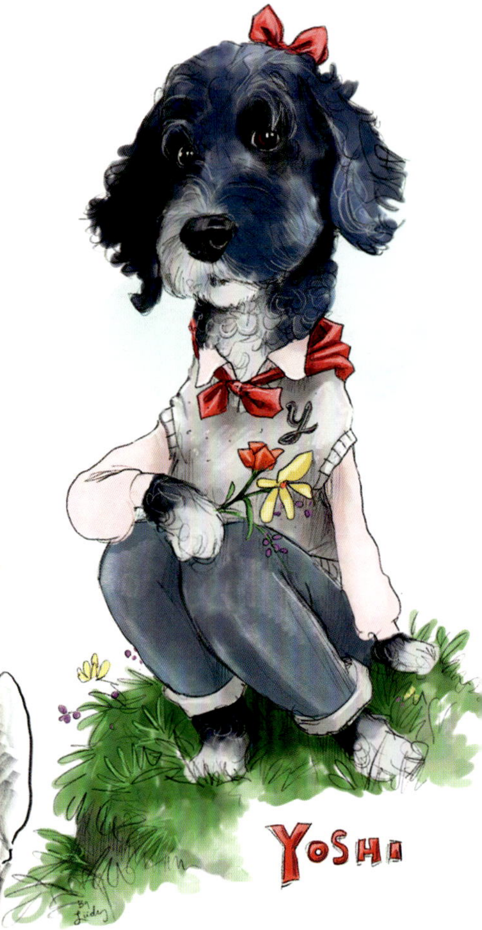
YOSHI

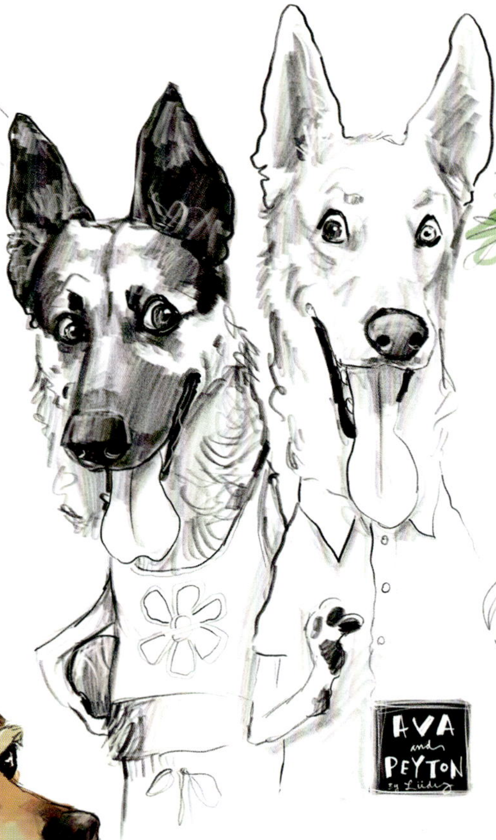
AVA
and
PEYTON

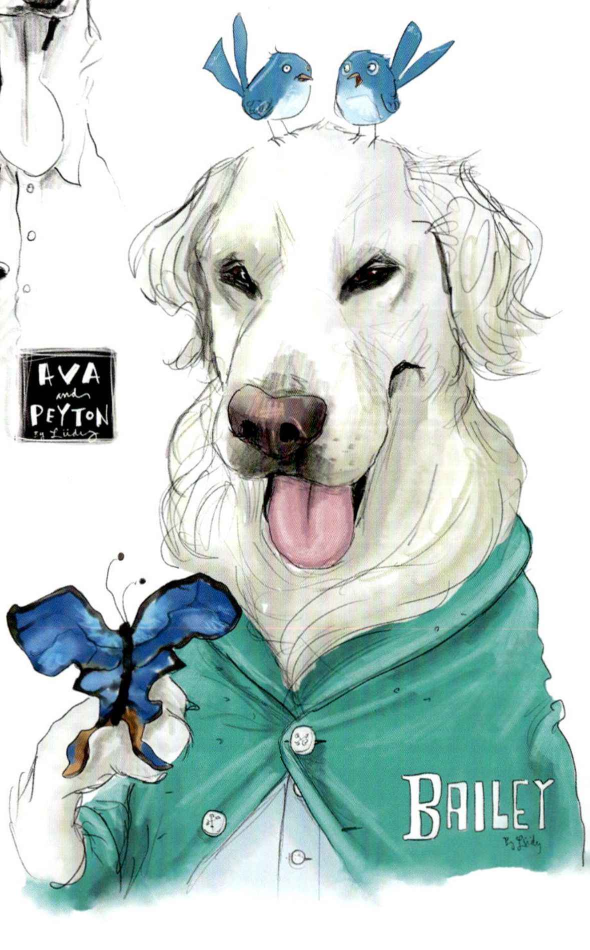
BAILEY

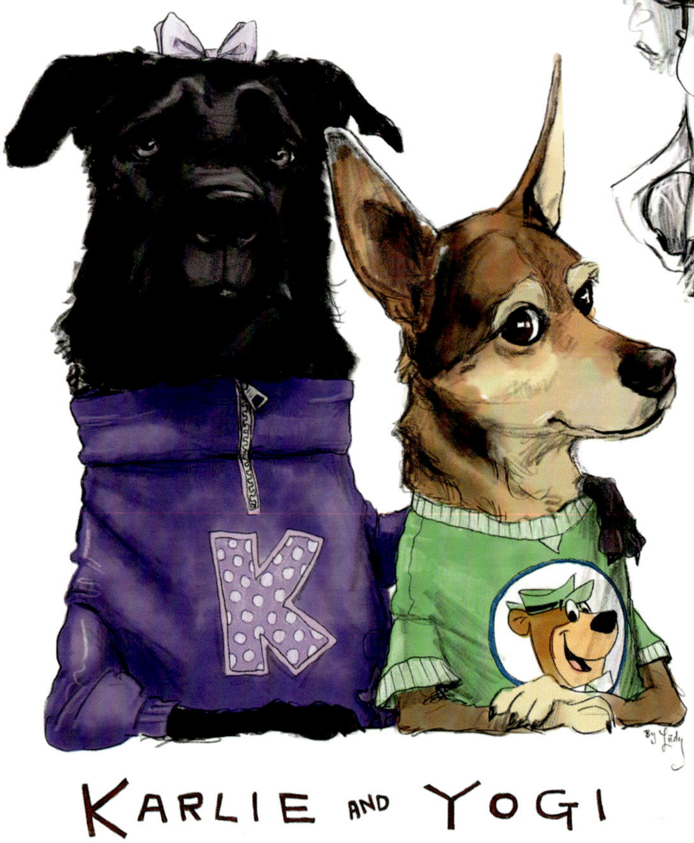
KARLIE AND YOGI

"Why wash what nature intended to be rolled in?"

– Every dog, everywhere

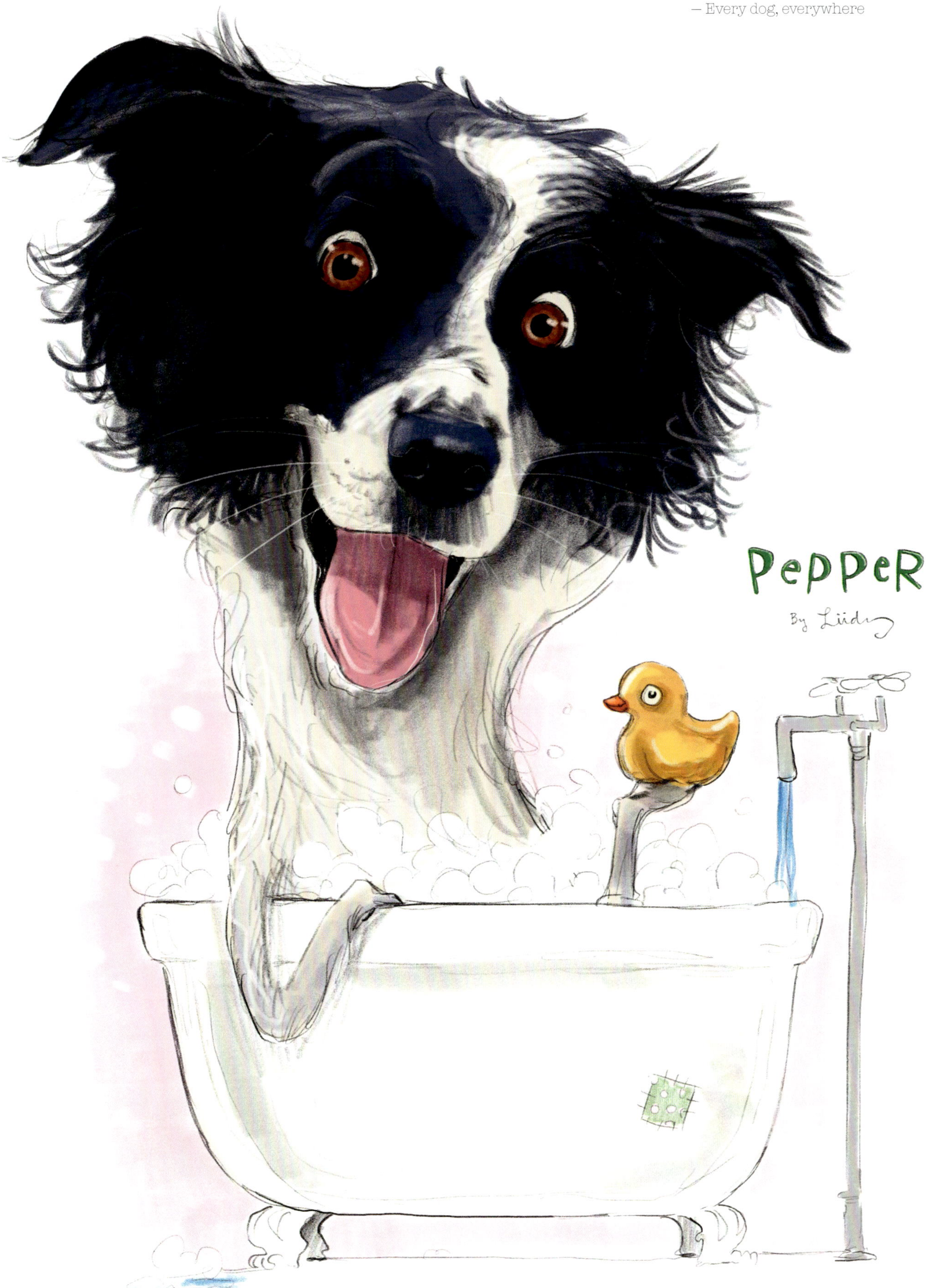

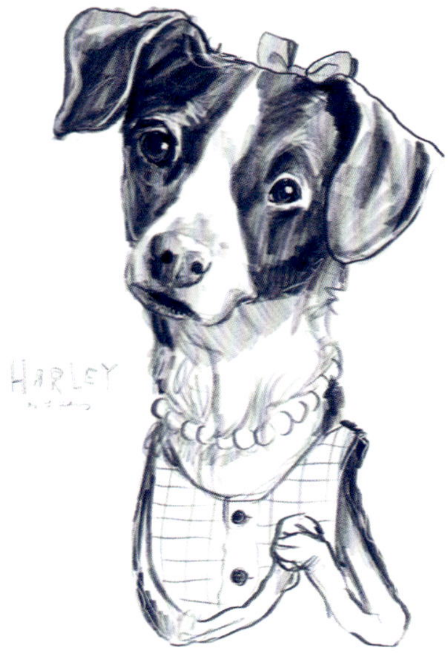
HARLEY

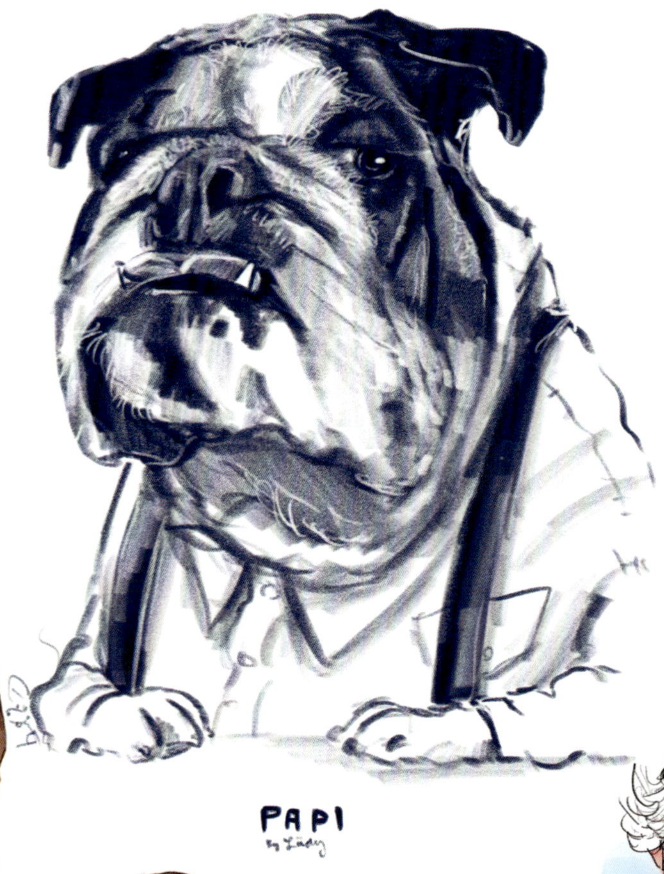
PAPI

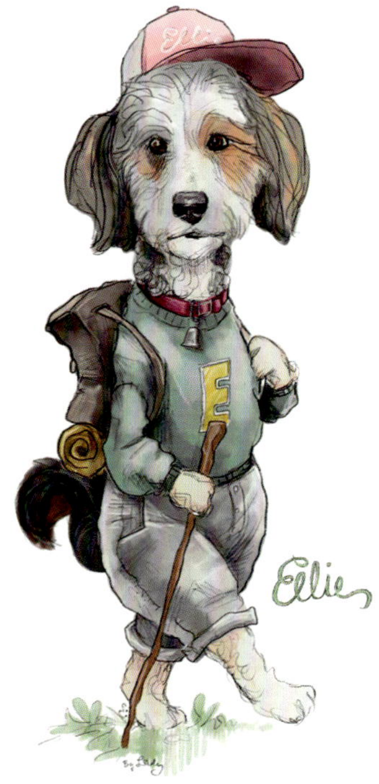
Ellie

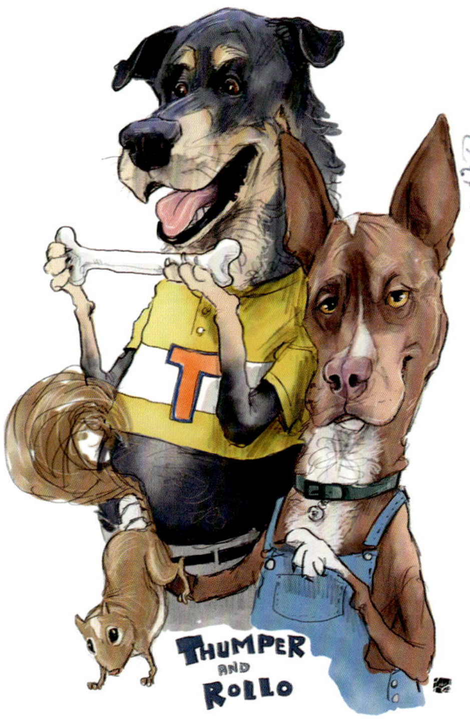
THUMPER
AND
ROLLO

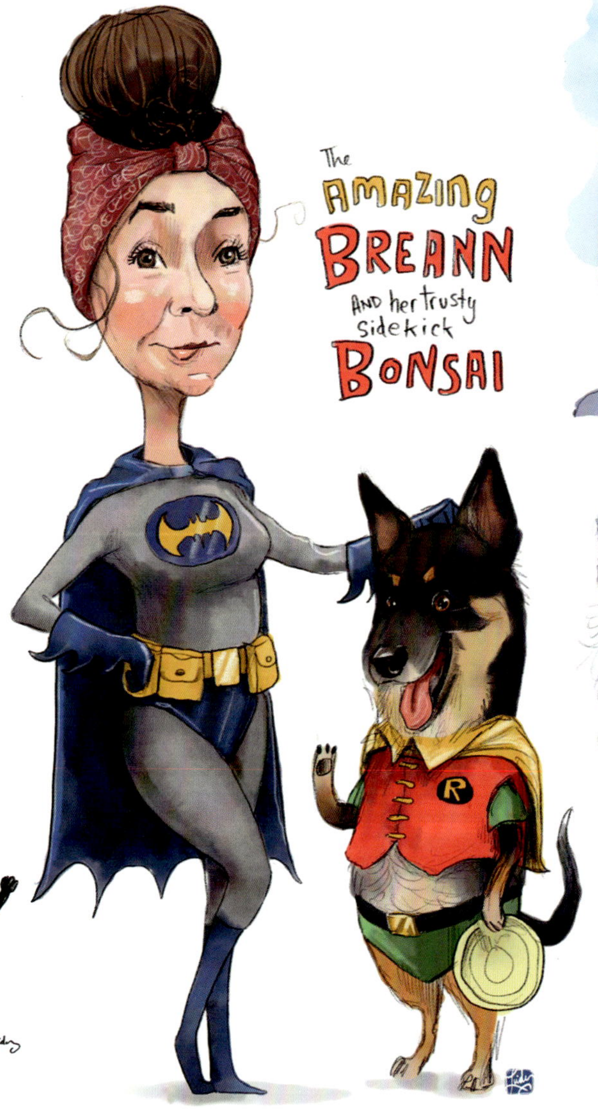
The
AMAZING
BREANN
AND her trusty
sidekick
BONSAI

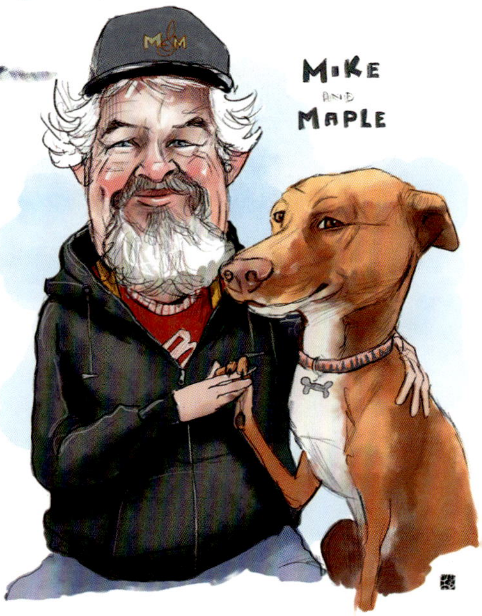
MIKE
AND
MAPLE

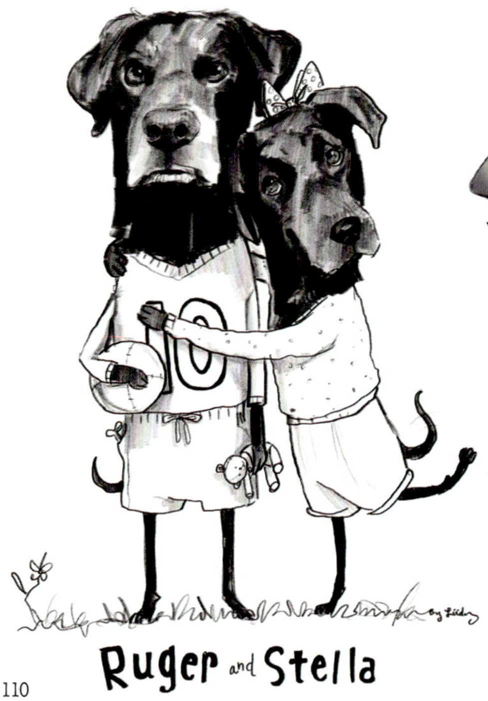
Ruger and Stella

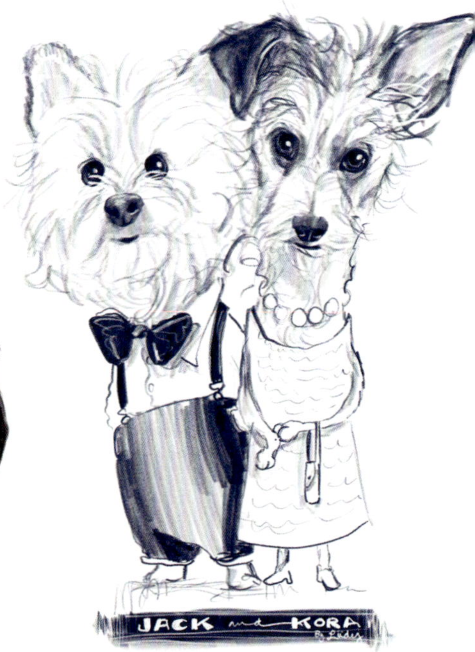
JACK and KORA

**"I have studied many philosophers
and many cats.
The wisdom of cats
is infinitely superior."**

—

Hippolyte Taine

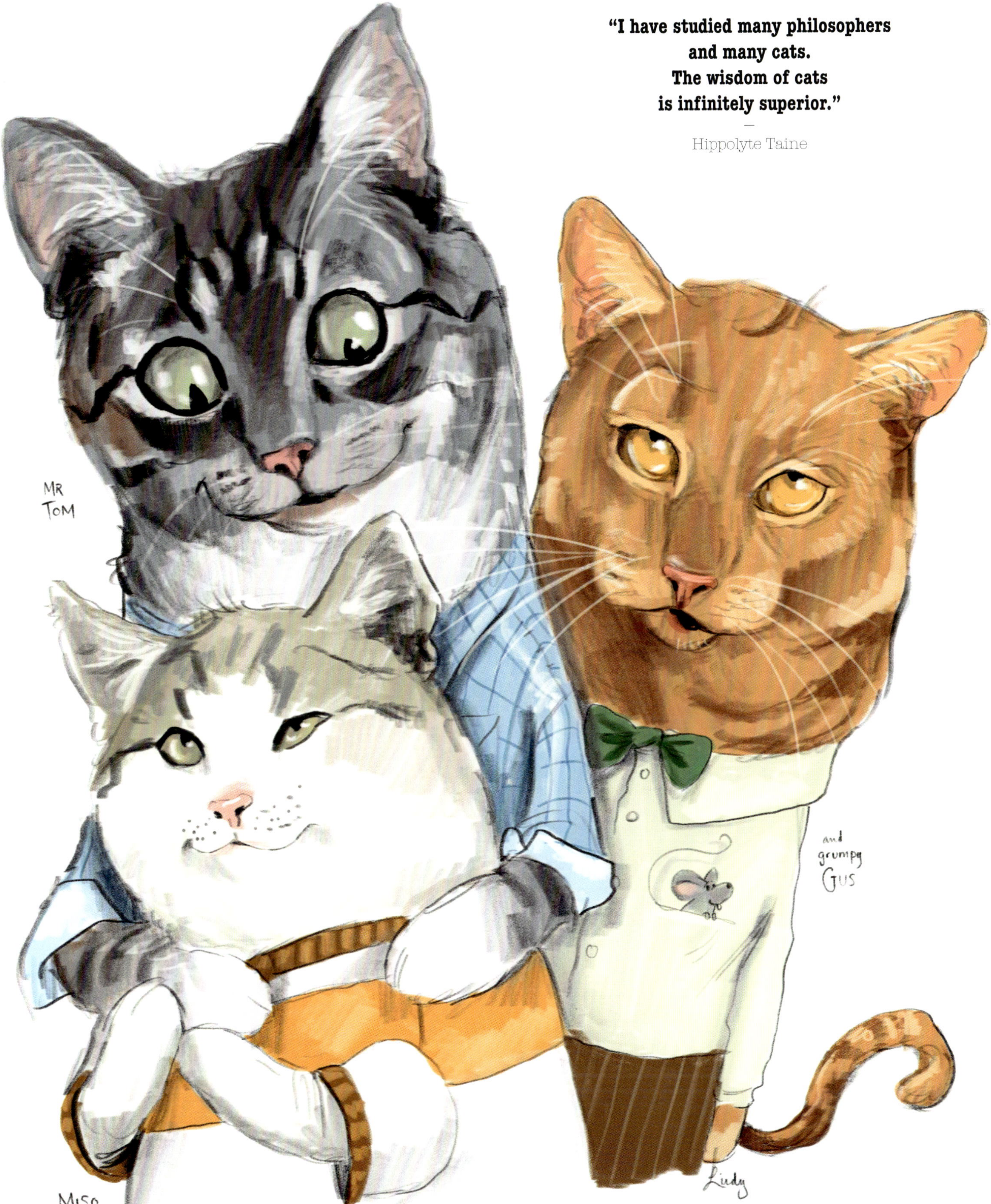

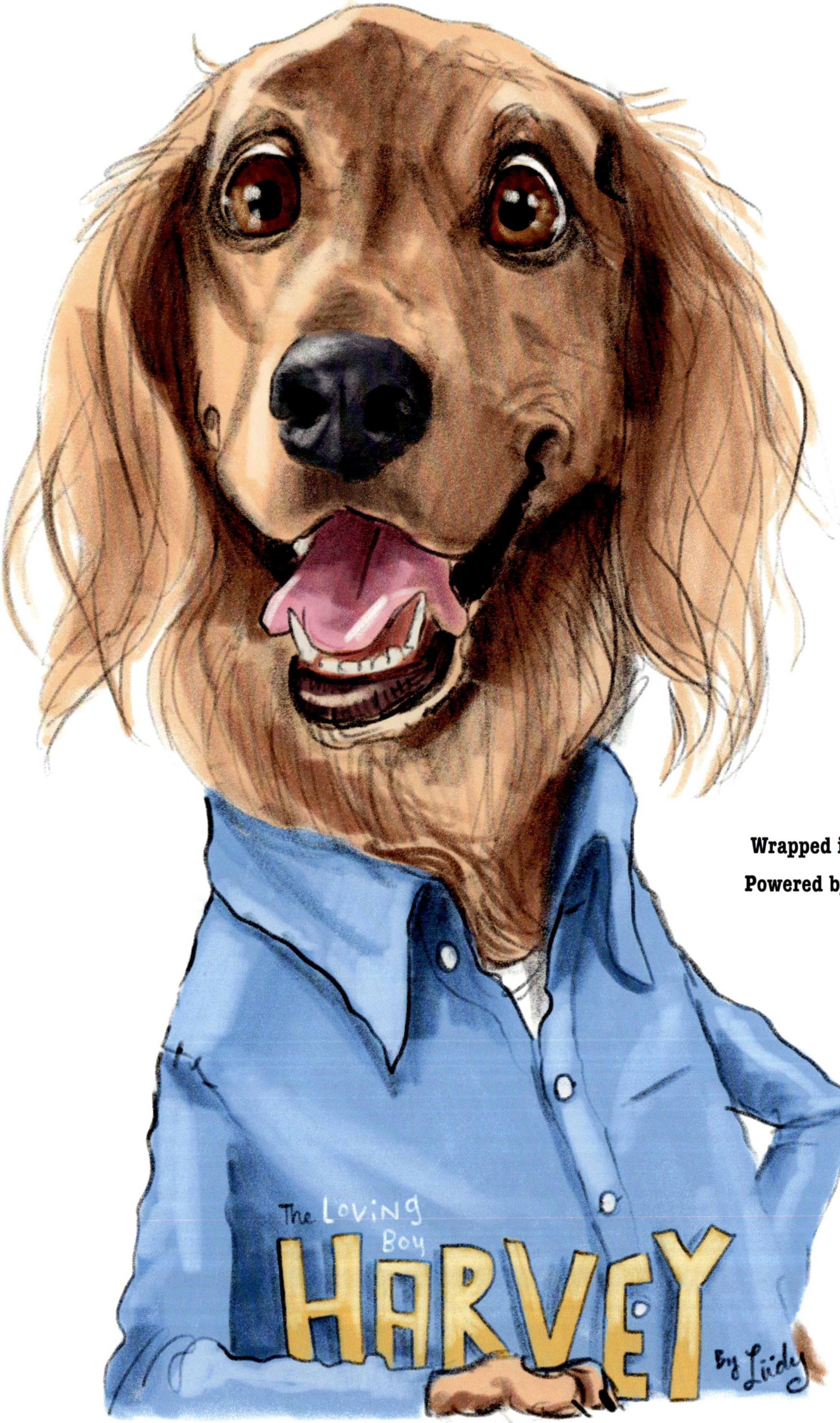

Wrapped in fur.
Powered by love.

Mark Ludy has been doodling since before he could spell it. An author, illustrator, and storyteller at heart, he's spent decades bringing characters to life—on the page and, more recently, through the unexpected joy of pet portraiture. What began as a quick sketch turned into hundreds of illustrations, each capturing not just a pet's likeness but its soul.

He lives in Colorado with his wildly creative household and three deeply opinionated dogs:
Kiwi – the grumpy, deaf old pug, singularly devoted to sleep, slumber, and snacks;
Tilly – the tootin', snortin' bulldog who keeps everyone in line; and
Opal – their scrappy little Frenchie, always up for a game of catch.

When he's not drawing, Mark is dreaming up stories, sipping strong coffee, and marveling at the everyday magic of being human.

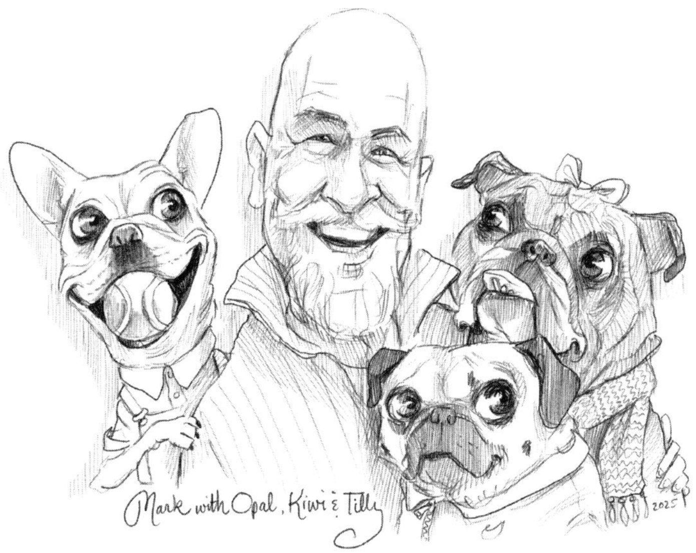

Want a portrait of your own curious companion? Visit MarkLudy.com to learn more.

Can you spot Squeakers the mouse—hidden 96 times throughout the book? (Yes. Ninety-six. The little guy's everywhere.)